STORY

OF

STONE

Post-

Contemporary

Interventions

Series Editors:

Stanley Fish and

Fredric Jameson

THE STORY OF STONE

Intertextuality,

Ancient Chinese Stone Lore,

and the Stone Symbolism in

Dream of the Red Chamber,

Water Margin, and

The Journey to the West

JING WANG

Duke University Press

Durham and London

1992

© 1992 Duke University Press
All rights reserved
Printed in the United States of America
on acid-free paper ∞
Library of Congress Cataloging-in-
Publication Data appear on the last
printed page of this book.
Second printing, 2000

For
Candice Rong-Rong Wei

CONTENTS

ACKNOWLEDGMENTS

Every author has his or her own moments of ecstasy and pain during the process of writing. This book opened up for me a space that gave me the pleasure of freedom, especially at those moments when I wrote about different forms of constraint in Chinese literary and cultural traditions. It is my craving for a continuous expansion of this space that underlies my double commitment to the field of classical studies: my commitment to reformulate the major theoretical issues with which sinologists of narrative fiction have dealt in the last few decades; and, no less importantly, my commitment to make classical Chinese studies relevant to contemporary theoretical concerns.

I am most indebted to Anthony C. Yu at the University of Chicago for his encouragement of my scholarly endeavors over the years, his invaluable suggestions for the revision of the manuscript, and his sharing with me his vision of "modern sinology" in labor. I remain deeply inspired by his commitment to scholarship that knows no geographical or disciplinary boundaries, and by his genuine appreciation of the clash of different ideas.

I would also like to thank Victor H. Mair at the University of Pennsylvania and Andrew H. Plaks at Princeton University for their reading of the manuscript. Professor Mair helped me fine-tune my portrayal of the "monkey king" Sun Wu-k'ung, and Professor Plaks provided constructive criticism for the revision of my first draft. Chapter 1 was written and revised in response to his criticism of the conceptual framework of this book.

I am grateful to my colleagues at Duke University for their generous collegial support and friendship: Miriam Cooke, Noriko Nagai, Hitomi Endo, Yüan Yao Lahusen, Roger Kaplan, Richard Kunst, and Yasumi Kuriya at

Asian and African Languages and Literature; Andrew Gordon in the Department of History; Mrs. Mavis Mayer at the Asian/Pacific Studies Institute; and Thomas Lahusen in the Department of Slavic Languages and Literatures. Special thanks are also due to Fredric Jameson in the Literature Program for his interest in my project, to Richard Kunst for letting me use his Chinese collection, and to Roger Corless in Religion for enlightening me on the concept of "karmic memory"; to Chi-sheng Kuo at the University of Maryland for providing me with bibliographical information on jade; to Hsin-yün Yeh at Mt. Holyoke College for his illuminating remarks on Lin Tai-yü's "genuine temperament"; to Ling-hsia Yeh at the University of Massachusetts for her friendship; and to Chih-p'ing Chou at Princeton University for his help in making the preparation of the final draft an easier task.

My gratitude also extends to Ch'ing-mao Cheng, Lucien Miller, William Moebius, Sarah Lawall, and Frederic Will at the University of Massachusetts (Amherst) for their guidance of my graduate work in comparative literature; to Leo Ou-fan Lee at UCLA for his unwavering support of my work and professional activities; to Hai-chün Huang, who helped in collecting materials for Chapter 2; to Yu-ch'eng Lee at Academia Sinica in Taipei for his help in locating Chinese typesetters; and to Reynolds Smith and the staff of Duke University Press for the editing and production of this book.

I would like to acknowledge the generous publication subsidy I received from the Center for International Studies at Duke and from the Pacific Cultural Foundation in Taiwan. I am also grateful to the Asian/Pacific Studies Institute for a research grant for the final preparation of the manuscript.

Mrs. Gail Woods at Asian and African Languages and Literature deserves my sincere thanks for typing part of the manuscript, copying one draft after another; for being a wonderful friend at difficult moments; and (together with Yasumi Kuriya) for being a surrogate mother to my daughter.

My affectionate thanks also go to friends in Durham—Aili Yang and Tao-shih Hsieh, Alice and Y. T. Chen, P'ing Tung, Jiahuan and Bingzhi Ding, Bibby Moore, Elmer Davis, and Xiaobing Tang.

To Professor Lin Yün of the Yün-lin Temple in Berkeley, I would like to express my appreciation of his wisdom and friendship. To Wei Young, my gratitude for his moral support.

My last word goes to my daughter Candy, who spent her childhood underneath my computer stand, and with whom I want to share the joy of "story-telling." To you, Rong-Rong, I dedicate *The Story of Stone* with love.

THE

STORY

OF

STONE

1

INTERTEXTUALITY
AND INTERPRETATION

There was not a single thing except a stone tablet in the center of the hall. It was about six feet in height, and was resting on a stone tortoise which was almost half in the soil. On the tablet were characters of the very ancient style, and they could not make out any of them.[1]

There was on top of that very mountain an immortal stone, which measured thirty-six feet and five inches in height and twenty-four feet in circumference. . . . One day, it split open, giving birth to a stone egg about the size of a playing ball. Exposed to the wind, it was transformed into a stone monkey endowed with fully developed features and limbs.[2]

Long ago, when the goddess Nü-wa 女 媧 [Nü-kua] was repairing the sky, she melted down a great quantity of rock and, on the Incredible Crags of the Great Fable Mountains, moulded the amalgam into three hundred and six thousand, five hundred and one large building blocks, each measuring seventy-two feet by a hundred and forty-four feet square. She used three hundred and six thousand five hundred of these blocks in the course of her building operations, leaving a single odd block unused, which lay, all on its own, at the foot of Greensickness Peak in the afore-mentioned mountains.[3]

This is how the three narratives begin: the excavation of an enigmatic stone tablet in the *Shui-hu Chuan* 水滸傳 (*Water Margin*), the miraculous birth of a stone monkey in the *Hsi-yu Chi* 西遊記 (*Journey to the West*), and the creation of a discarded sacred rock in the *Hung-lou Meng* 紅樓夢 (*Dream of the Red Chamber*). Read separately, each beginning appears to be a unique phenomenon of the fantastic, which conveys the aura of originality. Taken together, however, the three beginnings suggest a completely different strategy of reading that calls into question any appearance of the gratuitous. Take our reception of the Nü-kua stone: its seemingly idiosyncratic qualities appear less novel within the context of the image of the stone monkey. If we dig more deeply into the two narratives, we find analogies between these two stones that suggest that each text appropriates the other. Both the Nü-kua stone and the stone monkey bear the same epithet, *wan* 頑 (*wan shih* 頑石 in one case, and *wan hou* 頑猴 in another), and live up to the word's doubly shaded meaning—the spirit of "playfulness," and the qualities of "crudeness/ignorance." Any reading of the Nü-kua stone would have to reckon not so much with its derivative nature as with the presence of the literary antecedent of *wan hou*. One may even suggest that the prior text of the stone monkey is contained within the imaginative space of the Nü-kua stone and participates in the latter's signifying practices. This interpretive strategy suggests that "no text is ever completely free of other texts,"[4] a concept best captured in the name of "intertextuality."

Although the concept of intertextuality emerges as a post-structuralist idiom in the West, it is a universal phenomenon that defines the communicative relationships between one text and another, and, particularly in the case of age-old writing traditions, between a text and its context.[5] Such intertextual relations cover the entire spectrum of permutations, ranging between the poles of convergence and reversal. Whether a text converges with or diverges from a series of prior-texts, it must communicate with them in order to signify meaningfully. Textuality suggests pluralistic composition and presupposes the encounter between multiple volumes of texts and between heterogeneous signifiers. In the Chinese literary tradition, such intertwining patterns of communication are seen to characterize the definition of *wen*— literally, the "pattern or texture of a writing"—and are sometimes portrayed in the metaphor of sexual intercourse:

> The marrying maiden describes the ultimate meaning of heaven
>   and earth;
> If heaven and earth do not mate, a million phenomena in Nature
>   cannot be born.[6]

In various other passages, *wen* is perceived as a motley of tissues thrown together.

Two objects remain with each other [*wu hsiang-tai* 物相待]
therefore *wen* emerges; if the two objects depart from each other,
there can be no *wen*.[7]

Phenomena are entangled with one another [*wu hsiang-tsa* 物相雜],
this is called *wen*.[8]

A single phenomenon by itself does not create *wen* [*wu i wu-wen*
物一無文].[9]

[Ssu-ma] Hsiang-ju 司馬相如 once said, "Uniting multifarious
compositions to make up *wen*." [10]

These passages, some dating as far back as the Period of the Warring States
(480–222 B.C.) and the Ch'in (222–206 B.C.) and Han (206 B.C. to A.D. 220)
dynasties, indicate that the phenomenon of "intertextuality" has long been
embedded within the Chinese tradition of textuality in its broadest sense.[11]
For the ancient Chinese literati, the autonomy of text is indeed an alien concept. That no text escapes the confinement of its age-old literary tradition is
a truism so familiar to traditional critics that a notion such as "intertextual
relationship" has long been taken for granted and needs little justification.
In a culture where tradition and history hold such a privileged position, it is
hardly surprising that "intertextuality" is conceived more as the relationship
between a particular text and its larger cultural/historical context than as
that between one text and another. Since "context" is perceived as a fixed
magnetic pole toward which myriads of texts are continually drawn, traditional scholars are less interested in the study of the instantaneous movement
that characterizes the intertextual communication between individual texts;
instead, what defines intertextual relations in such a literary tradition is a
centripetal and *retroactive* movement that seeks to bring a text to an anchored context.

Such a highly structured view of intertextuality—a clearly delineated,
well-controlled, and recuperable totality of some sort—coexists with the
concept of a constrained and tamed "textual essence," which characterizes
the Confucian Canon. The formation of such a classical paradigm has provided traditional Chinese literature with a stable context to which later
writers constantly refer and return, in the literal sense.

The preoccupation with context, whether cultural, historical, or personal [12]—particularly with a single, stable, exterior, and ultimate text that

serves as the prototype for later texts—characterizes many treatises of poetics and theories of writing in ancient China. Not only do literati feel the anxiety of continuing the great heritage of the Five Classics,[13] their gaze turning backward to the past in awe and nostalgia, but in the same vein, this complex of return[14] is also one of the major characteristics of traditional evaluative criticism. Premodern commentators rely upon a small repertory of ancient texts as their aesthetic criterion, using them to assess classical and contemporary literary works. Throughout the literary history of imperial China, critics frequently return to these canonical texts, the orthodox and sacred stature of which encounters little challenge. Working in the name of evaluation, such critics are particularly fond of tracing the "source of influence" of an emerging poetic style to an older one, and in extreme cases, of identifying the moment of origination. "Source," "origin," "allusion," and "generic kinship" constitute the root concepts that permeate many evaluative poetics of greater or lesser importance.

The study of the intertextual relations of stone lore and the stone symbolism in literature recapitulates, to a certain extent, the same critical methodological assumption that privileges the notion of context in interpretation. For although it problematizes critical categories such as "source" and "influence" (categories derived from the author-centered perspective), the mechanism of intertextuality operates within a circumscribed system of signification that overlaps significantly with the idea of cultural constraint and literary tradition. Our recognition, for instance, of the referential function of stone lore in making intelligible such fictional constructs as *wan shih* ("the unknowing stone"), *san-sheng shih* 三生石 ("the stone of three lifetimes"), and the stone tablet, seems to reaffirm once more the boundary between context and text, structure and variants, the symbolic and the literal—even though "intertextuality" in theory assumes the form of boundary-crossing by challenging the notion of "generic and period distinctions."

The present book addresses both of these theoretical assumptions underlying the concept of intertextuality. On the one hand, the reconstruction of stone lore is based on the presupposition that context enjoys a boundary of its own and a certain stability that guarantees the textual intelligibility of, for instance, a particular manifestation of stone imagery. On the other hand, the study of the cross-referentiality of the stone symbolism in the *Dream*, the *Journey*, and the *Water Margin* challenges the notion of period distinctions and thus introduces the radical implication of intertextuality—namely, its potential to break down the limits between one text and another, and eventually those between text and context itself. Such a deeply subversive agenda, however, remains at best an unwarranted theoretical possibility, so long as one assumes that the meaning of a text is inseparable from its historicity. Thus within the scope of the present study, the investigation of the intertextual relationship among the three literary texts is undertaken with a view toward accounting for the local presence of each work's stone imagery, while at the same time determining the degree to which stone lore serves to constrain, if not to ground, the semantic play of stone symbolism. In other words, this book will not so much argue the priority of the contextualizing over the disseminating function of intertextuality, as it will zero in on those moments of interpretation at which an intertext intervenes to change our first reading of a given stone image and to prepare us for a second reading that will bring the historicity of such imagery into full play.

Eventually, one may argue, the challenge of intertextuality often results in a reflexive textual self-awareness that reminds us of, rather than disengages us from, our literary and cultural past. Such a textual self-reflexivity is often revealed at the very moment when the author/subject ceases to look for his or her own identity, as illustrated by a citation from Chiang K'uei (ca. 1155–ca. 1221), the famous *tz'u* 詞 poet in the Northern Sung dynasty (960–1127):

> In writing poetry, it is better to strive to be different from the ancients than to seek to be identical to them. But better still than striving to be different is to be bound to find one's own identity in them, without striving to identify; and to be bound to differ with them, without striving to differ.[15]

Chiang K'uei's remarks on the communion between the ancients and contemporaries sound revolutionary for his time. At one stroke, not only does he map out the intangible terrain of intertextuality as traces of both identity and differentiation, but, most significantly, he also challenges the notion of authorial intention ("without striving"). In so doing, he suggests the possibility of a text-oriented critical perspective that presupposes that every text, with or without the author's awareness, contains its referents elsewhere— whether these are quoted verbatim (*ho* 合, in Chiang's terms) or are already effortlessly transformed (*i* 異).

It is the subversion of the concept of the author and his or her intention that distinguishes the study of intertextuality from traditional source criticism, and that marks the viability of the term as a critical category distinct from the older term "allusion." While "allusion" occurs when an author, "recognizing the general necessity of making a literary work by building on the foundations of antecedent literature, deliberately exploits this predicament in explicitly activating an earlier text as part of the new system of meaning and aesthetic values of his text," [16] "intertextuality" goes a step further by encompassing those traces of the past that evade authorial consciousness because of their obscurity and anonymity. Thus while one can cite the metaphor of *san-sheng shih* as an allusion that Ts'ao Hsüeh-ch'in 曹雪芹 (ca. 1715–1763) [17] consciously exploited, the status of the epithet *wan shih* cannot be so easily determined. One could, of course, force the argument that authorial intention is at work in the citation of *wan shih*—and, for that matter, of *wan hou* as well—and treat both epithets as allusions to the folk legend of *tien-t'ou shih* 點頭石 ("the stone that nods"). [18] However, to recall Chiang K'uei's remarks, such an argument is quite beside the point since it is inherent in the nature of textual production that any two texts may converge without there arising the question of influence or authorial intention.

It is therefore on the ground of "intertextuality" rather than on that of "allusion" that we can undertake the study of cross-referentiality of our three literary texts without addressing the issue of linear causality introduced by the notion of source and influence. From the same perspective, the legitimacy of this project of constructing the stone lore is grounded on the premise that no conscious citation of the lore by the author is required in order to justify its presence in the literary stone symbolism. What "intertextuality" finally triggers is not only the dissolution of an anchored and identifiable authorial presence in the text, but, more importantly, the contextualizing process that our reading of such stone symbolism inevitably sets off. This is to suggest that the concept itself is as much a theoretical construct of the reader as an ideological purge of the myth of the "author." It sets the reader free, and it both invites and legitimizes the reader's self-projection into the text. The referential multiplicity of the stone symbolism in question does not so much unfold and grow out of the reader's vicarious experience of the "authorial intention"; rather, it is reconstructed through his or her own intertextual reading. It has always been the reader, rather than the author, who can activate and reactivate the intertext. [19]

When some critics cast a suspicious gaze upon the term "intertextuality" as critical jargon without substantial theoretical or ideological content, they only reveal their resistance to this new conceptual framework, which departs from the value system that has romanticized and sanctioned the concepts of "author" and "subjectivity." Indeed, any attempt to reduce "intertextuality" to a mere passing vogue misses the point entirely. The concept is hardly a value-free or innocent critical practice, whether in or out of vogue: it is an ideological instrument designed to attack the concept of the founding subject as the originating source of fixed meaning in the text.[20] Above and beyond the problem of voguishness (a stigma that the abusive citation of any critical idiom is likely to produce), the larger issue is the ideological representation that the term introduces and, no less significantly, the question of how the concept better serves the discussion of such perennial topics as "reference," "allusion," "imitation," and "parody." The emergence of the term in the general critical vocabulary within the past two decades tells us precisely that: we have found a new conceptual means to rejuvenate and reframe those topics. It is the nature of such rethinking and reframing that we will now turn to examine.

The critical issue addressed by older terms such as "allusion" and "imitation" (the relationship between a text and a prior-text) remains the fundamental locus from which the concept of intertextuality is germinated. The functional difference between the older terms and "intertextuality," as I have argued above, consists in the major shift of the privileged center of signification from that of author/subject to that of text/reader. What remains to be seen is the effect that such a shift produces on the formulation of the issue of historical consciousness (or, the role of tradition in textual production)—an issue that the older school takes to heart and emphasizes in its critical exercises. Much of the traditionalists' critique of "intertextuality," in fact, dwells on the "impending crisis" of historical consciousness to which the popularity of such a concept is said to contribute. This kind of critique delivers a double message: an objection to the so-called antihistorical drive of the new term, and a conclusion that older terms such as "allusion," "imitation," and "influence" serve a function that can by no means be replaced by "intertextuality." Any examination of the functional viability of the new term as an interpretive tool would then have to address the question of whether and how it reformulates the issue of historicity.

Instead of nullifying our sense of history, I would argue, the concept of intertextuality promises the opposite. It restructures the old agenda of historical continuity between a text and a predecessor-text by breaking down the abstract conceptual totality of "historicity" into two local manifestations: the reader's experience of his or her own contemporaneity through intertextual reading, and the text's experience of its own historicity as the rewriting and, more specifically, the recontextualization of the prior-text.

Our consciousness of our own contemporaneity is born at the moment when we encounter a certain unfamiliar sign in the text that speaks of a system of semantic, cultural, and ideological associations different from our own. While reading the *Dream of the Red Chamber*, for instance, we are perforce drawn into the myth of stone and jade, which does not agree with the reference (i.e., stone as a sterile and immobile object, and jade as an emblem of auspiciousness) presupposed by our own language. We become aware of the historicity of the text as we sense the gap that exists between the contemporary sign system of stone/jade and the system revealed in the eighteenth-century narrative fiction. Whether the reader is capable of locating and reactivating the intertext (in this case, the stone and jade lore) is not crucial. As Chiang K'uei so tellingly suggests, it is our presupposition, rather than our identification (i.e., "identity-seeking" in his terms), of intertextual homologues that makes both reading and writing possible in the first place. Our awareness of the unfamiliarity of the image of *wan shih* and that of Pao-yü's 寶玉 (Bao-yu)[21] mouth-jade already triggers our desire to decode, which instantaneously turns on the machinery of intertextual reading. Both our desire and our reading, it should be noted, presuppose that each image has a history of its own, and that its citation is never direct but is always transformed and edited in one way or another to better serve the new context—whether that context is ideological or historical.

And it is in this act of editing that we can locate the historicity of a given text. Inevitably any intertextual reference—a fragment taken out of the original context, a quotation, or the citation of a prior-text—resuscitates itself by relocating itself within another linguistic context. Even the seemingly direct quotation *san-sheng shih* falls short of faithfully reiterating the Buddhist theology of reincarnation as embodied in the temporal scheme of *san-sheng* 三生. Once contextualized, the cyclical drive underlying the original concept of "three lifetimes" is radically transformed in the *Dream* to a simple retroactive movement of returning to the past life (i.e., the source).[22] The metaphor in the *Dream* thus takes on the deceiving appearance of a verbatim quotation while it is already being tailored to reemerge as an ideological instrument serving a different context. The historicity of the metaphor of *san-sheng shih* is therefore located not so much in a recuperated fixed moment of genesis as in the rewriting and recontextualizing of the Buddhist concept of *samsara*. The concept of intertextuality argues that it is not in the recovery of its origin, but in the continual recontextualization of prior texts, that a text can ultimately claim and experience its own historicity. Our understanding of history is thus reformulated by the program of intertextuality as a transformative process rather than as an original point of departure that awaits to be retrieved.

The notion that a text can live its own historicity through recontextualization is not a familiar one to traditional Chinese writers and critics, for whom the standard practice of *yung tien* 用典 , "allusive borrowings," characterizes the conceptual mode of communicative relationships between the past and the present. The act of borrowing words and phrases from the venerated diction of the literary past, when exercised merely as a tradition, is often reduced to a ritual and is rarely conscious of its own double bind—aspiring to originality while practicing the act of imitation.[23] The Chinese penchant for *yung tien*, the conscious citation of a prior source, is a rather complex phenomenon that deserves full-length treatment elsewhere. However, it needs to be pointed out that "allusions" often appear as atemporal forms, particularly in their encounter with a reader oblivious to those unfamiliar markings. Inherent in the practice of *yung tien*, therefore, is the paradox that the historical context of an allusion is often both present and concealed in the new text. Thus while the use of allusions is a self-conscious act on the part of the author, it by no means guarantees the automatic retrieval of their historicity. It then seems all too possible for us to speculate that the conceptual framework of "allusion" contains the potential, despite itself, of repressing the past, and with it, the notion of temporality, and that such a potential cannot but undermine the function of allusion as a viable link between the past and the present.

We will, however, resist the temptation of getting more deeply immersed in an argument that would lead us to a thorough review of the entire classical Chinese writing tradition. Suffice it to say that the old concept of "allusion" deviates from the seemingly unfamiliar operation of "recontextualization" in that the practitioners of the former cite the reference to the past in order to *internalize literary models* (and, more often than not, to lend prestige and authority to their own texts), rather than bringing to our consciousness the specific historicity of such models, showing off their distance (both linguistic and ideological) from the vehicle into which they are being transformed, and thus rejuvenating the monumental moments of a specific literary and cultural past. Furthermore, the more successful writers in classical Chinese literature have always practiced "recontextualization" without being fully conscious of its radical strategy of *recontaining* an old reference, rather than internalizing a model, in a new context. It is in the light of the practice of recontextualization that the double bind of originality versus "allusive borrowings" finally loses much of its paradoxical poignancy—for an eloquent quotation comes to life only when it is neither original nor located in a determined moment of genesis (i.e., the identification of an allusion), but is relocated, reappropriated, and revalorized within a linguistically and ideologically different context. The process of relocation and revalorization is what makes a new text historically specific and self-conscious of its own fictionality. Inasmuch as an allusion or an intertext always contains the energy field of undergoing another recontextualization, the past to which we feel indebted reveals its deceptive clinging to the claims of fossil-like authenticity. Like the endless series of rewritten versions of literary texts, the past too is made up of re-creative impulses and fiction-making assumptions—a copy of older copies.

These illustrations should make it clear that as an explanatory scheme, "intertextuality" does not collapse period distinctions as much as it historicizes them in its own terms. It promises to fulfill the function traditionally performed by the study of influence and allusion, and to do so no less effectively. "Intertextuality" simply redefines the locus of "historical context" by shifting the burden of proof of historicity from the conscious speaking subject/author to the reader (whose intertextual reading is simultaneously an experience of his or her own contemporaneity) and to the text itself (which comes to life through the continual rewriting of previous texts).

Indeed, issues of historicity are so intimately woven into the theoretical apparatus of intertextuality that any study undertaken in its name, the present book included, will have to address a series of questions that bring into relief the global significance of context. Most importantly, through the study of intertextuality we may eventually gain better access to the writer's moral and ideological stance. What is relevant to interpretation is not simply the identification of a particular intertextual homologue, but also contemplation on the ideological articulation that a given text involuntarily yields. Taken at its widest scope, then, this book is written to demonstrate not merely how the stone and jade lore functions as a cultural context curtailing the free play of literary stone and jade imagery, but also how such lore will help us locate the ideological centers that a given text represses.

Thus while we should recognize the functional dependence of the dual discourses of stone and jade upon each other—the "moral" discourse of jade supplementing, and sometimes destabilizing, the "metaphysical" and "mythological" discourse of stone—it is even more urgent that we note Ts'ao Hsüeh-ch'in's valorization of stone as the privileged center of significance, and more specifically as the origin and ultimate identity of Precious Jade (i.e., Pao-yü). The reversion of Precious Jade to the Nü-kua Stone at the end of Pao-yü's spiritual journey reveals nothing other than the repressed content of Ts'ao Hsüeh-ch'in's ideological discourse. Instead of subverting the concept of "beginning," as the narrator claims in the first chapter, the *Dream* betrays its own radical philosophy by predicting and dictating the resolution of the hero's identity crisis (a split between stone and jade) by means of a simple retrieval of his stony origin. If the rifts in the dialogue between stone and jade reveal the struggle of the author against the ideological enclosure imposed by such culturally sanctified concepts as "homogeneity" and "identity," it follows that Pao-yü's final transformation back into stone reintroduces the privileged content of the concept of "beginning," and with it, the cultural and ideological constraint implicit in such a concept. Seen in this light, Ts'ao Hsüeh-ch'in's iconoclastic stance appears as no more than an ideological mirage.

Similarly, in the *Water Margin*, the intertextual reading of the stone tablet that falls from Heaven foregrounds the moral paradox that the narrative represses in depicting the Liang-shan-po 梁山泊 heroes' transition from bloodthirsty insurgents to loyalists. Such a paradox inheres in the problematic conversion of the 108 rebels from morally ambiguous anarchists to law-abiding subjects subservient to the imperial order that they have earlier undermined under the code of gang morality. As I will argue in the last chapter, by recognizing that the *feng-shan* 封禪 ritual serves as an intertext of the stone tablet dispatched by Heaven, we will immediately come to view such a conversion as morally and politically motivated rather than as an expedient and contingent measure. The political symbolism enacted in the ritual and inscribed into the couplet on the stone tablet—namely, the myth of the Mandate of Heaven and the identification of the human sovereign as the Son of Heaven—provides a powerful ideological justification for the rebels' denunciation of gang morality and cancels any ambiguity that may surround their voluntary subordination to an imperial decree endorsed by Heaven itself.

The reconstruction of the stone lore will eventually lead us to locate these moments of the ideological camouflage of a given text. Only by addressing the issue of the different forms of constraint, ideological as well as structural, with which the text cannot help reckoning, can we fully utilize the interpretive possibilities provided by the concept of intertextuality. I will argue that the appropriate objective of the study of intertextuality emerges at the moment when the analysis of the semiotic nature of a particular sign system (the stone lore, for instance) merges into the discussion of its place in the ideological discourse of the text.

Intertextual Reading

Now that we have mapped out the theoretical assumptions of "intertextuality," it remains to be seen how this serves the practical purpose of interpretation—in other words, how the concept assists us, often without our awareness, in coming to terms with both the familiarity and unfamiliarity of a given textual situation. In the pages that follow, I will cite examples from the three narratives to illustrate how our reading of a text is inherently intertextual.

This brings us back to the two viable mechanisms of intertextuality, convergence and divergence, which operate simultaneously to ensure the continuity of the old and the germination of the new. History itself is characterized by the dual movement of repetition and progression. In a similar manner, writing is the perpetual citation of words that form part of a pre-existing network of signification. A writer's choice of words depends upon the awareness of what they already signify. In this sense, writing is not a free creative exercise. The citation of each word in a new text not only evokes the entire spectrum of its semantic entries, it also involves the making of a decision that either deviates from or reinforces certain previously established entries.

Regarding the *Dream of the Red Chamber*, few traditional or modern Chinese readers would fail to recognize the mythical origin of the Nü-kua Stone in the well-known legend of the goddess's restoration of heavenly order. Relying on his reader's power of association, Ts'ao Hsüeh-ch'in adopted a curtain-raising technique characteristic of traditional Chinese professional storytellers, who always cited familiar poems or anecdotes at the very beginning of their storytelling sessions to settle the wandering minds of the restlessly gathering audience. The evocation of memories, whether racial or literate, seems never to fail to draw the audience into the make-believe world in which the laws of reality are temporarily rescinded and their place taken by the imaginary order of fiction. The name "Nü-kua" immediately conjures up the realm of the long-ago and the far-away when stones possessed healing powers and the broken firmament could be retrieved. Within this reactivated familiar framework, we renew our old acquaintance with the magic stones and hardly need to question how and why this block of stone has undergone the melting and moulding of a goddess.

However, the familiar traces of the mythical stone of Nü-kua become at once obscured, if not totally obliterated, when we confront the selfsame stone as it is now described: "it could move about at will and could grow or shrink to any size it wanted" (*Stone* I: 47).[24] Our attention is arrested, and we are aroused out of the comfortable lethargy resulting from a complete surrender to the composite texts of the Nü-kua myth. That this particular stone is cast aside unused by the goddess and is vested with such a delightful power of mobility and metamorphosis (as opposed to its passive attributes as a mere healing instrument in the original mythology) suggests that a radical conversion of the conventional stone imagery has taken place. It speaks of attributes of stone to which the average reader is a total stranger. Here the fictional stone seems to outgrow the mythical stone of Nü-kua and evolve into a new fictional character. At this point we are led into the unfamiliar world in which the fantastic story of the *Dream of the Red Chamber* is about to unfold. It is the natural recognition, by both the reader and the writer, of the Nü-kua myth, a corpus of extant texts from which the grand opening of the *Dream* originates and departs almost simultaneously, that allows the author-narrator to begin the narrative the way he does: he anchors the story of Pao-yü effortlessly in the mytho-logic of no known beginning and no known authorship, and in so doing he enables the reader to recognize where conventionality ends and where fiction begins. The disengagement of the Nü-kua Stone from the creation myth follows the law that intertextual divergence is not possible until the initial contact between the literary text and the composite of Nü-kua's creation myths has been established. The notion of intertextual convergence and deviation thus presupposes the existence of one or more prior-texts.

The concept of the prior-text—as either an ensemble of myths highly concentrated on a single mytheme (i.e., Nü-kua), or a myriad of texts diffused in their focus—evokes the idea of context. As mentioned earlier, "context" is a concept that transcends linguistic barriers and finds its expression in all literate cultures. Whether it is called, in structuralist terms, the "historical archive,"[25] "*déjà lu*,"[26] "sociolect,"[27] "hypogram,"[28] or "vraisemblance,"[29] or is vaguely associated with the concept of *yu-ch'ang chih-t'i* 有常之體 ("a body of constant essences")[30] and other loosely defined Chinese terms, "context" traverses the vast territory of tradition that incorporates cultural, historical, and literary paradigms regardless of the specific nature of the literate culture in which it operates. Loosely comprehended, "context" is an all-embracing term for conventions of all kinds.

It seems a paradox that some cultures, such as the Chinese, which continuously advocate the preservation and witness survival of their heritage, have taken the abstract system of "context" for granted and have devoted little effort to elaborating it in explanatory terms. Perhaps this is because the concept has always formed such an integral and significant part of the Chinese way of life that there is little need to examine its mechanism or justify its existence. Whatever the reason for this lack of interest in integrating the concept into the rich critical idiom of Chinese poetics, the notion of "context" pervades the mode of thinking and writing of traditional literati. The most articulate expression of their awareness of the relationship between context and the production of meaning can be found in the well-known aphorism about unreliable interpretation: *tuan-chang ch'ü-i* 斷章取義 ("to obtain meaning by truncating the text").[31] The aphorism, however, recognizes the fundamental working principle of contextuality—that the meaning of a word is by no means autonomous, but is generated through a complex network of reference. Throughout the literary history of China, we will find that the awareness of such a rudimentary concept of context underlies the writers' retrospective complex and continuously feeds their obsession with tradition and with the idea of *t'ung* 同 , "identity," and *t'ung* 通 , "continuity."[32]

The preexistent (con)texts, whether traceable or obsolete, are historical formations that make up the horizon and context of every text, often referred to as "the cultural unconscious"[33]—a reservoir of unconscious as well as conscious constraints. To comprehend a text is to bring it within the ken of those cultural constraints, to place it in contact with an order of reality that culture makes available and acknowledges as natural. When Ts'ao Hsüeh-ch'in says that Chia Cheng 賈政 (Jia Zheng) has lost much of his affection for his infant son ever since the son unwittingly picked up "women's things" at his first birthday celebration, Chinese readers (traditional ones especially) would hardly question the sensibility of such a fatherly vision. They would understand the father's lack of faith in his son at such an early stage of his development, and would take this seemingly insignificant and nonsensical ritual of "blind picking" as a powerful understatement of Pao-yü's later obsessive entanglement with his opposite sex. At the moment when Pao-yü chooses to play with "combs, bracelets, pots of rouge and powder and the like—completely ignoring all the other objects" (*Stone* I: 76), the reader could anticipate the father's disillusionment and his prediction that this unusually brilliant child would probably grow up to be a good-for-nothing. The reader would also be able to visualize the unnamed "other objects" randomly placed on the table and share Chia Cheng's disappointment when Pao-yü pays no attention to the swords, papers, ink stands, and brush pens—objects associated with the careers of knighthood and scholarship—that all Chinese parents secretly wish their children to toy with at such a ceremony. Those culturally prescribed objects are the symbols of the *ju-shih* 儒士 ("scholar-gentry"), the Confucian tradition that cultivates great men of impeccable physical stamina and moral/intellectual acumen. Chia Cheng's displeasure with his infant boy is therefore perfectly justified, for the rite of "drawing lots," superstitious as it may appear, has nevertheless become part of a collective knowledge that interprets reality, and turns the cultural and the symbolic into the natural and the real. Such a discourse requires little justification because it corresponds to a convention so completely assimilated into the Chinese mode of thinking that it is taken as "the text of the natural attitude of society (the text of *l'habitude*), entirely familiar and in this very familiarity diffuse, unknown as a text."[34]

When Pao-yü renders his first impression of Tai-yü 黛玉 (Dai-yu) as a maiden who is as still as "a graceful flower reflected in the water," and whose motion is as tender as "willow shoots caressed by the wind" (*Stone* I: 103), we do not have to rely on any specific explanation of these poetic allusions to understand that the heroine is a beautiful but physically fragile girl. The similes that evolve from the symbols of nature are made immediately intelligible because of their clichéd familiarity to the average Chinese reader. As Pao-yü continues to view Tai-yü with his inner eye,

> She had more chambers in her heart than the martyred Bi Gan 比干 ;
> And suffered a tithe more pain in it than the beautiful Xi Shi 西施 .
> (*Stone* I: 103)

A Chinese reader would be able to conjure up the image of the heroine as a sensitive and capricious beauty of nervous debility, unaware of the operation of cultural stereotypes in construing these two comparisons. In the mind of a foreign reader unfamiliar with Chinese historical personages such as "Bi Gan" and "Xi Shi," however, the metaphors would reverberate less forcefully.

Similarly, foreign readers who have not been brought into contact with the Chinese code of heroism and the deeply rooted Confucian scorn for sexually appealing women would probably frown and feel amazed, in turn, at the outburst of excessive violence and at the ineffable contempt that the "macho" heroes in the *Water Margin* express toward women. One may suggest that the historical legends of Pao Ssu and Hsi Shih, which help perpetuate the indigenous patriarchal myth that "beautiful women are sources of evil" (*hung-yen huo-shui* 紅顏禍水), underlie the author-narrator's thoroughly unsympathetic portrayal of beautiful women. The Liang-shan heroes' repressed hatred and their willful destruction of those women whose physical attraction provokes the male paranoia about seduction can also be attributed to the prevalent folk belief that the female principle—*yin* 陰, the arch-symbol of darkness and weakness—would absorb and impair the vitality of the male principle (*yang ch'i* 陽氣) upon contact. An understanding of the popularized interpretation of the Confucian virtue *i* 義, "righteousness," should also help a reader comprehend why Wu Sung 武松 and Shih Hsiu 石秀 would act with such fierceness to avenge their sworn brothers' death in one case, and the breach of honor in another: they obey the code of *i* and act with a sense of justice. Seen in this light, most of the slaughter and lynching that takes place in the *Water Margin* would raise the spirit of Chinese readers, especially traditional ones—for nothing more than the heroic striving for righteousness and military rigor would satisfy their vision of the ideal *hsia* 俠, "chivalrous knight." In contrast, a Western reading public often experiences revulsion in the face of the graphic delineation of bloodshed and the unambiguous condemnation of almost every beautiful female character.

Underlying this reading process—of recuperating the unfamiliar and the fictional in a text by bringing them within the grasp of intelligibility—is the search for intertextual similitude that bridges the elusive distance between fiction and reality. It is very often the phenomenon of the fantastic and the radically deviant in a text that serves as the powerful stimulus necessary to trigger the interpretive mechanism of intertextuality. The *Dream of the Red Chamber* may pose a worthy challenge to critics of all persuasions because of its structural complexity and rich allegorical implications, but it intrigues the reading public of all ages for a different reason. Their fascination is certainly not ignited by the real historical identity of the author and the commentator(s) and of the heroes and heroines in the narrative,[35] by the implicit antifeudal social critique of class struggle in eighteenth-century China,[36] or by high-minded critical concerns such as the depth of the mythical framework, the intricacy of the mixed mytho-mimetic mode, and the allegory of the garden and the dream. Rather, the average reader is most fascinated by the bewitching story of the fantastic claimed as its own by a stone—a divine relic cast aside by a legendary goddess, a well-inscribed rock that professes to narrate its own story,[37] whose sphere of action encompasses both heaven and earth. It is this encounter with the enigmatic symbol of stone that captures the readers' attention, engages them in an exciting bewilderment, and then lures them to play a riddle-solving game of reading. The readers are involuntarily led into a fabulous realm of mytho-logic that endows an otherwise unknowing and inanimate object with divine intelligence and human passions. It is an unfamiliar world full of surprises that constantly thwarts our expectations and invites us to reevaluate our own sense of reality.

What does this relic of stone signify? Shall we interpret it as a token of the gratuitous, or as an invitation to a deeper meaning? Is it a whimsical flourish, or part of a grandiose scheme? In other words, is the incredible stone a marvel wrought by an individual talent, a total fabrication sprung out of the fertile mind of the author, or is it a symbol that carries its own vestiges of cultural, historical, and literary context? These are legitimate questions that the interpretation of the unfamiliar inevitably invites.

If every word extends and reactivates the history of its own meaning, the study of the meaning of the Nü-kua Stone cannot but incorporate its intertextual relations with the preexistent semantic entries that stone has generated over the centuries. At this juncture we may recall the three different beginnings described in the epigraphs of this chapter, which should foster an even more acute interest in the interpretive puzzle of the stone. The very shock that we experience in confronting the versatile stone seems to speak against its perceivable correspondence to any socio-culturally conditioned context. That a stone talks and thinks in human fashion, gives birth, and falls from heaven, completely eclipses our expectation, since our habitual mode of thinking dictates just the opposite: stone is an earthly object, mute and immutable, crystal-hard and lifeless.

Our intuitive understanding of stone will most likely bring us to a premature conclusion that the authors of the three narratives write against our conventional knowledge of stone, and that by almost completely reversing our contemporary idea of what stone stands for, they exemplify their extraordinary creative genius. It is this initial impression of the originality of the stone imagery in question that may prevent a contemporary reader from perceiving certain patterns that unambiguously point to the existence of contextual constraints. Whether it takes the shape of a mysterious tablet, a sagacious monkey, or an eloquent storyteller, such stone imagery unleashes certain recurrent motifs, the meaning of which can be partly revealed if we look into the relations of reciprocal intelligibility discerned among a variety of preexistent texts in which stone figures prominently.

The prior-texts ensemble is an intimidating concept on its own. It seems to point to a continuously expanding, and therefore forever incomplete, repertory of both traceable and untraceable old texts. For the convenience of naming such an elusive entity, I call it "stone lore"—an intertextual configuration of stone. The intertextuality of stone lore emerges not as an exterior, but as an interior reference to the stone symbolism in the *Water Margin, Journey to the West*, and *Dream of the Red Chamber*. It seems impossible not to acknowledge the folkloristic character of the stone images therein, but at the same time it is important not to elevate such lore to the stature of an external constraint that serves to arrest the signifying practices of the literary stone symbolism in question. Everywhere we turn, the intimate parallels between the image of the folkloric stone and that of the literary stone are intermingled with signs of transformation and accretion. Where we expect to find traces of convergence, we encounter cryptic overlays where the folkloric and the literary symbols haunt each other, generating the fleeting mirage of integration, but producing nothing short of displacement—an outcome that can be expected of any such activity of reappropriation. It is the self-generated duality of intertextual appropriation that accounts for the similitude and difference between the mythological texts of the Nü-kua myths and Ts'ao Hsüeh-ch'in's recounted story of the Nü-kua Stone. The fable of totality embodied in the perfectly restored broken heaven undergoes a transformation that produces the new myth of debris—the tale of a leftover stone.

To function at all, the symbol—or in fact, any word—must be given over to repetition, which always implies alternation or becoming other.[38] We need not ask ourselves whether the author-narrator of the *Dream* consciously or unconsciously engages himself in making such difference, for it is in the very nature of intertextuality to perpetuate continuity and discontinuity at the same time. We need to remind ourselves frequently that no matter how much the stone lore may answer for the continuous coherence of the stone symbolism in literature, there always remains something irregular that cannot be rendered into a unitary pattern even by the most ingenious scientific intelligence. The three sets of stone imagery that invoke such an aura of gratuity and originality cannot help extending, while reactivating, the history of stone lore.

The Problematics of Stone Lore

Thus far we have seen how intertextuality underlies the activities of writing and interpretation. What follows is an examination of the intertextual relationship not only between the folkloric motif and the literary topos of stone, but also among the various manifestations of the literary stone imagery. In other words, we will take into account two sets of intertextual permutations: the presence of the folkloric stone within the literary stone, and the commentary of each text of the literary stone upon the other two.

The stone images presented in the mythical frameworks of the three narratives, although thematically divergent at first sight, share the following properties, which convey a momentary impression of consistency: the divine essence of stone; its function as a mediator between heaven and earth; the bipolar nature of its symbolic attributes; and its association with verbal activities, whether written or oral. In the *Dream*, we witness the return of the stone-incarnate Pao-yü to the realm of Disillusionment, and his reversion to his previous existence as stone after a long journey in the Red Dust; in the seventy-chapter edition of the *Water Margin*, the riddle-inscribed stone tablet that opens the story of the Liang-shan heroes emerges again at the end of the narrative to reinforce the Mandate of Heaven.

In contrast to the significant role played by stone in generating the underlying thematic structure of the above two narratives, the stone imagery in the *Journey to the West* fulfills a rather peripheral function. Although born from stone, the monkey, unlike Pao-yü in the *Dream*, does not resume the physical essence of stone after his successful quest for the Sutra. The narrative logic of the *Journey*, however, sanctifies other religious forms of symbolic return (as Anthony Yu suggests), even though Monkey's entrance into Buddhist sainthood is not supplemented by a mythical return to the moment of his origin. A quick review of Yu's argument is in order, since it should serve to illustrate that the narrative logic of circularity revealed in all three texts cannot but suggest a certain intelligible correspondence between the narrative structural constraint and cultural/religious philosophy. Given that the pilgrims, including their Master Tripitaka, are "delinquents from a prior celestial existence," their pilgrimage to the west appears more than just a spiritual quest. It is significant in particular as a home-bound journey.[39] "Home" in this context, as Yu cogently demonstrates, is saturated with Buddhist and Taoist symbolism. Underlying the twin concepts of Buddhist enlightenment and Taoist physiological alchemy is the notion of return: the recovery of one's original nature in one case, and the reversal of the natural course of physical decay in another.[40] Thus the "homecoming" of Monkey and his fellow pilgrims is seen as a double blessing: they acquire longevity and enlightenment simultaneously. But this form of return is framed in the logic of redemption—not in the unraveling of problematic identity myths, as in the other two narratives; and it is the heavy and knotty intertwining of the Buddhist and Taoist religious symbolism enwrapping every pilgrim that overshadows the single issue of whether Monkey's human essence is reversible to his original stony substance.

The case of the *Journey* serves to illustrate that "a single phenomenon by itself does not create *wen*" (*wu i wu-wen*).[41] I have already suggested that Monkey's stony origin does not occupy the central stage of the *Journey*. I should also go a step further by proposing that even the symbolism of stone reveals but one facet of the complex emotional and psychic makeup of Sun Wu-k'ung 孫悟空, whose identity remains an open and controversial issue to this day. To those scholars who insist on the transparency and homogeneity of Wu-k'ung's identity, Chapter 5 will demonstrate that what makes reading and writing possible is "not a single anterior action that serves as origin and moment of plenitude but an open series of acts, both identifiable and lost."[42] Although originating from the "single anterior action" of the transformation of a stone ovum, the stony identity of the monkey is supplemented, as illustrated in Chapter 5, by "an open series" of evocative mythological personae. It is the incorporation of these other personae—the trickster and the white ape in particular—that creates the indelible image of Monkey: his playful sagacity and transformative energy. The tenuous symbolism of stone with which the *Journey* starts cannot alone account for and sustain the popular fascination with Monkey; it is the intertextual communication of the folkloric stone with various other prior-texts that makes up the complexity of his character.

But if the *Journey* serves as a less distinct example of how the stone topos generates the circularity of narrative movement, the stone imagery therein has contributed to the making of the *Dream* in more than one respect. The reincarnation of the Nü-kua Stone echoes Wu-k'ung's transformation from the divine stone. The two beginnings bear a close resemblance to each other even in the description of the physical appearance of the two stones—each narrator has chosen to dwell meticulously on their measurement with the same mathematical precision. A traditional commentary even suggests that the source of inspiration for the allegorical device of Chen-Chia Pao-yü has to be sought in the *Journey*: "[The concept of the] Chen-Chia Pao-yü, the Real and Unreal Pao-yü, is evolved from the theme of the two pilgrims [Monkeys]." [43] All the speculations about the similarities between these two miraculous stones indicate that the image of the Nü-kua Stone in the *Dream* contains the trace of the monkey-stone. This is how intertextuality operates: a word, a symbol, or a text always brings back the residual and implicit (inter)texts of the past that never cease to reverberate in its textual space. And regardless of the marginal or central position that stone occupies in each of the three narratives, it shares a certain identity that suggests the ongoing infiltration into literary stone imagery of prior codes, historical context, cultural conventions, and unconscious practices. In other words, the text of the literary stone undergoes an incessant intertextual communication with the previous lore of stone.

When it comes to establishing the vast network of such multiple intertextual references in the global name of stone lore, we encounter several problems that accompany any enterprise aiming at systematization and incorporation. To reconstruct such lore is to set a boundary to the invisible space traversed by the infinite number of texts, both identifiable and unidentifiable, in which stone has ever participated in producing meaning. It is the open-ended character of intertextual space that seems to resist any attempt at recuperation. Although to produce or to analyze a text is necessarily to situate it within an inescapable intertextual network, it seems impossible to finish compiling and thus stabilizing such an archive. History, whether cultural history or the history of stone, includes unconscious as well as conscious materials and constraints; to reconstruct all such materials and patterns would amount to enclosing history within one textbook or paradigm. It is the inherent openness of intertextuality that contradicts the working principle of context as a complete and unified frame of reference. It exposes all contextualizations as limited and limiting.

Bearing this in mind, I do not claim to reconstruct stone lore in order to grasp in one heroic venture the sum total of all the historical and cultural conventions regarding stone. What I attempt to catalogue in the next chapter is a cluster of texts illustrating certain patterns of a distinctive "stone experience"—one facet of the highly stratified but recognizable interior of the intertextual network of stone—that includes a series of recurring attributes which will help illuminate the activities of both creating and interpreting stone imagery in literature. Such stone lore has already faded from the horizon of our common knowledge. It is a system of convention, the meaning of which has escaped our conscious grasp, but which can be retrieved by collecting and explicating a body of extant stone myths and rituals. The reconstruction of the stone lore will fulfill the demand of the critic for greater objectivity and will enable the reader to achieve a fuller perception of how the system of signification works—that is, what enables stone to signify the way it does in literary texts, and to what extent intertextuality both constrains and stimulates the assimilation of the folkloric stone into a literary theme. The explanatory value of such a frame of reference can hardly be dismissed, although we cannot hope to discover the convention of stone lore in its entirety.

Ferdinand de Saussure defends the concept of totality by arguing that language as a total system is complete and self-regulating at every moment, "no matter what happens to have been altered in it a moment before."[44] One may suggest that the same holds true for the stone lore in question—that although its contents shift and evolve incessantly, like any other system of metalanguage, it nonetheless assumes an immanent and general appearance of coherence composed of its current structural properties.[45] My proposal to recompose the grammar of stone lore thus represents nothing more than an attempt to derive a recognizable, albeit tentative, "mythological pattern" from a shifting and incomplete totality.[46] The stone lore reconstructed at each historical moment reflects just that—a recognizable structure comprising its previous properties and some newly emerged heterogeneous elements that have not yet been stabilized, the latter coexisting rather incongruously with the former in a kind of deceiving totality.

The elusive totality that a reconstructed stone lore inevitably evokes may create another false expectation that what I assemble in the next chapter will serve to account for all the various guises of stone imagery in the three narratives under discussion. As I will demonstrate in Chapter 5, the stone lore does not enjoy a hegemonic hold on the image-making of stone in literature. To ascribe to the lore an absolute authority in determining the significance of every manifestation of stone imagery is to subscribe to the same fallacy of interpretation to which dogmatic structuralists are often susceptible.[47] What we should recognize is that the freshness of great literature always escapes a strictly systematic reading and the tenacious grasp of conventional context. We should therefore carefully distinguish the legitimate pursuit of constructing a metalanguage from the dogmatic structuralists' assertion that an interpretive model exercises an absolute generative power and enjoys systematic completeness. At issue is how such an incomplete system can be properly used, not how it figures as the constitutive moment in the history of a particular word or symbol. We have to keep in mind that any scientifically appealing scheme serves its own purpose—as a kind of "discovery principle." But such a scheme, and in fact any scientific diagram, "cannot be guaranteed to replace intelligence or intuition."[48] I would even go a step further by suggesting that frequently "intuition" not only has the last laugh on scientific problem-solving techniques, it also ironically participates, however modestly, in the construction of what may appear to be a perfectly scientific paradigm.[49]

It is worth noting, at this point, that the construction of stone lore posits just such a preliminary way of "intuitive" seeing, a kind of presupposition that accompanies every critical approach to literature. What guides the folklorist's excursion into the immense mass of materials, and helps to locate more efficiently certain key myths and folktales, is exactly this "preunderstanding" of certain attributes of stone, a kind of trained intuition that continually formulates hypotheses. Proceeding from this foreknowledge, the folklorist is able to discover useful data from those sources which otherwise would not have appeared to bear any relevance to the topic under discussion. For instance, a preliminary understanding of the association of stone with divine power suggests its possible linkage to the rituals of *feng-shan* and of coercing rain deities. This kind of obscure yet evocative preconception also comes to our assistance in grouping clusters of recurrent stone-motifs and prevents us from experimenting with completely irrelevant combinations.

The reconstructed stone lore with its definable boundary suggests a certain conceptual closure. But as a "discovery principle," it has the capacity to generate a wide variety of possible combinations of its lexical entries. In so doing, it provides certain vantage points for interpreting the stone imagery that emerges in literary texts. On the one hand, it enables the interpreter of a stone-text to decide when to halt the potentially self-perpetuating process of the breaking up of larger meaning-units into smaller ones; on the other, it facilitates the explanation of how some meaning-units combine to produce certain prescribed structures that allow the individual stone-texts as such to emerge, to be read, and finally to be recycled into the existing stone lore. While the decision of the first operation often relies heavily on our intuitive intelligence, that of the second—the eliciting of principal meaning-units whose frequency of recurrence demonstrates a level of coherence pointing to the definability of an intertextual network of stone—cannot be accomplished without the aid of a highly technical solution. To derive such a definable but abridged lore, I turn to A. J. Greimas's theory of structural semantics, and particularly his concept of "isotopy"—"the level of coherence in a text." It is by means of such a theoretical paradigm, the operative laws of which I will introduce in a moment, that one can arrive at the portrayal of the shifting and often contradictory identity of the folkloric stone.

Stone is seen as an entity vacillating between stasis and dynamism. Its symbolic significance and physical attributes oscillate between fertility and sterility, and between liquidity and solidity. Most importantly, it displays characteristics corresponding to the stone imagery in the three classics: it has divine attributes, it functions as fertilizer and mediator, and it is a source of a special form of utterance. What has been regarded as anomalous, unmotivated, and outlandish, and has been tolerated as the indulgence of poetic license—such as the sacred stone embryo evolving into a monkey who undergoes a spiritual quest, the Nü-kua Stone acquiring the attributes of both "stupidity" and "intelligence," and the stone tablet falling from the sky bearing the Mandate of Heaven—appears in a new light when read against the intertext of the folkloric stone.

It is our awareness of such an intertext that enables us to interpret certain recurrent phenomena of fictionality in literary stone imagery as referents to the structural constraints inevitably imposed upon later texts by the intertextual model of stone lore. In this sense, intertextuality is seen as a contextual closure that enables a literary image to enter the system of signification and fall into certain intelligible patterns. Seen in this light, the points of contact between the different manifestations of stone imagery that we spot at every historical period and in different genres of writing, which taken separately might be regarded as coincidences, appear as structural variations of certain key motifs. Both the *Journey* and the *Dream* take as their point of departure the creation myth in which stone, emerging as the life-giving principle, transforms itself from a sacred object into a mundane human creature endowed with a potential for sagehood. The two primary attributes of the folkloric stone, divinity and embryonic fertility, are instilled into the stone monkey in the *Journey* and the lovesick stone in the *Dream*, respectively. The association between stone and cosmic design in the three narratives also appears as the transformation of the message-bearing and speech-making function of the ritualistic stone. The stone that *talks* in the mythological texts evolves into the stone that *knows* in literature. From the most primitive stone of five colors—an inanimate object, a healing instrument for a goddess—to the sound-making stone and the talking stone—an animate, language-making agent—we can fully recognize, and perhaps predict, the potential of the unknowing and inanimate stone to be developed into a conscious being endowed with acute cognitive faculty. It then seems conceivable that the fabulous monkey king in the *Journey* will be transformed from a dumb divine stone into an animal of human intelligence, and eventually to a Buddhist saint; and that the reincarnated stone in the *Dream* is blessed with a hidden divine intelligence despite its deceptive appearance of ignorance.

The study of these structural constraints constitutes the most important aspect of any project of intertextuality. Such a study can only follow the pattern of a spiral movement of cross-references, and this pattern will best characterize my strategy of interpreting the individual texts of the myths of stone in order to reach a composite picture of stone lore. In no other way can a meaningful coherence (i.e., "isotopy") be recuperated from the texts accumulated over different historical periods. Unlike the reading of literature that is governed by literary conventions and codes of genres, the reading of mythology has as yet found no rules to be applied to individual myths, which, when viewed separately, can hardly convey any concrete sense of meaning. The system of signification underlying mythology has to be established, if only partially, by a network of reciprocal intelligibility in which "the context of each myth comes to consist more and more of other myths."[50] The intelligibility of each myth is to be revealed slowly by the corresponding relations of enlightenment discerned among a set of myths.[51] In determining the significance of the mythical figure of Nü-kua, for instance, we accumulate myths of various activities in which she is involved; although each myth represents one syntagmatic sequence different from the others, a unified paradigmatic set can be deduced from the description of the goddess's metamorphosis, from her ritualistic acts of mending the heaven and creating human beings from mud and clay, from her identification with Kao Mei 高禖 (the divine matchmaker), and from the worship of her in times of drought—each a different version of the "fertility" theme. The discovery of the paradigm "fertility," which closely relates one set of the Nü-kua myths to the others, is crucial to our understanding of the global meaning of her legend. While a detailed discussion of the principal myths concerning the goddess will be undertaken in the next chapter, a few explanatory notes must be inserted here to elucidate several basic concepts of Greimas's semantic theory.

Greimas replaces the linguistic term "paradigm" with "isotopy" to define the pattern underlying a set of inflected forms or transformational texts. To derive the isotopy of a number of texts, one needs to work from the bottom up—in other words, from minimal semantic units to larger ones. Greimas's explanatory model comprises three concepts—seme, sememe, and classeme—which define the hierarchical relationship between different levels of semantic units. A "sememe," the general effects of meaning, is composed of an invariant core of semes and a set of contextual semes. The naming of "semes"—the minimal semantic units—is based on the naming of binary oppositions inherent in a lexeme (e.g., male/female, human/animal, fertile/sterile).[52] It is essential to identify recurrent semes in a text in order to derive a coherent meaning from the reading. The semes that are repeated in a text are called "classemes"; the repetition of classemes enables the reader to identify an "isotopy" that unifies the text.[53]

An isotopy is therefore unveiled by locating one or several recurrent semantic clusters—classemes—which are in turn constructed from the repetition of semes. If we examine the cluster of myths embodied in Nü-kua, for example, such a structural analysis will help us map out the constellation of texts into various sememes: "metamorphosis," "healing," "creation," "matchmaking," and "rain-evoking." Each sememe will then be transcoded into a congeries of semes. The repetition of certain semes will help us construe the classeme as "birth" and "sexual union," which in turn determines that the isotopy tying the cluster of mythical texts together is none other than "fertility."

While Greimas's theory of structural semantics may appear to be a satisfactory groundwork of anatomy, in its attempt to construct meaning by working from minimal units to higher semantic levels, it is worth noting that the discovery of isotopies often does not result from the mere totalizing of repeated semes. Perhaps Maurice Merleau-Ponty puts the matter most succinctly when he suggests that the meaning of the whole "is not a series of inductions—it is *Gestaltung* and *Ruckgestaltung* [the postulation and re-postulation of wholes]. . . . This means: there is a *germination* of what *will have been* understood."[54] That is, the meaning can be derived and defined only in the light of hypotheses about the meaning of the whole. It is this cross-referentiality of the parts and the whole, and the momentary glimpse of "truth," that enables us to map out the general semantic field of Nü-kua myths: the dialectical process of a reading that vacillates between the parts and the whole, supplemented by the native intelligence of the analyst, in swift succession triggers the dissolution of the diverse versions of the Nü-kua myth into a classeme closely related to the semes of "birth" and "sexual union," and simultaneously foretells the integration of sememes (e.g., creation, pro-creation, irrigation, healing, and matchmaking) into the single isotopy of fertility. It is obvious that although the homogeneous semantic level comes to assert itself through some definable interplay of semantic properties in a text, the recognition of dominant isotopies is nevertheless achieved "not so much by the intrinsic features of the text as by the intent at totality of the interpretive process,"[55] and by the aid of the "cultural grid"[56] that accom-panies the complex operation of interpretation. Thus a certain functional coherence of the goddess is envisaged to account for her unique position in Chinese mythology and is taken as an underlying organizing principle for the corpus of myths in which she plays a central role.

The acquaintance with the Chinese "cultural grid" also helps us form the preliminary hypothesis about the nature of symbolism that the name of Nü-kua evokes—such as our knowledge that Kao Mei is associated with Kao T'ang, a place known for its connection with sexual intercourse, and that she is consecrated in folk literature as the indigenous Mother Goddess. Furthermore, it is extremely significant that on the occasion of drought, it is to this particular goddess that our ancestors have chosen to dedicate their sacrificial rituals. By learning about the occasion we already know some-thing about what the rituals may mean. That the invocation of Nü-kua's name has the power of bringing forth rain is a telling testimony to her fertil-izing force. It is this sort of preliminary understanding of the referential code of our object of analysis that often qualifies the very claim of objectivity that the notion of "paradigm" and "isotopy" seems to command. We need to be constantly aware that while being useful as a discovery principle, the theory in question is not logically flawless. Even Greimas himself is well aware of the discrepancies of his model, for he acknowledges the obscurity of the idea of "totalité de signification."[57]

It is at this stage that we should be reminded once more of the hermeneu-tic emphasis on "preunderstanding" and the inescapably intuitive nature of interpretation. A competent interpreter often unwittingly understands a text in advance before analyzing it. By a dialectical process, a partial preunder-standing already contains the possibility of a global comprehension of the text. It is like arranging several pieces of a puzzle in order to figure out what is still missing. By this mutual interaction between the whole and the parts, each giving the others meaning, the act of reading is made possible in the first place.

Returning to our main thesis of intertextuality, I would point out that it is not only the unconscious recognition of the interdependent arising of the parts and the whole that defines the functional viability of preunderstanding. Preunderstanding does not work only in the name of presumed organic unity within a text, it also functions *across* the single textual space. Such preunderstanding is made possible by the omnipresence of *a concatenation of texts* that precede the target-text. Our potentially immanent understanding of the latter arises in part from the working of our involuntary recollection of many invisible frames of reference, that is, of a repertory of other texts sharing their lexicon with the one we are reading. In other words, preunderstanding is the reader's intuitive grasp of the intertextual relationship between the text and its "complementary or contradictory homologues"[58] in the preexistent texts.

So far we have focused our discussion on the "complementary" relations of the text to its prior "homologues," a relationship that characterizes the nature of closure inherent in the concept of intertextuality. As I explained earlier, intertextuality not only includes identifiable prior codes and conventions that help to ensure and constrain the production of meaning, it also incorporates unconscious signifying practices and lost intertexts that undergo infinite dissemination into other unidentifiable intertexts. The anonymous and dispersive nature of intertextuality cannot but continuously open up the enclosure formed by the recuperable intertextual network of signification. We need to recognize that insofar as the continuity of prior codes of signification implies extension and alteration at the same time, the convergence of meaning between a text and its predecessor-text always generates deviations and distances, however imperceptible these may be at first glance. This further reinforces the open-ended character of intertextuality, which is already perpetuated by the anonymity of obsolete texts. In this sense, intertextuality guarantees the continuity of cultural, literary, and historical context, but it also invites and triggers the transformation of such a context.

Our understanding of the transformative potential of intertextuality suggests that the stone lore constrains the meaning of the literary stone symbolism only to a certain extent. Although there exists in the Chinese cultural and philosophical tradition a deep-seated aversion to disruption and discontinuity, in the realm of narrative fiction the conformity to literary conventions has not always been strictly observed. The occasional resistance to conventional enclosure is made possible in the name of "poetic truth"; two notable examples of this are *Hsi-yu Pu* (*The Tower of Myriad Mirrors*) by Tung Yüeh (1620–89), and Ts'ao Hsüeh-ch'in's *Hung-lou Meng*.

In the following chapters, I will examine how the paradox of intertextuality—continuity versus change, convergence versus divergence—can shed light upon the continuous popular and academic fascination with the story of the Nü-kua Stone. The intertextual relationship of stone lore and the different variations of stone imagery inform us that the depth of a text depends upon the play of heterogeneous signifiers that resist total enclosure by any external constraint. Such is the everlasting appeal that the twin imagery of *wan shih/t'ung-ling shih* 頑石 / 通靈石 evokes. For while the imagery of the stone monkey in the *Journey* and the engraved stone tablet in the *Water Margin* reactivates the history of the folkloric stone in vivid reproduction, the semantic richness of their counterpart in the *Dream* surpasses the limitations imposed by the context of the stone lore. It does so by means of subtle deviations. Although the *Dream* eventually fails to escape the circular movement of narration or to realize its inner drive to flee from instead of returning to its starting point, the stone imagery therein is not brought within the confines of the intertext of stone lore. The Nü-kua Stone not only foregrounds and multiplies all the paradoxical attributes characteristic of the folkloric stone, but, more importantly, it also integrates the variant of jade and, by stimulating its intertextual relations with the latter, triggers a very complex process of semantic oscillation within its own field of signification. It is the intertextuality of stone and jade that distinguishes the *Dream* from the other two narratives in their relationship with the stone lore. It explains why the Nü-kua Stone has commanded a stronger hold on our imagination than the anonymous stone ovum that gives birth to Monkey. The stone-jade dialogue that serves as a significant thematic device linking the mythical and the mimetic, translates the implicit ethical code of the *Dream* in symbolic terms and makes up the shifting landscape underlying the ambiguous fictional truth that "Real becomes not-real when the unreal's real" (*Stone* I: 130).

The attempt to radicalize the stone imagery in the *Dream*, however, should not lead us into thinking that its author-narrator's good intentions are completely fulfilled. It should be noted that the subversion of context and conventions has rarely been attempted in the long history of traditional Chinese literature. Although a handful of scholar-critics, such as Wang Ch'ung 王充 (27–ca. 100), Liu Hsieh 劉勰 (465–522), Li Chih 李贄 (1527–1602), and

Yüan Hung-tao 袁宏道 (1568–1610), acknowledged *pien* 變 ("change") as the most vital principle of composition,[59] most Confucian literati subscribed to the concept of *che-chung* 折中 ("synthesis"), if not to that of *t'ung* ("homogeneous identity"), and condemned any signs of *i* ("difference") as the writer's sacrilegious attempt to defy tradition. A text's dependence on and infiltration by prior codes and conventions is therefore a deeply rooted phenomenon in Chinese literary culture, where intertextual constraints hold sway over the concept of textuality. The appropriation of one text by another is often a rendition rather than a violation or contradiction of the principles of the text that has been appropriated. In its struggle against the Confucian emphasis on the preservation of the classical heritage, the convention of *pien*, which promises intertextual dissemination, continuously undergoes a series of qualifications that serve to deradicalize its original subversive connotation.

Many scholars have argued that the indigenous Chinese notion of *pien* ("change") as conceived in the *I Ching*[60] by no means indicates progress in the Western image of the spiral.[61] The explication by Yang Hsiung (53 B.C. to A.D. 18) of the *hsüan* 玄, "the profound Tao," provides the best footnote to the Chinese paradox of the changing immutability of Nature:

> Heaven and earth were born amidst the alternate movement of opening and (en)closing; the rotation of sun and heavenly bodies reveals the alternation of "hardness" and "softness." The circulation returns to its point of origin—both the beginning and the end are definite [and definable] points [in time and space].[62]

Perhaps the composite metaphor of the ebb and flow of the tide can best capture the simultaneously static and dynamic nature of such a notion. The key image here is that of the "reflux" that always returns to its source the transformative and dispersive incentive, no matter how far the tide has rolled away from the heart of the ocean. Within the concept of *pien*, there hide the seeds of the return complex that never fails to compromise even the most intractable theory of transformation.

At this point, we need to pause momentarily to examine the solution of the Chinese "radicals" to the dilemma of eternal enclosure, a solution that takes a different route from that envisioned by Western deconstructionists. Based on an idealist understanding of language, the Ch'an and Taoist philosophers presuppose an original neutrality and innocence of the Tao. Thus instead of locating, foregrounding, and glorifying the elements of difference, debris, and irregularities, they go a step further by suggesting that the tyranny of enclosure is inherent in the very nature of language, and that true liberation consists in the destruction of both the linguistic medium and the attempt at conceptualization. In the message delivered in the Taoist and Ch'an poetics, the true textual experience—the Tao—appears not only impalpable and elusive, but also pure and natural—a sign neither to inform nor to be informed by the ideological signified.

The new ontological turn away from Confucian rationalism, which asserts the potency of the mind and the corresponding efficacy of language, arose with the emergence of the *hsüan-hsüeh* 玄學 tradition during the Wei-Chin period. Long before the works of Ssu-k'ung T'u 司空圖 (837–908) and Yen Yü 嚴羽 (fl. 1180–1235) came into being, the third and fourth centuries witnessed the burgeoning of the poetics of "emptiness" in its embryonic form. The epistemic orientation of the school of "Profound Learning" not only accentuates the "extralinguistic" essence of the Tao but also takes it as "self-evident."[63] The Tao—the authentic and the experiential—is to be found neither in the prescribed intertextual convergence with the Confucian classics, nor in some radical intertextual dissemination, but rather in a direct communion with the patterns, both pictorial and spiritual, of heaven, earth, and the myriad things in between. The highest level of intertextuality to the Taoists is just this—the translinguistic dialogue with the ubiquitous.

To be sure, such a philosophy of language—perceiving it as the artificial, and pitting it against the natural (i.e., the Tao)—contains the rudimentary notion of boundary subversion, verbal as well as conceptual. In its denial of any adequate linkage between *yen* 言 ("words") and *i* 意 ("meaning"), the Taoist poetics bears the semblance of the post-structuralist separation of the signifier from the signified. Yet despite its radical implications, the Taoist poetics is permeated with traces of the idealist philosophy that situates the human agent, language-making, and the Tao—each a given—as three entities seemingly independent of one another. Underlying the idealist stance is the assumption that the human agent is not only "free" to make and to interpret verbal signs, but is also able to withdraw from language-making activities self-consciously, and that the Tao, as the original and the ultimate sign, is in essence nothing other than a mystified homologue for the origin of meaning. Thus contrary to what the poetics advocates, the "unnamable" Tao cannot but be turned into a fixed center, rather than being a saturated moment in a process that can never take place without appropriating the verbal and the ideological "intervention" of the human agent.

Perhaps nothing better illustrates the idealist underpinning of the Taoist philosophy of language than an annotation by Wang Pi 王弼 (226–49) on the *I Ching*.[64] In the "Ming *Hsiang*" 明象 ("Elucidating the Image"), he provides a triangular explanatory model among three terms: *hsiang* ("image/sign"), *yen* ("words/signifiers"), and *i* ("meaning/the signified"). The main thrust of his explication of the Taoist paradox of language consists in the philosophy of instantaneous illumination and forgetting—*te-hsiang wang-yen* 得象忘言 , "once the image is grasped, the words [that convey it] can be forgotten," and *te-i wang-hsiang* 得意忘象, "once the meaning is grasped, the image [that carries it] can be forgotten." He concludes: "Therefore one establishes the image in order to discharge meaning. But the image can be forgotten. Therefore one draws sixty-four hexagrams in order to convey truth. But the hexagrams can be forgotten."[65] The surface significance of Wang Pi's explication of the concept of "image" (*hsiang* in the *I Ching* points toward the mimetic and the symbolic at the same time) seems revolutionary enough: the understanding of the sagely words, and eventually of the Tao itself, represents a tradition of *wen* that is not only independent of verbal analysis and contemplation, but, due to its tenuous link to any materialized verbal container (*ts'un* 存), is also free from (inter)textual enclosure in its flight toward a saturated silence.

What seems most disturbing about this approach to language is the underlying assumption that *i* preexists *yen*, and that *yen* in turn preexists *hsiang*. Thus Wang Pi's tripartite system of signification eventually privileges a fixed point and a singular essence—*i*—"meaning." Lacking from this system is the recognition, so vital to our understanding of how meaning is produced, that the sign, the signifier, and the signified remain interdependent, and that none of them preexists the others or has any meaning outside the complex network of their relationship. Although cloaked in the rhetoric of the ineffable and the innocent, the ultimate *i*—the Tao—is as artificial and arbitrary as its various human-made verbal carriers. It is by no means immune to the infiltration of social, historical, and individual practices that can only be understood as taking shape and taking place in language. This said, it becomes clear that what is absent from Wang Pi's Taoist poetics (perhaps deliberately left out) is a place for the language-using and language-making human agent. What appears problematic in Wang Pi's intuitive and experiential approach to the Tao is the concept that the ideal textual production is effortless and independent from language-making activities, and hence, from the language-making agent—the human individual.

The above discussion of Taoist poetics serves to bring our attention, if only momentarily, to the problematics of its translinguistic myth. And it illustrates once more the role of language as the locus of the construction of the social, ideological, and creative being. The following chapters will demonstrate, in various stages and to various degrees, the constraints of (meta)language, and the promises of momentary release from such an enclosure—the ongoing struggle of the story of intertextuality, a dilemma that the believers in the Ch'an and the Tao understand all too well. For them, the systematic reconstruction of stone lore only deepens the quandary. Perhaps the only possible salvation lies in being and becoming a stone.

石

Semantic Considerations

[stone]
1. n. Earth which is hardened into lumps, e.g., jade stone.
2. n. One of the eight musical notes, name of an ancient stone chime.
3. n. A substance that can be used to cure illness, e.g., medicine.
4. adj. Hard and solid.

[stone woman]
1. A woman with a defective reproductive organ.
2. A barren woman.

[stone falling into the sea]
(an idiomatic expression) Completely without information or response; without a trace.[1]

The stone entries recorded in any modern Chinese dictionary would consist of semantic categories similar to those listed above—the description of stone's dominant physical attributes and its less distinct medical and musical potency. These last two characteristics of stone, which assume prominent functions in the ancient stone lore, have remained latent in the modern usage of the word. The majority of contemporary Chinese speakers seem to have forgotten the melodious and healing potentials of stone; instead, they have fallen into the habit of associating it with something negative, as the idiomatic expressions of *shih-nü* 石女 ("stone woman") and *shih-ch'en ta-hai* 石沉大海 ("stone falling into the sea") both indicate. A similar evaluative orientation inherent in the standard definition of stone can be found in modern Japanese dictionaries:

固いもの、冷たいもの無情なもの、融通のきかないもの
などを比喩的にあらわす語²

For both Chinese and Japanese, it seems that stone conjures up the image of something hard, cold, heartless, and obstinate. The same holds true for the semantic entries of stone in a contemporary English-American dictionary:

[stone], n.
1. The hard substance, formed from mineral and earth material, of which rocks consist.
2. Any small, hard seed, as of a date; pit.

[stone-blind], adj. Completely blind.

[stone-cold], adj. Completely cold, as a radiator, a corpse, etc.

[stoned], adj. Slang.
1. Drunk; intoxicated.
2. Under the influence of marijuana or a drug.

[stone-dead], adj. Dead beyond any doubt; completely lifeless.

[stony], adj. Unfeeling; merciless; obdurate.³

Combinations such as "stone-blind," "stone-cold," and "stone-dead" operate under the principle of metaphor, with stone serving as the semantic vehicle and "blind," "cold," and "dead" serving as its tenors. The implicit comparison involved in these cases clearly indicates that stone elicits negative connotations in the extreme.

For the general reading public today, the word "stone" conveys a wide range of unpleasant meanings—it is hard, rigid, fixed, and barren. And most important of all, it is an earth-bound substance. This commonsense understanding of all that stone signifies in the contemporary context falls short of helping us interpret the heaven-bound magic stone that recurs in the *Dream of the Red Chamber*, *Water Margin*, and *Journey to the West*. Our expectations will be thwarted time and time again when we confront the stone images in these narratives with our preconceived notions of the mineral's negative qualities. In order to understand better how stone participates in the production of meaning in the literary texts in question, we need to acquaint ourselves with the ancient Chinese stone lore—a mythological dictionary of stone forever caught in the process of being completed. The concept of "process" is crucial to our understanding of the incomplete, and hence abridged, nature of such a dictionary. To reiterate what I have said in the preceding chapter, any logical system of richness entails the necessity of extension that renders the description of such a system incomplete. The system in question cannot be resolved in one final paradigmatic scheme; it therefore remains open-ended and potentially contradictory. The stone lore as a vast system of signification reveals the plenitude, and therefore the elusive totality, of such an ever-shifting structure. It thus testifies to the inherent limitations on consummating those projects that aim at constructing metalanguage of any kind.

As a "discovery principle," the stone lore can be perceived as an intertextual model, a system of literary conventions, that serves as a frame of reference for the creation and interpretation of the stone images presented in the three literary works. It not only naturalizes certain unfamiliar elements in the literary stone symbolism, but through the study of its point of disjunction with individual stone-texts, it also demonstrates how meaning is produced through the mechanism of making difference. Our study of intertextuality does not consist solely in the identification of intertextual convergence between the folkloric stone and the literary stone; more importantly, it also demonstrates that interpretation is made possible only through the construction of a network of relations, and that such relations are defined in transformational as well as in homologous terms.

Before undertaking the task of constructing the mythological dictionary of stone, we need to recapitulate our theoretical premise based on Greimas's structural semantics. In "Comparative Mythology," the investigation of meaning is perceived by Greimas as involving the translation of "mythological language" into "ideological language."[4] This technique of translation necessarily calls for a new descriptive model able to take into account the *relational concept of meaning.* The making of such a model involves a metalinguistic activity "that paraphrases and translates words and utterances by other words and utterances. It therefore follows that the first step in describing signification resides in the transposition of one level of language into another level, of one language into another language."[5] Taking the notion of transposition as the point of departure, we can understand why Greimas resorts to an analytical model of semantics based on a network of relational terms such as "seme," "classeme," and "isotopy." Description is thought of as the construction of a network of relations that can convert one level of signification into another level. The progression from minimal semantic units (e.g., seme) to higher ones (e.g., classeme and isotopy) is thus perceived as the translation of mythological language into a natural language shared by all. Such a methodology produces two sets of correlations: the formation of "semes" and "classemes" sets up microscopic correlations between the various meaning-units distributed throughout a single narrative, while "isotopy" works to affiliate one narrative with another, or with a series of other narratives. In the process of this continuous semantic transposition, we seek to explore the questions crucial to all interpretations: how is meaning produced, and how can it be described?

Methodology

In examining stone as a folkloric item, I will attempt to edit the dictionary of a single lexeme, "stone," which will in turn generate an analysis of a repertory of texts revolving around the motif of stone. The repetition of semes in a text enables us to name its "classeme," and the repetition of a cluster of classemes will enable us to identify a level of coherence, "isotopy," which will then serve to relate one text meaningfully to a bundle of other texts.

Before we can move on to compile the dictionary in question, two methodological problems need to be addressed. The first problem concerns the pseudo-scientific nature of the stone lore, which was discussed in Chapter 1 and needs only to be recapitulated here in a few words. As I pointed out earlier, Greimas's methodology of locating isotopies has its critics. Since the meaning of a text cannot always be automatically derived from the composite meanings of its lexical items, the question arises whether it is always possible to identify the level of coherence by depending upon a scientific model of semantic theory. The process of reading, we have shown, involves more than what a sound semantic theory can provide. The inadequacies of such a theory need to be supplemented by our "hermeneutic preunderstanding" of the text and by our reactivation of cultural context whenever the mechanistic adding up of semantic parts is of no avail in helping us arrive at a unity of any sort. In the process of composing the mytho-folkloric entries of stone, we will see how such preunderstanding and the cultural unconscious come to assert themselves at a particular juncture of a given text, so that their "intervention" in the semantic analysis will not appear as a convenient measure adopted by a cornered critic to resolve the deadlock of interpretation.

The second methodological problem involves some fundamental issues regarding semantic theories in general. Greimas has incorporated several basic concepts of general semantics into his own system of structural semantics without providing much explication; in exploring the semantic properties of stone, we will make cross-references to the concepts of general semantics to illumine the meaning of his terminologies and to fill in the gaps of his theoretical assumptions. We will start with the outline of general semantics, which will shed light upon the operation of our discovery procedures.

Semantic theoreticians look into two different aspects of meaning— "sense" and "reference," with unequal emphasis. "Sense" involves the intralinguistic relations among words, while "reference" deals with the relationship between linguistic data and the nonlinguistic context.[6] In the field of semantics, the study of "sense relations" seems to hold sway over that of context. For instance, J. J. Katz and J. A. Fodor direct their attention exclusively to the lexical structure of words. And even F. R. Palmer, who complains about the tilted balance, has evaded the crucial question and devotes only a flimsy chapter to the discussion of nonlinguistic context in *Semantics*.[7] It seems that linguists have happily relegated this problematic issue to pragmatics and semiology, preferring to work on the well-trodden ground of intralinguistic relations.

The study of sense relations inevitably includes the investigation of the syntagmatic and paradigmatic relations of a word.[8] Take the lexeme of stone: if we consider the sentence "the stone is making a resonant sound," we could discuss the syntagmatic relations between "stone" and "sound"; whereas if we compare this sentence with "the instrument is making a resonant sound," a paradigmatic relationship is established between "stone" and "instrument." The semantic representation of "stone" in the latter case will not be adequate without taking into account the paradigm of "instrument"; in this sense, "instrument" constitutes part of the linguistic context of "stone." Both the syntagmatic and paradigmatic relations of a lexeme constitute its linguistic text through which meaning can be stated and derived. Some linguists hold an extreme view of the importance of a narrow concept of linguistic context and tend to believe that the meaning of a lexeme is wholly statable in terms of the immediate context in which it occurs. A more modified response comes from J. R. Firth, who is not interested in the total distribution of a lexeme, but in its more obvious co-occurrences.[9] Take "stone" for instance: such co-occurrences as "stone-blind," "stone-dead," and "stone-deaf" are of high explanatory value, since the words collocated with stone share certain semantic properties. Similarly, "stone-woman" is also an interesting collocation, for the accompanying word "female"—a vehicle of reproduction, and hence a symbol of fertility—contributes to our collection of the lexical components of stone. The fact that we shall never find "stone" collocated with "male" reveals the significance of a broader linguistic context; one can know a word not only by the company it keeps, but also by the company it does not usually keep. The paradigmatic relations between "stone" and its various co-occurrences serve to indicate that "linguistic context" can be a very fluid notion that goes beyond the definable boundary of the immediate context of a lexeme.

Moving from the semantic representation of a single lexical item to that of myth, we will encounter the difficulty mentioned in the first chapter. While one can rely on one's "linguistic competence" to conjure up the paradigmatic set of stone ("stone-dead," "stone-deaf," "stone-woman," and so on) in a quick succession and to grasp almost intuitively the distinctive features (e.g., sterility) shared by all such paradigms, "mythological competence" is a far more elusive concept that is not easily accessible except by a privileged few. As Claude Lévi-Strauss argues, the context of each myth consists of other myths—so the structural analysis of a myth always involves the study of its cross-references to the other paradigmatic sets.[10] That is, the intelligibility of a particular myth is made possible by the setting up of its correlations with a number of units of the mythic signified, distributed across the textual space of a related set of myths. We will not be able to draw the semantic configuration of Nü-kua if we examine each myth related to the goddess separately. The signification of myth reveals itself through the paradigmatic (vertical) relations discerned between a set of myths, rather than through investigation of the syntagmatic (horizontal) structure displayed within a single narrative.

Greimas comes very close to Lévi-Strauss in his methodological approach to myth. He endorses the latter's paradigmatic definition of myth[11] by postulating that the mythic signified are "linked paradigmatically even though the story may make it appear otherwise."[12] He goes on to explain his position as follows: "One must not read myth syntagmatically in a way that is dictated by the story line; it is instead a grasping, in a way that is often unconscious on the part of the member of the community in which the given myth prevails, of the relation between the various units of the signified, distributed throughout the length of the story." [13]

The hierarchical relations established between semes and classemes, and between classemes and isotopy, serve as the best example of how the paradigmatic relations of signification actually work in Greimassian narrative analysis. What the mythological dictionary of stone incorporates in the following pages is nothing less than the complex network of paradigmatic relations discerned between the various sets of myths and rituals concerning stone.

Katz outlines four goals that a valid semantic theory should aim at achieving: (1) to construct a universal scheme for semantic representation; (2) to construct a dictionary that "specifies the sense of every syntactically atomic constituent in the language"; [14] (3) to relate the semantic components of the dictionary to the projection rules and to specify how the projection rules operate in a larger and more complex linguistic context; and (4) to spell out a set of definitions for semantic properties and relations such as semantic ambiguity, antonym, synonymy, and meaninglessness. [15] The present study of the stone lore will be focused on the first two goals: the representation of the semantic components of the lexeme of stone, and the construction of a dictionary that will assign its various lexical readings in minimal semic categories.

Since our dictionary will consist of only one lexeme, all the entries will then contain the various semantic components of stone. According to the ordinary entry, stone is composed of the following clusters of meaning: hard substance, mineral, tablet, medicine, and so forth. A lexical reading of the semantic nuclei of stone thus requires the decomposition of each nucleus into a series of semes represented by a set of semantic markers. For instance, "mineral" can be broken down into the following semes:

(nonliving)(concrete)(hard)(natural product)(underground). [16]

The structure of a conceptually complex sense is thus rendered into clusters of minimal units. According to Katz, this process of disintegration is meaningful in that "it is essential to treat a sense neither as atomic nor as monolithic but as a composite of concepts that can be decomposed into parts and the relations in which they stand." [17] What Greimas envisions in his structural semantics is not different from the proposals made by Katz and other semantic theorists; however, while the latter speak of decomposition, Greimas conceives the process of semantic analysis as one of *transposition*.

Although both parties bring our attention to the relational mechanism of meaning-making, Greimas goes a step further by suggesting that meaning cannot be decoded, it can only be transcoded. The implications of such a perspective will eventually lead us to the radical vision of which deconstructionists speak with such eloquence—that the process of "decomposition" is doomed to perpetuate itself indefinitely because there is no such a thing as a "stabilized signified" that may serve as the terminal point for this fatal quest of meaning.

We have seen how the Greimassian structural model of semantics incorporates the basic analytical strategies of segmentation and classification, and how it utilizes the familiar concept of syntagm/paradigm—two fundamental relations that characterize the signifying activity of a linguistic sign.[18] Bearing in mind the basic theoretical assumptions and the discrepancies of this explanatory scheme, we shall now return to the clusters of Nü-kua myths mentioned briefly in the previous chapter. The first step in constructing the global meaning of the goddess is to collect the semantic core of each myth in which she plays a central role. Such a core reveals itself in a series of semic categories. The dictionary of Nü-kua, as we have already seen, is composed of the following lexical items: the creation of humankind; procreation; irrigation; healing; and the covenant of matrimony. The semantic representation of each item can be figured as follows:

Creation: (causing to come into existence)(birth)
*contextual semes: (animate beings)(inanimate beings)(god)(human)(nature)(culture)

Procreation: (causing to come into being)(birth)(nature)(sexual union)

Irrigation: (fluid)(passage)(entering)(causing to grow)
*contextual semes: (human fluid)(natural fluid)

Healing: (causing to become whole)(bringing back into existence)(rebirth)
Matrimony: (culture)(sexual union)

As this analysis shows, each lexical item consists of an invariant core of a variety of semes and a possible series of contextual semes. Take the lexeme of "irrigation," for instance: its semantic core is made up of "fluid," "passage," "entering," and "causing to grow." One should note that the seme of "fluid" takes "human fluid" and "natural fluid" as its contextual variants. If "irrigation" occurs in a context in which a female or male subject serves as the object of the act of irrigation, then our reading of the sememe will call for the selection of "human fluid" as the dominant contextual seme. To determine the correct reading of "irrigation" in this given context, we combine "human fluid" with the semantic invariants of "passage," "entering," and "causing to grow" to produce the semantic effects of "sexual union"—a metaphorical reading of "irrigation."

This ànalytical model also enables us to detect the recurrence of certain semes and helps us identify "birth" and "sexual union" as the classeme, which in turn leads us to recognize "fertility" as the isotopy for the set of mythic texts focused on Nü-kua. Although this structural model of semantics seems to yield nothing other than what the cultural unconscious dictates—namely, that the goddess is consecrated as the symbol of fertility—it is important to recognize that one of the goals of semantic analysis is to "account for the data in a way that is compatible with speakers' intuitions." [19] A good semantic theory lays bare the operation of our intuitions in forming familiar concepts; it provides descriptions of how reading works, step-by-step; and above all, it enables us to give a full account of how familiar expressions such as "stone-woman" and "stone-dead" are in fact semantic anomalies that should not be taken for granted.

Sources

A few comments need to be made here regarding the nature of the sources on which I will rely to establish the groundwork of the mythological dictionary of stone. I will be using both pre-Han and post-Han texts, up to the Yüan Dynasty (1271–1368). It is important to note that the concept of intertextuality has rendered irrelevant Bernhard Karlgren's point of contention made in his *Legends and Cults in Ancient China*: the question of the authorship of the post-Han materials is crucial to the study of the religion and social history of ancient China, a project that Marcel Granet attempted to achieve in his *Danses et légendes de la Chine ancienne*,[20] but it loses its legitimacy in any study of intertextuality, since what traverses the vast intertextual space includes unidentifiable and spurious texts as well as identifiable and so-called authentic texts.

Thus, for instance, the data needed to reconstruct the mythology of Nü-kua and the deluge hero Hsia Yü 夏禹 will first be culled from the pre-Han texts, which Kalgren states provide the most trustworthy documentation of early beliefs and rituals. Supplementary and miscellaneous materials will also be drawn from early Han and later literatures, such as the *Huai-nan-tzu* 淮南子, *Lu shih* 路史, and many other sources. By examining these different kinds of sources, we shall establish a wide spectrum of intertextual references to the mythological personae of the two legendary figures. In the process of reconstructing the cult of Nü-kua and Hsia Yü, we will also witness how certain embryonic mythemes undergo subsequent transformations, filled out by later embellishments and often ruthlessly trimmed by the systematizing interpretation of Confucian scholars. The problem of deciding upon the degree of genuineness of a particular text appears irrelevant to our study of the growth and transformation of myths and legends. In folklore scholarship, anthropologists have come to the conclusion that the search for ultimate origin can yield results only in terms of probability, rather than as proven fact—and there is the danger of being enticed into the realm of pure speculation, for which no concrete supporting evidence could be found. It is therefore necessary to differentiate the problem of origin from that of accretion and intertextuality, in the present discussion.

The particular myths and legends collected in the following pages include the myths of Nü-kua, Hsia Yü, the *feng-shan* rite, ceremonies of coercing the rain deities, the talking stone, the sonorous stone, the stone that nods, and other closely related stone lore.

Nü-kua and Stone

The myths of Nü-kua revolve around three well-known mythemes: the repair of heaven, the creation of humankind, and her mating with Fu Hsi 伏羲. Other more fragmentary aspects of the goddess that bear relevance to our study of her intimate relationship with stone include the correspondence of her name to Kao Mei—the goddess of matchmaking—and her identification with Yü's wife T'u-shan 塗山.

Creation

Nü-kua's name first occurs in an ambiguous question in the *Tien Wen* 天問: "Nü-kua had a body. Who formed and created it?"[21] While Karlgren places more emphasis on the object "it" and takes the question as a statement of marvel at the goddess's peculiar shape,[22] both Yüan K'o 袁珂 and Andrew

Plaks shift the focus to the subject "who" and rephrase the question as follows: "Who created Nü-kua if she created mankind?"[23] To this vague text the Han commentator Wang I 王逸 (A.D. 158) added the following annotation: "It is said Nü-kua had a human head and a snake body. She made seventy transformations a day."[24] In the chapter "Shuo-lin" 說林 of the *Huai-nan-tzu*, it says:

> Huang Ti 黃帝 begat *yin* and *yang*. Shang P'ien 上駢 created ears and eyes, Sang Lin 桑林 created arms and hands, that was whereby Nü-kua made seventy transformations.[25]

The character *hua* 化 in the two texts evokes different interpretations, which do not necessarily contradict each other. Yüan K'o follows the suggestion of Hsü Shen[26] in construing the "seventy transformations" as a reference to the creative power of the goddess.[27] In the *Shuo-wen*, Hsu Shen defines the character *kua* 媧 as "an ancient divine goddess who created a myriad of things."[28] Karlgren and other interpreters, however, favor the explication of *hua* as a reference to the metamorphosis taking place in the body of the goddess herself. The source in the *Shan-hai-ching* seems to support this argument:

> There are ten gods named as the bowels of Nü-kua. They were transformed into spirits, dwelling in the wilderness of Li Kuang 栗廣 and blocking the road.[29]

This particular text of Nü-kua's transformation seems to confirm the idea that her creative resources are inwardly centered. Despite the controversy surrounding the character *hua*, a composite picture of Nü-kua's creative energy can only be accomplished by drawing both the internal and external manifestations of her creativity. As a matter of fact, both her own metamorphosis and her creation of the universe point in the same direction: they signify the dynamics and versatility of the goddess with the same emphatic tone.

Nü-kua's creative impulse and her innate power of transmutation clearly indicate the domination of the transformative character of the feminine within the archetype of the Great Mother. In his study of the psychic structure of the mother archetype, Erich Neumann carefully differentiates the transformative from the elementary character of the feminine: "In the transformative character, the accent is on the dynamic element of the psyche, which, in contrast to the conservative tendency of the elementary character, drives toward motion, change, and in a word, transformation. The transformative character is already clearly at work in the basic function of the Maternal Feminine, in the Gestation as well as the bearing of children." [30] First and foremost, women experience their transformative character naturally in pregnancy and childbearing. In the case of Nü-kua, this particular aspect of her feminine principle is manifested both in the biological birth of the ten gods from her bowels, and in her involvement in a symbolic labor that took place outside her body—the creation of humankind.

Nü-kua's creation of humankind from a handful of mud is seen in the extant version of the *Feng-su t'ung-i*:

> It is said that when Heaven and Earth had opened forth and no human creatures could yet be found, Nü-kua created human beings by patting yellow earth together. But the work taxed her strength and left her no free time. So she dragged a string through the clay and made into human beings the mud thus shaken off. Therefore the rich and the noble are those made of yellow earth, while the poor and the lowly—all ordinary people—are those cord-made creatures. [31]

Underlying this passage is the intimate association between earth and the maternal principle. Earth, out of which human beings are made, embodies the real mother of humankind. The goddess plays no more than a supplementary role—as the "spreader" of the seeds that originate in Mother Earth. Through her magic touch, her crafts(wo)manship, and most importantly, her intent of molding the clay in the image of human beings, Nü-kua becomes the surrogate mother of humankind. [32]

To sum up Nü-kua's creative capacity, the birth of ten gods and that of human beings is made possible only through the power of transformation—in one case, through the transformation from the inexhaustible resources of Nü-kua's own body, and in the other, through that from the cradle of earth. In the act of her self-transformation, and in her ability to give life and shape to human beings, the goddess experiences her own creativity and the bliss of motherhood. The transformative attributes of the goddess serve as telling evidence that Nü-kua is not only a primordial cosmogonic deity, but also a female goddess—an embodiment of the Chinese Great Mother. This confirms Hsu Shen's intuition in determining Nü-kua's gender as female in the second century A.D. [33] It is indeed a wonder, as Karlgren suggests, that there is no indication in any of the pre-Han texts that Nü-kua is a woman. [34] The association between the symbolism of fertility and the female gender seems an issue that did not surface in those earliest classical writings.

Healing

Having discussed the creation mythology, we will now turn to a second set of myths closely related to the name of Nü-kua. When one speaks of the self-generating creativity of which the goddess is known to be possessed, an equally significant feat that attests to her celestial grandeur also calls for our attention. Among the various complimentary titles Nü-kua enjoys, the most familiar to the common folk is that of the "healing goddess" who rejuvenates the disrupted heaven. The earliest source of this popular legend in ancient Chinese mythology can be found in the *Huai-nan-tzu*:

> In very ancient times, the four pillars (at the compass points) were broken down, the nine provinces (of the habitable world) were split apart, Heaven did not wholly cover (Earth), and Earth did not completely support (Heaven). Fires flamed without being extinguished, waters inundated without being stopped, fierce beasts ate the people, and birds of prey seized the old and the weak in their claws. Thereupon Nü-kua fused together stone of the five colors with which she patched together azure Heaven. She cut off the feet of a turtle with which she set up the four pillars. She slaughtered the Black Dragon in order to save the province of Chi. She collected the ashes of reeds with which to check the wild waters.[35]

Nü-kua has revealed her role as a cosmic fashioner in Han reliefs, where she is pictured with serpent tails, holding a compass or a moon in either hand.[36] The emphasis of the present text is on her power of arresting subversive movements ("being extinguished," "being stopped," "to check") and restoring order to the universe that has already come into existence, rather than creating one from scratch as indicated by the carpenter's tool in her portrait. It is strongly suggested, however, that the goddess is closely associated with cosmic design in both cases.

In the above text quoted from the *Huai-nan-tzu*, there is no mention of the cause of the heavenly disorder, which is later attributed in the *Lun Heng* 論衡 and in "San-huang pen-chi 三皇本記 "—the supplement to the *Shih Chi*—to the rage of Kung Kung 共工, an arch-demon viewed in traditional light,[37] but whose antiauthoritarian spirit has impressed Chinese Marxist critics.[38] The fusion of the myths of Kung Kung and Nü-kua serves as a good example of how ancient people attempted to interpret portentous disasters of nature in terms of human motivation. The operation of this kind of mytho-logic seems to account for the occurrence of Mount Pu-chou 不周 (cf. *ti pu chou-tsai* 地不周載) in the texts of Kung Kung's infamous battle:

> According to the Sacred Books, Kung Kung and Chuan Hsü 顓頊 fought for the throne. Kung Kung was defeated and bumped into Mount Pu-chou in anger. The pillars of Heaven were broken, and the four corners of Earth were severed. Nü-kua fused together stones of five colors to patch the sky.[39]

We shall put aside the variations of Kung Kung's myths, since his combat with Chuan Hsü or Chu Jung 祝融 is of little relevance to our study of Nü-kua's association with stone. Let us now return to the main text of Nü-kua's heroic deed of revivifying the disjointed Heaven and Earth.

In this particular myth, the stone of five colors serves as the most important instrument for retrieving the dislocated Heaven and Earth. It has come to be associated with the name of Nü-kua much more closely than the other remedies mentioned (the feet of water tortoises, and the ashes of reeds). The five colors of the stones signify the hues of five elements—earth, water, fire, metal, and wood. The balanced arrangement of the five elements provides the spatial orientation required for environmental harmony. The alchemical flavor imbued in the stones is brought to our attention in the *Lieh Tzu* 列子, which indicates that it is the harmonious fusion of the five elements in the stones that enables Nü-kua to reestablish order.[40] We should note that it is only after the smelting procedure is completed that the stones of five colors, now in their liquid substance, acquire and assume the healing function. This healing quality of the mystic mineral in question recurs in many other myths of stone and appears to be one of its constant attributes. The heaven-bound character and the divine aura of stone are also subtly but unmistakably revealed in the text, since it is far from accidental that the goddess chooses stone rather than wood or metal to mend Heaven.

In "San-huang pen-chi," Ssu-ma Chen 司馬貞 wrote of Nü-kua as ruled by "the virtue of wood."[41] Nü-kua is also known as the inventor of reed pipes.[42] It seems only natural that with the aid of the ashes of reeds, the goddess of the wood principle holds the deluge in check—the vanquishing of water by the element of wood. Andrew Plaks even suggests that the word *yin-shui* 淫水, "uncontrollable waters," finds its echo in the theme of libidinous obsession in the *Dream of the Red Chamber*.[43]

We may suggest that a subtler correspondence between this mythic text and the *Dream* can be detected in the complementary occurrence of Nü-kua's two curing instruments—the stones of five colors that mend the breach of Heaven, and the ashes of reeds, the element of vegetation/wood, that curb the terrestrial floods. Wood plays a complementary role in several other legends of stone. In this particular myth, its subtle interplay with stone seems overshadowed by the intervention of the third element, that of fire—the stones are "molded," and the reeds are burned into ashes.

In the *Dream*, the association between stone and wood finds its most eloquent expression in the idea of the "union of wood and stone" (*mu-shih chih meng* 木石之盟), a motif that underlies the mythical framework of the narrative fiction. The interplay between these two elements originates in the karmic encounter of a precious stone and a divine plant. The insatiable desire of the plant and the stone to consummate their fated union haunts their human reincarnations and sows the seeds of a tragedy that gradually unfolds in a logocentric world hostile to the unadulterated purity of mythical instinct. The intimate conjunction between stone and wood in the literary text may appear to be one of the many fictions that are relevant only within the self-sufficient domain of the narrative in question. However, our recognition of a similar motif in folkloric texts leads us to view the stone-wood affiliation not merely as a fictional device, but also as the haunting appearance of a mytho-folkloric (inter)text.

Kao Mei

The close relationship of Nü-kua to stone is further shown in the sacrificial ritual to Kao Mei, the Divine Matchmaker (who also appears with several alternate names, such as *Chiao Mei* 郊媒, *Shen Mei* 神媒, and *Kao Mei* 皋媒).[44] The Mei rituals were merry spring festivals on the day of the vernal equinox, on the one hand, and religious ceremonies for the divine matchmaker Kao Mei on the other. The description of the ritual is found in the *Chou Li*:

> In the month of mid-spring men and women are brought together. At this time license is not prohibited. Whoever refuses to comply without reason is to be punished. All unmarried men and women are mustered and brought together.[45]

It is important to note that the rite of Kao Mei, which is remembered primarily as a folk festival that celebrated the matching of young men and maidens, also served as an occasion when barren couples prayed for progeny at the temple of Mei, *mei kung* 媒宮：

> She who in the beginning gave birth to the people,
> This was Chiang Yüan 姜嫄 .
> Well did she sacrifice and pray
> That she might no longer be childless [*i fu wu-tzu* 以弗無子].[46]

The association between Chiang Yüan's sacrificial prayer and the Mei ritual is established in the annotations of Mao Kung on the *Shih Ching*:[47]

> *Fu* 弗 means "to dispel." In order to dispel barrenness and to pray for progeny, the ancients built the Mei Temple in the countryside.[48]

The Mei deity therefore assumes the double role of the Divine Matchmaker and that of the birth-giving Mother Goddess.

It is said that a rock or a stone was placed at the altar for Kao Mei.[49] In the time of the Southern Dynasties (420–589), the place of worship for the goddess was also identified as a rock:

> In the sixth year of Yüan-k'ang 元康 reign period of Emperor Hui 惠 of Chin Dynasty [A.D. 296], the stone on the altar of the Mei Temple was split in two. The Emperor inquired whether another stone should be obtained to replace the broken one. . . . Shu Hsi 束皙 proposed, "The stone was placed on the altar to preside over the Tao. Once the sacrificial implement was worn out, it should be buried and replaced. Now [the old stone] should be buried and its place taken by a new one. It was improper to speak of abolishing it." At that time Shu Hsi's proposal was not taken by the Emperor. Hence the story of Kao T'ang-lung 高堂隆 was derived. During the reign period of Green Dragon [Emperor Ming of Wei [A.D. 233–237], the stone was erected [in the temple]. And the Emperor issued an order to place an inscribed stone on the Kao Mei altar as in the past. The old broken stone was buried ten feet deep underground.

It was said that on the west side of a path in the north gate of the ancestral temple of Liang Dynasty, a stone was found with an inscription like bamboo leaves. It was housed in a small shelter. This stone was discovered during the construction of the temple during the reign year of

Yüan-chia 元嘉 of Liu Sung Dynasty [A.D. 424–453]. Lu Ch'eng 陸澄 thought that it was the altar stone of Emperor Hsiao-wu's 孝武 Mei temple. However, it was said that the downstream area of the Yangtze River also observed this sacrificial ritual.[50]

The placing of a stone at the altar of Kao Mei is reminiscent of the primeval stone cult. It serves as an understatement of stone's alliance with divinity and procreative power. There is widespread evidence in China,[51] as well as in the rest of the world, of rocks serving as the locale for sacrifices.

The identification of Kao Mei still remains a subject of dispute. It has been asserted, according to Wen I-to, that Kao Mei is identical to Kao Mi 高密 and is closely associated with Kao T'ang 高唐, and that other names for the goddess are *San-hu* 三尸 ("Three Doors") and *San-shih* 三石 ("Three Stones").[52] The last two names probably imply a well-secluded place surrounded by three walls as the locale for sexual revels on the festive day. The character *mi* 密 seems to evolve from *mei* 媒, just as *chiao* 郊 seems a variant of *kao* 高. Kao Mi is identified with Yü according to the *Shih Chi*,[53] *Shih Pen*,[54] and *Wu-yüeh ch'un-ch'iu*.[55] The male gender identity of Kao Mi by no means indicates that Kao Mei is a male deity—for Kao Mei is also closely associated with the name Kao T'ang, a southern place connected with sexual activities, the well-known home of the legendary divine maiden of Kao T'ang,[56] which clearly suggests its liaison with the female gender. To complicate the gender controversy, Kuo Mo-jo 郭沫若 and Wen I-to came to yet another interpretation of the term *kao t'ang* by tracing its phonological variation to *chiao she* 郊社.[57]

The real issue, however, is neither the identification of Kao Mei with a specific personage or a specific gender, nor the phonetic association with *chiao she* ("the she temple"), but rather the significance of the spectacular array of guises that Kao Mei assumes in the image of famous mythological personae. In the *Lu Shih*, the celestial matchmaker is named Nü-kua:

> Nü-kua prayed to the temple god for the divine office of Matchmaker [*nu-mei* 女媒]. Thereupon she established the marital system.[58]

> Since [Nü-kua] was the vehicle of matchmaking, the posterities of later countries worshiped her as the Goddess of Matrimony [*kao-mei* 皋媒].[59]

According to the source in the *Cheng Chih*, Kao Mei takes on yet another identity in Chien Ti 簡狄:

> After swallowing the egg of a phoenix, Chien Ti [the daughter of Yu-Jung] was consecrated by the Emperor as the Divine Matchmaker and enshrined side by side with the emperors in the ancestral temples as the Goddess of Kao Mei.[60]

Wen I-to argues that the divine goddess of Kao T'ang bears close resemblance to yet another quasi-historical personage, the first empress of Hsia Dynasty, Yü's consort T'u-shan.[61] All these references make us wonder why Kao T'ang assumes the legendary figures of Nü-kua, Chien Ti, and T'u-shan all at once. Wen I-to's analysis of the subject has broken new ground and provides illuminating clues to the mystery. After examining the sources of Kao Mei's various appellations—Nü-kua/T'u-shan in the court of Hsia (ca. 2100–ca. 1600 B.C.), Chien Ti in the court of Shang (ca. 1600–ca. 1100 B.C.), and Chiang Yüan in the court of Chou (ca. 1100–256 B.C.)—he concludes that the consecration of the tribal ancestress of each dynasty in the name of Kao Mei serves to prove that in ancient China it was a standard practice to identify the sacred title in question with the matriarchal progenitors of the people.[62]

Wen I-to's analysis helps us link Nü-kua with T'u-shan through their common association with Kao T'ang/Kao Mei. And I would suggest that due to the crucial ritualistic functions that stone and rock play in the Kao Mei sacrifices, they have become more and more intertwined with the personified images of Kao Mei—the legendary matriarchs. It then seems only natural that stone/rock recurs in the myths evolving around Nü-kua and T'u-shan.

The use of stone in the Kao Mei ritual seems to be based on the former's symbolic association with fertility and procreation. One has to acknowledge, as Karlgren implies in his analysis, that there exists in primitive cultures a mysterious association between stone, fertility, and motherhood, and that this primordial unconscious seems to pervade the earliest ritual practices of humankind. In many ancient civilizations, stones serve as the oldest symbols of the Great Mother goddesses—from Cybele and the stone of Pessinus to the Islamic kaaba and the omphalos, the navel stone.[63] In China, the legends of both Nü-kua and T'u-shan seem to attest to and reinforce this association. As the goddess of matchmaking and birth-giving, Nü-kua is closely identified with the altar stone. T'u-shan's affiliation with stone is no less strong, since she is physically turned into a stone which then gives birth to the royal blood. While one perceives in Nü-kua attributes of symbolic maternity, the legend of T'u-shan materializes such a symbolism through the act of childbearing. However, while Nü-kua is recognized as the cardinal Chinese Mother Goddess and elevated to a pedestal for human worship, T'u-shan, in contrast, enjoys no such deification. Although she is designated as the tribal mother of the Hsia people, the story about her transformation into a rock and the rock's subsequent giving birth to a son is not well integrated into the lore of Chinese Mother Goddesses. One might say that Nü-kua is consecrated regardless of her association with stone, while T'u-shan's status as a Mother Goddess probably suffers from that very association.

This is hardly the place to speculate on why T'u-shan enjoys a lesser mythological stature than Nü-kua. The issue is further complicated by the fact that the identities of these two matriarchal figures merge into each other in early historical writings. In the following section, we will look into the confusion of identity between Nü-kua and T'u-shan. It is interesting to note that although Nü-kua evokes the manifold association of stone with fertility, it is actually in the myth of T'u-shan that we find the earliest Chinese reference to the concrete image of the childbearing stone. It should also be noted that it is in the obscure legend of T'u-shan's stony transformation that one finds the most dramatic reference to the coexistence of two contradictory attributes of the folkloric stone—fertility and sterility.

T'u-shan and Nü-kua

In the light of Wen I-to's analysis, the sources in which Nü-kua is equated to the Kao Mei of Hsia Dynasty imply that the goddess is the ancestress of Hsia, and thereby the royal spouse of Yü, totally identical to T'u-shan Shih. A variety of texts seem to support this argument. In "Hsia pen-chi 夏本紀," it is said that "the name of T'u-shan Shih is Nü-chiao 女憍."[64] In the text of the *Shih Pen*, we have a slightly different variation on the name: "Yü married T'u-shan's daughter whose name was Nü-kua."[65] In the *Wu-yüeh ch'un-ch'iu*, it is said that "thereupon Yü married T'u-shan whose name was Nü-chiao 女憍."[66] T'u-shan is also recorded as Nü-chiao 女憍, Nü-ch'iao 女趫, Yu-chiao Shih 有蟜氏, and Yu-kua Shih 有媧氏.[67] It seems obvious that *chiao*, *ch'iao*, *chiao*, *kua*, and *chiao* (媧) are interchangeable and refer to a single personage.[68] Wen I-to brings to our attention another piece of evidence indicating that Nü-kua's and T'u-shan's identities are indistinguishable from each other: "Based on the 'Lan-ming 覽冥' chapter of the *Huai-nan-tzu*, which describes Nü-kua's collection of the ashes of reeds for the purpose of restraining the uncontrollable waters, we can thus infer that Nü-kua's role as the helpmate of Yü in his flood-control task is an ancient folk belief."[69] Based on such a variety of sources, we can assume that Nü-kua and T'u-shan are identical beings under two different names.

Let us now turn to the fascinating episode about T'u-shan's transformation and her miraculous giving birth to Ch'i 啟 :

> Yü went to appease the floods. He pierced through Huan-yüan 轘轅 Mountain, and transformed himself into a bear. [Earlier] Yü had said to T'u-shan, "At the sound of the drum, you would bring me food." Yü jumped on a piece of rock, and thus hit the drum by mistake. T'u-shan [brought the food and] went. She saw the transformed bear. Feeling embarrassed and distressed, she went away as far as the foot of Sung-kao 嵩高 Mountain where she was transformed into a stone. Yü said to her, "Return my son." Facing north, the stone split open and gave birth to Ch'i.[70]

Wen I-to postulates a theory to account for T'u-shan's transformation in the myth. He finds a close connection between this text and the Kao Mei ritual: "I supposed that because T'u-shan Shih is an ancient Kao Mei Goddess, and because stone is the embodiment of Kao Mei, the legend about T'u-shan's transformation into a stone was thus formed later."[71] By highlighting T'u-shan's association with the Kao Mei ritual, Wen I-to brings into focus the fertility symbolism of stone in this particular myth. Wen's mytho-logic seems to be based on his awareness of the intertextual relationship between Kao Mei and the ancestress of the Hsia people, and that between stone and Kao Mei—a set of paradigmatic relations of which the present T'u-shan text seems to form a part.

However, a closer scrutiny of the T'u-shan legend reveals a far more complex picture of the stone's function in the text and thus challenges Wen I-to's interpretation of the T'u-shan stone as a dominant emblem of fertility. In this particular myth, the function of stone as life-giver is embodied in its capacity to give birth. However, the symbolism of fertility contains within itself images of sterility at the same time. T'u-shan's story is one of the rare instances where one finds stone possessing both positive and negative connotations. First, T'u-shan's transformation into a rock can be interpreted as an act of tacit rebuke and retaliation, a strong reaction to Yü's turning into an animal and thus making any prescribed sexual relations with a human spouse unlikely. Upon the appearance of the bear, it is possible that

T'u-shan's aversion to sodomy embarrasses her and triggers her subsequent metamorphosis through an instantaneous self-withdrawal into an inanimate object totally deprived of sexuality. The connotation of sterility is therefore present in the traumatic encounter between Yü and T'u-shan. The impossibility of any form of communication, whether physical or verbal, between the wife and her husband, finds its most eloquent manifestation in the metaphor of stone. However, with a curious inversion of such a negative content, the T'u-shan rock retrieves its sterile image at the end of the myth by emerging as a stone that is not only communicative but also fertile in the literal sense. Thus Yü comes forth (there is no indication as to whether he resumes his humanity or still remains an animal), and makes a request for his son. The stone answers him by opening itself up, and in that very act it gives birth to Ch'i—a character that literally means "to open up." The split of the stone symbolizes the simultaneous opening of its mouth and its womb. It suggests the realization of verbal communication between Yü and T'u-shan, and most significantly, it serves as the reminder of their earlier sexual communication. In fact, it is the strong connotation of procreation in the second part of the myth that leads us to presume that T'u-shan's initial metamorphosis is sexually motivated. Both through the act of symbolic speaking and that of childbearing, the stone has recovered from its former closed, inanimate, and sterile substance.

This myth serves as a cogent footnote to the pluralistic symbolism of which the five elements are characteristic. Although stone was a predominant symbol of fertility in prehistoric times, it emerged as early as the Han Dynasty as a substance of contradictory attributes. Erich Neumann will probably argue that the qualitative transmutation of symbols such as stone, fire, and wood manifests the process of differentiation triggered by the dawning of a human consciousness that seeks to break down the continuum of the unconscious into a series of binary opposites. Thus the image of darkness is distinguished from that of light, and sterility from fertility.[72] Whatever the psychological or sociological cause for the emergence of such binary entities, the ambiguity of stone symbolism that we witnessed in the T'u-shan legend is to be carried over into other myths and will culminate in the twin imagery of the *wan shih/t'ung-ling shih*, "the unknowing stone/the stone of divine intelligence," in the *Dream of the Red Chamber*.

The Dictionary of Nü-kua

Having examined the cluster of Nü-kua myths, we shall now reconstruct the lexical entries of the goddess for the purpose of identifying the dominant isotopy of the Nü-kua myths ensemble. The mythological dictionary of Nü-kua is composed of six sememes that are in turn made up of a set of semes, several of which contain secondary instrumental semes:

> Self-transformation: (innately motivated) (divine will) (change by increasing)(giving birth)
>
> Creation of humankind: (motherhood) (divine will) (giving birth through artisanship)
> *instrumental seme: clay/earth
>
> The repair of heaven: (divine will)(healing)(rebirth)(causing to become whole)
> *instrumental seme: stone of five colors—(harmony)(heaven-bound) (solid-liquid transformation)(healing)(fire)
>
> Suppression of floods: (divine will)(excessive motion arrested)(healing)
> *instrumental seme: ashes of reeds—(wood)(fire)
>
> Kao Mei ritual: (birth)(sexual union) (tribal motherhood) (spiritual communion with divinity)(healing [sterility])
> *instrumental seme: stone
>
> T'u-shan: (matriarch/mother)(sexual union)(change by hardening)(enclosure)(birth)
> *instrumental seme: stone—(fertility) (giving birth) (sterility) (speech act)

Based on the above lexical readings of Nü-kua, the semantic representation of the goddess can be derived from the repetition of the semes of "giving birth," "healing," "divine will," and "motherhood," which in turn lead us to the formulation of the classemes of "healing" and "divine motherhood." We are thus able to name "fertility" as the isotopy that ties together all the variants of the Nü-kua myths.

According to the above semantic scheme, stone stands out as the most dominant instrumental seme in all the Nü-kua myths. It therefore forms an intimate affiliation with the goddess. Although designated as the ruler of wood,[73] Nü-kua is more strongly attached to stone, the element of earth, an archetypal symbol of fertility, than to any other element in the cycle. One should also note that stone's alliance with the Mother Goddess of fertility has triggered the gradual transposition to itself of all the semic properties of Nü-kua. It is this semantic transposition that helps to strengthen stone's association with the sacred and to consolidate its elevation from an earth-bound to a divine stature in ancient folkloric texts.

Yü and the *She* 社 Ritual

Stone's association with the *She* ritual is intricately woven into the myths of Yü and Kao Mei. Yü, the first emperor of Hsia Dynasty, is a renowned deluge hero in ancient Chinese legends. The most comprehensive account of his feat of subduing the inundations is seen in the *Shu Ching* 書經 .

Karlgren recapitulates Édouard Biot's theory that the elaborate account of Yü's feat recorded in the *Shu Ching* indicates the "scholastic endeavor to make history out of a deluge legend."[74] Moreover, he emphasizes the need to distinguish Yü's legend from those of Kung Kung and Kun 鯀 — common deluge legends—by recognizing the former as a systematized hero myth. The catastrophe of the flood therefore emerges not so much as the center of the myth as one of the many episodes of which a hero myth is made up. In successfully overcoming the inundations as well as many other ordeals, Yü appears larger than an ordinary flood hero. He emerges as the quasi-divine sage-king—one of the primeval milestones of the dawning of human ego-consciousness upon the chaotic waters of the unconscious.[75]

By examining Yü's deluge legend in the light of the global conception of the hero myth, we can account for the emergence of a cluster of legends that are integrated into the Yü myth proper. The first such legend that attracts our attention is the story of Yü's miraculous birth. According to Neumann's reconstruction of the archetype of the hero myth, the birth of the hero is very often attributed to a virgin. The virgin mother and the leviathan whom the hero has to vanquish during his quest constitute two dominant motifs of the hero myth.[76] We shall return to the theme of the leviathan later; let us now examine the mythological account of Yü's birth.

Neumann seems to have overlooked an equally important form of the hero's supernatural birth: the self-procreation of the hero's father. In Greek myth, Athene was not born of a woman, but sprang from the head of Zeus. And not surprisingly, Yü was also said to be born from his father Kun, according to the following sources:

> Kun was *dead* for three years. His body was not putrefied. *Cut* open by
> a magical sword of Wu, it was *transformed* into a yellow dragon.[77]

> Kun was *cut open* by the magical sword of Wu. Hence Yü was born.[78]

> Kun was *imprisoned* under Mount Yü 羽 —why did his body not decay
> for three years? Kun was pregnant with Yü—how was Yü *generated*
> after all?[79]

Each of these three different versions of Kun's death is pervaded by images of
violence and enclosure—the cutting open of his body in the first two legends,
and the allusion to his rough imprisonment in the third. But the negative
imagery of death coexists with the signs of life—the birth of Yü from his
father's cleaved bosom, and the dead body's transformation into another
form of existence ("yellow dragon"). Life is created through death. It takes
its shape only after the ritual of mutilating the body of the life-giver has been
accomplished.

The myth of Kun's giving birth to Yü provides but one solution to the
mystery of Yü's parentage. The mythic origin of Yü is more commonly ascribed to his virgin mother Hsiu-chi 脩己 . "Virgin mother" refers either
to a woman who has not copulated but gives birth, or to a woman who
conceives children after experiencing a suprahuman communion with some
supernatural force. In the *Huai-nan-tzu*, it is proclaimed:

> Yü was born of a stone.[80]

Commenting on this text, Kao Yu 高誘 (2nd century A.D.) says:

> His mother was moved [to pregnancy] by a stone and bore Yü; breaking
> her bosom he came out.[81]

In the *Lun Heng*, it says that Yü's mother swallowed the seed of lotus-fruits
and became pregnant.[82] The source from the *Ch'ien-fu lun* gives a slightly
different description of Yü's birth, according to which it was the sight of
a comet that moved Yü's mother to pregnancy.[83] The *Shih Chi* provides a
combination of both themes:

> His father is Kun. His mother, Hsiu-chi, saw a meteoroid pass through
> the Mao constellation; she dreamt that she received it. Her spirit was
> thus moved [to pregnancy]. She also swallowed the divine pearls and
> seeds of lotus-fruits. Her bosom burst open, and she bore Yü.[84]

We should note that the meteoroid contains the seme of stone—the "stony" essence of a fallen meteor. We can also assume that by the time of the mid-Han, the theme of Yü's preternatural birth had cropped up to complete the cycle of his hero myth. It seems obvious that in ancient beliefs, Yü's divine progenitor no longer takes the form of the personal mother: it appears as a suprahuman element in the guise of different variations of the ovum-motif—pearls, the seeds of lotus-fruits, a meteoroid, or a real stone.

The divine power that plays a significant role in the birth-myths of Yü also manifests itself through the medium of jade in the legends about his formidable task of flood-control. Yü was said to have been awarded by the gods a piece of black jade on one occasion, and a jade slip on another:

> According to the *Annotations on "Shui Ching,"* Yü went west as far as the upstream of River Yao 洮. He saw a tall man and received a black jade from him. This man was probably the god [Ch'ang Sheng 長乘].[85]

The black jade in question seems to remain an unmotivated motif in this text. It is most likely the self-same object that Emperor Shun 舜 or Heaven bestows upon Yü as a reward for the successful completion of his mission:

> Emperor [Shun] bestowed a black jade on Yü, announcing his exploits to the entire world.[86]

> After Yü succeeded in subduing the waters, Heaven bestowed upon him a black jade, announcing Yü's feat to the world.[87]

In the *Shih-i chi*, however, the jade tablet is said to be a magic gift Yü receives from a mystical being to help him accomplish the heroic task of suppressing the floods:

> Yü bored through the mountains of Dragon Pass, which was also known as the Dragon Gate. He arrived at an empty crag . . . [he] saw another god with a snake-like body and a human face. Yü talked to him . . . was offered a slip of jade of one foot and two inches long which co-incided with the number of a cycle, for the measurement of sky and earth. Holding this slip of jade, Yü was able to restore order to land and waters.[88]

The jade in these legends serves as a token of the imperial acknowledgment of Yü's heroism, as well as a celestial instrument for the restoration of human order. The sacred gift reaffirms Yü's divine origin and strengthens his bond with Heaven. In this sense, jade serves to mediate between the world above and the world below. Yü's affiliation with jade, the quintessence of stone, seems to stand in certain relationship to the flood hero's intimate connection with the element of stone.

When we come to the second stage of the cycle of hero myth, the slaughter of the leviathan, we encounter even more diverse versions of the Yü legend. Yü's antagonist, or the mythical beast, is referred to as Kung Kung in the *Huai-nan-tzu*[89] and *Hsun Tzu*,[90] and as Wu-chih-ch'i 無支祁 in the *T'ai-p'ing kuang-chi*.[91] The evil water god is also referred to as Kun's chief minister Hsiang Yao 相繇 or Hsiang Liu 相柳 in the *Shan-hai ching*:

> Kung Kung's vassal is named Hsiang Yao who had nine heads, self-intertwined snake body. He ate on the nine soils. What he spat out and deposited became springs and marshes. And if they were not pungent they were bitter, the animals could not endure them. When Yü dammed up the flooding waters, he killed Hsiang Yao, his blood was rancid, one could not grow the grains there. . . .[92]

The combination of both themes, the slaying of water monsters and the extraordinary birth of Yü, elevates an otherwise primitive deluge legend to an archetypal myth of the cultural hero who is worshiped as the guardian deity of his people according to the ancient folk belief. This again sheds light on the source in the *Huai-nan-tzu* that refers to Yü as the consecrated *She* deity:

> Yü labored for the world. After his death, he became *She* [the God of Earth].[93]

In ancient Chinese society, *She* was the guardian deity of Earth. The ritual is therefore a fertility ritual in essence. *She* temples were usually built in forests, or surrounded by woods:

> The Hsia people used pine trees; the Yin people used cedar trees; the Chou people used chestnut trees.[94]

Most interestingly, what was worshiped in the *She* temples was nothing other than a rock—the same token used to represent the divine goddess in the temple of Kao Mei:

> Stone was used to embody the host-god of the *She* temple.[95]

> According to the rituals of the Yin people, stone served as the *She* deity.[96]

The *She* temple was not sheltered indoors. It consisted of an altar, exposed to frost, dews, wind, and rain, for the purpose of absorbing the spirits of Heaven and Earth. Because of its hard and durable substance, stone was therefore used as the host image [of the *She* Deity] on the altar.[97]

Since all the pre-Han texts invariably designate Hou T'u 后土 as the *She* deity, Karlgren is led to look upon the source in the *Huai-nan-tzu* (in which Yü is identified with *She*) as a "very curious item."[98] What Karlgren fails to see, however, is that the intricate relations between Yü and stone, and between stone and the *She* ritual, inevitably pave the way for the merging of these two sets of myths.

In addition to worshiping stone as the altar deity, the rituals of Kao Mei and *She* share one more characteristic that further reinforces their intimate association with each other. Both rituals fulfill the function of harmonizing marital relationships, according to the *Chou Li*:

Lawsuits that concerned marital problems of men and women were offered a hearing at the *She* temple of the subjugated country.[99]

Based on this source, we can assume that in ancient society, the *She* deity also listened to all the pleadings and complaints of men and women related by marriage. The peacemaking function that the *She* deity fulfilled served to restore the harmonious bond between estranged couples and to ensure the continuity of procreation—a function similar to that of the Kao Mei goddess in the matchmaking and birth-giving rituals. I would suggest that Yü's connection with stone appears as intimate as Nü-kua's with the Kao Mei rock, and that this connection undoubtedly reinforces his identification with the fertility deity of *She*.

We have shown that the *She* ritual intersects the legends of Yü and the Kao Mei ritual at certain peripheral points. For instance, stone and marital relations serve to link the Mei and *She* rituals, while Yü's heroism and his role as the tribal ancestor seem to justify the association of his name with the *She* deity. Two sets of relationships are thus established—*She* and Kao Mei, and the *She* ritual and Yü's legends. Instead of incorporating the lexical readings of Kao Mei and Yü into the dictionary of the *She* ritual, we shall analyze the semantic representation of each mytheme—*She*, Kao Mei, and Yü—and then decide upon their point of convergence later.

She Stone, Kao Mei Stone, and Yü Stone

She: (earth) (matrimonial/natural harmony) (guarding/promoting growth)
*instrumental semes:
1. stone—(arresting of change)(tribal motherhood)
2. pine/cedar/chestnut trees—(wood)(evergreen/fertility of Nature)

Kao Mei: (birth)(sexual union)(tribal motherhood)(spiritual communion with divinity)(healing sterility)
*instrumental seme: stone

Yü: (stony origin and affiliation)(birth-in-death)(arresting of water) (slaying of water monsters)(restoring harmony)(tribal fatherhood)
*instrumental seme: jade slip—(stone) (heaven-bound) (overcoming waters)

When we take a close look at the map above, we find that stone emerges as a dominant seme, and that all three sets of myths/rituals involve the semes of "harmony," "healing," "birth/growth," which again point to the isotopy of fertility. It is worth noting that a certain degree of cultural understanding serves as an important clue for our preliminary experiment of juxtaposing the *She* ritual with the Yü legend and the Kao Mei ritual. Equipped with our preanalytic knowledge that the *She* ritual is dedicated to Earth, and hence has immediate connection with the seme of fertility, we are able to predetermine the *She*'s possible intertextual relationship with other similar fertility rituals, such as the Kao Mei.

The close affiliation of Yü with stone that evolves around a threefold manifestation—his own origin, his spouse's stony transformation, and his son's birth from stone—seems to account for the mysterious bonding between the deluge hero and Nü-kua. For just as Yü leads an existence intertwined with stone, the goddess herself never ceases to participate in an intense communication with it, regardless of the different mythical personae she assumes in various rituals. The bonding between the male hero and the female deity is further reinforced by their similar roles in restraining the floods—the one with the aid of a jade slip, the other with the five-colored stones. It is probably due to the convergence of such semic categories that there emerges the inexplicable legendary belief that Yü's spouse T'u-shan Shih is none other than the Goddess Nü-kua herself.

Rainmaking Rituals

As seen in the Kao Mei and *She* rituals, stone assumes an instrumental role in the human petition for fertility and harmony. In ancient times, sacrificial petition was the most primitive form of the spiritual communion of human beings with supernatural forces. By means of the prayers and sacrifices made to the altar-stones at such rituals, human beings performed the act of verbal and symbolic communication with stone—an emblem of both Heaven and Earth. The association between stone, petition, and speech act will take a slightly different form in the following accounts of the rituals of the supplication for rain.

Since it is not my purpose to study all the rainmaking rites practiced in ancient China, I will focus only on those procedures in which stone serves as an important ritual instrument. According to Wang Hsiao-lien, stone magic forms an integral part of the fertility cults of ancient agricultural societies.[100] In fact, it is not difficult for us to hypothesize that the belief in the potency of stone evolves from the heavy reliance of human beings on the stone implements used during the Paleolithic and Neolithic periods. Rain, on the other hand, appears as another indispensable natural resource upon which harvest, food, and livelihood depend. Not surprisingly, the deification of rain in ancient cultures took place side by side with the worship of stone.

The Chinese rain deities assume various guises. It is commonly believed that dragon gods are the providers of rain.[101] In the *Lun Heng*, the familiar figure of Nü-kua emerges as the rain goddess:

> People offered sacrifices to Nü-kua if it did not stop raining.[102]

It seems reasonable that the Han people would designate a fertility goddess as a rain deity. Based on the same mytho-logic, the *She* temples are often said to be the locale where the emperors prayed for rain.[103]

The *Ching-chou chi* gives us the earliest account of a ritual performed in the fifth century that involved the whipping of two magic stones to induce rain:

> In Heng-shan [county] there is a solitary mountain standing high and precipitous. On its north east side there is a stone cave. If one takes a candle and goes in about one hundred paces there will be two big stones standing about ten feet apart. The common name for one is the Yang Stone, and for the other the Yin Stone. When there is calamity from

drought or flood, one whips the Yang Stone and then it rains, or one whips the Yin Stone and the sky clears.[104]

Alvin Cohen argues that a cult of this kind is built upon the laws of sympathetic magic. He also concludes that one whips the stone that is overactive in its function: "Since Yang produces heat and dryness, when it produces too much it must forcibly be caused to reduce its energy and allow the Yin, which produces cold and wetness to function, and vice versa."[105] The *T'ai-p'ing yü-lan* quotes a passage from the *Ching-chou t'u* 荆州圖 that records a ritual of similar nature:

> There was a cave in I-tu 宜都 in which were found two big stones situated more than ten feet apart from each other. It was said that one was the Yang Stone, the other was the Yin Stone. When there was a drought, people whipped the Yang Stone. And the rain would come. When the Yin Stone was whipped, the day would clear up. They were the so-called Lin-chün 廩君 Stones. However, he who whipped the stones would not live long. Therefore people were frightened, reluctant to execute the ritual.[106]

In the *Kuang-chou chi* 廣州記, we find a rain-petition ritual in which an equally aggressive measure was resorted to. A stone bull is regarded as the substitute deity:

> Southeast of a mountain in the prefecture of Yü-lin 鬱林 was a pond. On its edge stood a stone bull which was worshiped by the people. When the drought came, people killed an ox and painted the back of the stone bull with the mixture of ox blood and mud. After the ritual was over, the rain would pour heavily. As soon as the stone bull's back was cleaned, its mud [and blood] washed away, the sky would then clear up.[107]

As "blood" is the vital essence of human life, so is "mud." The semantic representation of both lexemes contains the seme of water, an element indispensable to the growth of vegetation. As life-giving symbols, it is hardly surprising that both blood, the fluid of human energy, and mud, the combination of earth energy and water, are instrumental in bringing about the heavenly waters.

Seen in this light, the ceremony of coercing rain deities is but a variation of the ancient fertility ritual, part of the age-old stone cult. The rain-inducing rituals, however, depart from the Kao Mei and *She* rites in their means of petition. The success of the former seems to require certain acts of violence. And the imagery of death precedes that of life. It seems that in appeasing the alienated natural forces, sacrifices have to be made in return for good harvests and the uninterrupted cycle of birth and growth. Thus in one account, the human petitioner often suffers an untimely death, and in the other, the killing of an ox serves as an indispensable prelude to the ritual proper. The blood of the ox that is painted on the back of the stone bull thus symbolizes both life and death at the same time. The symbolic reenactment and celebration of the natural cycle of life and death in the rain-coercing rite and many other fertility rituals of ancient civilizations manifests the mytho-logic of the "savage" mind—life and death form a single continuum of existence.[108] The efficacy of fertility cannot be achieved without assimilating the violent energy of death.

It is also interesting to note that in the rainmaking rituals, stone serves to induce as well as to subdue waters. Stone symbolizes fertility in either case, since both drought and flood are detrimental to the harvest. Like the temple stone of *She*, which listens silently to the complaints and supplications of human creatures, the Yin-Yang stones and the stone bull also serve to mediate between Heaven and Earth. Any such form of petition is based on a contractual relationship and mediated by an emblem of divinity. The fulfillment of the request is usually accompanied by a requital: the rain deity claims either the life of the supplicant or that of an ox as a return of favor. In this framework, the transaction between the two parties seems fairly executed and faithfully observed.

The semantic representation of rainmaking rituals is made up of the following lexical readings:

> petition/irrigation: (symbolic speech act)(communion with gods)(contract) (violent energy: whipping/killing) (death) (life: mud/blood) (water)(earth)(vegetation)(harmonizing: Yin-Yang Stone)(fertilizing) *instrumental semes:
>
> 1. *Yin-Yang* Stones—(element of earth)(reactivating the inanimate principle)(harmonizing)(human sacrifice)
>
> 2. stone bull—(animate principle: blood and mud)/(inanimate ritual-object: stony statue)(element of earth)(element of water)(animal sacrifice)

As ritual objects, both instrumental semes (the Yin-Yang stones and the stone bull) serve as the recipients of petition and the active rainmaking agents. The close association between stone and speech act gradually evolves as the former participates more and more in rituals that consecrate the contractual relationship between the human sovereignty and the heavenly one.

The *Feng-shan* 封禪 Ritual: The Imperial Sacrifices to Heaven and Earth

The instrumental nature of stone that mediates the communication between the human and the divine/supernatural in the rainmaking ceremonies is further strengthened in the *feng-shan* ritual. According to early historical accounts, *feng-shan* rituals were performed by emperors in person on the summit of T'ai Shan 泰山 —Mount T'ai—the Eastern holy mountain in ancient China. The *Shih Chi* provides us the following definition of the ritual:

> On Mount T'ai, people piled up soil as an altar to worship Heaven in requital for His divine blessings. This was called *feng*. On the little hill at the foot of Mount T'ai, people weeded the ground in requital for the blessings of Earth. This was called *shan*.[109]

> With the change of each dynasty and the arrival of new order and peace, [the new emperor] had to observe the *feng* ritual on Mount T'ai and the *shan* ritual on Mount Liang-fu 梁父 . In so doing, he received the Mandate of Heaven as the [new] sovereign. He then ruled the people, declared the peace of his reign to Heaven, and rewarded gods for their blessings.[110]

Feng-shan is therefore an imperial ritual conducted by the emperor and his subjects for the purpose of consolidating the Mandate of Heaven and establishing the cosmological justification for his regency. The occasion was in essence a celebration of the successful reign of his dynasty. Although sacrifices were made to both Heaven (*feng*) and Earth (*shan*), it seems obvious that this was primarily a power ritual rather than a fertility ritual, and that the emperor was more anxious to reinforce his bond with the male sovereignty of Heaven than with the chthonic-feminine Earth.

According to Li Tu, the concept of the Mandate of Heaven, and of the unification of heaven (*t'ien* 天) and sovereign (*ti* 帝) in one entity *t'ien-ti* 天帝 ("the Sovereign of Heaven"), seems to have been introduced by the

Chou people.[111] The *Shih Ching* and the *Shu Ching* abound with the idea that Heaven chooses the virtuous man to rule and sanctions the kingship of he who obeys the Mandate of Heaven:

> Ah, the gracious and glorious King Wen,
> Our reverence for him is boundless;
> He received the Mandate from Heaven,
> To him all the descendants of Shang were subjugated,
> Their number far surpassed ten millions;
> The Sovereign in Heaven has passed His Ordinance,
> The Shang people thus paid homage to Chou;
> Ah, the Shang yielded to Chou,
> The Mandate of Heaven was never possessed by one king.[112]

> The Almighty Heaven charged His Mandate,
> King Wen and King Wu accepted it.[113]

> The Sovereign of Heaven learned about this. He was pleased, and thus bestowed upon King Wen the Mandate. . . .[114]

The identification of Heaven with sovereignty can also be found in both the *Shu Ching* and the *Shih Ching*:

> Ah, the Almighty Sovereign in Heaven would not spare my people.[115]

> The Great Sovereign of Heaven revoked His Mandate and eliminated the mandate of His elder son [King Chou 紂 of Yin Dynasty]. . . .[116]

Therefore, as *t'ien-tzu* 天子, "the Son of Heaven," the emperor manifested the legitimacy of his monarchy and announced the prosperity of his throne by virtue of the *feng-shan* ceremony. The political significance of such a ceremony will reveal itself as we examine the ritual proper and analyze the role that stone performs therein.

Emperor Shih-huang 史皇 (r. 246–210 B.C.) of Ch'in Dynasty was said to be the first ruler to have carried out the *feng-shan* ceremonies.[117] The incident was described in "Ch'in Shih-huang pen-chi 秦始皇本紀" of the *Shih Chi*:

> On the twenty-eighth year of his throne, Emperor Shih-huang went east to the prefecture of Chün 郡, climbed Mount Tsou-i 郰嶧, and erected a stone tablet there. He consulted with the scholars of Shan-tung and inscribed the stone with a eulogy praising the virtues of Ch'in. After he decided to observe the *feng-shan* ritual and the ceremony of sacrificing

to the mountains and rivers, the Emperor ascended Mount T'ai, erected the stone, and offered sacrifice at the temple.[118]

In Shih-huang's time, the ritual was quite simple. It consisted in inscribing and erecting a stone tablet that recorded "the virtue of Ch'in." By the time of Emperor Wu of Han dynasty (r. 141–87 B.C.), the ceremony had become more complicated—as seen in the text of the *Han Shu* and in Ying Shao's annotations:

> "In the April of 110 B.C., Emperor Wu returned. He climbed Mount T'ai and offered sacrifice there. . . ." Meng K'ang 孟康 annotated [on this passage]: "The Emperor has completed his exploits and ruled his kingdom. He announced his success to Heaven, engraved and marked down his reign title on the stone. Sacrifices consisted of the sealing of gold registers and stone sheaths, gold clay and jade slips."[119]

> Ying Shao said, "What is the *feng-shan* ritual at Mount T'ai? [Later emperors] went to the place where Emperor Wu of Han used to make his offerings, piling up stones, building the altar, sealing books of jade plates inside the stone, and then covering up the stone slips again."[120]

As shown in the above description, in addition to setting up the engraved stone tablet, the *feng-shan* ceremony of Emperor Han-wu also incorporated the sealing (*feng*) of stone coffers containing the emperor's secret prayers written on jade plates. The ritual act of enclosing the royal message consummated the private covenant made between the earthly and heavenly sovereigns. In theory, this particular imperial cult solicits the prosperity of the empire and the welfare of all the king's subjects. Therefore the message is in nature a well-motivated prayer addressed to a specific recipient—the Sovereign on High. And like any other form of communication, the sender of the message hopes to invoke favorable responses from the divine recipient. It is the potential fulfillment of all the terms enumerated in the request that underlies the discursive logic of prayer. The dispatching and sealing of the message written on jade plates thus indicates the potential realization of a speech act.

The discourse inscribed on the stone tablets, however, embodied a different speech pattern. Unlike the engraved imperial prayer, which was sealed and thus concealed from public scrutiny because of its intimate and private nature, the carvings on the stone tablets called for no such discretion: they catalogued the military exploits of the emperor and served to testify to the glory of the dynasty. While the jade plates were buried within stone coffers, the stone tablets were erected near the altar and exposed to the examination of the public. The code engraved on the tablets was therefore not transmitted to a single recipient, such as Heaven, but to the general public. It is the public function of the *pei-shu* 碑書 ("scripts on stone tablets") in general that guarantees the perpetuation of the legend of the virtue and splendor of a ruler from one generation to the next. As the sealing of the jade plates symbolizes the consummation of an esoteric covenant, the erecting of a stone tablet bears public testimony to the success of an imperial reign.

Despite the different functions of verbal transmission they played in the *feng* and *shan* rituals, both the jade plates and the stone tablets were chosen as message-bearers for various reasons. Apart from being durable and weatherproof, both jade and stone possess an aura of sacredness. In our discussion of the rainmaking rituals and the Nü-kua/Yü myths, we have shown how stone's divine stature emerges as its constant attribute. Let us now take a quick look at the characteristics of jade.

The *Shuo-wen* defines "jade" in the following manner:

> Jade, the quintessence of stone, has five virtues. Smooth and warm, it can be compared to *jen* 仁, "human-heartedness"; one can tell its inner texture and essence from the outside, it can thus be compared to *i* 義, "righteousness"; its sound is eloquent and far-reaching, it is thus regarded as a token of *chih* 智, "wisdom"; one cannot bend it without breaking it, thus it is compared to *yung* 勇, "bravery"; bright and clean, yet not covetous, it is an emblem of *chieh* 絜, "purity."[121]

The five virtues of the perfect gentleman are conveyed by the jade pendants he wears. As early as the Yin Dynasty, jade was already taken as a badge of the virtuous man. According to the *Li Chi*,

> In ancient times, a gentleman must wear a jade pendant.[122]

> A gentleman would not put aside his jade [pendant] without a good reason; the gentleman competes with jade in virtue.[123]

Its peculiar somber tint, sonority, smooth texture, and most important of all, its flawless quality, have made jade the favorite Chinese symbol of purity and perfection. In view of all the rare and precious attributes jade is known to possess, it is hardly surprising that it should be adopted as an imperial token and as a favorite ritual emblem in many ancient Chinese rituals.

The jade seal, *hsi* 璽 , of the emperor serves as the token of sovereignty to be passed down to his successors. In the *Chou Li*, we find an account that delineates the functions of various sacrificial vessels made of jade:

> [The ancients] used jade to make the six ritual implements to worship Heaven and the four corners of Earth. The deep green jade was used to worship Heaven, the yellow jade for Earth, blue jade for the East, red jade for the South, white jade for the West, and black jade for the North.[124]

It was believed that the jade embodied the "qualities of solar effulgence," and that heaven was epitomized in the tangible form of a perforated disk of jade—*pi* 璧 .[125] The perfection of the physical properties of jade is thus considered a manifestation of divinity, and it is therefore closely connected with the powers of Heaven. As a result, jade was frequently used by the ancients in sacrificial observances made to Heaven.

Returning to our discussion of the *feng-shan* rite, we can break down its ritual content into the following sememes and their respective semic categories:

> Sacrifices to Heaven and Earth: (communion with gods) (Heavenly Mandate)(prayer)
> Announcement of a successful reign: (verbal transmission) (power) (prosperity)
> *instrumental semes:
> 1. stone tablets—(public)(written statements)(testimony)(eulogy)(communication with human beings)(erected)
> 2. jade plates—(prayer) (written statements) (private) (covenant with Heaven)(sealed)

The instrumental function that stone and jade serve in bearing two different patterns of verbal imagery generated by the *feng-shan* cult continues to find an echo in a variety of stone imagery portrayed in narrative fiction, including the fiction-inscribed Nü-kua Stone in the *Dream of the Red Chamber*, and the enigmatic underground stone slab and the Heaven-dispatched engraved slate in the *Water Margin*. It is worth noting that such stone symbolism emerges as a variation of the ritualistic stone tablet and jade plates.

Shih kan-tang 石敢當:
The Evil-Warding Stone

The legendary *shih kan-tang*—literally, the "stone that dares to undertake formidable tasks"—is usually placed in front of the main gate of a house or at the entrance of a street, or else at places under malign influences. Some of the local guardian-stones bear the inscription "T'ai-shan Stone Takes upon Itself 泰山石敢當," appealing to the protective spirit of the sacred Mount T'ai in Shan-tung Province. Stone statues of men, stone animals, and pillars have been erected in front of imperial tombs since the Ch'in and Han dynasties.[126] We find the earliest account of *shih kan-tang* in the *Chi-chiu p'ien*:

> In the kingdom of Wei 衛 [ca. 1022–241 B.C.], there were men named Shih Ch'ueh, Shih Mai, and Shih O; in the kingdom of Cheng 鄭 [ca. 806–375 B.C.], there were Shih K'uei, Shih Ch'u, and Shih Chih, all of whom were of the Shih clan. In Chou 周 Dynasty there was Shih Shu; in Ch'i 齊 [ca. 1122–221 B.C.], those who were named after *shih* 石 were numerous. And in later dynasties, people also adopted the character for surnames. *Kan-tang* means "invincible in the face of enemies."[127]

In the *Yü-ti chi-sheng*, we have a clear description of the exorcising function of such stones:

> During the reign period of Ch'ing-li, Chang Wei governed P'u-t'ien. As he reconstructed the County, he discovered a stone on which were inscribed the following words—"Shih kan-tang: the stone which suppressed all evil spirits and calamities."[128]

This miraculous stone was also said to serve as the guardian deity of villages:

> . . . now it became clear to me why at the houses located at the end of a thoroughfare toward which the traffic of the street converged, there was always erected a stone statue or a stone tablet carrying the inscription of the name of *shih kan-tang*. It was meant to exorcise evil spirits. This local custom truly had its basis.[129]

Wang Hsiao-lien attributes the worship of this apotropaic stone to its relationship with the *She* ritual.[130] As *She* is the deity of Earth, and stone is the host of the *She* temple, it seems natural that the ancients took stone as a substitute Earth deity who protected the good fortune of village folk.

The spell-binding formula of the inscription on the stone is another phenomenon that calls our attention. It appears that the magic power of the *shih kan-tang* must be reinforced by some verbal charm to guarantee the success of its mission. It is as if with the advance of civilization, human beings have alienated themselves from the wonder of natural magic, and the loss of that primitive innocence has weakened the faith of human beings in the self-generated omnipotence of stone. The plain stone sitting in the She temple no longer seemed sufficient for the needs of civilized humankind; the potency of its sacredness gradually waned, as the stone myth faded from our collective memory. It is thus hardly surprising that in later epochs the primordial naked stone was brought to carry the emblems of human intellect as a reinforcement of its magic power. It seems predictable, therefore, that the semic composition of this particular folk custom should be dominated by the recurrent seme "written expression."

Shih kan-tang: (written message)(exorcising/curing)

The Inscribed Stone

The inscriptions on stones are sometimes natural pictorial patterns whose unusual beauty and strange design resulted in their being worshiped as auspicious emblems sent from Heaven;[131] accounts of the discovery of such stones have been found in many local legends. In most cases, however, the engravings were verbal messages that spoke the Mandate of Heaven and were regarded as prophetic discourses; thus the mediating function of the stones is clearly implied. In the "Wu-hsing chih 五行志" of the *Chiu "T'ang-shu"*, Emperor T'ai-tsung 太宗 worshiped an inscribed stone by identifying its engravings with the Mandate of Heaven (*t'ien yu ch'eng-ming, piao jui chen-shih,* 天有成命，表瑞貞石).[132] According to the *Hsi-ching tsa-chi*, Dowager Empress Tou 竇 of Han Dynasty found a stone of finger size, which, after being cut in half, revealed the inscription *mu-t'ien ti-hou* 母天地后 ("Mother and Empress of Heaven and Earth").[133] The prophecy later came true and Lady Tou became the Empress of Han. She kept the precious stone and designated it the "disc of Heaven." The *Shen-i chi* 神異記 reported the discovery of a turtle-shaped stone on which were written the four characters *Li Yüan wan-chi* 李淵萬吉, "Li Yüan [the founder of T'ang Dynasty] has every fortune on his side"[134]—a sign that spelled out the heavenly sanction of Li Yüan's kingship. The *Han-chin ch'un-ch'iu* 漢晉春秋 recorded the finding of a huge stone block standing in the river that carried the written command *ta-t'ao Ts'ao shih* 大討曹師 , "to quell the troops of Ts'ao [Ts'ao]," [135] a decree of Heaven demanding to be executed by human beings.

As the messages conveyed in the writings on the stone became more and more cryptic and metaphorical, they fascinated the literati and posed an intellectual challenge to imperial astrologers and fortune-tellers. The explicit message given by the magic stone was gradually replaced by riddles waiting to be deciphered. The unaccountable puzzle that stone engravings embody seems to evolve from the ancient Chinese folk belief that the cosmic design and divine will is always shown enigmatically. And human beings have always found it difficult to resist the temptation of interpreting such verbal mysteries:

> After the Kan-lu 甘露 plot [of Li Hsün] failed, Wang Fan's 王璠 whole family were executed.

> Earlier, Wang Fan was building the city wall and city moat on an official duty in the province of Western Che-chiang. His subjects dug up a square stone on which twelve words were inscribed:

> On the mountain there is a stone.
> Within the stone is a jade.
> On the jade there is a flaw.
> And the flaw is the end.

> Fan read the inscription without being able to understand its meaning. An old man from Ching-k'ou 京口 [in Chiang-su Province] interpreted it as follows: "This stone cannot be taken as an auspicious sign for Your Highness the Imperial Secretary. Your great grandfather was named Yin 崟 [a character made up of a "mountain" radical and a "metal" phonetic root]. Yin gave birth to Ch'u 礎 [a character made up of a "stone" radical and a "ch'u" phonetic root], hence the riddle that 'there is a stone on the mountain.' Ch'u gave birth to Your Highness, the Imperial Secretary Fan 璠 [a character made up of a "jade" radical and a "fan" phonetic root], hence the riddle that 'there is a jade inside the stone.' Your son is named Hsia-hsiu 退休 [*hsia* (退) is made up of the same phonetic root as its homonym *hsia* (瑕), which literally means "flaw"]. *Hsiu* means the 'end.' This is by no means a good omen."

> Indeed, as it turned out, Wang Fan's entire clan was exterminated.[136]

As the mediator between Heaven and Earth, the inscribed stone is usually identified with a particular form of utterance—written or oral—that either foretells strange incidents or bestows divine blessings upon the privileged. The mytho-logic at issue here depends upon the curious interplay between a real divine revelation and the fabricated human justification.

We have noted that the earlier belief in unadorned stone as the immediate embodiment of pure divine essence gradually eroded. In its place arose an interest in the engraved stone that revealed the divine order through the medium of written words—signs of human verbal activities. In other words, the primordial stone, whose divine efficacy seems to require no mediation of language and little justification of human intelligence, gradually evolved into the engraved stone, which underwent the processing of the human and the artificial/cultural in the written form of riddles. The increasing affiliation of stone with human activities paved the way for the emergence of magic stones bearing dominant features of animate beings, and eventually the characteristics of human beings in particular. Thus the stone that makes sounds and the stone that talks should be considered manifestations of the gradual personification of stone, a tendency already shown in the legends of the engraved stone.

The evolution of the folkloric stone from a silent object that represents an impersonal deity to a fully developed animate *subject* capable of performing speech acts did not take place as an unexpected and isolated phenomenon in ancient Chinese folklore. I believe that this transformation occurred side by side with the increasing popularity of a large corpus of legends related to the fertilizing power of stone. The emphasis of the latter texts on the internal creative drive of stone may have facilitated, if it did not actually give rise to, stone's metamorphosis into a voluntary entity that took upon itself the burden of verbal activities. As we shall observe in the following sections, legends about the talking stone date as far back as Chin Dynasty (A.D. 265–316), while most of the fertility legends were found in the sources of the T'ang (A.D. 618–907) and the Sung (A.D. 960–1279). As a result, I would discredit the evolutionary theory that the talking stone can be taken as the supreme consummation of the fertile stone. We need not, however, be too hasty in abandoning the hypothesis that the outgrowth of stone's verbal potential is intimately associated with the folk belief in its innate dynamic principle celebrated in various other legends. I suggest that it is the interlocking of these two clusters of folkloric texts that maps out the energy field of stone. The personification of stone has to be examined in the light of other legends that highlight the fertile capacity of stone.

Folk Legends about Stone's Fertilizing Capability

1. The *Tung-ming chi* 洞冥記 provides us an account of stone's magic power of changing gray hair, a sign of aging and decline, to black hair, the symbol of youth and energy (note that the function of curing and restoring is a familiar semic attribute of the primordial stone, to be traced back to the mythological era of Nü-kua):

> During the reign period of Yüan-ting 元鼎 [116–111 B.C.], a country named T'iao-chih 條支 offered a Horse-Liver Stone as a tribute [to the Court of China]. It could be mixed up with the nine-winding cinnabar. Those who brushed their gray hair with this stone could change it into black again.[137]

2. The healing function of stone is most active in various accounts of stone medicine. The *Pen-ts'ao kang-mu* gives a long catalogue of stones that serve as either tonics, disease remedies, or elixirs of immortality.[138] Stones of this kind are also said to be able to dissipate harmful spells:

> There was a stone known as Ti-t'ai's 帝臺 Chessman on the top of Mount Hsiu-yü-chih 休與之. It was in five colors and beautifully streaked, with a shape like a quail's egg. It was this stone that was used in the sacrificial rituals to the gods. Those who ate it would never be bewitched.[139]

In this short anecdote, the curing function of stone is clearly connected with the semes of five colors and ovum. The medicinal properties of such a stone carry the same significance as the divine essence of the ritualistic stone. In fact, the medicine-stone often fulfills both a curing and a ritualistic function, as manifested in the above text. Both the *Pen-ts'ao kang-mu* and Shen Nung's 神農 *Pen-ts'ao ching* 本草經 provide us a long list of mineral substances such as azurite, mica, limonite, sulphur, and cinnabar—valuable medical stones—the knowledge of which helped develop an important branch of native therapeutic science no less significant than pharmaceutical botany. The popularity of this medicinal tradition is attested by such contemporary idiomatic expressions as *yao-shih wang-hsiao* 藥石罔效 , "even stone-medicines are of no avail."

3. The act of eating, which forms an instrumental seme of stone-medicines, dominates the set of legends about the edible stone. The *Huan-yü chi* provides an account of *nun-shih* 嫩石 "tender stones" that served as food.[140] The *T'ang hui-yao* records a miraculous episode about stones that were changed into noodles.[141] The nourishing function of such stones seems to be derived from the healing dynamics of the stone described in the above category.

4. The *Yu-yang tsa-tsu*, compiled during the T'ang, records a strange incident of *chang shih* 長石 , "the growing stone":

> At the time when Yü Chi-yu 于季友 was the provincial governor of Li 利 Prefecture, there was a temple beside a river, a gathering place for all the fishermen. A fisherman cast the net and felt the weight in the net as he pulled it back. Breaking the net, he found a stone the size of a fist. He therefore asked the monks to place it in the Buddhist temple. The stone did not stop growing. In a year's time, it grew as heavy as forty *catties*.[142]

The text seems to suggest that the Buddhist temple, an abode of holy ambience, generates the living organism of the magic stone in question. It is also interesting to note that the growing stone is affiliated with the instrumental seme of "water," a recurrent motif in the legends of *ming-shih* 鳴石 , "the resonant stone" (see below).

The folk belief of the ever-growing stone is also seen in the *Chi-ku lu* 集古錄 of Sung Dynasty:

> Li Yang-ping 李陽冰 stated that the inscribed seal-types of the three tablets at the prefecture of Chin-yün 縉雲 were the thinnest. It was said that the three tablets were all alive, growing slowly as years went by. The engraved seal-types were thus closed up gradually. This accounted for the slenderness [of the characters engraved on the tablets].[143]

5. The *Yu-yang tsa-tsu* gives another fabulous account of a stone that not only moved but grew feet:

> According to Tuan Ch'eng-shih's 段成式 several retainers, Tuan often destroyed birds' nests when he was little. Once he got hold of a black stone as big as a swallow's egg, smooth and lovely looking. It was later accidentally put into a utensil filled with vinegar. Suddenly the stone

seemed to move. Peeping into it, they saw four feet growing out of the stone like threads. When picked up, the feet recoiled immediately.[144]

The association between ovules and stones seen in the earliest birth myths of Yü and Ch'i recurred frequently in the folk legends of the T'ang and the Sung. Such an association must have emerged from such ancient fertility cults as the *She* and Kao Mei, giving rise in turn to the interesting folk legends about *ch'i-tzu shih* 乞子石 , the "birth-giving stone." Before looking into the cult of the *ch'i-tzu shih*, we shall examine a tale of the sixth century about a miraculous birth that seems to have been inspired by the myth of the impregnation of Yü's mother:

> Kao-lin's mother once had an ablution in the Ssu 泗 River. She came across a stone of shiny colors and smooth texture, and brought it back with her. That night she dreamed of a man dressed as an immortal addressing her, "The stone is the sperm of the floating stone chime. If you treasure it dearly you will surely give birth to a son." Awakened from the dream in a shock, she sweated all over her body. In a short while, she became pregnant and gave birth to a son who was named *Lin* 琳 , bynamed Chi-min 季珉 .[145]

Whether the mother was moved to pregnancy by the floating stone chime or by her symbolic intercourse with the river gods during her ritual bath cannot be easily determined. However, in each case the seme of water seems to complement the stone and plays a significant role.

6. The popular belief of the birth-giving stone appears to be widespread in China. The *Chün-kuo chih* 郡國志 gives the following account:

> The birth-giving stones were found in the southeastern bank of Lake Horse. The stone in the east gave birth to a little pebble; the stone in the west was pregnant with a pebble. This was where the Chi 犁 people asked for their offspring and got their wishes fulfilled. They were thus named the birth-giving stones.[146]

The procreative power of stone in this story no longer serves as an abstract attribute like that of the Kao Mei stone—it is materialized in the actual pregnancy of the stones. It is interesting to note that such magic stones always exist in pairs, and that this symbolic conjugal relationship is evidently crucial to the mytho-logic of the fertility cult revolving around the legends of birth-giving stones. In the *Huan-yü chi*, we find a similar account of such stones:

> There were the so-called birth-giving stones in Chi-tao 僰道 County [Ssu-ch'uan Province]. The two stones, separated by the Ch'ing-i 青衣 River, faced each other like man and wife. According to ancient legends, the stone in the east prayed for a child from the stone in the west, and returned with one. Therefore people who did not have offspring used to go there to pray. Their prayers were answered efficaciously.[147]

The potency of this cult depends upon the ambivalent interplay between the two stones, which seem to assume human sexuality and take part in the act of procreation.

The various anecdotes about stone discussed above manifest its dynamic capability in different guises. In the following section, we shall look into a set of magic stones that embodies the same animating principle characteristic of the fertile stone.

Ming-shih 鳴石 : The Sonorous Stone

The messages given by stones that make resonant sounds vary from the musical to the verbal, from the nonsensical—content-free noises—to the intelligible, a certain kind of verbal signification. At first sight, the legends about the sonorous stone take root in the belief that natural phenomena possess consciousness and are therefore self-sufficient organisms. However, the extreme case of the sonorous stone (as well as the riddle-inscribed stone) crystallizes the internal tension between its autonomous nature and its subordinate capacity as the mouthpiece of Heaven. When taken as a token of divine prophecy, the sonorous stone serves as a convenient human device of self-justification, and its self-generated life force is to a great extent nullified.

The earliest account of the *ming-shih* can be found in the *Shan-hai-ching*,[148] on which Kuo P'u commented:

> In the first year of Yung-k'ang 永康 reign period [A.D. 300] of Chin Dynasty, the prefecture of Hsiang-yang 襄陽 offered a sonorous stone as a tribute [to the court]. It looked like a jade in deep green color. When people knocked at it, the sound it emitted could be heard seven or eight li [one *li* equals about ½ kilometer] away. This was the particular kind of stone [mentioned above].[149]

There is no discussion of the nature of the sound that the sonorous stone makes, except that it travels far. More elaborate descriptions of the stone in question are found in the following sources:

M1: At the time of Emperor Wu of Han, the coast of Lin-p'ing 臨平 in the prefecture of Wu 吳 cracked up, and a stone drum emerged. It made no noise when struck. People asked Chang Hua 張華 . Hua said, "Go and fetch the timber of paulownia in Shu, and make it in the shape of a fish. Strike the drum with this stick, it will surely make sounds." They did according to his instruction. The drum could be heard several *li* away.[150]

M2: In the fourth year of Hsien-ch'ing 顯慶 , a fisherman caught in his net a blue stone from the rivers. It was four feet long and nine inches wide. Its shiny colors were very different from those of other stones. They hung it up and struck it. It made clear and far-reaching sounds. Every passerby would come to a halt upon hearing the sounds. Governor-general Prince T'eng 滕 made a report and sent the stone to the court as an auspicious token.[151]

M3: At the end of Western Chin Dynasty, there was a magistrate of Ching-yang 旌陽 County named Hsü Hsün 許遜 . He obtained Taoist magic at Mount Hsi at Yü-chang 豫章西山 . At that time in a certain river there was a water dragon which brought disasters [to the people] and made the river overflow the whole country. Hsü Hsün wielded his sword and killed the dragon. The sword disappeared afterwards. Later on, a fisherman caught a stone which made resonant sounds. When struck, the stone would make sounds that could be heard miles away. Prince Chao 趙 of T'ang Dynasty was then a provincial governor of Hung 洪 County. He broke the stone apart, and found a pair of swords with the inscriptions *hsü-ching-yang* 許旌陽 on one sword, and *wan-jen* 萬仞 ("eighty thousand feet high") on the other. Hereby was derived the title of the *Wan-jen* ("formidable") Troops.[152]

An analysis of the semic composition of the sonorous stones indicates that each version contains the seme "water." This provides ample evidence that the *ming-shih* is probably identical to the floating music stone-chime seen in the "Yü Kung 禹貢 ."[153] It is this very same music stone that is imbued with the essence of ovum, which impregnates Kao Lin's mother. Since water is a powerful symbol of fertility, its familiar fusion with stone is hardly an accident. The appearance of the instrumental seme of water in various guises in the stone legends serves to strengthen the positive connotation of stone as a life-giving principle.

The sonorous stone in the three versions cited above either plays the role of a neutral sound-making agent (M1), or delivers some implicit verbal signals—"good fortune," in M2 and M3. M3 illustrates a very complicated variation of such a stone, whose verbal messages include the inscriptions on the swords as well as the sound produced by the stone. As the message-bearer of the remnants of the past—the sword of the renowned general—the sonorous stone makes a sound to indicate that it carries the burden of historical relics. Its music therefore appears as the most meaningful of the three versions.

The message-bearing sonorous stone is seen again in the *Chia-shih t'an-lu* 賈氏談錄. Its sound-making function, however, appears in a less naturalistic light. The sound takes on a symbolic significance as the stone is turned from an object of its own integrity into a spokesman of the will of Heaven. Thus the message no longer sounds as innocent as the wild call of Nature itself, but carries the weight of divine prophecy:

> The stone tablet which was made by the order of Emperor Hsüan-tsung 玄宗 [of T'ang Dynasty] and placed in the temple of King Chin-t'ien 金天王 [the prehistorical legendary emperor Shao Hao 少昊] suddenly made sounds by itself during the first year of the Kuang-ming 廣明 reign period [880–881]. The sound could be heard indistinctly for several *li* and died away after ten days. The following year the rebel Huang Ch'ao's 黃巢 army invaded the imperial palace. The temple was burned down by bandits. And the main gate was also destroyed.[154]

What emerges in this legend is the seme of the talking stone, which is developed more elaborately in an anecdote found in the *Ch'ia-wen chi* 洽聞記:

> There was a sonorous stone on the Chü-lou 岣嶁 Peak of Mount Heng 衡. When called upon, the stone would respond, as though conversing with human beings. However, its response could not be comprehended. A sonorous stone was found in the Tan Creek 丹溪, thirty *li* away to the southeast of the Nan-ho 南河 County in the Nan 南 Prefecture [Ssu-ch'uan Province]. It was thirty-five feet tall, twenty feet wide, look-

ing like a reclining beast. It responded to human voices and laughter. Sitting there alone, it was also named the Solitary Stone.[155]

We have here a fabulous account of the personified stone that not only echoes human voices, but also converses with human beings in unintelligible terms. The neutral sound-making function characteristic of the earliest versions of the *ming-shih* inevitably evolves into the more advanced phase of verbalization—speech-making.

The fact that the stone is situated on a mountain suggests that what it utters may simply be the echoes one often hears in the wilderness and in mountainous areas. It follows that the stone's "response" to human speech is not necessarily endowed with human intelligence. Perhaps a talking stone presents such an extreme case of the strange and the extraordinary that the storyteller has to neutralize it somewhat so as to make it seem more plausible.

Shih Yen 石言 : The Talking Stone

In the *Tso Chuan* we find the earliest reference to the talking stone, which in its own light seems to belong to the genre of the fantastic—a literary genre that, according to Tzvetan Todorov, occupies the space of uncertainty between the natural and the supernatural:[156]

> In the spring of the eighth year, a stone made an utterance at Wei Yü 魏榆 of the State of Chin. The Marquis of Chin asked Shih-k'uang 師曠, "Why did the stone talk?" Shih-k'uang answered, "Stone cannot talk. It is perhaps a pretext, or else an absurd hearsay from common folk. However, Your Servant has also heard of the saying, 'If the rulers fail to carry out the right orders at the right moments, people below would be stirred to complaints and hatred, then things that cannot talk would speak up.' Now Your Court is in pursuit of luxury. Your subjects and people are exhausted of energy. Enmity is arising. You have failed to abide by Nature. Isn't it proper that the stone should talk?"[157]

Here we have an example of the naturalizing process of a supernatural phenomenon. The anecdote is made up of two texts—the hearsay about the talking stone, and the minister's interpretation of it. The emphasis is obviously laid upon the latter text, for the appearance of the strange occurrence is not accepted at its face value but is taken as a sign to be deciphered. The legend of the talking stone thus loses its supernatural aura and assumes the function of an allegory. It serves as the mouthpiece of an agent external to itself. In light of the allegorical interpretation, the miraculous stone-talk can be seen as the collective voice of the discontented, as well as a portent sent by Heaven. The crux of the matter is not *whether* the stone talks, but *why* it talks and what such talk represents.

Shih-k'uang's political censure is based upon the contradictory logic that although "stone cannot talk," it will nonetheless talk when the human order is upset. Implicit in this logic is the ancient Chinese belief that human order corresponds to the natural order, and that the subversion of the former is reflected in natural disorder or calamities. This tendency to find human justification for natural phenomena that appear to be inexplicable is characteristic of Confucian rationalism: every strange occurrence, whether auspicious or ominous, delivers a moral message and serves as a commentary on human affairs. Inasmuch as the talking stone is a static object verbalizing a borrowed speech, it can be viewed as a rectifying device created by human beings themselves. Shih-k'uang's effort to naturalize the strange phenomenon serves his own political interest. This legend provides a good example of the Confucian systematization of the mythic and the supernatural.

References to the talking stone are rare in the myths and legends of traditional China. The *Shih-i chi* records a legend about a stone statue built by Emperor Wu of Han Dynasty to honor his deceased concubine Madame Li. The statue was able to "transmit and interpret human language. It makes sounds but does not have breath."[158] In both legends, we witness the progression of stone from a static object to a subject endowed with the capacity to speak and to communicate. The cognitive potential of both the sonorous stone and the talking stone is equally emphasized in the following folk legend, which dwells on a different aspect of the stone's evolution into a full-fledged conscious entity—its intellectual capacity:

> Wu-lu Ch'ung-tsung 充宗 was tutored by Mi Ch'eng-tzu 彌成子. Mi Ch'eng-tzu had once received an ovum-like streaked stone. Swallowing it, Ch'eng-tzu became very intelligent. Later on in his illness he spat it out and gave it to Ch'ung-tsung. The latter swallowed the stone, and became a great scholar.[159]

We witness in this legend the merging of two most important semes of the folkloric stone—the stone ovum, and stone-intelligence. It documents the subtle interplay between fertility (physical reproduction) and intelligence (mental reproduction).

Chao-shih 照石 and Shih-ching 石鏡: The Stone That Illuminates and the Stone Mirror

In addition to the stone that nourishes and accelerates the growth of human intellect, we find in ancient lore another cluster of texts focusing on the *chao-shih* 照石 , the stone that illuminates, which reinforces the numinous qualities of the folkloric stone and reflects yet another aspect of its spirituality. The *Hsun-yang chi* 潯陽記 provides the following account of such a stone:

> East of the Stone-Mirror Mountain, there was a round rock hung on a cliff. It was shiny and lucid to such an extent that it could reflect human faces. Every single detail of human facial expressions could be easily seen.[160]

It is noteworthy that the shiny stone not only sheds light upon concrete things, it is also capable of detecting the smallest details on human faces and even the most minute changes of its surrounding scenery. The stone's impeccable reflectibility evokes the impression that such stone mirrors are endowed with certain supernatural qualities. This mysterious power of stone mirrors, which the above account and other similar legends vaguely suggest, is brought to the fore in the following anecdote in which the seemingly natural wonder wrought by such "natural" mirrors appears in a supernatural light:

> It was said that there were several stones at the side of Lake Kung-t'ing 宮亭 . Shaped like round mirrors, they were very shiny. Since they could reflect human faces, they were thus named stone mirrors. Later on a passerby burned one of the mirrors. All the other stone mirrors then lost their brightness. That person also turned blind.[161]

In this anecdote, the mystical potency and the animate qualities of the stone mirror are manifested in its response to the human destructive force. What is at work here is not only the enactment of sympathetic magic, which triggers the chain reaction in which the destruction of one mirror leads to that of the others, but also the execution of a moral law—the punishment of the human culprit—by those forces of which the stone mirrors form a part. Within such a symbolic universe we find the connection between stone and visual perception, which in turn intensifies the symbolic meaning of the stone mirror as the animate eye of Nature itself.

We shall now move to a Buddhist tale that illustrates the summing up of nearly all the semic properties of the animate stone endowed with human consciousness. It combines the divine character of the mythic stone with the enlightening capacity of the folkloric stone.

Tien-t'ou Wan-shih 點頭頑石：
The Enlightened Crude/ Unknowing Stone

It was said that in Chin Dynasty of the fifth century, a renowned Buddhist monk Chu Tao-sheng 竺道生, also known as Master Sheng Kung 生公, preached beside a stream at the foot of Mount Hu-ch'iu 虎丘. His audience numbered as many as one thousand, yet none comprehended his sermons. Strange to tell, only the *wan shih*, the "crude and unpolished stones" lying motionless in the stream, rose up, bowed to him, and nodded in response. From this comes the popular saying, *Sheng Kung shuo-fa, wan-shih tien-t'ou* 生公說法，頑石點頭, "Master Sheng Kung preached the scriptures / The crude stones nodded in agreement."

This miraculous anecdote is found in an account collected in the *T'ung-su pien* 通俗篇, which in turn evolved from the extant text of the *Kao-hsien chuan* 高賢傳：

> The Buddhist master Chu Tao-sheng of Chin Dynasty once gathered stones at Mount Hu-ch'iu as his disciples. He preached the Nieh-p'an 涅槃 scriptures, and all the stones nodded their heads in unison. Nowadays the idiomatic expression *wan-shih tien-t'ou*, "the crude/unknowing stones nod," refers to the powerful influence of spiritual illumination.[162]

The dramatic twist of this legend rests on the ambiguity of the act of communication between the Buddhist preacher and his stone-disciples. The stones' response seems to defy any clear-cut distinction between "silence" and "speech"—they are "silent," because inanimate objects such as stones are incapable of making speech, but "expressive," since as a form of "body language," "nodding" represents a potent means of communication. The absence of verbal activity and the enacting of body language interact with each other to produce a dramatic tension that is the source of whatever piquancy the metaphor of "the nodding of the crude/unknowing stone" manifests.

The modern interpretation of this legend highlights the irony of the metaphor, for the semantic entry of "stone" in modern dictionaries clearly emphasizes its inanimate qualities. We may ask: How are inanimate objects endowed with human intelligence? And how can they make such voluntary movements as "nodding"? A modern semantic theorist would probably regard the metaphor in question as a "deviant expression," since two semantically incompatible lexemes, "stone" and "nodding," are arbitrarily collocated. In another light, however, the enlightenment of the unpolished stones is nothing spectacular. The association of stone and enlightenment abounds in Buddhist legends. Bodhidharma is known to have spent nine years facing a rock in meditation. In the Shao-lin 少林 temple of Ho-nan Province today, one can view the legendary rock that bears the vague impression of the meditating saint. The portrayal of eccentric arhats seated on rock platforms lost in meditation can also be seen in paintings. In the hand scroll *The Sixteen Arhats*, dated 1591, one finds a figure "absorbed in a tree trunk that is transmuted into a rock grotto." [163]

The connection between stone and spiritual illumination appears less mysterious if one bears in mind the primordial myths and rituals in which stone serves as an emblem of divinity and a source of fertile energy. Only a small step needs to be taken to transform the imagery of stone from a source of reproductive energy into one of spiritual energy. The myths and legends of stone's fertile power therefore provide the missing link that renders meaningful the seemingly contradictory semantic units in which stone, an inanimate object, is combined with such semic categories as speech-making and intelligence.

Shih-nü 石女 : Stone Woman

Shih-nü, now commonly understood as a metaphor for barren women,[164] is not so strongly endowed with negative semantic attributes in ancient folk legends. Its earliest occurrence is found in the popular myth of T'u-shan, who, after being transformed into stone, gives birth to a son. As discussed earlier, T'u-shan's metamorphosis is composed of two contradictory semes, "fertility" and "sterility," with the former seme slightly overshadowing the latter. Inasmuch as stone is closely associated with such fertility rituals as the She, Kao Mei, and rainmaking, its positive semantic properties assume predominance over the negative ones in ancient lore. This is not to suggest, however, that legends about stone's static and sterile qualities do not exist— they are found sporadically intermingled with the rituals of the fertile and dynamic stone.

The transformation of stone imagery from overwhelmingly positive attributes to extremely negative ones seems to have taken place over a long period of time. Although the process of this change can hardly be recuperated, the simultaneous existence of the attributes of virility and sterility in one single entity may well have paved the way for its later semantic reversal. Both Mircea Eliade and Erich Neumann regard the coexistence of bipolar opposites as an archaic formula for the expression of wholeness and primordial unconsciousness. Mythical thinking, as postulated by Eliade, presupposes the prior existence of an undifferentiated unity; and the "primordial situation" is such a neuter and a whole mode of being. In studying the phenomenon of androgyny in ancient religions, Eliade pointed out that "the phenomenon of divine androgyny is very complex; it signifies more than the co-existence—or rather coalescence—of the sexes in the divine being. Androgyny is an archaic and universal formula for the expression of wholeness, the co-existence of the contraries, or coincidentia oppositorum." [165] This special phenomenon of androgyny is found very often in the great divinities of vegetation and fertility, a symbol of the perfection of the primeval undifferentiated mode of existence. The coexistence of positive and negative attributes perceived in the mythic accounts of such elements as fire, water, and stone is based on the same principle.[166]

Seen from this perspective, the symbolic polyvalence of stone represents the original unity of the opposites of *yin* and *yang*, of heaven and earth, of the static and the dynamic, of cave and grave, and of fecundity and fruitlessness. As human consciousness comes into being and dictates the separation of the self from the other, the primordial unity undergoes an endless process of differentiation, in which the imagery of fertility comes to be distinguished from that of sterility and emerges as a separate entity diametrically opposed to the latter. The perpetual cohabitation of opposites in the polymorphic stone thus gradually gives way to dualism. The increasing alienation of humankind from Nature accelerates the demythologizing process of the mythic stone: it is split in two, and eventually becomes dominated by its negative semantic properties.

Folk legends about stone women seem to be inspired by the nuclear myth of T'u-shan, but the seme of fertility that dominates the earlier text is totally lacking in the present context. Indeed, stone in later legends is seen as a static and nonliving object that symbolizes chastity—a total absence of procreative activities. Both the *Yü-ti chi-sheng* and the *Shih-shuo hsin-yü* give us accounts of women longing for their absent husbands, of their anguish and their transformation into stones sitting at the top of mountains.[167] A more interesting legend is seen in the (*T'ai-p'ing*) *Huan-yü chi*, in which the stone is entitled *chen-fu shih* 貞婦石 , "the stone of the chaste woman":

> There was a rock known as the Stone of the Chaste Woman in Chi-tao County. It was said that in older days there was a chaste woman, childless and bereaved at the loss of her husband. She served her mother-in-law with strict observance of filial piety. The latter forced her to remarry; however, the woman did not obey. She then served her mother-in-law for life. After she died, a big stone emerged from her room. People admired her chastity and thus named the stone "Chaste Woman." [168]

We can probably trace the evolution of the modern concept of stone woman to the sudden transformation of an animate being (who is capable of reproductive function) into a static substance—a stone—deprived of sexuality, and hence of fertility. We should note that in this particular text, although the woman is known to be "childless" and "bereaved," she is by no means biologically sterile. It is a fertile woman's conscious choice for chastity that turns her into a heroine, and the legend into a morality tale.

In the mythological past, the stone woman poses a perplexing semantic contradiction. Like T'u-shan, *shih-nü* is a deviant expression in which two incompatible semes ("fertility" and "sterility") coincide. As mentioned above, upon closer scrutiny we find that what is forbidden and thus denied in the legends of the "chastity stones" is by no means sexuality, much less a woman's reproductive capacity. The modern definition of "stone woman" has changed greatly since T'u-shan's time: today it refers to a woman "with a defective reproductive organ." [169] The chaste woman who consciously restrained her procreative power has been turned literally into a barren woman deprived of her fertility functions. What merely remains inactive in the former is seen as absent in the latter. While the myth of the stony T'u-shan giving birth to Ch'i still evokes the powerful image of motherhood, the stony image of a modern *shih-nü* conveys nothing but the stark picture of sterility.

The Mythological Dictionary of Stone

The analysis of the semantic inventory of "stone" demonstrates for us that a lexeme in mythology can signify only when it is transcoded into its semic components. While it may be true that a lexeme in any context, mythological or otherwise, calls for the same kind of analytical operation, such an inventory needs to be distinguished from the one compiled in an ordinary dictionary. To map out this distinction, let us return to the beginning of this chapter where various semantic entries of "stone" are cited from a modern dictionary. Each entry, whether it be "an ancient chime," "medicine," "hard and solid substance," "barren woman," or "gone without a trace," appears as an abridged and isolated unit of meaning that bears little connection to the others. It is the autonomous nature of the entries as such that creates the impresson of completeness of the semantic field given in an ordinary dictionary. It also contributes to the general effect of enclosure, since each entry is unambiguously defined in an insulated form.

When we turn to mythology, the situation is different. The semantic field of "stone" is seen as a vast network in which each text of the mytho-folkloric stone serves as a reciprocal context for the other paradigmatic sets of stone myth. The semic category of "birth-giving" in the myths of the T'u-shan Stone is meaningless mythologically speaking, unless it is seen to partake of the global context from which we derive the seme of "tribal motherhood" (in the Kao Mei and She stones) and the conflicting semic set of "fertility/ sterility" (in the legends of the stone woman). The cross-referentiality of each semic category to the others establishes a hierarchy of analytic levels— combinatorial, sequential, or contradictory—that enables us to identify and measure redundancy, and to achieve the maximum readability of any set of stone imagery found in mythological and literary texts.

To map out such a hierarchical network is to undertake a never-ending process of evoking an illusory image of the folkloric stone in its unfinished totality. The incomplete idiom of stone displays itself in a series of substitutable names and categories that are themselves the result of transformations, displacements, and reversals. The study of Nü-kua thus leads us through the labyrinth of the intertwining mythologies not only of T'u-shan, Yü, Kao Mei, the She rituals, and rainmaking ceremonies—homogeneous ensembles of the fertility stone—but also of folkloric texts such as the stone woman—clusters of semic categories that contradict and eventually reverse the homogeneous content of the fertility stone. Suffice it to say that the mytho-folkloric texts interact with each other in the process of generating the potentially ever-expanding discursive space of the folkloric stone. Such a space comes into existence and extends itself continuously whenever the texts crisscrossing therein intersect each other. The construction of the network of meaningful intersections brings us to a collective mythological vocabulary of the folkloric stone that consists of recurrent as well as unclassifiable semic entries. In what follows, the semantic inventory of stone will display a configuration that does not resemble the seemingly exhaustive scheme of an ordinary dictionary. It enumerates various sets of semic categories that can best be described in the name of "mythological dictionary."

The Mythological Dictionary of Stone

Stone of Five Colors: (heaven-bound)(harmony)(solid/liquid transformation)(healing)(fire)

Kao Mei Stone: (birth) (spiritual communion with divinity) (healing [sterility])(tribal motherhood)(sexual union)

T'u-shan Stone: (change by hardening)(enclosure)(birth)(fertility)(giving birth)(sterility)(speech act)

The She Stone: (earth)(tribal motherhood)(arresting of change)(matrimonial/natural harmony)(guarding/promoting the growth of vegetation)
*instrumental seme: pine/cedar/chestnut trees—(wood) (fertility of Nature)

Yü and Stone: (heaven-bound)(stony origin [divine stone/pearls/seeds/meteoroid]) (birth-in-death) (arresting of water) (restoring harmony) (tribal fatherhood)(the She-identity)
*instrumental seme: jade slip—(stone)(heaven-bound)(arresting water)

The Rainmaking Stone: (communion with gods)(symbolic speech act) (contract)(violent energy: whipping/killing)(death)(life: mud/blood) (water) (earth) (growth of vegetation) (harmonizing: *yin-yang* stones) (fertilizing)
*instrumental semes:
1. *Yin-Yang Stones*—(earth)(reactivating the inanimate principle)(harmonizing)(human sacrifice)

2. *stone bull*—(animate principle: blood and mud)/inanimate ritual-object: stony statue)(earth)(water)(animal sacrifice)

Feng-shan Stone: (communion with gods: Heaven/Earth)(Heavenly Mandate)(prayer)(verbal transmission)(sovereign power)(prosperity)
*instrumental semes:
1. stone tablets—(public)(written statements)(testimony)(eulogy)(communication with human beings)(erected)
2. jade plates—(private)(prayer)(sealed)(covenant with Heaven)(written statements)

The Evil-Warding Stone: (written message)(exorcising/curing)

The Inscribed Stone: (written message)(prophecy)(riddle)(Mandate of Heaven)

The Horse-Liver Stone/Growing Stone/Stone-Ovum/Birth-Giving Stone: (fertilizing)(animate)

The Sonorous Stone: (sound-making) (written statement) (animate) (Mandate of Heaven)(prophecy)
*instrumental seme: (water)(striking)(fishing-net)

The Talking Stone: (speech act)(Mandate of Heaven)(mental reproduction: stone-intelligence)

The Shining Stone/Stone Mirror: (animate)(visual perception)

The Nodding/Enlightened Stone: (consciousness) (intelligence/ignorance) (crudeness/perceptiveness)(nodding as a speech act)

The Stone Woman: (fertility/sterility)

The above vocabulary entries reveal a cluster of classemes that sum up the recurrent semes of the folkloric stone: "animate," "heaven-bound," "fertilizing," "harmonizing," "healing," "birth-giving," "growth of vegetation," "reactivating the inanimate principle," "communion with divinity," "speech act," "prayer," "contract," "covenant," "written statements," "prophecy," and "the Mandate of Heaven." The classemes in turn lead us to the discovery of isotopies (levels of coherence) that relate one particular stone myth to the others. Thus the stone of five colors, the Kao Mei stones, T'u-shan Stone, the She stones, the stones that impregnated Yü's mother, the rainmaking stones, the evil-warding stones, the legendary horse-liver stone, the growing stones, the birth-giving stones, and the stone mirrors are all bound together by the isotopy of the animate characteristic of stone and its fertilizing/healing function. The various ways in which our ancestors used stone to communicate with deities also give rise to two other isotopies that serve to associate the Kao Mei stones with the rainmaking, the *feng-shan,* the inscribed, the sonorous, the talking, and the nodding stone—namely, stone's mediating function between heaven and earth, and its being a source of a special form of utterance. The folkloric stone is also affiliated with two dominant instrumental semes, "water" and "wood"—elements that embody different aspects of cosmic energy and the potentials of growth.

The association of stone with wood and water is not simply ritualistic and mythological but aesthetic as well. In China and Japan, stone and rocks are appreciated as aesthetic objects that are used to enrich the visual appeal of gardens. The art of rock-arrangement in the gardens of gentry and the imperial house flourished as early as the Western Han Dynasty (206 B.C. to A.D. 8).[170] A sophisticated rock culture continued to hold the attention of artists, poets, and literati until the Ch'ing Dynasty (1644–1911). Andrew Plaks has suggested that the aesthetic appeal of juxtaposing stone and moss may depend upon our awareness of the garden artist's manipulation of complementary bipolarity—the coexistence of hardness and softness, stasis and growth.[171] One can indeed speak of the metaphysics of "bonsai," for the microscopic view it cultivates is said to evoke the internal landscape of the mind's eye and, as a result, to afford us an instant's glimpse of the patterns of cosmic energy. The association of rocks with water is just as persistent as the combination of stone and plants in garden art, and in paintings in general. The fluidity of water and its image of movement and change form a stark contrast to the hardness of rock and its association with stillness and immutability—thus suggesting, again, a metaphysical vision based on the logic of complementary bipolarity.[172]

John Hay offers a different interpretation of the cosmological vision underlying the arrangement of rocks, water, and plants in Chinese gardens. According to him, the garden art reveals the unique Chinese worldview, which perceives Nature as a "system of interactions between patterns of energy."[173] In his opinion, "The Chinese were much more interested in generic structural qualities, such as hardness or softness, permeability or impermeability, and often delighted in exploring these qualities by deliberately transgressing the borders between objects, by reproducing one material in another."[174] According to this view, the transformational principle between natural elements underlies the art of carving rocks out of old wood. And the rocks created naturally by trees were objects of aesthetic delight for garden artists as early as the Northern Sung Dynasty (960–1127).[175] Underlying this theory of transformational process is the recognition that a natural element like stone contains within itself different forms of energy, and that at the core of its physical existence is its continuous transition from one state of energy to another. Rather than displaying a sharp contrast between substances of clearly defined bipolar representation, the combination of rocks with plants and water in a garden evokes the vision of an energy that flows not only between different entities but also within the amorphous structure of a single entity itself.

In garden art as well as in ancient Chinese myths and rituals, it seems that stone illustrates one such amorphous entity. It does not convey one single image, such as solidity and immutability. In fact, it is hardly conceived as a static and tangible object, but rather as the *ch'i*, "breath," of the concentrated energy of heaven and earth.[176] The Chinese seem able to transcend the material concreteness of stone by perceiving it as a symbol in either ritualistic or aesthetic terms. It is thus the stone's gaseous qualities and the different degrees of its spirituality, rather than its autochthonous nature, that account for much of the stature it enjoys in art and literature. It is worth noting, however, that the structural complexity of stone as an embodiment of natural energy is primarily derived from its transformational character, that it breaks the boundary between earth and heaven and lives through its continuous transition from earthbound nature to the empyreal, from a mineral to a mental image, from solid substance to the aerial, and from stasis to mobility.

The same transformational attribute that is characteristic of the aesthetic stone can also be witnessed in the composite makeup of the folkloric stone. It is significant that in the above dictionary we find the contradictory coexistence of several binary terms, such as solidity and liquidity (the five-colored stones), fertility and sterility (T'u-shan Stone and stone women), animation and the arresting of movement and change (Yü and stone, the She stone, and the rain-evoking stone bull), life and death (the rainmaking stones), and finally, silence and speech, senselessness and intelligence (the nodding stone). Rather than interpreting the convergence of bipolar concepts as a contradictory phenomenon, we can appreciate stone's structural indeterminacy in light of its transformational facility.

It is probably due to its capacity to transgress fixed boundaries that stone also emerges in the folkloric texts as an agent that facilitates communication between the human and the supernatural. As a mediator between heaven and earth, stone is usually associated with a particular form of verbalization— either written or oral. Anxious to communicate with the unfathomable, our ancestors turned to a go-between to bridge the distance between heaven and earth and that between the wishful thinking of human beings and the arbitrary ordinance of divine authority. In classical narrative fiction, stone partakes of the cosmic design, assumes the role of the spokesman of heaven, and carries the riddle-like message to challenge the wisdom of earthbound creatures. And just as the solution of the riddles on the stone archway in the Land of Illusions would pave the way to Pao-yü's enlightenment in the *Dream of the Red Chamber*, so would the engravings on the two stone tablets in the *Water Margin*, once deciphered, reveal the subtle mechanism of karma and divine will. Both the transitional status of the folkloric stone and its mediating function in rituals and mythological texts continued to reverberate in the imagery of the literary stone for centuries. In the chapters that follow, we will examine the nature of such reverberations, in terms of both echoes and disruptions, and the relationship between the mythological diction of stone and its literary manifestations/variations in the *Dream of the Red Chamber*, the *Water Margin*, and the *Journey to the West*.

The *Dream of the Red Chamber* evolved from the *Journey to the West*, trod the path of *Chin P'ing Mei* 金瓶梅 (*The Golden Lotus*), and drew its spirits from *Shui-hu Chuan*.[1]

At first glimpse, there seems nothing original about this statement. Influence-studies of the *Dream of the Red Chamber* in the past seventy years have so exhausted the topic it is difficult to discover any untrodden ground. To undertake such a study is to find oneself quickly falling into the tedious recapitulation of old discoveries. Therefore, if the "influence" in question is viewed in terms of characterization, mood-building and the coexistence of the mythic and the mimetic in the four novels, the above statement is indeed nothing more than a cliché. Yet this critical statement contains within itself a hidden insight of which even the critic himself may not be aware— the matrix of a subtle *dialogue* between the *Dream of the Red Chamber*, the *Water Margin*, and the *Journey to the West* generated by the composite symbolism of stone.

Many critics have noted the traces of earlier literary conventions in the *Dream*. Drama, *ch'uan-ch'i* 傳奇 tales, and the colloquial *hua-pen* 話本 stories all find crisscrossing repercussions in the encyclopedic narrative in question. Most critics have taken *Hsi-hsiang Chi* 西廂記 (*The Romance of the Western Chamber*) and *The Golden Lotus* to be Ts'ao Hsüeh-ch'in's primary models.[2] Pao-yü and Tai-yü frequently engage in lovers' repartee by alluding to the erotic passages from *The Romance of the Western Chamber*.[3] Chih-yen Chai 脂硯齋 (The Red-Ink Studio),[4] the most distinguished commentator on the *Dream* in the eighteenth century, also identified Ts'ao's various allusions in the narrative to several episodes in the drama and pointed out his adroit imitation of *The Golden Lotus*.[5] Yet strange to say, the influence of the *Water Margin* and the *Journey to the West* on the *Dream* is mentioned only in passing in earlier criticism—either in ready-made conclusions, or in casual remarks such as the one quoted at the beginning of this chapter. It seems that the issue in question has been prematurely closed, precluding any efforts to elucidate the nature of an intertextual connection among the three narratives. This interconnection, I argue, derives its dynamics from an intricate network of stone imagery that finds its way into the three literary works under different guises.

Let us now return to the quotation that sets us off on the trail of literary antecedents. The comment by Chang Hsin-chih 張新之 on the subtle relationship between the three narrative texts appears in an intriguing light precisely because it opens up the narrow focus of the traditional type of influence-studies and offers us the possibility of a multiple reading of the intertextual activities that take place between the *Dream*, the *Journey*, and the *Water Margin*. When Chang Hsin-chih speaks of the influence of the *Water Margin* on the *Dream of the Red Chamber*, he uses the term *shen* 神, "spirits"—a critical concept too elusive to be brought into clear focus. It could refer either to the overall structural design of the narrative, to character portrayal, or to narrative style in general. It is the ambiguity and fluidity of such a concept that sets our imagination afloat in a hitherto uncharted direction. Chang's elusive suggestions lead us to envision an intertextual space drawn between the inscribed Nü-kua Stone in the *Dream of the Red Chamber* and the two stone tablets that emerge at the very beginning and end of the seventy-chapter edition of the *Water Margin*.

Several modern Chinese critics have discerned a structural correspondence between the *Water Margin* and the *Dream* based on the hypothetical existence of the Goddess Ching-huan's 警幻 (Fairy Disenchantment) *ch'ing-pang* 情榜 ("Roster of Lovers") in Ts'ao Hsüeh-ch'in's original unfinished manuscripts.[6] From Chih-yen Chai's fragmentary commentaries on the earlier chapters,[7] we learn that the Roster lists all sixty female characters in Five Grades of Beauty. The now-lost Roster is viewed by many as a supplement to the Twelve Songs in chapter 5,[8] and as a structural device completing the mythic cycle of the narrative.[9] In light of its structural function of enclosure, both Hu Shih and Yü P'ing-po conclude that the originally conceived denouement of the *Dream* is very similar to the frame-device of the

"Stone Tablet" in the *Water Margin*.[10] It is important to emphasize that the *Water Margin* referred to just now is the truncated seventy-chapter edition, in which the fall of the stone tablet from heaven brings the novel back to its mythological overture. It is a cyclical movement that would also be seen to characterize the *Dream of the Red Chamber*, had one kept in mind the hypothetical existence of the "Roster of Lovers."

At the present moment, it seems that due to the textual corruption in the *Dream*, the study of the structural similarity of the Roster to the enigmatic stone tablets in the *Water Margin* remains a highly hypothetical project and one that can yield little tangible result. But as I will argue in Chapter 6, the narrative circularity of both narratives may be accounted for by a *different* structural design. In studying the Stone Record and Pao-yü's encounter with the stone arch in the Land of Illusions, and in examining the episodes of the underground and heavenly stone tablets in the *Water Margin*, we can hardly ignore the recurrent motif of the stone that bears enigmatic and oracular messages. And in each case, the narrative logic depends upon the hero's failure to decipher the inscriptions engraved on the stone.

While the relationship between the *Water Margin* and the *Dream of the Red Chamber* is characterized by Chang Hsin-chih as one of "resemblance in spirit," the intertextuality of the *Journey to the West* and the *Dream* is seen in a less subtle light: Chang uses the maternal imagery of *t'ai* 胎, "fetus," thus unambiguously referring to the *Journey* as the literary antecedent of the *Dream*. Both the *Journey* and the *Dream* open with an account of the creation myth, a curtain-raising stock-in-trade of medieval professional storytellers. Yet their most significant point of contact resides less in their oral heritage than in the myth of the magic stone: one assumes the shape of a stone egg; the other, that of an engraved precious stone. Both attain enlightenment at their journeys' end. Yet no matter how obvious the resemblance between these two stones may seem to us, the significance of such an intertextual relationship rarely grips the attention of traditional critics. Chang Hsin-chih's commentary appears to fill up this gap, for it calls our attention to how these two narratives begin—in both the literal and symbolic sense. When read symbolically, the word *t'ai* points to the source of the work under discussion; when read literally, it points to its beginning. The comparative vision that Chang Hsin-chih conjures up is built on his recognition of the point of convergence between the two beginnings—the beginnings not only seen in terms of the creation myths that set off the two narratives, but also seen as the "beginnings" of the two protagonists, Wu-k'ung and Pao-yü.

Thus without any mention of the word "stone," the commentary already contains a subtle reference to it, since stone figures predominantly in the two creation myths and is the literal "fetus" of both heroes.

Chang Hsin-chih's commentary thus serves as the point of departure for the study of intertextuality of the three narratives in question. In each set of such intertextual relations, the presence of stone imagery looms large—imagery that evokes the phantoms of the folkloric stone, while often transgressing the impalpable constraints that such phantoms inevitably induce. Yet although we cannot help acknowledging the pivotal role that stone assumes in the study of intertextuality of the three narratives, we must avoid stretching the stone imagery in the *Journey to the West* and the *Water Margin* beyond what it serves—it functions marginally in one narrative, and remains a decorative frame-device in the other. It is in the *Dream of the Red Chamber* that we witness the incorporation of stone imagery into a full-fledged symbolic discourse that carries the main burden of the narrative logic. The dynamic manifestation of such a symbolism conjures up a wide spectrum of meaning that transcends the intertextuality of the folkloric stone. For the Nü-kua Stone not only evokes the haunting presence of the latter, it also triggers the subtle dialogue between stone and jade.

It is in the signifying possibilities of the jade symbolism and in the contradictory relationship between stone and jade that one can locate the sociomoral didacticism of a literary work that is said to subvert the concept of dualism, and therefore, of such bipolar value systems as *chen* 真 ("the true") and *chia* 假 ("the false"). The subtle infiltration of the jade symbolism into the stone imagery deserves a thorough investigation, for it introduces the issues of ideology and ethics into a work that has long been lavishly appreciated for its pure metaphysical vision. If the imagery of stone evokes the mythical and folkloric past, that of jade conjures up the ritualistic, the political, and the moral order of the Han Confucian culture with a history almost as long as its jade connoisseurship.

The following chapters will map out the intertextual space of the literary stone in the three narratives, and that of stone and jade in the *Dream*. By taking the divine stone and the inscribed stone tablet—the two pivotal variations of stone imagery that define the intertextuality of the *Journey* and the *Dream*, and the *Dream* and the *Water Margin*, respectively—as the two primary axes of interpretation, I hope to look into the process of how meaning is produced, and to illustrate the illusory nature of fictionality. This dialogue between the folkloric stone and the literary stone is accompanied by an account of the Chinese jade symbolism that serves to supplement, and sometimes to disseminate, the stabilizing presence of the folkloric stone within the symbolism of the Nü-kua Stone.

We will begin with the two celestial stones in the *Journey* and the *Dream*, the stone egg and the Nü-kua Stone, images that create an ambivalent effect upon those readers who have gained access to the ancient Chinese stone lore. It is an impression that cannot be better conveyed than in Pao-yü's puzzling comments upon his first encounter with Tai-yü: "but her face seems so familiar that I have the impression of meeting her again after a long separation" (*Stone* I: 103).

The Sacred Fertile Stone

> . . . Beyond the ocean there was a country named Ao-lai. It was near a great ocean, in the midst of which was located the famous Flower-Fruit Mountain. This mountain, which constituted the chief range of the Ten Islets and formed the origin of the Three Islands, came into being after the creation of the world. . . .

There was on top of that very mountain an immortal stone, which measured thirty-six feet and five inches in height and twenty-four feet in circumference. The height of thirty-six feet and five inches corresponded to the three hundred and sixty-five cyclical degrees, while the circumference of twenty-four feet corresponded to the twenty-four solar terms of the calendar. On the stone were also nine perforations and eight holes which corresponded to the Palaces of the Nine Constellations and the Eight Trigrams. Though it lacked the shade of trees on all sides, it was set off by epidendrums on the left and right. Since the creation of the world, it had been nourished for a long period by the seeds of Heaven and Earth and by the essences of the sun and the moon, until, quickened by divine inspiration, it became pregnant with a divine embryo. One day, it split open, giving birth to a stone egg about the size of a playing ball. Exposed to the wind, it was transformed into a stone monkey endowed with fully developed features and limbs. (*Journey* I: 67)

Long ago, when the goddess Nü-wa was repairing the sky, she melted down a great quantity of rock and, on the Incredible Crags of the Great Fable Mountains, moulded the amalgam into three hundred and six thousand, five hundred and one large building blocks, each measuring seventy-two feet by a hundred and forty-four feet square. She used three hundred and six thousand five hundred of these blocks in the course of her building operations, leaving a single odd block unused, which lay, all on its own, at the foot of Greensickness Peak in the afore-mentioned mountains.

Now this block of stone, having undergone the melting and moulding of a goddess, possessed magic powers. It could move about at will and could grow or shrink to any size it wanted. Observing that all the other blocks had been used for celestial repairs and that it was the only one to have been rejected as unworthy, it became filled with shame and resentment and passed its days in sorrow and lamentation. (*Stone* I: 47)

The pivotal role of stone in the creation myths cited above seems self-explanatory if one bears in mind the familiar associations of stone with various rituals of procreation in ancient China. The phenomenon of stone-birth accompanies the legends of birth-giving stones and the myths of Yü and his son Ch'i. In Chapter 2, I showed how various legends merge to constitute the mythology of Yü's birth from different forms of stone—from a meteoroid, fruit-seeds, and a divine pebble—and how the generative capacity of stone works its miracle on the stone pillar of T'u-shan through the birth of Ch'i from its voluntary rupture. The evolution of Wu Ch'eng-en's 吳承恩 (ca. 1506–82) monkey from the stone ovum reveals such a striking correspondence to the T'u-shan/Ch'i legend that the mechanism of intertextuality here requires little explanation. The mythological imagery of stone as an embryo reverberates in the description of the evolution of the stone egg in question. The pregnant stone conjures up in quick succession the images of the T'u-shan rock that conceives a son inside its stony womb, and of the two birth-giving stones sitting face-to-face ceremoniously like a couple. The procreative stone egg in the *Journey* and the fertile folkloric stone in ancient lore are twin images that share the same symbolic attributes. The power of Wu-k'ung—the incarnation of the stone egg—can thus be viewed as stemming from the dynamic principle of fertility. When Wu-k'ung dazzles us with his treacherous seventy-two physical transformations, we are actually confronted with the pageant of an endless permutation of stone's self-generated energy field. In the folk legends of the ever-growing stone, we already detect the emergence of a restless, fully animated creature that is capable of evolving itself into an agile stone monkey endowed with an overflowing vitality and an unquenchable life force.

As we move from the Flower-Fruit Mountain to the foot of Greensickness Peak, we behold an equally versatile and magic stone possessed of the power to "grow and change" its size at will—attributes that likewise reveal a strong folkloric orientation. Yet we shall look in vain in the Nü-kua Stone for an unreserved glorification of the stone's primitive vitality similar to that in the beginning chapter of the *Journey*. What greets our eyes in the *Dream* is a stone block deprived of the opportunity to exercise its fertilizing power. By casting the stone aside,[11] the goddess has not only exiled it from the restored sky and left it earthbound, she has also ridiculed its healing and fertilizing potency. As a result, a curious displacement of the myth of the five-colored stone takes place. The "precious stone" inverts the major semes of its folkloric antecedent and yields the following reading:

(earthbound)(disharmony)(nonhealing)

At the end of this first episode we are informed that the stone, saddened by this unexpected turn of events, indulges itself in lamentation—until one day it comes to the Sunset Glow Palace and encounters a beautiful, yet fragile, plant. Here we seem to encounter the problem of a textual gap, or, one might even say, a fictional corruption of the text. The two episodes are widely separated from each other by the insertion of a lengthy dialogue between Stone and K'ung-k'ung Tao-jen 空空道人 (Vanitas), and by the introduction of the mundane world—the Ku-su 姑蘇 City. The transition from the first episode to the second seems abrupt and arbitrary. We feel hardly prepared for the sudden transformation of the self-deprecating Stone into a carefree and tender nurturer in the Sunset Glow Palace. Some readers may accept the transition, not questioning what might happen between the two episodes to account for the emergence of Stone's new persona. Others may want to dismiss the new nourishing personality simply as an unmotivated whimsical idea. I would suggest, however, that the love-sickness of *shen-ying shih-che* 神瑛侍者, the Divine Luminescent Stone-in-Waiting, should hardly be considered unmotivated and purely fictional. The significance of the newly emerged passionate nature of our Nü-kua Stone can only be unraveled and interpreted in light of the first episode.

The clue to the new psychic makeup of Stone is actually submerged in the mythic prelude, where Stone has just fallen out of divine favor and is indulging in self-pity. The desire to heal the broken heaven has been held in check, yet it never dies away completely. The subdued fertilizing energy craves a different outlet. Internalized, this thwarted wish of Stone is finally materialized in the mythic locale of the Sunset Glow Palace:

> There, by the Rock of Rebirth, he found the beautiful Crimson Pearl Flower, for which he conceived such a fancy that he took to watering her every day with sweet dew, thereby conferring on her the gift of life. (*Stone* I: 53)

This act of irrigating the Flower can be seen as nothing less than a surrogate act of repairing the firmament. It is to be viewed as the retrieval of Stone's fertile efficacy once denied by the careless Goddess Nü-kua. And it is interesting to note that the intense anguish of Stone over fulfilling and verifying its life-force not only animates Crimson Pearl Flower, but most importantly, also *motivates* its own descent into the Red Dust.

The incarnation of the "precious jade" in the first chapter poses a problem complicated by the existence of different print copies[12] of the *Dream*. The sixteen-chapter transcribed copy (*Chih-ts'an-pen* 脂殘本 in Wu Shih-ch'ang's terms, and *Chia-hsu-pen* 甲戌本 in Hu Shih's terms) and Ch'eng Wei-yüan's 程偉元 second printed edition (1792) give two different versions of Stone's encounter with the Buddhist and Taoist immortals, and thus provide different motivations underlying Stone's descent into the human world.

Ch'eng's edition inclines more toward interpreting Stone's incarnation as the relentless carrying-out of a predestined cosmic design, while the sixteen-chapter transcribed version attributes Stone's journey on earth to its own doing—in other words, to the fulfillment of its own willpower. One emphasizes the divine scheme, the other Stone's voluntary action. Let us now take a close look at the passage in Ch'eng's edition:

> One day, in the midst of its lamentings, it saw a monk and a Taoist approaching from a great distance, each of them remarkable for certain eccentricities of manner and appearance. When they arrived at the foot of Greensickness Peak, they sat down on the ground and began to talk. The monk, catching sight of a lustrous, translucent stone—it was in fact the rejected building block which had now shrunk itself to the size of a fan-pendant and looked very attractive in its new shape—took it up on the palm of his hand and addressed it with a smile:

"Ha, I see you have magical properties! But nothing to recommend you. I shall have to cut a few words on you so that anyone seeing you will know at once that you are something special. . . . After that I shall take you to a certain

brilliant
successful
poetical
cultivated
aristocratic
elegant
delectable
luxurious
opulent
locality on a little trip."
The stone was delighted.

"What words will you cut? *where is this place you will take me to?* I beg to be enlightened."

"*Do not ask*," replied the monk with a laugh. "You will know soon enough when the time comes." (*Stone* I: 48; italics mine)

Here the Buddhist and the Taoist provide little justification for letting Stone embark on its earthly journey, except on the grounds, as explained later, that "this stone is fated to go into the world" to repay the "debt of tears" (*Stone* I: 53). The stone thus appears nothing more than a mute recipient of the karmic design in the Ch'eng edition.

In the transcribed copy, this simple account is expanded into an elaborate argument between Stone and the two immortals over the former's request for reincarnation. The petition is eventually granted, but not without some laborious efforts on the part of Stone to change the mind of the reluctant immortals. The conversation between the three characters occurs right after the Buddhist and the Taoist sit down at the foot of the Peak:

Now speaking, now smiling, they arrived at the base of Blue-Channel Peak, sat themselves down beside the Stone, and began to chat in a gay bantering fashion. At first they spoke of 'Cloud and Mountain,' 'Fog and Sea,' 'Divinity and Sylph,' 'Mystery and Illusion,' later they came to 'Splendor and Riches' among mortals of the Red Dust. As the Stone listened, worldly desires were unconsciously aroused, and *it longed to go among mortals to savor their splendor and riches.* While it regretted being a coarse fool, it nevertheless could not resist sputtering out human words:

"Great Master!" said the Stone to the Monk, "I happened to overhear you both discussing the magnificence and luxuries of the mortal world and *my heart is filled with yearning.* Although in substance I am only a coarse fool, my nature partakes of some spirituality—upon seeing the divine forms and immortal bodies of you two Masters, I became certain you are uncommon. Surely you have the material to patch Heaven and to regulate Earth, and the virtue to benefit all things and to save men. Should you show some compassion and carry me to the Red Dust where I may enjoy myself for several years in the realm of wealth and in the homeland of soft, warm affection, I would cherish forever your vast favor and not forget you for myriad ages."

When the two Divines heard this, they both giggled like idiots. "Bless you! Bless you!," they exclaimed. "There actually are some happy affairs in the Red Dust, it's just that one cannot depend on them forever. Then again, there is 'discontent within bliss, numerous demons in auspicious affairs,' a phrase of eight words all of which belong tightly bound together. In the twinkling of an eye, sorrow is born of utter happiness, men are no more, and things change. In the last analysis, it's all but a dream and the myriad realms return to nothingness—really, it's better not to go at all!"

But the Stone was already aflame with worldly desire. How could it obey such advice? It began to plead pitifully again and again. The two immortals realized there was no forcing the Stone:

"There too is a destiny of *non-being giving birth to being (wu-chung sheng-yu), and a situation where, when quietude reaches an extreme, thought of action arises (ching-chi ssu-tung),*" they said with a sigh. "Since that's how it is, we will carry you to enjoy yourself—but when you become dissatisfied—absolutely no later regrets!"

"Naturally," replied the Stone. "Naturally."

The Buddhist then spoke again: "One may say your nature partakes of a divine spirit, yet you are also a plain fool. Moreover, there is nothing about you which would indicate you are rare or precious—you're just a stepping stone, and that's about it! Well then, now I shall display the Buddha Dharma and help you a bit. When the kalpa ends you will be returned to your original substance and your case would be settled— what would you say to that?"

When the Stone heard this, it could not thank the Immortals enough.

The Monk then chanted incantations and wrote charms, unfurled his magic arts, and in an instant the slab of stone became a piece of lovely jade, fresh and lustrous, gleaming and pure.[13] (italics mine)

The passive stone in the Ch'eng edition has now been changed into a strong-willed agent burning with *fan-hsin* 凡心 , "worldly desires." We have witnessed how Stone discharges its fertile healing power by watering the celestial plant. Here the insatiable life-force is seeking to be released once more. The sprouting of this "desire" is vividly embodied in the words of the immortals: "out of stasis evolves mobility, and out of nothing, being is given birth."[14] The urge to be reincarnated originates in nothing other than the driving force of dynamics (*tung* 動) that is best characterized in terms of *sheng-yu* 生有 , "giving rise to being"—a self-generated incentive in biological evolution. Such an urge embodies yet another outlet for the life-giving energy of Stone. Willpower issues from the energy of the mind. In the face of such single-minded concentration of mental energy, even the two immortals have to give in. In contrast to the passive stone in Ch'eng's passage, the Stone we now encounter initiates the request for reincarnation and conquers by its autonomous willpower.

The sixteen-chapter version thus provides us a rather detailed manifestation of Stone's willpower, which saves the mythic prelude from the reductionist view of predestination. The active participation of Stone in its own downfall, in both the literal and the symbolic sense, weakens the arbitrary mytho-logic of the Mandate of Heaven and paves the way for the unfolding of the human tragedy whose eloquent ambivalence rests on the subtle interaction between cosmic design and individual choice. In highlighting Stone's subjectivity, the sixteen-chapter version fully exposes the mechanism of *yü* 欲 ("desire"), which is downplayed in the Ch'eng edition. Seen in this light, the descent of Stone into the human world can be viewed as motivated by the same dynamic principle that compels the honorable Divine Luminescent Stone-in-Waiting to irrigate the celestial plant. It is a principle that flows from the fertile potential of the mythic stones molded by Nü-kua. Stone's passion journey in the Sunset Glow Palace and on Earth reenacts the old tale of the sacred stones. Each of these journeys is a transformed literary version of ancient fertility cults. As the sweet dews showered on Crimson Pearl are reminiscent of the heavenly waters invoked by the rainmaking stones, the familiar echoes of the reproductive stones can also be heard intermittently in the laments of the Stone Outcast and in the arguments of the Stone-in-Waiting who cries aloud the desire to be reborn. Whether under the guise of the irrigator or that of the orator, Stone casts the spell of fecundity and generates the thirst for life.

It is worth noting that Wang Kuo-wei's little treatise on the *Dream* dwells on the implicit connection between the word "desire" and the word "jade"; based on Schopenhauer's philosophy of free will, his interpretation comes very close to my proposition that Stone's reincarnation is self-motivated.[15] However, while I view such a desire as an archetypal recurrence of the kinetic energy of the primordial stone, Wang Kuo-wei envisages it as a sin resulting from human free will: "Thereupon we know that the desire for living exists before our earthly life. And our earthly life is nothing other than the discovery of this desire. Thereupon our downfall is sought for by ourselves. It is a sin of the free will."[16] That is to say, Stone plunges itself voluntarily into the sea of desire and courts its own downfall. Wang Kuo-wei's theory of willpower thus provides a footnote to Chih-yen Chai's cryptic commentary on the dispirited Stone: "it conceives of itself as the fallen root of passion, therefore it is useless for the repair of sky."[17] Seen in this light, the *Dream of the Red Chamber* is ultimately a story about self-delusion and a tragedy of will power: "The so-called jade [*yü* 玉] is nothing other than the emblem of the desire [*yü* 欲] for living. Therefore its descent into the Red Dust is not initiated by those two [the Buddhist and the Taoist] but by the unknowing Stone itself. And he who ushers the Stone into the other shore of Nirvana is not the two immortals, but the unknowing Stone itself."[18]

Only by interpreting jade as the embodiment of desire can we decipher the mystery of *huan-yü* 還玉, "returning the jade." In chapter 117, the enigmatic conversation between Pao-yü and the monk holds the clue to the solution of the riddle:

> ". . . May I venture to enquire, Father, whether you have recently re-turned from the Land of Illusion?"

> "Illusion, my foot!" exclaimed the monk. "I come whence I come, and I

go whither I go. I came here to return your jade. But let *me* ask *you* a question: where did your jade come from?"

For a minute or so Bao-yu could think of no reply. The monk laughed.

"If you know nothing of your own provenance, why delve into mine?"

Bao-yu had always been a sensitive and intelligent child, and his recent illumination had enabled him to penetrate to a certain extent the veil of earthly vanity and illusion. But he still knew nothing of his own personal "history," and the monk's question hit him like a whack on the head.

"I know!" he exclaimed. "It's not the money you're after. It's my jade. I'll give you *that* back instead." (*Stone* V: 301–2)

The monk's riddle-like rhetoric triggers Pao-yü's discovery of his true identity and completes his illumination. The unknown origin (*ti-li wei chih* 底裡未知) of the precious jade dawns upon him in a flash, as he ponders the paradox of "coming whence I come, and returning whither I go." The answer to the paradox hits home as Pao-yü realizes that the jade does not descend from the Land of Illusion or from Nü-kua's celestial collection of stones, but is generated by the fluttering of the wings of desire. Hence the land of "whence and whither" is not the literal Greensickness Peak, but the invisible locale in the mind that gives birth to desire. The jade is nothing other than the very incarnation of this craving. Born from desire, it shall be taken away from Pao-yü with the extirpation of this desire. The sixteen-chapter copy thus reinforces the subtle connection between jade and desire by informing us that the physical transformation of Stone into a lustrous jade takes place only after Stone has experienced the longing for life. "Returning the jade" then symbolizes the extinction of this desire. Pao-yü's determination to sever his ties with the Red Dust makes his keeping of the jade (desire) totally meaningless. Thus his words to the monk: "Let me return the jade to you." The loss of desire and the return of the jade mark his journey's end.

Following this line of argument, Pao-yü's loss of consciousness on every occasion when his jade disappears indicates a momentary loss of desire, which in turn engenders the transitional status he then assumes between enlightenment and dull-wittedness. If "desire" is seen to define the mythological persona of the Nü-kua Stone before its reincarnation, it is a spiritual limbo—half *wan* and half *t'ung-ling*, yet neither—that characterizes

Pao-yü's mode of existence on earth. At this juncture, two possibilities of interpretation emerge to change the direction of our critical discourse. One such possibility is to move from the discussion of the cult of the fertile stone to an analysis of the cult of the liminal stone,[19] which will shed light upon the transitional status of the fictional Nü-kua Stone. In both the *Dream* and the *Journey*, the symbolism of the *reproductive* potency of the mythical stone becomes quickly overridden by issues related to the cognitive potency of the folkloric stone—that is, to the stony mode of *production in thinking*. Issues such as the problematic nature of knowledge and the paradoxical act of knowing are so closely intertwined with Pao-yü's and Wu-k'ung's stony mode of existence that one cannot interpret the meaning of the two heroes' spiritual quest without taking into account the full spectrum of the cognitive metaphors that stone is capable of engendering. The primordial fertility rituals present stones that give birth—but the meaning of the fertile stone remains hollow until it incorporates the image of stone that conceives in thinking.

However, while an examination of the liminal stone will reveal the particular mode of thinking characteristic of the ritualistic and folkloric stone and will thus serve to elucidate the theme of the mind-journey and spiritual enlightenment central to both narratives in question, another possibility of interpretation is equally viable—and perhaps even more compelling, in light of its obscure status in the critical discourses on the *Dream of the Red Chamber* in the last two decades. This critical concern has been consistently overshadowed by the issue of enlightenment. It presents an interpretive possibility that brings us to a close encounter with jade: jade not merely as a metaphor for *yü*, "desire," as Wang Kuo-wei perceives it, but also as a locus that can generate discourses of all kinds—ritualistic, political, moral, and perhaps even metaphysical ones.

I have discussed above one facet of the metaphorical significance of Pao-yü's birth-stone. This tiny jade amulet, which Wang Kuo-wei takes as the emblem of the desire to live, recurs throughout the narrative whenever Pao-yü undergoes a spiritual crisis. In fact, after chapter 1, the narrator seems to have lost sight of the Nü-kua Stone: it has been upstaged by the jade. The *Dream* may be a story told by the stone, yet it is the story of Pao-yü—how he acquired, lost, regained, and returned the jade. One cannot but wonder what it means that Pao-yü is not only a stone but also literally a precious jade, the object he is named after. Perhaps the symbolism of his double identity is part of the authorial intention—or perhaps it is simply an accident. For one can easily justify the whim of putting into our hero's mouth a piece of jade rather than a stone pebble. Regardless of the authorial intention, however, the stone-jade interaction gives rise to an ambiguity that opens up the textual space of stone symbolism and multiplies the signifying possibilities of the narrative. Let us leave the issue of the liminal stone suspended for the time being, and pursue the second possibility of interpretation by turning to the discourse of jade.

Precious Jade

Jade, rich in ritual significance, has found a unique place in Chinese poetic diction. If the human appreciation of stone carries residual memories of its mythical potency, the appeal of jade seems to be due to its aesthetic rather than its ritualistic value. The symbolism of jade bears close relevance to the aesthetic. Its fine texture, lustrous surface, and hard substance are qualities soon associated with, and finally transformed into, ethical terms such as "purity" and "tenacity." As the symbol of purity, jade can generate in a narrative an innate moral criterion on which is based the narrator's implicit assessment of fictional characters. The thematic significance of jade consists largely in the *evaluative* function it serves. One might say that if the story of stone is *descriptive*, that of jade is double-edged.

While the folkloric stone of ancient fertility cults would appear to play an active role in the creation of the stone egg and the energetic Monkey in the *Journey*, the Nü-kua Stone in the *Dream* seems to shed its mythical attribute of fertility once it has been transformed into a piece of jade. One can almost attribute the mythical origin of Wu-k'ung to Wu Ch'eng-en's acute awareness of the ritualistic intertexts in which the self-generating ova of the Yü Stone, the T'u-shan Stone, and the birth-giving stone contain within themselves the seeds of endless motion and change. Yet if Wu-k'ung betrays a rather explicit folk identity, the stone under Greensickness Peak shares few characteristics of the fertile stone. Except for the episode in the Sunset Glow Palace, the salient features of fertility do not appear to have occupied a significant place in the miraculous incarnation of the Stone Outcast; departing from the cardinal intertext of the myth of Nü-kua, it has wandered further and further away from the heaven-bound image of the fertilizing five-colored stones.

The shedding of the folk identity of stone in the *Dream* is an ambiguous act, however. On the one hand, one can argue that it never completely casts off the shadow of the ancient mythic stone. The implicit intertexts of the life-giving stone continue to reverberate in the underlying theme of desire, and the image of the fallen stone as the root of passion echoes the sexual understatement of Kao Mei and many other fertility cults. The imagery of the conscious "*t'ung-ling shih*" has indeed evolved a long way from the unconscious reproductive cell. The story of Pao-yü relates his sowing of the seed of passion and unfailingly reminds us of his fervent appetite for life, which extends from the self-renewing vitality of stone in primitive rituals. On the other hand, what makes the Nü-kua Stone a more potent fictional character than the stone monkey is precisely its departure from the folkloric antecedents that reproduce the latter verbatim. And one such departure (or, arguably, one such radical venture) consists in the interplay of the discourse of stone and jade in the symbolic space within which the personal identity of Pao-yü is constructed—or, as the narrator so frequently promises, deconstructed. As the narrative of the *Dream* unfolds, the Nü-kua Stone cannot but participate in the signifying activities that the jade motivates. Although jade shares many traits of the stone family, it is distinguished by many attributes that prevent its complete integration into stone. The encounter between the two gives rise to various textual gaps in the narrative, as the appropriation of one by the other is continuously interrupted by the emergence of attributes that distinguish rather than incorporate each other. The Nü-kua Stone thus becomes ambiguous as it is engaged in shedding its singular and homogeneous identity. The psychic journey that Pao-yü undertakes can be understood as the process of his attempt to resolve the ongoing conflict created by this double identity.

Tsang-yü 葬玉 and *Han-yü* 唅玉: The Burial Jade and the Mouth-Jade

Just as stone was closely associated with fertility rituals, jade in ancient China was first put to use as ceremonial emblems—but while stone celebrates the potency of reproduction, jade primarily partakes in rituals consecrating political authority. This is not to imply that jade does not share the curative and fertilizing attributes of stone; rather, from the very beginning of its emergence in Chinese history, its miraculous power was mainly brought to serve the sovereign and his royal subjects. Even after the emphasis on its ritualistic role shifted to the aesthetic, jade was clearly a product of an elite aristocratic culture, supplementing the stone lore with a long history of the craft of carving, the connoisseurs' meticulous account of its nomenclature, and an embryonic religious symbolism.

There is little in the jade lore to clearly account for the supernatural essence that gives rise to the religious symbolism associated with the *liu-ch'i* 六器, the six jade vessels, used in the imperial ritual for the worshiping of heaven, earth, and the four corners. It is a common belief in ancient China, however, that jade is not only the "quintessence of heaven and earth," but also the "crystallization of the *yang* principle."[20] The Taoist medicinal cult of jade and the burials of jade implements in the royal graves during the Chou period (ca. 1100–256 B.C.) must have been due to the belief that as the ultimate source of the *yang* on earth, jade was endowed with the power to heal the sick and preserve the body after death. The practice of taking jade potions was thus viewed as a "rite of holy communion," for it put a person "in tune with the infinite" from which he or she derived a renewed life force.[21] Berthold Laufer even suggests that the jade hammer with which the Chou emperor worshiped the sun corresponds to the "actual image of the solar deity"; the ceremonial placing of burial jades in the Chou period was thus interpreted as a last survival of this ancient cult of the sun.[22]

The role assumed by the ritual jades in the royal burials is similar to that assigned to the *yü-pi-hsieh* 玉辟邪 —a carved jade figure of a ferocious winged feline that became popular during the Eastern Han Dynasty (A.D. 25–220)— which served as an averter of evil when erected at the entrance to important tombs. Such practices are predicated upon a rudimentary religious mysticism that ascribes to natural objects a mythical potency to mediate between life and death. Whether one associates jade with the sun god or with some inexplicable healing capacity of supernatural origin, it is believed to share the quality of a divine life-force that can dispel darkness and demons, bring immortality to the living, and prevent the dead from decaying. The mediating role that jade plays in matters of life and death reminds us of the liminal characteristics of stone. But as we have already seen, since all archaic symbols such as stone and the other four elements are susceptible to permutations of symbolic reversal, stone imagery has gradually become more associated with the concept of sterility than with that of fertility. In the case of jade, the permutation in question took a different form: the symbolic significance of jade in the cult of the dead gradually overshadowed the mythology that paid tribute to its generative force. With the passage of time, as the images that jade invoked related more often to the grave than to the elixir, it became bound intimately to the lore of death, antiquity, and excavation. This subtle transformation of the symbolic significance of jade appears closely connected with the rise and fall of religious Taoism: with the waning of the influence of Taoist mysticism after the Han, and resulting decline of the art of alchemy, the connection between jade and vitality, and thus the conception of jade as a symbol of immortality, grew indistinct and gradually lost much of its validity. What prevails in the early religious symbolism of jade is its link to the burial ritual. And it is in the nature of this link that one can perceive the close correspondence between the cosmic cult and the religious symbolism of jade.

According to the *Chou Li*, the various burial jades to be placed in the coffin of a deceased member of the imperial house included the six jade implements that represented the cosmic deities of heaven, earth, and the four corners.[23] Surrounded by these six ritual objects, the dead were believed to be able to continue their communion with the cosmic forces. It is therefore impossible to separate the relations of jade images to the cult of cosmos from those to the grave. The bond between jade and the image of death is seen in the prevalent folk belief that jade amulets dispel evil spirits. The strength of this belief is manifested by the kind of jade carving that artists after the Han continued to produce: although the T'ang and the succeeding dynasties steered further and further away from ritualistic formulas in favor of naturalistic portrayal, their production of jade pieces was dedicated to two main purposes—the utilitarian, and the amuletic.[24] The protective and punitive properties of jade thus prevail over those associated with life-giving.

This part of the jade symbolism survived the various functional changes that the symbolism underwent throughout Chinese history. The engraving on Pao-yü's miraculous birth-jade testifies to the popularity of the folk belief that remains efficacious up to the present day:

1. [It] dispels the harms of witchcraft.
2. Cures melancholic distempers.
3. Foretells good and evil fortune. (*Stone* I: 189)[25]

It is interesting to note that although Pao-yü's precious jade dutifully performs each of the folkloric functions literally prescribed on its reverse side, the significance of the jade symbolism in the *Dream* in fact transcends this explicit citation of the folkloric intertext. Beneath the visible text engraved on Pao-yü's jade amulet, which yields the semblance of a homogeneous identity of the folkloric jade, there looms in the narrative fiction an enigmatic textuality of the mouth-jade, *han-yü*: a ritual object turned into an ambiguous imagery, once fictionalized.

Among the burial jades employed to close the nine openings of the body, a practice developed from the Chou burial rituals but perfected during the Han,[26] those placed on the tongue were the most significant. Here the metaphor of rejuvenation is delivered through the vicarious act of eating. The culinary symbolism is derived from the Taoist lore that, as the food of mana, jade guarantees immortality.

Our recognition of the custom of those burial rituals which were known to have persisted up to the Ch'ing Dynasty (1644–1911) gives rise to a different reading of the range of signification that Pao-yü's birth-jade can convey. We cannot dismiss the play of intertextuality that the ritualistic mouth-jade triggers in the symbolism of the precious jade. We are led to wonder what it means for our hero to be born with a piece of jade deposited in his mouth. Early in chapter 2 of the *Dream*, we are given a reading of the significance of this event, summarizing the general reaction of those in the Chia family to Pao-yü's birth: it was considered "remarkable," "extraordinary," "strange," and "an event of the fantastic."[27] The birth of the jade is regarded as a miracle signifying "something very unusual in the heredity [*lai-li* 來歷] of that child" (*Stone* I: 75).

The word *lai-li* pinpoints the gist of the mystery. Literally, it means "where it [the subject/object] came from"—its place of origin. In Pao-yü's case, the concept of *lai-li* stretches itself in two directions: it applies to both *where* and *what* he was before he underwent metamorphosis into a human being. The presence of his birth-jade constantly reminds us that Pao-yü's original identity is none other than the mythical Nü-kua Stone. The mouth-jade is capable of generating such an association because it reactivates our memory of the episode in the sixteen-chapter *Chih-pen* where there is a detailed account of how the stone in question was transformed into a tiny jade pendant through the magic incantations of the Buddhist monk.[28] It is also by means of such a reminder that we are able to evoke the image of the place that the stone used to inhabit—the mythical realm. The birth-jade, then, holds a key more crucial than any other clues in the *Dream* to our understanding of Pao-yü's *lai-li*, for it serves to remind us, and eventually Pao-yü himself, not only of the *previous* existence he led, but also of the *transformation* that has taken place in both the mode and the abode of his existence. By serving as the reminder of such a temporal and spatial transition, the jade pendant unfailingly triggers the memory of the past and, by doing so, connects the human reality of Pao-yü with the mythical reality of the Nü-kua Stone.

It is thus interesting for us to take note of one crucial factor indispensable to the symbolic function that the miraculous birth-jade assumes in the narrative—namely, that the jade amulet can signify only if and only when a change of abode takes place. In other words, it is the transition from one place or from one form of existence to another that makes the insertion of the jade piece in the human body meaningful. This reminds us of the ritualistic formula contained in the historical burial jades mentioned earlier: for the grave signifies a change of habitation, and it is this transition that enables the jade objects to mediate between life and death. The burial jades not only sanctify the transition from the hearth to the grave, they also guarantee the continuation of an after-life affiliation of the dead with those cosmic forces that shaped and blessed life earlier. It is this liminal symbolism, characteristic of the burial jades in general, that imparts to the imagery of Pao-yü's birth-jade an esoteric aura that casts a mystifying spell over those who look at it and elicits from them an inexpressible admiration for its fantastic qualities.

Just as in the burial ritual the jades were placed only *after* the transition from life to death had been completed, in Ts'ao Hsüeh-ch'in's story the birth-jade was deposited in the child's mouth at the moment of his *reincarnation*, which coincided with the disappearance, and thus the symbolic demise, of the mythic Nü-kua Stone. Both rituals—the real and the fictional—manifest the human obsession with the meaning of death and the craving for regeneration. However, while in real life the burial jade is an oxymoron, a silent *sign* buried in the grave, in fiction it comes to life as an *agent* acting upon the transition between life, death, and resurrection.

Throughout the *Dream*, the periodic disappearance and reemergence of this jade amulet always serves to predict either the beginning or the end of Pao-yü's spiritual limbo. On the one hand, it is the making of the transition that enables the amulet to signify that whoever owns it is neither here nor there, but between this world and the other world, and eventually between life, death, and rebirth; on the other hand, it is the jade amulet alone that is endowed with the power to provoke the liminal chain reaction. No longer simply a precious object worn by a human subject, it comes alive as something internal to Pao-yü's very existence, regulating the momentum of his spiritual quest. Here one can perceive the intriguing permutation of the symbolic significance of the burial jade. Leaving the grave, where it was an immobile object, an accessory, something completely exterior to the body, it now takes on an enigmatic guise in the *Dream*, turning itself into something that transcends the boundary between subject and object, between inside and outside, between spiritual and material substance. And finally, it is transformed into a catalyst of both life and coma. Once fictionalized, the ritual jade thus multiplies its signifying activities by extending its liminal spectrum. Although Pao-yü was born with, not lying dead with, a piece of jade "buried" in his mouth, the twist of intertextuality by no means represses the metaphor of burial. And it is our awareness of the intertext of the burial amulets that sheds light on the inherent paradox on which rests the symbolism of Pao-yü's mouth-jade—that the signification of the (re)birth-jade is efficacious only if it already contains within itself the imagery of the mortuary jade. While the symbolism of eating is virtually lost in the *Dream*, the mortuary mouth-jade (which usually took the shape of a pupa, an insect known for its capacity to transform[29]) reactivates the theme of rebirth and reinforces the regenerative potency of Pao-yü's tongue-amulet.[30]

Bearing in our mind the haunting image of the burial jade, we will probably relish the unreserved admiration of the entire Chia clan for Pao-yü's precious jade with a kind of ironic sympathy. Those who take delight in the extraordinariness of this jade envision the living present, not as a continuum, but as an opposite, of the past. But there exists another time prior to and after life, and even after death itself, a temporal order that knows no meaning other than that of mediation. It exists in between and feeds a vision that is tragicomic. It never ceases to trigger the play between contradictory levels of expectation, interpreting the precious jade no less as an auspicious sign than as a prodigy of ominous significance. The reading of the supernatural sign by those surrounding Pao-yü is rooted in the comic vision. The expectations aroused about the boy are of a spectacular kind. Thus we are told, "that is the reason [i.e., that he was born with the jade] why his old grandmother thinks him such a treasure" (*Stone* I: 76).

With the growth of the child there develops a fetishism of this jade, which assumes a steadily increasing significance that even usurps that of the human subject in possession of it. We only need to recall how Hsi-jen 襲人 (Aroma) throws a fit over the loss of the jade: "if it is really lost, it is even worse than losing Pao-yü's life itself" (*HLM* III: 1333). This level of expectations— that the jade unambiguously signifies good fortune and good health, the very source of Pao-yü's life, *ming-ken-tzu* 命根子 —comes into conflict with another level of expectations based on our awareness of the liminal incongruity of the imagery of the mouth-jade. With the second set of expectations it is no longer possible for us to draw premature conclusions about the signification of the jade; instead, we view any such attempt as an invitation from the narrator for an ironic reading. The grandmother's reading of the propitious potency of the precious jade is meant to be read as both an overstatement on her part and an understatement on the part of the narrator. Not only does it foretell the possible frustration of such great expectations, but it also serves as a signal intentionally given by the narrator to trigger our skepticism of the literal interpretation of an enigmatic sign. The apparent statement of the text, that the jade amulet is a propitious gift from heaven, is subverted by a contrary set of expectations that as a sign of transition, the amulet also conjures up the images of the dead and the dust. The sign of Pao-yü's mouth-jade is thus meant to generate an uncertainty, for it immediately calls into question the intelligibility of the human vision. Our sense of irony is aroused as we ponder the vulnerability of a vision that stakes everything on the literal reading of the sign. The force of dramatic irony that consists in the intrusion of this other level of expectations is what animates the imagery of Pao-yü's precious jade and enables it to transcend its immediate function as an unmotivated phenomenon of the fantastic.

The Political and the Ethical: The Ritual Jade Reinterpreted

It is a true marvel when the glowing five-colored jade meets the eyes of those awaiting the birth of the child. The grandmother may not be well aware of the intertextuality of the mouth-jade, but she nonetheless reads into this beautiful object a simple truth that has sustained the unfailing admiration of jade by generations of Chinese people: it is rare, and therefore a precious material. The literal reading of Pao-yü's mouth-jade, that it is something precious and auspicious, is unambiguously registered in the very name of our hero—Precious (*Pao* 寶) Jade (*yü* 玉).

The journey of jade from the imperial ceremonial altar to the jade-carver's studio was a short one. The evolution of the ritual vessel into a precious material began as early as the third century B.C., toward the end of the Chou period, when jade took on a more worldly use as its religious significance began to diminish.[31] After the Han Dynasty (206 B.C. to 220 A.D.), the religious aura surrounding jade continued to wane gradually; the interest in its symbolic function in ceremonies was replaced by an increasingly pragmatic appreciation of its aesthetic appeal. But it was not until the T'ang

(618–907) and the Sung (960–1279) that the functional change of jade was fully achieved, and that it was viewed as a precious material rather than as some substance of semimagical or spiritual qualities reminiscent of its earlier ritual symbolism.[32] The predominantly ceremonial use of the object was then superseded by the human aesthetic delight in it as something precious and beautiful, and therefore worth preserving. Small objects and personal ornaments were the two major varieties of jade sculpture produced during the T'ang. The art of jade carving was further refined during the three succeeding dynasties, while the aesthetic motif shifted its focus back and forth between archaism and naturalism.[33]

By the time of the Ch'ing Dynasty, when Ts'ao Hsüeh-ch'in was engaged in writing the *Dream of the Red Chamber*, the technical level of jade carving had reached its acme and jade connoisseurship had established itself as a field in its own right. In the eighteenth century, jade pieces bore a distinctly worldly imprint, which, as Berthold Laufer describes it, "[had stripped them] bare of that deep religious spirit which had instigated the great early masters to their transcendental and spiritually impressionistic motives. The emotional idealism and sentimentalism had vanished. The exigencies of the life here had come more and more to the front and the old-time rigid sacredness was redeemed by a more human and social touch."[34] The receding sacred aura of jade in real history was manifested in the increasingly secular taste of both those who made and those who appreciated the jade ornaments. The *Dream of the Red Chamber*, as a masterpiece of the century, captured this changing trend in fictional terms. It is not merely fictitious that the grandmother and the other characters in the narrative have grown ignorant of the spiritual and religious symbolism of Pao-yü's mouth-jade, choosing to interpret it as a sign that pertains to immediate human reality—a sign of beauty. But is the "human and social touch" mentioned by Laufer engendered by a vision dedicated to artistry alone and simply confined to what the aesthetic eye beholds? And most important, is that vision clearly distinguished from the earlier one that was characterized by a kind of "emotional idealism," in Laufer's words?

The rigid contrast between the human/social and the religious implied in the passage above presents a picture too simplistic to account for the intriguing evolutionary process that the jade symbolism underwent throughout the ages. It is deceiving, in the first place, to assume that the sacred and the secular embody two opposite poles of cultural development. The secularization of the jade imagery throughout the centuries is not a phenomenon generated in reaction against, and thus grown contrary to, the religious connotation of the ritual jade. The human and social aspect of jade, although distinctly different from its religious guise, is by no means something altogether foreign to the latter; it was in fact originally incorporated into, and only later evolved away from, the symbolism of the ritual jade vessels.

I have shown earlier that the Chou imperial ritual that paid tribute to cosmic deities was both religious and political in nature. Performed by the Son of Heaven, it was a state ceremony that celebrated the consolidation of his power and invoked the divine spirits for the continuous prosperity of his kingdom. The bonding between the human and the cosmic not only signified the renewal of the energy of both realms, it also gave sanction to the political order that prevailed on earth. The performance was therefore a highly politicized event. And the six jade vessels, emblems representing each cosmic deity, had acquired a political significance that gradually transcended the thinning religious symbolism underlying the ritual, and had come to be associated with authority and royalty. It is not surprising that the symbol of jade should accommodate references to the profane and the political. The central position of jade in the ritual symbolism thus incorporates an intensely human and highly political vision, which remains from the very start inseparable from the sacred and the religious.

Both the archaeological evidence and records in ancient texts such as the *Shu Ching* and the *Li Chi* emphasize the importance of jade in ceremonies related to the social and political organizations of the Shang (ca. 1600–ca. 1100 B.C.) and Chou dynasties.[35] The ceremonial exchange of jades was widely practiced among rulers and their royal subjects as a way of bargaining for political power. By the time of Western Chou (ca. 1100–771 B.C.), state rituals had become highly systematized. According to the *Chou Li*, the *kuei* 圭 —a jade tablet, one of the six ritual vessels—came to serve as an official emblem designating the specific rank of those who held it.[36] It was given to a noble at his enfeoffment as a token of contractual authority from his superior. The possession of this token thus signifies the ownership of power and status. It was also said that those who had won imperial favor might receive the right to use a certain number of jade vessels of specific kinds in sacrificial rites dedicated to their ancestors.[37] It seems only natural that as time went by, jade became more and more associated with the human imagery of those who were possessed of it. By the time of Eastern Chou (770–256 B.C.) and throughout the period of Spring and Autumn (*Ch'un-ch'iu* 春秋) (770–476 B.C.) and the Warring States (*Chan-kuo* 戰國)

(475–221 B.C.), the ritual jade was undergoing a significant transformation as its referentiality came to rest more and more on human rather than cosmic imagery.

It was probably due to the connection of the political symbolism of the *kuei* with the imagery of its aristocratic owners that there evolved by the time of Confucius an anthropomorphic symbolism of jade. The characteristics of jade, both the tangible and the intangible ones, came to be associated with the human attributes embodied in an idealized power elite. It was Confucius who assigned to jade all the virtues appropriate to the *chün-tzu* 君子, the ideal gentleman in an ideal state. When asked by one of his disciples why the *chün-tzu* valued jade more than any other precious stone, Confucius explained that the ten attributes jade is possessed of should be viewed as metaphors of virtue for the ideal man.[38] Although it is not clear whether jade was assigned human attributes or the ideal man was brought to assimilate the properties of jade, the union between the two grew stronger during the Han period when Confucianism held ideological hegemony over the other schools of political philosophy. Under the influence of Confucian indoctrination, the ethical symbolism of jade not only found a legitimate place in statecraft, it also became deeply rooted in social mores and was absorbed into folk wisdom. The definition of jade in the *Shuo-wen* (ca. A.D. 100), the first lexicon of Chinese language, provides a summary of the Confucian view of jade that remains valid even today:

> Jade is a certain kind of fine stone possessing five virtues:
> (1) It is moist and glossy, possessing the characteristics of *jen*, "kind-heartedness."
> (2) Upon examining its exterior, its interior is revealed to those who understand the stone, for it resembles the character of *i*, "righteousness."
> (3) Its sound is musical and far-reaching, like the character of *chih*, "intelligence."
> (4) Although it may be cut, it retains to itself completeness, thereby displaying an inherent characteristic of self-defense like unto the character *yung*, "bravery."
> (5) It is without blemish when clear, similar to the character *chieh*, "purity."[39]

One can argue that the marriage of the political and ethical symbolism of jade is partly attributable to the prevailing Confucian ideology that politi-

cal acumen and personal cultivation go hand in hand. When the emblem
of power is cast into the paragon of virtue, the political symbolism of jade
reinforces its potency. The association between jade and the Confucian in-
telligentsia was in fact so strong that jade became an integral part of their
everyday life. Jade pendants were attached to their belts, and calligraphy
sets and accessories made of jade were placed on their studio desks. Jade
was even carved into small objects that the gentry fondled in their hands at
leisure.[40] The imagery of *yü* thus evokes the figure of the Confucian elite who
formed the backbone of the state establishment.

Such a class-oriented imagery seems at first glance to fit perfectly well in
the *Dream*—for one can hardly imagine that Pao-yü would have been born
with a plain stone in his mouth, given his aristocratic lineage. The precious
mouth-jade, however, becomes quite a problematic symbol as it goes on to
assume a cardinal role in the story of the iconoclastic Pao-yü. A symbol like
jade, no matter how radical its process of fictionalization may turn out to
be, does not start as an empty sign waiting passively to be filled up anew:
not only is it a well-saturated sign at any historical moment, it is also riddled
with ways of speaking that impose a specific frame of social position, political vision, and ideological stance. While jade is brought to constitute the core
identity of Pao-yü, who continuously questions the validity of the ideological establishment of Confucianism, it does not leave behind all the historical
references to its inseparable ties with Confucian values.

The relationship between language and ideology is a complicated one. It is
not my intention to review the entire literature of the debate on the issue, for
it is beyond the scope of this writing to give a full account of the interaction
of the Marxist, structuralist, post-structuralist, and Lacanian psychoanalytic
perspectives. My sympathy lies with the theoretical position that integrates
the Marxist and psychoanalytic perspectives. Ideology does not hold complete hegemony over language, for the language-using subject is also sub-
mitted to processes that escape the total enclosure of ideology—processes
that take place in the unconscious, a repressed interior that contradicts and
subverts more often than it conforms. A sign, whether written or verbal,
paradoxically stops signifying and is turned into a dead sign as soon as it
is cut off from the continuous permutations of those unconscious processes
and brought to represent and to be identified unequivocally with a certain
ideology. It is interesting to note, however, that the expression of repressed
subjectivity does not usually assume the simplified form of either total sub-
mission or total negation in its relation to ideology. Very often its expression

is ambiguous, resisting a rigid categorization based on the binary formula of assimilation versus rejection. It is riddled with gaps, in that the encounter between the subject and ideology generates the mechanism of a dialogue as well as hostile appropriation on both sides. The relations therefore cannot be easily grasped as either positive or negative.

Thus although the status of language is not subsumed under ideology, as those who are critical of dogmatic Marxism would argue,[41] we should recognize that language is nonetheless subjected to the process of ideological articulation. While the language-using subject interacts as much with the unconscious, the unpredictable, as with an outside system of signification that bears the burden of established ideological discourse(s), he or she is not only produced in those existing representations, but is also engaged in working on, if not in working out, the contradictions between an infinitely free imaginary space of subjectivity and the function of ideological limits that overdetermine the construction of such an individual subject. In the *Dream*, such contradictions take shape in the potential conflict between the anti-Confucian worldview constructed by Pao-yü and his identification with a symbol that contains within itself an ideological discourse that is predominantly Confucian. Whether or not Ts'ao Hsüeh-ch'in was aware of the existence of this contradiction, does not concern us here. What needs to be looked into is whether he transgresses the structural limits of the ideological discourse inherent in the imagery of jade, and whether the contradiction under discussion produces enough tension to trigger a transformation of the ideological articulation in the jade symbolism. This inquiry, which concerns the engaging of one text in a dialogue with a prior-text, and the engaging of subjective processes with the signifying practices of a culture, poses the issue of intertextuality. To examine such intertextual relations, it is necessary to map out the sites of interaction between the literary imagery of Pao-yü's jade and the cultural symbolism of jade. In other words, we need to address a series of questions that pertain to the issues of intertextuality. For instance, does the jade imagery in the *Dream* radically depart from the symbolism of the ritual jade? Does the new imaginary order of jade articulate an ideological discourse different from the previous one? How much of the old ideological content is appropriated into the legend of Pao-yü's mouth-jade? Must the relationship between the old discourse and the new be characterized in conceptual terms of binary opposition? Is it possible that such a relationship may transcend the either/or—the compatibility or conflict—pattern?

The Unfolding of a Moral Vision:
Chieh 潔 and *Chen* 真

I have mentioned earlier the grandmother's obsession with, or rather her illusion about, the auspicious potency of Pao-yü's mouth-jade. Inasmuch as such an obsession testifies to the folk belief in the talismanic magic attached to the ritual jade, we probably cannot help feeling sympathetic toward her restrained vision. When such an intertextual reference is explicitly engraved on the reverse side of the jade, it unambiguously invites readers to take the meaning of those written signs literally. We also need to recall that not only the mundane creatures but also the celestial beings in the *Dream* fall equally under the spell of this folk belief. Thus when Pao-yü falls victim to the Taoist sorceress Ma 馬道婆 (Mother Mah), the supernatural Buddhist monk mysteriously appears to remind Chia Cheng of the amuletic power of his son's jade to dispel the harms of witchcraft (*HLM* I: 357). This explicit citation of the folkloric intertext easily reinforces the impression, and in fact gives rise to the prevailing interpretation, that the jade imagery in the *Dream* unequivocally coincides with the folkloric amulet stone, and that the intelligibility of the meaning of Pao-yü's mouth-jade is confined within the signification of the latter.

Such an impression, however, proves to be deceptive. We have seen that the significance of the birth-jade in the *Dream* surpasses that of the amuletic stone. In examining Pao-yü's jade in the context of ancient burial rituals, I discussed how the ritual symbolism of liminality pertains to the inherent ambiguity of the literary jade imagery. And as the ritual charm gradually evolves into a political and ethical emblem of power and virtue, we have seen how it enriches the cult symbolism by incorporating into it a vocabulary that carries the vestiges of a dominant political ideology and a set of well-defined moral standards. The historical interaction of the ritualistic with the politico-ethical imparts to the jade symbolism two predominant dimensions of signification: it is read as both a descriptive and a *prescriptive* sign. For jade not only signifies the class status of its holders, it also anticipates certain character traits that justify such ownership. The most obvious traits that have come to be associated with it are those closely related to the image evoked by its physical substance: it is translucent and hard, and thus a perfect symbol for purity and tenacity. The association of jade with purity—and, by extension, with virginity—has taken such a strong hold on the cultural (un)conscious that not only the character *yü* itself, but also the characters composed of jade radicals have constituted a small repertory of favorite categories from which Chinese parents or grandparents choose to name their infant girls. Although the prescriptive connotation of such naming rituals has today probably escaped the awareness of both the name-givers and the named, the naming practice of heroes and heroines in narrative fiction, especially in the genre of boudoir romances (*feng-yüeh hsiao-shuo* 風月小說), very often reflects the moral order consciously dictated by their fiction-makers.

Naming in Chinese culture indeed embodies the act of fiction-making. It is as if by bestowing a name (e.g., *yü*) that strongly suggests the attribute of purity, the authorities (whether parental figures or, in this case, the fiction-writer) have already succeeded in confining the named individual within a preconceived behavioral code dictated by the name itself, and can indeed anticipate that she or he will grow increasingly attached to, and eventually become identified with, that attribute—the value of purity. What starts as pure fiction often predicts and overdetermines the pattern of development that is to follow. As if by one stroke, the name-giver closes the gap between the name and the named and turns into reality an imagined participation of the named in the signifying activities of the name. The liaison between the two is tightly sealed. And it surprises no one if those who bear the name of *yü* are turned into the very model of all the qualities that purity evokes.

When we turn to the *Dream*, it is not difficult to perceive the same kind of symbolic logic at work in the naming of major characters. Although the last names of Tai-yü, Pao-yü, and Pao-ch'ai 寶釵 (Bao-chai) have hitherto attracted much attention,[42] the jade character, *yü*, that is embedded in the names of the former two characters, seems to have been taken for granted and is mentioned only in passing in some critical treatises. Perhaps the association of naming with the symbolism of jade appears too peripheral to the thematic framework of the narrative to have invited major critical discussion. I would argue, however, that the examination of such an association is indispensable to our understanding of the evaluative standpoint assumed by the narrator in appraising the personality of his fictional characters. In a manner similar to that in which the ambiguity of Pao-yü's jade is significantly informed by the ritual symbolism of the tongue amulet, the characters named "jade" in the *Dream* embody a set of values that contain intertextual references to the ethical symbolism of jade. And since naming is an art of prescription, particularly in the hands of those who write fiction, the ethical value attached to fictional names very often reveals the moral vision of the one who designates them. In the case of the *Dream*, the naming device in particular holds an important clue to our discovery of the ideological orientation of the author-narrator, who often betrays a partiality in the treatment of his characters by assigning, through the symbolic act of naming, a certain privileged position to one particular group of characters instead of another.

Tai-yü and Pao-ch'ai

Although both modern and traditional commentators of the *Dream* have bickered among themselves about the personality appraisal of these two heroines,[43] it seems indisputable that the narrator's sympathy tilts toward Lin Tai-yü. To make the issue more controversial, the competition between Tai-yü and Pao-ch'ai takes place in various planes: it is a contest of their poetic talents, physical appeal, and moral sensibility. The narrator's judgment of the first two categories often betrays the difficulty one experiences in choosing between the apple and the peach—neither is dispensable since both are equally favored. Thus, in various poetry-writing bouts, the heroines take turns in winning the championship. As early as in chapter 18, the Imperial Concubine Yüan-ch'un 賈元春 (Jia Yuan-chun) summarizes the results of the talent match by naming both Tai-yü and Pao-ch'ai superior to their female companions in the Chia family. The result of the beauty tournament proves to be equally unsettled. Here the role of arbiter is naturally and appropriately assigned to the one who is not only a male connoisseur of femininity, but also the man with whom both maidens have fallen in love. Seen through Pao-yü's eyes, Pao-ch'ai's earthy, sanguine physique is certainly as appealing as the ethereal fragility of Tai-yü; on more than one occasion, we find our hero pleasantly surprised by Pao-ch'ai's physical appeal and lost in an ecstatic reverie about her sensuality. So it seems that the winner's title in the contest of the first two categories remains unclaimed.

The inconclusiveness of the matter, however, is far from being conclusive. For while the narrator takes pains to create the impression of impartiality toward both maidens, what he thinks silently gives the lie to such an impression. His own subversion of this deceiving impartiality can be located here and there between the lines. A contradictory (and sometimes a corrective) statement often emerges right after a verdict has placed the two on an equal footing. Thus, after Yüan-ch'un acknowledges the commensurability of Tai-yü's and Pao-ch'ai's poetic sensibility, the narrator slips in a note of explanation as a supplement to her verdict:

Dai-yu had confidently expected that this night would give her an opportunity of deploying her talents to the full and amazing everyone with her genius. It was very disappointing that no more had been required of her than a single little poem and an inscription; and though she was obliged to confine herself to what the Imperial Concubine [Yuan-chun] had commanded, she had composed her octet without enthusiasm and in a very perfunctory manner. (*Stone* I: 367)

So Tai-yü was half-hearted when she composed the "single little poem" at the command of the Imperial Concubine. The poetic talent she exhibited on this occasion by no means measured up to what she would have fully deployed if she had felt duly challenged. The narrator's apology for Tai-yü subtly betrays where his real empathy lies—for if Tai-yü could so easily match Pao-ch'ai while feeling so "confined" and unmotivated, it goes without saying that her genius is far superior to the latter's. The narrator's supplementary note thus subtly overrules the decision reached by Yüan-ch'un.

When we examine the matter of physical attraction, we find that here, too, in a no less involuntary manner, the narrator allows his partisan understatement to prevail over a carefully disguised and seemingly dispassionate narrative voice. At his grandmother's funeral, Pao-yü is carried away by the sensual looks of Pao-ch'ai in her unadorned mourning attire. Yet no sooner is he immersed in her natural charm, than the haunting image of Tai-yü dressed in the same appealing simplicity overtakes his thoughts:

> "But if only Cousin Lin were alive, and if she were to dress like this, how could one even imagine how sensual and beautiful she would have looked!" he cannot but feel saddened in this thought. With tears dripping down his face, and knowing that the funeral occasion would serve as a good disguise, Pao-yü burst into a loud wail. (*HLM* III: 1524)

The lover's partiality for his beloved is quite obvious. Even after her death, Tai-yü still gains the edge over her rival in the competition of beauty. Pao-yü's preference for the languid comeliness of Tai-yü actually reveals an aesthetic criterion unique to Chinese culture: the frail, the delicate, and the vulnerable convey a kind of charm to the male gender that the plump, the hale and hearty—the kind of physique possessed by Pao-ch'ai—cannot equal.[44]

This speculation on the culturally prescribed feminine model underscores the problematic nature of the narrator's evaluative stance toward Tai-yü and Pao-ch'ai. The narrator himself is probably unaware that the criteria for ideal femininity are not value-free, but manipulated by sexual politics and constructed by cultural categories. In his own innocent and subtle way, he bestows upon Tai-yü an aura of superiority to all the other maidens in the story—and especially to Pao-ch'ai, her rival in the art of poetry and love. We need to remember, however, that although the narrator's assessment of Tai-yü's physical beauty betrays a cultural bias and may thus cripple the persuasive power of his point of view, the privileged position of Tai-yü is solidified by yet another consideration that overshadows, and eventually outweighs, the criteria of physical appeal and intellectual acumen. The narrator's favoritism could not have stood its ground and attained its full significance if the subject in his favor had not also excelled in the last category of the personality contest—namely, moral sensibility.

The Metaphor of *Chieh* 潔 ("Purity")

As a social being functioning within the complex hierarchical structure of the traditional Chinese family, Tai-yü undoubtedly loses the popularity contest to Pao-ch'ai. She is ignorant of the mechanism of the power-struggle and awkward in her relationships, not only with the matriarchal authority above, but also with the female domestics on the lower rungs of the social ladder in the Chia clan. Pao-ch'ai, in contrast, is a master of the art of interpersonal relations. Always serving the eclectic function of mediator, she wins approval from her elders, admiration from her social inferiors, and even genuine friendship from her peers—including her distrustful rival Tai-yü. We are presented with a perfect paragon of virtue and beauty in the image of a maiden who exercises restraint and practices propriety. Indeed, her exquisite demeanor, well-tempered wit, and self-deprecating gestures embody the ideal womanhood—that is, the femininity generated and endorsed by Confucian teachings. Just as we have earlier seen the ethical and the political mutually engendering and reinforcing each other's initiative, so is Pao-ch'ai able to turn those prescribed ethical standards successfully into subtle political maneuvers. To go a step further, we see in her the merging not only of the political into the ethical, but also of her intimate self-image into a highly refined public profile. Here is a genteel Confucian gentlewoman who is acutely aware of the advantage of highlighting her public self at the expense of her private one. We are scarcely allowed to enter into her inner world to get a glimpse of her secret joys or sorrows. Even at the climactic moment of her final separation from Pao-yü, what we behold is still a self-restrained lady who succeeds in repressing the genuine expression of her inner self. Although her tears stream down her face as if this were "a separation in life and parting at death," she holds back the outburst of a cry that "was almost on the verge of being set loose" (*HLM* III: 1621). Such a well-polished public image has persisted throughout the narrative. Only once are we given a fleeting close-up of the well-guarded private self whose expression will suffer a gradual erosion and become increasingly muffled, as Pao-chai's tug-of-war with Tai-yü for the man they both love evolves into more intense phases. Such a rare occasion occurs in the early period of the paradisiacal life in the Garden when the innocence of the young maidens has not yet been shattered by the politics of reality. A more relaxed and vulnerable Pao-ch'ai greets our eye. She can still afford to trip and err, and yield to her impulses occasionally, and she does so despite her vigorous mental discipline. In this episode, Pao-ch'ai withdraws early from her brother's birthday party because she cannot stand the heat. An innocent remark inadvertently made by Pao-yü allows us to see her precarious balance tilted momentarily:

> "No wonder they compare you to Yang Gui-fei, cousin. You are well-covered like her, and they always say that plump people fear the heat."

> The colour flew into Bao-chai's face. An angry retort was on her lips, but she could hardly make it in front of company. Yet reflection only made her angrier. Eventually, after a scornful sniff or two, she said:

> "I may be like Yang Gui-fei in some respects, but I don't think there is much danger of my cousin becoming a Prime Minister."

> It happened that just at that moment a very young maid called "Prettikins" jokingly accused Bao-chai of having hidden a fan she was looking for.

> "I *know* Miss Bao's hidden it," she said. "Come on, Miss! Please let me have it."

> "You be careful," said Bao-chai, pointing at the girl angrily and speaking with unwonted stridency. "When did you last see *me* playing games of this sort with anyone? If there are other young ladies who are in the habit of *romping about* with you, you had better ask *them*."

> Prettikins fled. (*Stone* II: 98)

Her brief explosions are followed by a smiling but malicious taunt targeted at Tai-yü, who secretly enjoys the sight of her rival's loss of self-control. This is the Pao-ch'ai whom we hardly know—a private creature exposed to public scrutiny. The image evoked by her repartee falls short of being the portrait of a diplomat in the making. It reminds us, instead, of the pattern of petulance with which Tai-yü is usually associated.

If Pao-ch'ai can be viewed as a victim of her obsession with the public self, Tai-yü's mental trap is of a different kind. The delicate and enervated maiden is enclosed in a private space shielded from sight. Her inner domain is spacious, for it is not subject to public constraint. She subscribes to no rules except those dictated by her heart and her natural proclivities. She pleases very few in the family who view societal naiveté in a bad light. But she has achieved an intimate emotional and spiritual empathy with Pao-yü exactly because both of them dwell in this unadulteratedly private sphere, and both are waging a solitary battle against the hegemony of the public interpretation. It seems that in honor of such a dear comradeship, the narrator has given them names suggesting a common spiritual identity: the nominal reference to the character "jade" (*yü*) carries a significance that can hardly escape our attention. It is perhaps due to the self-explanatory nature of such visible signs, that most critics have skimmed over the first layer of symbolism implied in the names of Pao-yü and Tai-yü. Although it is commonly recognized that the character *yü* points to the mystery of the karmic association between the two and their shared root of origin—namely, the myth of the stone and the celestial plant—the naming device in question cannot reveal its symbolic function to the full if it is not brought to participate in the signifying practices of jade symbolism.

In discussing the association of jade with the naming device, we can hardly ignore another female character in the *Dream* whose first name also contains the magic word. This is the talented and beautiful Miao-yü 妙玉 (Adamantina), a nun who befriends very few in her self-secluded mode of existence in the Garden. When we examine the three characters all at once, many personality traits that appear idiosyncratic if viewed separately, will display palpable traces of a behavioral pattern dictated by the ethical symbolism of jade prescriptively installed in their names by the narrator.

We have already noted one of the characteristics they all share: namely, the inclination to retreat to a private space where they can find either an emotional refuge, as in the case of Tai-yü, or a spiritual shelter from all worldly desires, in the case of Pao-yü and Miao-yü. All three of them attain the airy temperament of the recluse, for each has escaped in one way or another from the "confinement of social values"[45] that binds the rest of humankind to earth. This private microcosm is not only an imaginary free space in which the three nonconformists roam without constraint, but also a space insulated from the pollution of worldly ways, and swept *clean* of the "red dust." Miao-yü's spotless abode and her neurotic aversion to dirt conjure up an idealism of self-preserved purity, which she believes to be impenetrable by the befouled forces outside her clean and sacred nunnery. To her, the public embodies all that the private is not: it is obscene, unfamiliar, tarnished, and forever engaged in the hostile act of subverting the well-defined boundary that the self takes such pains to draw and defend. But ironically, the symbolism of "cleanliness"—*chieh*—which is so meticulously woven into Miao-yü's way of thinking and living, proves to be nothing but an illusive metaphor, a fragile verbal sign, which escapes her grasp in the end. For the autonomy of such a clean and sequestered space cannot possibly withstand the brutal intrusion from the outside. What was enclosed is doomed to open, and what was clean, to be helplessly contaminated. The eventual shattering of her physical and spiritual enclosure testifies to an earlier prediction engraved on the Goddess's Main Register in the Land of Illusions:

> For all the spotlessness you yearn for,
> How can you ever have been clean? [*yü chieh ho-ts'eng chieh*
> 欲潔何曾潔]
> For all your would-be otherworldliness,
> Deeply sunken in this world you truly are.
> Ah you that were born with jade and gold
> Shall end up in dirt and mud.
> (*HLM* I: 79)

This verse serves as a good example of one of the most illuminating moments that the narration provides us: it introduces a narrative voice that is able to transcend the simple dichotomous view by suggesting that the reversal from jade to mud, and from the other world(liness) to this world(liness), is in fact anticipated from the very beginning. For Miao-yü's desire for cleanliness (*chieh* 潔) and otherworldliness (*k'ung* 空) already contains within itself the seeds of their opposites. What particularly interests me, however, is not the complementarity of bipolar pairs implied in the verse, but the phenomenon of mutual arising between jade and mud, and the implicit symbolism of purity versus contamination. As a sign, "jade" is endowed with the potential of assuming a generative and reactive function with regard to "mud" only when it is capable of activating the signification of *chieh*—"spotlessness" and "purity." It does so quite effortlessly, for the cultural unconscious vividly retains the connection between the precious stone and the virtue in question. In the ethical symbolism of jade, it is the reference to the particular virtue of *chieh*, "purity"—a symbolic trait intimately connected with the unblemished and translucent qualities of jade—that has been most frequently cited in traditional poetry, narratives, and folk literature. Such popular citations have undoubtedly left an indelible imprint on the mind of the people. Throughout Chinese history, *chieh* has been celebrated as the most noble virtue among all the "five virtues" that jade represents in the Confucian tradition. Idiomatic expressions such as *yü-chieh ping-ch'ing* 玉潔冰清 ("as pure as jade, and as limpid as ice") have survived even today as the standard metaphor for chaste and virtuous women.

The network of interactive referentiality in which *yü*, *chieh*, and the synonyms of "mud" participate in the *Dream* serves as a significant footnote to certain eccentric acts and mannerisms to which both Pao-yü and Tai-yü are subject. Readers who appreciate frail beauty will be particularly moved by the tragic awareness that Tai-yü acutely feels while she gathers the fallen peach blossoms and buries them in the flowers' grave. She experiences such unrelieved grief over this seemingly leisure activity because the fate of the dropped petals reminds her of the irrevocable fate of the fair maiden. Her elegy to the flowery remains is thus self-addressed, and their burial a vicarious one for herself. The symbolic identification between the fallen blossoms and Tai-yü herself reaches a dramatic intensity as she concludes her elegy with a reference to the burial as a ritual of purification:

> Pure substances to the source of purity return, [*chih pen chieh lai*
>   *huan chieh chü* 質本潔來還潔去]
> Rather than leaving them soiled and sunken in a foul ditch.
> (*HLM* I: 383)

This couplet, which merges the imagery of the pure maiden into that of the fallen flowers, reveals the inner motivation of Tai-yü's self-destructive mode of thinking. The "source of purity," a realm that the foul living cannot reach and touch, is also the terminal point for the flowers and the pure—the grave. The yearning to return to this source, a clean space not spoiled by the dust of earth, is also a yearning for the grave, the locale best able to guarantee the privacy necessary for the continuous preservation of one's "pure substance." The journey to the grave is thus a homeward journey. When the rationale of living is based solely on the wish of self-enclosure, the wish to remain intact eventually becomes indistinguishable from the wish to die. In her futile struggle to safeguard her self-contained purity, Tai-yü inevitably follows the steps that hurry her off to the journey's end—the return to the origin. It is this unconscious death wish that underlies her obsession with the ritual of burying the flowers. The desire to purify herself is paradoxically the desire for self-destruction. What begins as a ritual of purification ends up in self-motivated martyrdom. Emerging from behind the remnants of faded peach blossoms is the image of an uncompromising heroine who dares to pursue the ideal of *chieh* at all costs.

The immaculate image of the pure feminine, which attains a narcissistic intensity in Miao-yü's and Tai-yü's mode of existence, provides a source of inexhaustible inspiration to Pao-yü. The desire to grasp, savor, and then arrest such an image defines the very core of the meaning of existence for him. Pao-yü's total immersion in such a feminine image manifests itself in various guises. Seen through his eyes, men are shamelessly contaminated and driven from the realm of the pure and the clean. He himself is overcome with a sense of self-degradation and acutely aware that having been born as a male, he is nothing but filth in contrast to his female companions in the Garden. This awareness is reflected in his self-designation as a *cho-wu* 濁物, "a foul thing" (*HLM* III: 1499). It also gives rise to some peculiar personality traits that distinguish Pao-yü from the rest of his lot. The fervent adoration of both Chen Pao-yü 甄寶玉 and Chia Pao-yü for virgin maidens is carried to such an extreme in the case of the former that he commands all his male servants to observe a certain ritual:

> "The word 'girl' is very precious and very pure. It is much more rare and precious than all the rarest beasts and birds and plants in the world. So it is most extremely important that you should never, never violate it with your coarse [dirty] mouth and stinking breath. Whenever you need to say it, you should first rinse your mouths out with clean water and scented tea. And if I ever catch you slipping up, I shall have holes drilled through your teeth and lace them up together." (*Stone* I: 80–81)

Chia Pao-yü is no less pious than his double in his ritualistic worship of the pure femininity:

He'll say, "Girls are made of water and boys are made of mud. When I am with girls I feel fresh and clean, but when I am with boys I feel stupid and nasty [feel and smell their filth]." (*Stone* I: 76)

Boys and girls, men and maidens, are conceived as two different species— one is polluted, and the other pure. The metaphor of mud and dirt, which Miao-yü and Tai-yü vaguely perceive as representing the public realm opposed to their own clean private space, is here unequivocally identified by Pao-yü with the male image ensemble. Intensely aware that the purity of delicate femininity is constantly encroached upon by aggressive and coarse masculinity, Pao-yü dictates the ritual of mouth-rinsing as a symbolic purifying act.

It is no wonder that Pao-yü is seized with the anxiety to cleanse, for as a man deeply rooted in the essence of jade, he has been born with a penchant for purity. It is he who comes to the rescue of Hsiang-ling 香菱 (Caltrop) when her pomegranate skirt is spoiled in the foul water. While the other maidens leave her alone, it is only Pao-yü who cannot stand the sight of the badly stained skirt. His natural aversion to contamination renders him an unusually sensitive spectator of Hsiang-ling's dilemma. It is possible to detect a certain exasperation in his voice when he asks Hsiang-ling not to move:

"Stop moving!" said Bao-yu. "If you don't keep still, you'll get the dirty water on your trousers and pantaloons and the tops of your shoes. . . ." (*Stone* III: 213)

It is this same inherent antipathy to dirt that enables Pao-yü to appreciate anything that conjures up the image of purity. At his grandmother's funeral, he indulges himself in the aesthetic delight of watching Pao-ch'ai and Pao-ch'in 寶琴 (Bao-qin) dressed in pure white. And he realizes that the aesthetic category of "pure white/clean fragrance" (*chieh-pai ch'ing-hsiang* 潔白清香) far outshines that of "a myriad of reds and purples" (*HLM* III: 1524). The poignant empathy that Pao-yü feels for pure maidenhood may create the impression that he alone is exempt from the pollution inherited by the male gender. In both physique and temperament he is seen as effeminate. Even his name befits a maiden. Does this strong feminine identity suggest, then, that Pao-yü is the male embodiment of female purity—as unadulterated as the piece of the "translucent and pure" (*HLM* I: 3) jade he was born with?

"The Story of the Stone," however, is anything but a tale of the jade as a pure spectator of the human drama enacted in the Chia family. The one who is transformed into the very symbol of purity is not exempt from the process of post-originary degradation. One might say that Pao-yü's earthbound journey is seen through the narrator's eyes as a continuous history of degradation, from origin to fall.

In Chapter 1 I mentioned briefly that the *Dream* is based on a narrative logic that privileges the point of origin (i.e., the identity of stone) as an implicit ideological center, and I shall examine this concept in detail in the next chapter.[46] It seems imperative, from the narrator's point of view, that the mythical reality, the original point of departure for Pao-yü and Tai-yü, be recovered and regained in order to derive any meaning from the secondary human reality. Once having left the realm of his origin, Pao-yü is seen as inevitably deviating from his "true" identity. The original is identified as the authentic; it follows that any departure from such a privileged position entails deterioration.

In a similar manner, the fall from the original is also a fall from innocence, for Pao-yü cannot but move toward the cesspool of human desire. His reincarnation is a literal descent as both his birth-jade and he himself are subjected to the pollution of the Red Dust. It is this symbolic fall from original grace that necessitates the periodic "renewal" of the purity of Pao-yü's jade. And we recall the sudden appearance of the Buddhist monk during his illness to perform such a ritual: the supernatural machinery needs to recur at every critical moment of Pao-yü's earthly sojourn to *recover* the original potency of his jade. When asked by his father why the jade has lost the "power it lays claim to," the monk responds:

> "That is because the world and its temptations have confused [polluted] it," said the monk. "It certainly used to have the power. If you will have the goodness to fetch it for me and allow me to hold it in my hand and say a wee prayer over it, I think I can undertake to bring the power back again." (*Stone* I: 505)

Here the "power" of the jade is conceptually indistinguishable from its original "sheen" (*Stone* I: 505)—its pure essence. The ritual of purification performed by the monk is intended to bring back the sheen of the jade, which has been "besmirched" by the "vain sensual joys" (*Stone* I: 505) it has experienced. The uttering of incantations, a ritual of verbal cleansing, is therefore supplemented by a corresponding rite of nonverbal purification:

When the monk had finished apostrophizing the stone, he rubbed it and polished it between his hands and muttered some strange-sounding words over it.

"There! Its power has now been restored." He handed it back to Jia Zheng. "But you must be careful that it does not become contaminated again." (*Stone* I: 505)

The stroking and smoothing of the jade is a symbolic act of wiping off, and thus eradicating, the traces of dirt that have covered it up and canceled the original potency of its purity. The point of origin enjoys its privileged position not only because it is primary and authentic, as opposed to the spurious and artificial, but also because it is perceived as the absolutely pure as opposed to the polluted. The narrator's obsessive return to the original thus incorporates a purity complex. It is in this episode of the *Dream* that we find the most palpable reference to the interactions that exist among the point of origin, the metaphor of recovery, and the endorsement of *chieh* as the most privileged fictional ethics in the story.

It is probably not too far-fetched to suggest that Pao-yü, Miao-yü, and Tai-yü, who are named after the symbol of purity, are turned into strategic positions that motivate the enactment of the ritual of recovery. Their yearning to fulfill the prescriptive content of their names—that is, the imagery of purity—renders them susceptible to the compulsion to recover the source. The periodic cleansing of Pao-yü's jade and Tai-yü's longing to return to the "source of pure essence" (*huan chieh ch'ü* 還潔去) should be seen as variations of the same motif: the original is pure. In a similar symbolic gesture, Miao-yü interrupts the improvised recital by Hsiang-yün 史湘雲 (Shi Xiang-yun) and Tai-yü of linked pentameters at the Concave Pavilion in a cold mid-autumn night. Sensing that the two maidens are being carried further and further away into bizarre and decadent poetic imagery, Miao-yü reveals her presence in her concealed spot in an attempt to prevent the momentum of their evolving poetic mood from deviating too far from their start:

"Now to conclude what you have done so far," said Miao-yü, "it is necessary to return the poem to what we Buddhists call its 'root-origin' (*kuei-tao pen-lai mien-mu shang chü* 歸到本來面目上去)...." (*HLM* III: 1094)

Only by bearing in mind the context of the intertwining relations between the two categories—the origin, and the pure—can we account for Miao-yü's unusual involvement in such a worldly affair as poetry composition, can we perhaps appreciate why a detached and presumptuous nun like Miao-yü is suddenly seized with the urge to interfere in what she would normally consider a lay(wo)man's business. Hers is the same kind of anxiety that Tai-yü experiences in her little ritual of burying the fallen flowers—the anxiety to return to the point of departure, the zero degree that signifies plenitude and emptiness at the same time.

I have discussed the subtle interaction among different value-categories (the private, the pure, and the point of origin) whose primary point of contact evolves around the metaphor of *chieh*. The interior space is clean because it is private. The moral dilemma for those who dwell in the increasingly contaminated Garden is the preservation of *the purity of the within*. The within does not simply refer to the enclosed Garden itself, but to a room within one's own mind. It is particularly in the latter locus that the narrator of the *Dream* inscribes his moral vision and builds his implicit scheme for the evaluation of the moral caliber of his fictional characters. This "purified personal within" is what distinguishes Tai-yü, Miao-yü, and Pao-yü from the other inhabitants of the Garden. Pao-ch'ai may be viewed as a chaste resident within the larger confines of the Garden; on the scale of the personal interior, however, the narrator is relentless, albeit subtle, in his condemnation of her compromising philosophy. Pao-ch'ai is so concerned with and adept at polishing her public image that in the end she is pared down to merely a public self that obliges and accommodates. Her private self—which, in the narrator's moral vision, is where one preserves one's purity—recedes further and further into the background and finally disappears altogether. Hers is a mere semblance of uncontaminated innocence, compared to the intensely concentrated purity of Tai-yü and Miao-yü.

That Pao-ch'ai is perceived as a moral being far inferior to Tai-yü depends upon the working of the ethical symbolism of jade, which prescribes the virtue *chieh* as one of the most important criteria for a highly cultivated moral being. It is the prescriptive content of this symbolism that provides the raw material for the built-in evaluative order of the narrator. The intertextual reference to the unblemished quality of jade and to what it signifies symbolically is internal to the makeup of his moral vision. To discuss the meaning of the rivalry between Pao-ch'ai and Tai-yü only in the descriptive terms of the *yin-yang* philosophy is to sidestep the issue of the evaluative scheme of narration—an issue of substance to a narrator who was deeply embedded in a cultural tradition preoccupied with personality appraisal.[47] Our recognition of the intertextuality of *chieh* thus sheds light on the nature of the intricate evaluative framework within which the contest between the two heroines takes place.

Our awareness of such intertextual relations in the *Dream*—namely, those between the naming device and the ethical symbolism of jade—does not merely provide us a frame of reference within which the seemingly unmotivated imagery of Pao-yü's birth-jade sheds much of its apparent gratuitousness: more significantly, it also opens up a door to the internal landscape of the narrator's moral consciousness. It is important to note that by highlighting the essence of purity rather than any of the other four virtues in the jade symbolism, the narrator involuntarily reveals his perception of where the true meaning and worth of humanity lies. Is the significance of life to be found in serving one's public image, or in saving one's private one? in yielding one's spiritual innocence, or in keeping it intact? Eventually the author-narrator perceives the choice as being either to give up one's own private space, and thus one's individuality, to a homogeneous outside, or to tenaciously preserve that clean little space in defiance of the public totality. The choice is not a difficult one for a nonconformist. The value of a human being, for the narrator in the *Dream*, lies unambiguously in individuality— an individuality that is defined and assessed by one's capacity to sustain and shelter the private and the pure. The other, more public virtues traditionally ascribed to jade, such as *jen, i, chih*, and *yung*[48]—attributes that characterize the Confucian gentleman—find no privileged position in a fictional moral universe that endorses self-withdrawal and identifies the innately good with purity.

The metaphor of *chieh*, however, carries a certain ambivalence that saves the *Dream* from being enclosed by the structural constraints inherent in the operation of intertextuality. Although the ethical symbolism of the pure jade is clearly based on the visual image of its unblemished quality, in reality such perfect purity is rare in the jade discovered underground or in rivers. The real jade is actually tarnished. It is usually stained by the interpenetration of such metals as magnesium, chromium, and iron, which can form streaks and create a rippling effect that gives jade an "impure" look.[49] In fact, during the Ming and Ch'ing dynasties all jade excavated from the earth had to undergo a special process of purification known as *p'an-yü* 盤玉, "uncovering jade."

The metallic alloy that infiltrated the jade was extracted from it in order to restore its original pure essence. The process, which was described in metaphorical terms as that of *t'o-t'ai* 脫胎,[50] "shedding the shell," subjected jade to a gradual qualitative transformation through smoking, boiling, distillation, and intensive rubbing techniques. The jade that emerged from such a lengthy and complex process of recovery was said to be born anew. The image of the flawless jade is therefore a myth perpetuated by the ethical symbolism of Confucianists. Like stone, jade is also a liminal emblem, existing between the categories of the pure and the impure, the artificial and the natural, and identical to neither.

The inherent ambiguity of the essence of jade does not escape the narrator of the *Dream*. The underlying conceptual framework of the narrative fiction subverts the notion of identity, and with it, the act of identification. Its fictional potency depends upon the confusion of values, which results in the breaking down of all boundaries between binary opposites. Thus, Miao-yü serves as the best embodiment of the liminal ambivalence of the *chieh* metaphor. The verse that predicts her destiny delivers the message that the seeds of the impure are sown in the soil of the pure, and that the bipolar opposites are mutually transformative for they coexist in the mind of Miao-yü. In a more complicated manner, the mind-journey that Pao-yü undertakes in the Red Dust is symbolically the self-same process that the real jade has to undergo to retrieve its original purity. It is a winding journey of self-recovery, a transition from the impure to the pure. In this process of transformation, the categories of *chen*, the "authentic/natural," and *chia*, the "derivative/artificial," overlap and are interchangeable. As an integral part of nature, the blemished jade is authentic, on the one hand; however, as an object containing the presence of the other—namely, some external metallic substances—it is seen as derivative, on the other hand. The same paradox applies to the jade that undergoes processing: it is artificial because it has been worked on, and yet at the same time, what the process of distillation restores is nothing other than its original authenticity.

Many commentators and critics of the *Dream* have elaborated on the theme of complementary bipolarity that blurs the concept of *chen* and *chia*, "the real and the unreal." But such discussion often rests on the plane of metaphysics and leads us to contemplate the macroscopic vision of human existence in general. In reading such high-minded criticism we can become entangled in abstruse terms that the dramatic is pared down to a treatise of philosophy without our awareness. I would argue that only by exploring the theme of *chen* and *chia* in the context of the narrator's moral vision can we bring ourselves back from the attic in the air to the central stage where the human drama of the *Dream* is enacted. This is not to downplay the significance of the self-contained conceptual system that underlies the human reality in the narrative fiction—but the metaphysical framework remains only a void if it is not inhabited by the physical presence of human beings. And those of us whose professional activity is confined within the domain of the mind forget only too frequently that human beings not only think, but also act as well. Seen in the light of behavioral ethics, the concept of *chen* and *chia* carries a different set of signification, which enriches the narrator's moral vision by extending its prescriptive category beyond that of *chieh*, purity. The complexity of the jade imagery in the *Dream* will then further unfold as we move from the ethical symbolism of the ritual jade to another set of behavioral modes: the authentic and the artificial, value-categories drawn from the transformative metaphor inherent in the craft of *p'an-yü*— "uncovering the true essence of jade."

The Behavioral Ethics of *Chen* and *Chia*: The Genuine versus the Artificial

> "Sister Lin is such a clever soul," said Hsi-ch'un 惜春 [Xi-chun]. "But she cannot see through things and go beyond them. She takes everything so seriously [*jen ch'i chen lai* 認起真來]. But really how can there be so much genuineness in the world" [*t'ien-hsia shih na-li yu to-shao chen te ne* 天下事那裏有多少真的呢]! (*HLM* III: 1187)

Here we are given the portrait of a maiden who indulges herself in taking things as real and expects them to be true—*jen chen* 認真—a philosophy of life that makes her an anomaly in the Chia family. Hsi-ch'un's observation of Lin Tai-yü points to the one personality trait—*chen*—that is considered her flaw. The possession of this particular trait not only causes her continuous disillusionment with life, it also serves to distinguish her from the rest of humankind. Tai-yü is perceived as a different species from the other maidens in the Garden exactly because, unlike them, she has not reconciled herself to the reality spelled out by Hsi-ch'un in the above passage—that one cannot and should not expect everything in the world to be genuine. As a sign of difference, *jen-chen*, "taking things in earnest," represents a value that cannot but endear itself to the nonconformist narrator of the *Dream*.

One who cherishes the worth of the inner space invariably respects all that bears the mark of difference. The intimate self is very often the locus where differences reside. One might indeed suggest that the moral vision revealed in the *Dream* arises from the appreciation of all that is different from what is publicly perceived. It follows that such a vision cannot but be a private one, nourished by a narrator who resists the notion of submitting that which is both intimate and different to public exposure, which often provokes public condemnation at the same time. Thus we often get a glimpse of the narrator's subtle endorsement of certain values through innuendos and veiled comments, such as Hsi-ch'un's.

Hsi-ch'un's lament for Tai-yü pinpoints the issue of social code, which dictates behavioral patterns that are publicly legitimized. In the context of such a code, individual gestures are either made unintelligible or rejected as idiosyncratic. The viewpoint reflected in Hsi-ch'un's words clearly represents public wisdom, for it implies the existence of a social code that frowns upon the idealistic naiveté embodied by Tai-yü. Although the nature of such a social code is never explicitly spelled out by our narrator, we know through Hsi-ch'un's words and the other negative comments directed at Tai-yü throughout her short life in the Chia family that the code embodies everything that our sentimental heroine is not. Hsi-ch'un's final exclamation reinforces this impression: "But really how can there be so much genuineness in the world!" This mildly taunting remark about Tai-yü's unrealistic vision amounts to nothing less than a strong insinuation that the reverse is true—that not only should one not expect so much genuineness on earth, but, on the contrary, one should also realize that the world is submerged in deceptiveness (*chia*)!

As categories of ethics, *chen* and *chia* are diametrically opposed to each other. One may say that on the surface level, the moral vision in the *Dream* reveals an inner logic different from its metaphysical vision: while *chen* and *chia* are perceived in the latter as mutually transformative, in the moral vision they are turned into distinct binary poles that enter into confrontational rather than complementary relationships with each other. The opposition between these two terms is solidified when the specific behavioral patterns assigned to them elicit diametrically opposed evaluations. One's moral vision can be defined by the nature of one's evaluation of the behavioral manifestation of each term.

To illustrate how the binary pair functions in the implicit evaluative scheme of the *Dream*, let us now consider a dialogue that takes place between a loyal retainer of the Chen 甄 family and Pao-yü's father, Chia Cheng. The two are involved in a conversation in which Pao Yung 包勇 (Bao Yong) tries to enlighten Chia Cheng as to why the fortune of the Chen family has so quickly declined:

> Pao Yung said, ". . . I am not in a position to say this. But our Master is too nice. He deals with people with true feelings [*chen-hsin* 真心]. That is why he has brought so much trouble on his family."
>
> Chia Cheng said, "But being true to others is a great virtue."
>
> Pao Yung replied, "But he is too true [*t'ai chen le* 太真了]. That irritates every one. . . ." (*HLM* III: 1320)

The downfall of Pao Yung's Master—Master Chen—is thus attributed to the same tragic flaw that Tai-yü is known to possess: *chen*. We know through Pao Yung's description that the cultivation of such a genuine temperament is viewed suspiciously in the public eye; it is a behavioral pattern that offends "everyone." And in the realm of human justice, what the public condemns must be put down. The popular viewpoint dictates that the attribute of *chen* embodies nothing other than a stigma on Master Chen's reputation. But the above conversation provides us with two different interpretations, two contrasting evaluations, of the behavioral code of "acting genuinely." The alternative reading is given by Chia Cheng, who challenges the public verdict by changing the negative connotation of *chen* into that of "a great virtue." Known as a character of rectitude and good conscience, Chia Cheng establishes himself in the narrator's evaluative scale as someone whose voice carries the weight of authority—in terms of both the patriarchal and the moral jurisdiction of the Chia family. In this particular instance, the narrator has borrowed Chia Cheng's voice to counter public opinion and to subvert the legitimacy of public justice. The oppositional relations between the public and Chia Cheng's interpretation suggest that the inversion of the apparent is true—that it is those who subject themselves to the behavioral code of *chen* who are the ultimate recipients of poetic justice.

As the paragon of both virtues, *chieh* and *chen*, Lin Tai-yü emerges unambiguously as the main heroine among the Twelve Beauties on the Main Register. Her ethereal bond with Pao-yü is strengthened on earth for he too shares the two most essential personality attributes. When we turn to Pao-yü, what is merely implied in the above conversation—namely, the contradiction between *chen* and *chia*—emerges as the primary axis of the behavioral code that assists him in differentiating his own species from that of the profane. We need only recall his meeting with Chen Pao-yü to understand that his disillusionment with his double arises from a deep-seated aversion to anything that falls into the category of *chia*—the artful, the affected, and the disingenuous. The symbolism of inversion that underlies the narrative framework of the *Dream* is ingeniously manifested in this fateful, albeit belated, encounter between the *Chen* and *Chia* Pao-yü. The literally "real" Pao-yü turns out to be anything but *chen*. Through "Chia" Pao-yü's eyes, we perceive, to his horror and surprise, a young man adept in the art of "mundane rhetoric" (*shih-lu te hua* 世路的話), which produces only "false meanings" (*hsü-i* 虛意) accompanied by affected gestures (*HLM* III: 1574). Chia Pao-yü's disenchantment with his namesake is doubly acute, for not only has he not found in Chen Pao-yü the obstinate defender of the value of *chen*, but he has also discovered in the latter the complete opposite of such a self-image. The oppositional relation between *chen* and *chia*, on which Chia Pao-yü bases his own criterion of personality appraisal, serves to convince him during their symbolic confrontation that his double belongs to the category of *lu-tu* 祿蠹 (*HLM* III: 1576), the "fortune-eating worms," a materialistic species in direct contrast to his own.

But if Chen Pao-yü embodies the unreal, how do we define the behavioral pattern that conveys the meaning of the real? Throughout the *Dream*, we find Pao-yü reveling in idiosyncratic behaviors that perplex the elders in the family, but for which he offers little apology. In his childlike innocence during the early period of his life in the Garden, Pao-yü indulges himself in the pure delight of acting strangely. It would be futile for anyone to ask Pao-yü, in this stage of his existence, to conceptualize his idiosyncrasy in the abstract terms of *chen* and *chia*. What greets our eye is a carefree hero who is not yet aware what motivates his behaviors. He acknowledges no connection between an action and its rationale, between the experiential and the conceptual. In his natural world, the latter category is superfluous—for he sees no gap between the intuitive and the cognitive. Tai-yü's death opens up that gap and shatters the undifferentiated existence that Pao-yü has so far experienced. He now enters the realm of the conceptual and perceives with poignant insight the invisible incentive that has always driven him to behave eccentrically. A mellower Pao-yü emerges, toward the end of the *Dream*, to philosophize on the meaning of human action, and to decipher his own actions in particular.

In the following episode, Pao-yü provides us his own perception of what it means to behave "genuinely." The episode takes place during a pensive night when he has retired to an outer room but has stayed awake, hoping that Tai-yü's spirit will appear to alleviate his intense love-sickness for her. While waiting listlessly, he is carried away by stray thoughts of another deceased maiden, Ch'ing-wen 晴雯 (Skybright). His interest then shifts suddenly to Wu-erh 五兒 (Fivey), a newly employed housemaid whose close resemblance to the short-lived Ch'ing-wen catches his attention for the first time. In a moment of emotional vulnerability the curious Pao-yü wakes Wu-erh up with the vague intention of befriending her, believing her to be Ch'ing-wen's "shadow." He initiates a conversation with the reluctant maid, who mistakes her master's genuine feelings for a flirtatious gesture:

> ". . . This is a long story. Why don't you sit down next to me, I will tell you in detail," said Pao-yü.
>
> Wu-erh blushed. She said with a smile, "You are lying down in your bed. How can I sit down?"
>
> "So why does that matter? Some years ago, I remember it was Ch'ing-wen frolicking with She-yüeh (Musk) in a cold winter night. I was so afraid that she would catch cold that I held her in my arms and warmed her up in my cotton comforter. What's wrong with that? A human being shouldn't act like an affected egg-head [*suan-wen chia-ts'u* 酸文假醋]."
>
> Wu-erh interpreted this as Pao-yü's intention to dally with her. How could she know that the silly Pao-yü was in fact genuine [*shih-hsin shih-i* 實心實意] about what he said? (*HLM* III: 1505)

A clear-sighted Pao-yü can now perceive in retrospect that the inner motivation for his earlier "philandering" activities did not grow out of lust and some peculiar disposition, as everyone assumed, but out of "a genuine heart/mind" (*shih-hsin*) and "genuine intentions" (*shih-i*). Following one's own instinct and yielding to one's heart are the behavioral codes that Pao-yü holds superior to the affected mannerisms of pedants. But in a social code dominated by "false meanings," the category of *chen*, "genuine naiveté," invites only misunderstanding and apprehension—for it appears not only anomalous but also hazardous to the social arbiters in whose well-ordered world only the tamed are considered virtuous.

This brings us back to the issue of Confucian ideology, which emphasizes the importance of self-cultivation. In that context, the cultivation of the mind is nothing more than the laborious process of domesticating the unruly, the instinctual, and the natural in human temperament. In the case of Monkey in the *Hsi-yu Pu*, what is repressed extends even to the imaginative, the creative, and the libidinal. In the late Ming Dynasty (1368–1644), however, there arose a voice challenging the evaluative system embedded in the old dichotomy between nature and artifice, and between spiritual laissez-faire and mind-cultivation. At issue, eventually, was the hegemony of a Confucian worldview that privileged collectivity at the expense of individuality. This alternative voice emerged to articulate a different vision, both metaphysical and moral/ethical, couched in the inversion of old values. Underlying this seditious vision is a different interpretation of the wild and the tame: the former is seen as the natural, and therefore the authentic; the latter, as the polished and the artificial.

T'ung-hsin 童心 and *Chen-hsin* 真心

As John Hay indicates, the issue of artificiality and artifice grew increasingly complex in the seventeenth century.[51] By the time of the writing of the *Dream of the Red Chamber*, the concept of "natural" versus "artificial" had become loaded with ambiguities. A discussion that refers to the inversion of the evaluative content inherent in both concepts takes place between Pao-yü and his father Chia Cheng, a faithful proponent of Confucian values. In this episode, Pao-yü has accompanied his father at his command to inspect the newly built Garden. Chia Cheng intends to take advantage of this occasion to test his son's flair for versification. With this in mind, he orders Pao-yü to compose impromptu inscriptions for the stone tablets erected at the entrance of each building in the Garden. When asked whether he likes "Apricot Village," a rustic little thatched hut that pleases his father immensely, Pao-yü gives the unexpected answer that he prefers a much fancier retreat, "The Phoenix Dance." The angry father retorts,

> "Ignoramus! You have eyes only for painted halls and gaudy pavilions— the rubbishy trappings of wealth. What can you know of the beauty that lies in quietness and natural simplicity? This is a consequence of your refusal to study properly."

> "Your rebuke is, of course, justified, Father," Bao-yu replied promptly,

"but then I have never really understood what it was the ancients *meant* by 'natural.'" . . .

"Why, fancy not knowing what 'natural' means—you who have such a good understanding of so much else! 'Natural' is that which is of *nature*, that is to say, that which is produced by nature as opposed to that which is produced by human artifice."

"There you are, you see!" said Bao-yu. "A farm set down in the middle of a place like this is obviously the product of human artifice. . . . It isn't even a particularly remarkable view—not nearly so 'natural' in either form or spirit as those other places we have seen. The bamboos in those other places may have been planted by human hand and the streams diverted out of their natural courses, but there was no *appearance* of artifice. That's why, when the ancients use the term 'natural' I have my doubts about what they really meant. For example, when they speak of a 'natural painting,' I can't help wondering if they are not referring to precisely that forcible interference with the landscape to which I object." (*Stone* I: 336–37)

That which seems natural therefore appears artificial in the eyes of Pao-yü, in whose perception the concept of *chia* is tantamount to any form of "forcible interference." It is significant that his disquisition on the "natural" serves as a rebuttal of Chia Cheng's view, which embodies what the "ancients"— in other words, the Confucianists—conceived of as "the natural" (*t'ien-jan* 天然). Implicit in this critique of interference is Pao-yü's deeper skepticism about the Confucian tradition of mind-cultivation. To cultivate is to tamper with the original pure essences that one is born with, and to process the natural into a product of artifice.

The anti-Confucian moral vision that the *Dream* implicitly endorses is not completely novel in the late imperial history of China.[52] Taking "intuitionism"[53] as a point of departure, Li Chih 李贄 (1527–1602), a late Ming radical who belonged to the idealist tradition of the Wang-Lu School, anteceded Ts'ao Hsüeh-ch'in in his elucidation of the moral implications of the unfolding of a mind that "knows about itself naturally," a mind whose purity is defined in terms of autonomy—in other words, in terms of its resistance to the act of conscious cultivation. A nonconformist disillusioned with the socio-political order of his time, Li Chih engaged himself in revitalizing the moral vision underlying the neo-Confucian notion of *hsin* 心 —the mind-and-heart. The concept of the translucent mind unburdened by pre-conceptions in the Wang-Lu philosophies seemed to him to still fall short of conveying the harmonious and effortless merging of the mind and the heart—the cognitive and the intuitive. To close that gap, he found a meta-phor for the mind that highlights the essence of its immediate potency, and in so doing, he transformed the philosophical concept into literary imagery. The metaphor thus created reflects the originality and imaginative power of a daring maverick. Although it may appear ideologically neutral to many, Li Chih's metaphor of *t'ung-hsin*, the mind-and-heart of the child, contains within the simplicity of its expression the seeds of an ideological subversion long overdue in the cultural and intellectual history of old China. It is no accident that he chose to privilege the period of one's life that is the least significant in Confucian ethics,[54] and the least immune to the ideology of self-control—namely, childhood. Let us look at two excerpts from Li Chih's well-known treatise "On *t'ung hsin*":

> . . . "*T'ung hsin*," the mind of the child, is *chen hsin*, the true heart. If one opposes the idea of *t'ung hsin*, one is actually opposing the idea of "true heart." The mind of the child is completely disengaged from falsehood [*chia*]. It is the original mind [*pen hsin* 本心] before thoughts emerge. If one loses the mind of the child, one loses one's true heart; if one loses the true heart, one loses one's true identity.[55]

> . . . That is to say that if a person is false, then everything he/she does will be false. It follows that one makes the untrue person happy by talk-ing to him/her in false language; one makes the unreal person delighted by giving him/her false information; and one pleases the artificial per-son by communicating with him/her in insincere writing. If nothing he/she does is not false, then nothing will fail to please him/her.[56]

It is interesting that in Li Chih's conceptual framework, the terms *t'ung hsin*, *chen hsin*, and *pen hsin* ("the original mind") are variations of the same motif. Not only are these three concepts interchangeable, each of them also depicts one important profile of the ideal mind-and-heart that Li Chih holds to be characteristic of authentic individuality. The categories of the innocent, the genuine, and the original, which used to be subjugated to the opposing set of value-concepts—the sophisticated, the artificial, and the derivative—now serve as a privileged point of reference for a new aesthetic and moral vision that denounces the Confucian principle of imitation and cultivation in favor of the idea of noninterference. In this utopia of spiritual freedom, artifice and falsehood give way to a self-perpetuating simplicity that finds its place not only in the realm of the letters but also in that of human behaviors.

The antiintellectualism and romanticism reflected in Li Chih's treatise had great influence on his contemporaries and provided a source of inspiration for the late Ming and early Ch'ing literati and intellectuals. The repercussions of such an influence were no doubt still felt in Ts'ao Hsüeh-ch'in's time.[57] In view of the narrator's preoccupation with the concept of *chen* as a unique behavioral code to which Pao-yü and Tai-yü faithfully subscribe, one might suggest that the *Dream* has carried on the heritage of the *t'ung hsin* theory by presenting a fictionalized version of the moral vision prescribed in Li Chih's treatise, a vision built on the oppositional relations between the bipolar terms of *chen* and *chia*.

The intimate relationship between the concepts of *t'ung hsin* and *chen hsin*, which serves as the central theme for Li Chih's treatise, finds its place in the *Dream* in various guises. The reference to "the mind of the child" appears in one of Pao-yü's final conversations with Pao-ch'ai, during which he alludes to Mencius's concept of *ch'ih-tzu chih hsin* 赤子之心, an alternate term for *t'ung hsin*, as a footnote to the awakening of his religious consciousness. In the final stage of Pao-yü's journey on earth, his yearning for the return to the origin colors his perception of mundane matters. For the first time it dawns on him that the religious connotations of Buddhism are embedded in the nature of the child and in the concept of *chen*. In his newly awakened religious vision, the child, the authentic, and the Buddha are commingled:

> "... Do you know that some ancient sage has said, 'Not losing the mind of the child'? What does the word 'child' refer to other than the state of not knowing, not discerning, not desiring, and not envying? Since we were born, we have been sunken deeply in greed, anger, stupidity, and passion, as in dirt. How could we jump out of this snare of the Red Dust? ..." (*HLM* III: 1613)

To someone who holds on to the value of "naturalness" and "genuine naiveté" as tenaciously as Pao-yü, the concept of *chen* evokes the image not only of the beginning but also of the Ultimate. The beginning is the child, while the Ultimate is embodied in the Buddha who corresponds to the state of mind beyond the reach of the Red Dust. As the zero degree of humanity, the child is an empty vessel, defined by the state of *wu* 無, "nonbeing," specified by Pao-yü as "not knowing, not discerning, not desiring, and not envying": a complete absence in itself. This creative nothingness is none other than the state of Nirvana—the elusive mind of the Buddha—*fo hsin* 佛心. In a moment of illumination, the image of the child's mind merges into that of the Buddha, and the differentiation between the beginning and the end is vitiated.

I have discussed in the above Pao-yü's attempt to conceptualize the ethical code that guides his behavior. This is the grown-up hero who has gained philosophical understanding of the inner motivation that drives the child Pao-yü to perform what others perceive as eccentric behavior. Whenever he reveals his "authentic" nature, he provokes public reaction to the inexplicable. The perception of the others consistently reinforces the hegemony of public opinion over individual expression, sanctioning the former as collective wisdom while rejecting the latter as behavioral anomalies whose very irrationality seems to speak of "stupidity." Throughout the *Dream*, the public image of Pao-yü evokes epithets contrary to "reason" and "sagacity": he is seen by almost everyone except Tai-yü as helplessly *feng* 瘋 ("crazy"), *sha* 傻 ("silly"), and *tai* 呆 ("stupid").[58] The public interpretation of Pao-yü's private ethics, *chen*, is often delivered by minor characters in a tone of light-hearted ridicule and condescending tolerance. The following comments made by two old female servants in the Garden represent the most involved and articulate response of the mundane world to the childlike hero who is not yet conscious of the meaning of his own behavior:

> "Well, I've heard people say that this Bao-yu is like a bad fruit—good to look at but rotten inside," said one of them, "and I must say I'm not surprised. He certainly does seem a bit simple [*tai ch'i* 呆氣] [stupid]. Fancy scalding his own hand and then asking someone else where it hurt! He *must* be a simpleton [*tai tzu* 呆子]! Heh! heh! heh!"

> "He really and truly *is* a bit simple," said the other one. "A number of them told me about it when I came here last. Once when he was out in the pouring rain and himself as wet as a drowned chicken, he says to someone, 'It's raining,' he says, 'run inside and get out of the rain.' What a laugh! Heh! heh! heh! And he often cries or laughs when no one else is by. They say that when he sees a swallow he talks to the swallow, and when he sees a fish in the river he talks to the fish, and when he sees the stars or the moon, he sighs and groans and mutters away to himself like a crazy thing. And he's as soft as a *baby* (italics mine). Even the little

maids can do what they like with him. If he's in the mood for saving, he'll make a fuss over a piece of thread; but other times they can smash things worth a fortune and he won't mind a bit." (*Stone* II: 188–89)

The mood that the two old women fail to appreciate is precisely that of the innocent child who is always true to his original nature. That the typical public opinion is here conveyed and endorsed by two ignorant old chatterboxes cannot but deepen our impression that the credibility of their viewpoint is highly problematic. Our awareness of the intertextual reference of *t'ung-hsin* comes to shed a different light on what is revealed in this passage. The reciprocal relations between *t'ung hsin* and *chen hsin*, which Li Chih elaborates in his treatise, provide us a clue that what is condemned in Pau-yü by the two old hags is not only the mind of the child, but also the genuine and authentic mind. Viewed in this light, the so-called proper behavior is revealed as the artificial and the false. The narrator's moral vision is made intelligible through the contrast between the public and private readings, and through the inversion of the privileged viewpoint. We now know that the narrator chastises what the old hags recommend. What is unacceptable according to such a moral vision is the kind of sophistication that would forbid Pao-yü to reveal his true emotions and preclude him from entering into communion with Nature and his fellow human beings. In defiance of the will-to-cultivation—and, in essence, of the will-to-artifice—a certain practice of "stupidity" is not only innocuous but also emancipatory. The epithet *tai* 呆 used by the old women to designate improper behavior is thus a correlative of *chen*. The implicit correspondence between these two words occurs so often in the *Dream* that the former quickly acquires the status of signifier for the latter—that is to say, the adjective "crude/ignorant" is capable of conjuring up the entire referential network of *chen*: "the authentic," "the original," and "the genuine." The recurrence of *tai* in the first eighty chapters of the *Dream* serves as a constant reminder for the reader not only of the ethical code of behavior to which Pao-yü unconsciously subscribes, but also of the implicit moral vision of the narrator.

Chia 假

The narrator's appreciation of "true feelings" and the authentic mood unfolds itself gradually during Pao-yü's sojourn in the Red Dust. At first it is well disguised, in intimations such as Hsi-ch'un's comments on Tai-yü and the old women's criticism of Pao-yü. Only toward the end of Pao-yü's quest does the narrator allow our hero to meditate on the moral implications of his behavioral code. Thus the episodes with Wu-erh and Pao-ch'ai reveal a grown-up Pao-yü who engages in the belated reconstruction of the meaning of his early childlike behavior. Finally, as if afraid that his moral vision will elude the public eye, the narrator provides us a conclusive evaluation, in the last chapter, of his hero's "true" temperament as epitomized in the meritorious title conferred upon him by the emperor. To the title of *wen-miao chen-jen* 文妙真人 ("the wondrous true man of letters"), a Buddhist epithet, the traditional commentator Chang Hsin-chih contributes the following annotation: "The most wondrous attribute of a human being consists in his/her authenticity. That quality of the true and the authentic is what distinguishes a human being from beasts."[59]

The tragic flaw that Hsi-ch'un finds in Tai-yü, her stubborn belief in genuine self-expression, is in fact the selfsame trait that moves Pao-yü to spontaneous laughter and tears. In contrast to these two genuine souls, whose karmic bonding is strengthened on earth by their absorption of the same moral vision, there emerge a number of characters who follow the socio-ethical code endorsed by the public. Pao-ch'ai and Hsi-jen, who share the same man, not surprisingly also share the same spirit of *chia*—the false and the artificial. Hsi-jen is concerned only with appearances, while Pao-ch'ai is evaluated, in the narrator's words, as being good at *ts'ang yü* 藏愚, "hiding/disguising one's intelligence" (*HLM* I: 123).[60] Hsi-jen on one occasion instructs Pao-yü to act as if he genuinely enjoyed studying, in order to win his father's favor (*tso-ch'u ko hsi tu-shu te yang-tzu lai* 作出個喜讀書的樣子來) (*HLM* I: 271).

Pao-ch'ai's betrayal of the code of genuineness can be found in more than one account. Her soul has grown too cultivated and sophisticated to be able to understand what a genuine gesture or verbal expression signifies. When she fails to decipher Pao-yü's language, she dismisses it as either *tai hua* 呆話 , "silly words" (*HLM* III: 1576), or riddles beyond the comprehension of her practical mind (*HLM* III: 1615–16). As the paragon of Confucian eclecticism, she reacts against any nonconformist view and finds herself constantly struggling to hold Pao-yü's free spirit in check. Her long lecture to Tai-yü on good maidenhood reveals a viewpoint that borders on abusing one's true nature (*HLM* II: 582–83). She knows how to manipulate the power relations in the Chia family by ingratiating herself with the elderly superiors and the young maids at the expense of the others. In chapter 27, Pao-ch'ai accidentally overhears a conversation between two maids about a secret love; instead of revealing herself, a genuine move that would inevitably involve her in some trouble, she extricates herself from the difficult situation by deliberately involving the innocent Tai-yü through her acting out of "a getaway technique" (*HLM* I: 374–75). On another occasion, we witness the working of her devious mind in a subtler manner. In this episode, Pao-ch'ai appears at the right moment to comfort a distraught Lady Wang who has just found out that a maid she dismissed from her service committed suicide by throwing herself into a well. A hypocritical Pao-ch'ai greets our eye, as she feeds Lady Wang a lie at the expense of the dead maid:

> ". . . but in my opinion Golden would never have drowned herself in anger. It's much more likely that she was playing about beside the well and slipped in accidentally. . . . There's no earthly reason why she should have felt angry enough with you to drown herself. If she did, all I can say is that she was a stupid person and not worth feeling sorry for!" (*Stone* II: 139)

For someone whose sole concern is to accumulate her political capital and climb up the social ladder, the death of a maid or the emotional vulnerability of others only provides an opportunity for her to experiment with falsehood. Chin-ch'uan 金釧 (Golden) and Tai-yü are mere victims of Pao-ch'ai's Machiavellian exploitation.

Much of the discussion of the meaning of the *Dream* in the past has been primarily focused either on Pao-yü and Tai-yü's love, or on Pao-yü's spiritual quest alone. But the concept of *chen* acquires its definition not only by its own positive content, but also negatively by its relations with the other term of the moral language—*chia*. The genuine expression of Pao-yü and Tai-yü makes sense only when it is contrasted with the artificial mentality of Pao-ch'ai and her like. The moral vision of the *Dream* is therefore built on the differential relations between *chen* and *chia*, and between *chieh* and *cho* 濁 ("filth"). While we can appreciate other critics' exploration of the metaphysical implications inherent in the allegory of the Garden and in the metaphor of the dream, we also need to remind ourselves that the ontological vision of the *Dream*, painstakingly derived from such critical pursuits, cannot sustain the weight of meaning-making alone without incorporating the equally potent moral vision of the narrator. The intricacy of the story of the stone is built precisely on the elusive encounter between these two visions. While the metaphysical vision blurs the boundaries between this world and the other world, dream and reality, the authentic and the artificial, and the pure and the impure, the moral vision yields a different interpretation of the human relations among the main characters in the Garden. It differentiates, evaluates, and concludes. From such a viewpoint, Pao-yü and Tai-yü's ill-fated love is no longer seen as the fulfillment of their karmic obligation, but as the tragedy of two individuals who dare to defend their private space of purity and authenticity against the imposition of a public code that pollutes with falsehood. The spiritual affiliation between these two resides less in their unresolved karmic ties than in their conviction that the value of *chieh* and *chen* is different from, and superior to, that of *cho* and *chia*. The rivalry between Tai-yü and Pao-ch'ai will also appear in a different light if we bear in mind the partiality of this moral vision: the rivalry is no longer seen as a confrontation between the elements of wood and metal, but rather as an incompatibility between two different ethical codes—authenticity, and artifice. It is only when we discover the concept of difference, from which the moral vision of the *Dream* is derived, that we can appreciate the story of the stone as a *tragedy* rather than as an allegory. What the human drama of the Garden reveals is the tragic vision of a nonconformist—the irrevocable destruction of everything that is pure and genuine.

Chieh, *Chen*, and Confucianism

We have seen how purity and authenticity, two value-categories identical to physical attributes of jade, have participated in the making of a moral discourse. We have also seen that jade long served as a symbol for the Confucian gentleman. What, then, is the relationship between the moral discourse in the *Dream* and the Confucian worldview? The adoption of Confucian imagery for the symbolic identity of a hero who incarnates the arch-rebel against everything that Confucianism stands for sounds paradoxical, to say the least. The potential discrepancy between Pao-yü's mouth-jade and the ideological repercussions of jade symbolism inevitably gives rise to inquiries concerning the problematic relations between language and ideology. One cannot help wondering what can result from such a clash between a fictional image and the ideological content embedded therein.

To examine this problem, we need to start with the content of the moral discourse derived from the jade imagery in the *Dream*, namely, the concept of purity and authenticity. It is worth noting that although the essence of purity, *chieh*, is named as one of the five virtues in the *Shuo-wen*, it is not one of the ten Confucian virtues enumerated in the *Li Chi*. Its absence from

the latter suggests that as a virtue, *chieh* is a variable, occupying a peripheral status in the ritual symbolism of the Confucian tradition. One might
even hypothesize that the noninclusion of this particular virtue in the *Li Chi*
is the result of an ideological censorship. The composition of the *Li Chi* is
now commonly recognized as dating back to the Period of Warring States.
Confucius himself was known to have edited the document. Undoubtedly,
compared to the *Shuo-wen*, the *Li Chi* is a much earlier document bearing
more of a historical imprint of the time of Confucius. It is interesting to note
that in this document a completely different virtue—*chung* 忠, "loyalty"—
takes the place of *chieh* as the symbol of the unblemished characteristic of
jade.[61] If one compares "purity" with "loyalty," it becomes clear that the
former is differentiated from the latter on the basis of the private/public dichotomy: "loyalty" is perceived as a public virtue, and "purity" as a private
one. The omission of "purity" from the repertory of Confucian virtues in
the *Li Chi* not only indicates the downplaying of the private domain in Confucianism, it also serves to underscore the moral vision of an ideology that
considers human relations in hierarchical terms by stressing the relationship
between individual parts and the whole, rather than dwelling on the individual entity itself. The quality of "purity," which embodies the centripetal
drive, finds no place in the Confucian macrocosm where meaning is defined
by a network of relations rather than by the self-generating content of an
autonomous entity.

It is also worth noting that the connotation of the "purity of one's moral
composition," originally implied in the *Shuo-wen*, suffered a qualitative
change in the hands of later Confucianists. *Chieh*, "cleanliness," is brought to
assimilate the meaning of its homophone *chieh* 節, "honor." When "honor"
(*ming-chieh* 名節) is applied to Confucian gentlemen, it signifies "loyalty"
to the imperial sovereign. In this context, the substitution of *chung* for *chieh*
in the *Li Chi* seems less gratuitous than it at first appears. In the *Hsun
Tzu*, the concept of *chieh* ("honor") is not only perceived as a companion
virtue to *chung* and *i* ("righteousness"),[62] it is also considered a matter of
life and death.[63] The intimation of martyrdom is so intermingled with the
concept of honor that the desire to preserve one's good "name" often precipitates the heroic action of self-sacrifice—in extreme cases, masochistic
self-crucifixion—among the faithful followers, both male and female, of
Confucianism. In a patriarchal ideology such as Confucianism, "loyalty to
one's monarch" is equivalent to "fidelity to one's husband." When it applies
to women, the concept of *chieh* 節 ("honor") is even more tightly bound to

that of *chieh* 潔 (purity). Legends of martyrdom serving as examples of the female version of moral fortitude abound in traditional literature, such as the *Lieh-nü chuan* 列女傳 .

All these semantic permutations of the original concept of *chieh*—the flawless quality of jade—suggest in one way or another that the later derivations of *chieh* ("purity") have never quite departed from the Confucian context. The concepts of "loyalty" and "chastity" both appear as the public presentation of honor. They are perceived as public virtues, in contrast to the cardinal virtue endorsed by Pao-yü and Tai-yü—purity of the within. The innovation of the imagery of "pure jade" in the *Dream* consists in its close adherence to the embryonic concept of *chieh* crystallized in the *Shuo-wen*, and in its resistance to the ideological infiltration of Confucianism that motivates the semantic transfiguration of *chieh* and gives birth to the twin Confucian virtues of *chung* ("loyalty," as the dominant form of male honor) and *chieh* ("chastity," as the dominant form of female honor). Although capable of evoking the intertext of *chieh* 節 ("honor"), the concept of *chieh* 潔 ("purity") manifests itself as different from its homophonous double and subtly announces its flight from the ideological enclosure of Confucianism.

Thus although *chieh* is clearly named in the *Shuo-wen* as one of the five virtues of a Confucian gentleman, its inner contradiction to the Confucian scheme of values opens up the possibility of expanding the discursive space of the literary jade imagery. The ambiguous position that the virtue of purity occupies in Confucian ideology renders the symbolism of "pure" jade susceptible to radical transformations of all kinds. The gap between symbol and ideology in this particular case results in the liberation of the symbol and creates the possibility of relative autonomy for the symbol-maker. In a subtle manner, the imagery of the "pure" jade in the *Dream* contains within itself the potential to reactivate a defunct ideological initiative, but at the same time it attempts to obscure such a historical memory through a continuous fictional self-transformation.

If one can thus free the imagery of the "pure" jade from the ideological constraint of Confucianism, that of the "authentic" jade fares even better. This is a category that rarely emerges in the Confucian Canons. The author-narrator enjoys an even freer hand in molding the symbolism of *chen* in the jade imagery. He does so by exploring the possibility of delving into the metaphysical and moral dimensions of such a symbolism at the same time. As I mentioned earlier, the mutual arising, or rather the bipolar complementarity, of *chen* and *chia* gives rise to a metaphysical vision that celebrates the continuous subversion and blurring of the boundary of each term. When such an ambiguous vision comes into contact with a moral vision based on the clear differentiation between these two binary poles, a problem arises as to which reading one should subscribe to. The complexity of the *Dream*, however, cannot be reduced to the simple choice of one of these two seemingly incompatible visions. As a literary work that was interpreted by different schools over a century, the *Dream of the Red Chamber* embodies a linguistic construct that continually generates new signifying activities under the examination of changing critical perspectives.

In the present context of the study of intertextuality, it is important to investigate not only the intricate network of relations between the stone lore and the stone imagery in literature, but that between the stone lore and jade symbolism. The interaction between stone and jade constitutes one of the most abstruse narrative drives in the *Dream*. Jade is undoubtedly affiliated with the stone family, but at the same time it distinguishes itself as a unique mineral that occasionally enters into contradictory relations with stone. The encounter between these two objects proliferates the signifying possibilities of the text, since each provides a stimulus to challenge the self-sufficient conceptual closure of the other. A rudimentary binary pair, jade/stone, is thus formed, and it is sustained by the attraction and tension that each term simultaneously generates in the other. It is worth noting that there is an infinite capacity inherent in any such pair to multiply its conceptual combinations. The formation of such a binary schema provides a spatial structure within which the jade/stone affiliation can map out all the possible combinatory positions the pair is capable of generating. At different moments of their engagement, the two terms may generate the relations of synthesis, complementarity, opposition, and contradiction. And nowhere can one find a better locale to examine such a complex relationship than in the problematic of Pao-yü's identity that shifts between jade and stone. I suggest that it is in the ambiguity of this double identity that one can find the point of contact between the two seemingly contradictory visions—the moral and metaphysical visions—of the *Dream of the Red Chamber*.

Between Stone and Jade: An Issue of Authenticity
and Artificiality—from the Moral to Metaphysical Vision

> A deity came down to the Capital of late,
> He sowed a pot of white Lan-t'ien 藍田 jade.
> (*HLM* I: 511)

This couplet is composed by Shih Hsiang-yün at one of the poetry-writing bouts in the Garden, a joyful occasion at which Pao-yü and his female companions gather together to celebrate the founding of their new poetry society, the "Crab Flower Club." The allusion to the "Lan t'ien jade" in Hsiang-yün's verse requires some explanation. It refers to a folk tale of divine retribution recorded in the *Sou-shen Chi* composed during the Chin Dynasty (265–420). The legend relates how a man in Lan-t'ien Province is rewarded for his good deeds by an immortal who brings him a load of pebbles to be planted on the mountains. The man follows the divine instruction and sows the pebbles in a stony area. Later on, as the immortal has promised, the man harvests a crop of white jade and makes his fortune with the divine gift.[64] This legend reflects the folk consciousness that distinguishes jade as a precious object utterly different from common stone. It is thus considered a miraculous event that such a precious object could have been born from the common stock of lifeless stone. What the Lan-t'ien legend mystifies is not only the fertile potency of stone but also something that to us seems natural—the stony origin of jade. By viewing the natural birth of jade from stone as a supernatural happening, the story pares down the complex and elusive relationship between these two species to that of differentiation.

The immortals' prophecy, that "jade will grow out of the stones," might have appeared as a phenomenon of the fantastic to the folk tradition that perceived jade unambiguously as a different species from stone. During the Six Dynasties, however, there emerged simultaneously an elite literary tradition which acknowledges the ambivalent relations that exist between jade and stone—a recognition that surpasses the simplistic logic of the *Sou-shen Chi*. This ambivalence, which results from the simultaneous existence of an affiliative as well as a differential relationship between these two objects, triggers a conceptual disorder characteristic of paradoxes in general. In the *Wen-hsin tiao-lung*, Liu Hsieh adopts the idea of the potential categorical confusion between jade and stone as a metaphor for the evaluative disorientation that he considers characteristic of the literary criticism of his time:

Those who are intensely interested in literary composition often vie with one another in creating new elegant phrases. Most of them are obsessed with the desire to refine their linguistic expressions, but none wish to attend to the fundamentals of the art. As a result, brilliant jade is often lost in a pile of rocks, while common stones take on the appearance of jade.[65]

Liu Hsieh goes on to illustrate how difficult it is to distinguish the erudite and profound mind from the confused and pretentious mind, since the latter too often conceals its identity by finding the same expressions as the former in literary compositions. When the distinction between binary opposites grows thus unintelligible, it follows that the function of appraisal will lose its momentum, and eventually, its own justification. For someone as preoccupied with evaluation as Liu Hsieh, the prospect of blurred boundaries must have appeared a dilemma. In fact, one of his primary concerns in writing the *Wen-hsin* was to remedy such a disarray by establishing a critical criterion that would enable later writers and critics to make distinctions between the superior and the inferior literary mind. To set up this evaluative scale, he starts with a privileged point of reference—the Confucian Canons—as the fixed touchstone for appraisal. The jade/stone metaphor cited above serves to illustrate the fundamental logic underlying an evaluative system that subscribes to the dichotomous way of thinking—the peripheral is weighed against the center, the bad against the good, and the artificial against the authentic. In such a dichotomous scale of values, jade is identified as the extraordinary and authentic, and stone as the spurious and banal. One should not be tempted, however, to conclude that the metaphor of jade/stone is sustained merely by oppositional logic. The metaphor makes sense only if one also recognizes the potential danger of displacement triggered by the perceptual analogy between stone and jade, a similitude that can lead to the conceptual confusion of one term with another. It is the relationship of analogy no less than that of difference that binds stone and jade to each other meaningfully in the paradoxical compound.

The emergence of the *yü-shih* 玉石 ("jade/stone") compound is not a novel phenomenon credited to Liu Hsieh. The allusion to the binary pair as the embodiment of opposite values can be traced back to the Period of Warring States (475–221 B.C.). In the legend of the "Ho Shih pi 和氏璧" ("the jade disc of Ho Shih") recorded in the *Han-fei tzu*, we already find the suggestion that jade and stone evoke two different readings, since they represent two opposing sets of values.[66] The same allusion recurs in Ko Hung's 葛洪 (284–363) *Pao-p'u-tzu*:

> The true and the false are turned upside down,
> Jade and stone are entangled with each other
> [*chen-wei tien-tao, yü-shih hun-yao* 真偽顛倒，玉石混淆].[67]

The parallelism invoked in this couplet is still valid in Ts'ao Hsüeh-ch'in's time. Conventional wisdom continues to reinforce the correspondence of jade to authenticity, and that of stone to artificiality. Underlying the parallelism is the hierarchical axiology that privileges the first term over the second one: just as the "false" is secondary to what the "true" connotes, so is stone a lesser term subordinate to jade within the binary system. Moreover, the second term is perceived as a potentially subversive force that awaits its chance to usurp the first term. Like Liu Hsieh's metaphor, Ko Hung's reference to the jade/stone imagery betrays a conceptual framework based on the rigorous hierarchical division separating two terms that originally share many familial traits. Difference rather than similarity is brought to serve as the focal point of reference in defining the relationship between jade and stone. What is left to be unraveled in the examination of such a relationship is the potential reciprocity between these two species, a potential already implied in the suggestion that the one is often "entangled with," and thus mistaken for, the other.

For centuries, the paradox of jade and stone remained unresolved. The growing linguistic affiliation between *yü* and *shih* is revealed in the popularity of such idiomatic expressions as *yü-shih hun-yao* and *yü-shih chü fen* 玉石俱焚 ("to destroy indiscriminately, be it jade or stone"), yet the likelihood of the conceptual mix-up of these two terms was not fully explored until Ts'ao Hsüeh-ch'in wrote the *Dream of the Red Chamber*. In discussing the issue of Pao-yü's identity, critics of the past often lost sight of the ambiguity embedded in the transformation of Nü-kua's stone block into the tiny mouth-jade our hero was born with. I have shown how the moral being of Pao-yü and Tai-yü is made intelligible by the twin concepts of *chieh* and *chen*—symbolic attributes inseparable from the imagery of jade. But if the precious jade is Pao-yü's birthmark and namesake, and taken as the emblem of his moral consciousness, stone has an even more intimate bond with him: it is his original mode of being, and both his incipient form and substance. We are tempted to ask, then, What characterizes Pao-yü's true identity—the jade, or the stone? What is the relationship between his name and his original substance? What can it mean when the narrator inadvertently describes the jade as the "illusory image," *huan-hsiang* 幻相 (*HLM* I: 123), of the Nü-kua Stone? How does the mirror-image of the Chen-Chia Pao-yü—a symbolic naming device—figure in the jade/stone puzzle? And finally, what does such an ambiguous double identity signify?

The Issue of Identity

As we ponder the ethical symbolism of jade and turn our gaze to the meaning of the tragic flaws that pertain to human beings of flesh and blood (Pao-yü and Tai-yü) rather than to celestial beings of mythical origin (the Nü-kua Stone and the Crimson Pearl Flower), we must not lose sight of the fact that the *Dream* is a story told by the stone, and that the meaning of the human tragedy in the Chia clan is from the very beginning inseparable from that of the Nü-kua myth, which takes its roots in the suprahuman Land of Illusions. The human and the divine, jade and stone, the mimetic and the mythical have become so intricately intertwined in the *Dream* that it seems inconceivable that a critic could discuss one without taking into account the other. Strategically, however, this task has frustrated generations of Western scholars of *HLM* studies who have been trained since the 1950s to accept the concept of organic unity as the critical canon, and to adopt those interpretive schemes that can best deliver, and in most cases re-create, such preconceived unity in a literary work.[68] Methodologies such as the traditional Chinese commentaries, which do not aim at transforming textual disparities into an intelligible conceptual center, were viewed throughout the sixties and early seventies as reflecting an inferior critical spirit—a spirit that is held to be characteristic of the "unscientific" Chinese mind. It is therefore not surprising that the encounter of Western-trained critics with the encyclopedic plenitude that a full exploration of the *Dream* promises often engenders an anxiety of interpretation that takes the form of a transposition of the narrative fiction onto a highly conceptual and metaphysical plane of vision. Theoretical issues such as "narrative structure,"[69] "allegory" and "archetype,"[70] "myth" and "persona"[71] serve as the embodiment of a critical orientation preoccupied with the taming, rather than the interpretation, of the literary text in question. The illusion arises that by crystallizing a literary discourse into a single concentrated form, a critic can discover the correct vantage point—from the outside and above—and thus prevail over the discourse.

Indeed, the mixed narrative mode of myth and mimesis in the *Dream* poses just this problematic: in order to present a highly coherent critical discourse unriddled with conceptual gaps, critics are often reluctant to leave textual incongruities intact. Instead, they tend to focus on one explanatory model that commands a centripetal movement by stabilizing the multifarious signifying activities and arresting the often irreconcilable textual interplays in a static and homogeneous pattern.

Thus in discussing the stone—the emblem of Pao-yü's mythical substance—critics often choose to ignore the jade, the token of his mundane identity. In a similar manner, the analysis of allegory takes place at the expense of the examination of the human reality of the *Dream*. The discussion of the mythical narrative mode seems to call for a critical discourse that precludes the discussion of the mimetic, and vice versa. It seems that the major difficulty of incorporating the two potentially contradictory critical discourses lies in the formidable task of locating a point of convergence that can facilitate the smooth transition of one discourse into the other.

While I hold suspect the notion of a smooth transition and seamless integration whose semblance of totality is achieved at the expense of incompatible, but often viable, fragments, this hypothetical point of convergence is nonetheless present in the narrative fiction, serving to bridge, if only momentarily, not only the narrative of myth and that of realism, but also the discourse of jade and of stone. And most significantly, it is at this particular point of convergence that the merging of the moral and the metaphysical vision of the *Dream* is initiated and accomplished. This vantage point is none other than the issue of Pao-yü's identity: it is precisely the problematic of Pao-yü's identity that subverts the rigid boundary between the discourse of stone and of jade, and that between the moral and the metaphysical discourse of the *Dream*.

The quest for identity—*chi* 己 ("the self")—emerges as an anomalous phenomenon in the Chinese tradition. In both Confucianism and Buddhism, "the self" is conceived as identical to desire, inimical both to the socio-moral order and to the pursuit of spiritual enlightenment. While Confucius dictates in the *Lun Yü* the importance of *k'o-chi* 克己, "to hold one's self in check,"[72] the Buddha preaches the extinction of selfhood in order to attain Nirvana. Both the practice of self-cultivation and that of religious asceticism stress the eradication of self-identity as a prerequisite for salvation, be it moral or spiritual. Chinese culture abounds with rituals of self-repression and self-mortification. The distinction of the self from the other and its emergence as a unique entity belong to the philosophical tradition of Chuang Tzu 莊子, a tradition that made only sporadic appearances in cultural history waging war against the Confucian triple alliance of "totality," "collectivity," and "homogeneity." The collective body appears not only homogeneous and totalized but also stable and resistant to the infiltration of that which is different.

In the genre of narrative fiction, the quest for identity emerges as a theme in its own right during the late Ming Dynasty. What Wu-k'ung experiences in the *Hsi-yu Pu* is a symbolic process of self-discovery. Tung Yüeh is well aware that among the major characters in the original legend of Tripitaka's pilgrimage to India, Sun Wu-k'ung alone reveals a psychic makeup sufficiently complex for him to possess the kind of individuality able to revolutionize the stereotyped concept of hero. The inadequate psychological portrayal of Wu-k'ung in the parent novel *Journey to the West* (*Hsi-yu Chi*) gives Tung Yüeh the opportunity to explore the issue of concealed identity. To unveil the invisible and remove the disguise, the narrator of the *Hsi-yu Pu* sends the hero upon a journey into his own mind, a mind more riddled with unresolved anxieties than preoccupied with heroic schemes and adventurous fantasies. The self-discovery takes place, not in metaphysical contemplation during his wakeful hours, but in the unconscious realm of dream, where the restrained self loses its control. What emerges in Wu-k'ung's dream is the repressed self, the other self, which not only contradicts the semblance of the visible and self-possessed subject but also shatters it into incompatible fragments. This is a discovery whose significance could go beyond its fictional logic and enrich the undernourished Chinese ontological tradition, insofar as the existence of the repressed self challenges the Chinese notion of a coherently structured and well-unified self-identity. But Tung Yüeh the fiction-writer fails to transcend the boundary of his fictional imagery and to transform the allegory of the mind-monkey into a philosophical vision. He is not yet prepared to acknowledge the radical significance of the challenge he himself has posed to the conventional association of identity with unity. At the juncture when Wu-k'ung's quest for identity evolves toward the ominous emergence of a disruptive self who engages in the continual dispersal of a fixed center, the narrator cuts short the self-winding discourse of the dream with an explanatory note that dismisses the autonomy of Wu-k'ung's dream and his helpless entanglement in schizophrenia as a predetermined plot designed by a demon to beguile and ensnare the invincible hero. What could have triggered a revolution from the within is thus attributed to the manipulation of an exterior machinery. The adventure of *discovery* loses its momentum as it is turned into the routine of *recovery*. Wu-k'ung wakes up from the nightmare. And without further ado, he retrieves his original persona—a holistic and invulnerable entity. The quest for identity gives up its radical implications and turns out to be nothing more than a quest for unity again, reiterating the formula familiar to the old tradition.

The *Dream* takes up the issue of identity with the same innovative imagination that the *Hsi-yu Pu* promises. The hero's problematic journey on earth and his dubious encounter with his double point to the central position occupied by the motif of identity-quest in the structural and thematic development of the narrative fiction. However, the impression of unity, which the *Hsi-yu Pu* recuperates faithfully at the end, is subverted in the *Dream* in a less dramatic and yet more sustained fashion. The narrative fiction unfolds with the urgent issue of identity as the leftover stone block ponders the meaning of being left *alone*:

> She [the Goddess Nü-wa] used thirty-six thousand five hundred of these [stone] blocks in the course of her building operations, leaving a single odd block unused. . . . Observing that all the other blocks had been used for celestial repairs and that it was the only one to have been rejected as unworthy, it became filled with shame and resentment and passed its days in sorrow and lamentation. (*Stone* I: 47)

This single block turns out to be the mythical stone that enacts and tells its own story. It is interesting to note that from the very beginning such a stone appears as a surplus and a remainder of a totalized scheme. The stone interprets its primordial loneliness as the refusal of the goddess to recognize its worthiness. The notion that it is being excluded from the rest arouses such an agitation in it that one wonders whether its lamentations are simply induced by the sense of humiliation, as it openly professes. One might in fact argue that Stone's failure to merge into the interior signifies nothing other than the "rejection" of the application for membership in a totalized society. The stone's "sorrow" and "resentment" can therefore be understood in terms of its failure to cope with the meaning of differentiation. I would suggest that it is not the impaired self-image but the fear of being a heterogeneous, and thus an individual, entity, that provokes such an outburst of emotionalism from the Nü-kua Stone. The problematic of individual identity thus looms large early in the mythical prelude. In the sense that Stone is the author-narrator-protagonist of its own story, the *Dream* can be viewed as a fictionalized account of an autobiography that explores the meaning of self-identity.

Stone's discovery of its polymorphous identity unravels in a more problematic manner than Wu-k'ung's. While the latter's identity crisis ends in an instant recovery of a single, unified self, the concept of a totalized identity emerges consistently as a paradox throughout the *Dream*. Pao-yü is reincarnated from a mythical stone that undergoes a simultaneous transformation into a birth-jade that serves as his identity token. We are tempted to ask: is his original nature, to which the narrator is so anxious for him to return, identical to the essence of jade or to that of stone?

Because jade and stone are categories traditionally seen as divided from each other, as the true from the false, Pao-yü's double identity poses the problem of unity. By alternating between the symbolism of jade and that of stone in the characterization of Pao-yü, the narrator of the *Dream* builds his work on an internal disorder that could lead to a total dissolution of the hero. But the outrageous contradiction is turned into a rich paradox, as the narrator continues to question the conventional wisdom that clearly differentiates the true from the false, and the authentic from the artificial. This challenge to the pattern of conceptual oppositions gives rise to a metaphysical vision that is based on the idea of mutual arising which undoes the hierarchical pairing device. Not only is the priority of the first term over the second overruled, but the content of each term is also set free and held to be transferable. Thus in his insightful comments on the scenery in the Garden, Pao-yü perceives the potential reversal of such notions as "naturalness" and "artificiality." The painted halls and gaudy pavilions of the "Phoenix Dance" that seem so artificial may actually appear more natural than the simple rustic look of the "Fragrant-Rice Village," which, according to Pao-yü, can only achieve the impression of naturalness due to the working of human artifice.

The arbitrary division between "nature" and "artifice" insisted on by "the ancients," which provokes Pao-yü's skeptical remarks, also serves to distinguish the value of jade from that of stone in the system of thinking that has not recognized the validity of relativism. Both Han Fei and Liu Hsieh represent such an intellectual trend by subscribing to the hierarchical conceptualization: they ascribe a lesser value to the plain-looking stone by identifying it with the concept of the false. Jade, in contrast, enjoys a privileged position, for it is not only rare but also precious. To make the parallelism work, the positive value-content of jade is further reinforced through its bonding with the concept of the authentic. The stability of the hierarchical order within each binary pair—in this particular case, the priority of jade over stone, and that of the true over the false—is considered indispensable to the maintenance of order, be it moral, political, or literary. To most Confucian philosophers, the possibility of inversion would inevitably pose a dangerous threat to order, rationality, and the entire system of evaluation. Thus Liu Hsieh laments the confusion of aesthetic standards at his time and condemns the reversibility of the symmetrical matrix formed between these two binary pairs—truth/falsity and jade/stone.

As a relentless critic of Confucian ideology, the narrator of the *Dream* finds no better target than the conceptual pattern of rigid symmetry to subvert the structured epistemology that the Confucianists have developed. In chapter 5 he spells out his own metaphysical vision in a frequently quoted couplet that challenges the traditional, well-differentiated view of knowledge and existence:

> Truth becomes fiction when the fiction's true;
> Real becomes not-real when the unreal's real.
> (*Stone* I: 130)

Whether we name the topsy-turvy vision "complementary bipolarity," in Andrew Plaks's terms, or "supplemental differentiation," in deconstructionist terms,[73] or even "dialectical," in Marxist terminology, it suggests an indefinite discursive movement and opens up the enclosed space of every conceptual realm. The relations of difference and identity that characterize the ambiguity of bipolar pairs are seen to relate to each other *within* each other. When we turn to the jade/stone polarity and reexamine it in the light of this radical vision, we encounter a potential inversion of the old value system embedded in the compound. The way in which the narrator describes the diminished form of Pao-yü's mouth-jade will thus help us achieve a new understanding of the jade/stone relationship in the *Dream*. Seen through the narrator's eyes, this tiny piece of jade is but an "illusory image" of the Nü-kua Stone. Both *huan* 幻 ("illusion") and *hsiang* 相 ("image") connote the unreal and the elusive—the copy of something authentic. Contrary to what the traditional bipolar structure dictates, the jade in the *Dream* contains the potential of reversing its conventional image by interchanging its value-content with stone. It can appear as a semblance, a transcript of the original, both artificial and derivative in nature—in short, a mere illusion of the stone. The Nü-kua Stone also contains the potential of turning upside down the old value-categories arbitrarily assigned to it. As the original from which the mouth-jade is reproduced, the stone represents the natural and the authentic. It is the root of Pao-yü's identity and the source of his life-force— a kind of source that the Taiwanese critic Kang Lai-hsin describes as suggestive of the primeval purity that is both spontaneous and immanent.[74] The affiliation with jade, on the other hand, gives rise to a different mental picture. Of stone and jade, Kang Lai-hsin clearly favors the former, for she perceives the difference between the two as that between authenticity and artificiality, and between the intrinsic purity and extrinsic sophistication: ". . . stone and jade are in fact two sides of the same coin. Their boundary is marked by the presence or absence of the artistry of carving. Wood/stone and gold/jade are opposed to each other—the former represents an uncultivated naiveté, the latter the fortune and prosperity that a worldly cultivation promises."[75]

The connection of stone with the original and the authentic is perhaps a truism that coexists in folk wisdom with the opposite view that it is inferior in nature to jade. The old saying in the *Li Chi* that "jade must be cut and chiseled to make it a useful vessel" (*yü pu-chuo pu ch'eng-ch'i* 玉不琢不成器)[76] testifies to the equally popular association of jade with artifice. But while a Confucian gentleman appreciates jade as the emblem of cultivated perfection, the Taoist rustic turns to stone for its natural simplicity. The dialectical relations between jade and stone implied in the *Dream* reflect in part the interaction between the Confucian and Taoist perspectives. That which the Confucianist considers to be the privileged point of reference—jade— is subordinated to stone, the symbol of artless naiveté, in the Taoist referential framework. For someone as antagonistic to the Confucian advocacy of self-cultivation as the nonconformist disguised under various personae (the stone-narrator, Pao-yü, and the author-narrator), the effortless simplicity of stone must have appeared far more appealing than an object whose beauty is so often associated with refinement and artistry.

But the nature/culture bipolarity is too simplistic a conceptual scheme to account for the complexity of Pao-yü's shifting double identity that the paradox of stone and jade generates. For just as jade is associated with purity (*chieh*), authenticity (*chen*), and artifice all at once, so is stone a subject vacillating ceaselessly between the poles of nature and culture. Assimilating the imagery of *t'ung-ling shih*,[77] the stone in the *Dream* cannot simply be identified with uncultivated pure nature. The dogmatic Taoist worldview that ascribes superiority to nature renders itself equally susceptible to subversion by the metaphysical vision according to which the content, as well as the privileged position, of nature and culture are as reversible as those of any other binary pairs. Suffice it to say that as the metaphysical vision of the *Dream* emphasizes the continuous evolution of binary poles and recognizes neither perspective as the ultimate representation of truth, the narrator's suggestion that the mouth-jade is nothing more than a replica of the Nü-kua Stone should by no means indicate an endorsement of the Taoist view. The reversal of the privileged order of jade and stone should rather be interpreted as the narrator's implicit critique of the supreme authority of the Confucian standpoint.

The paradoxical vision that underlies the *Dream* reveals the radical perspective of a nonconformist who keeps on uncovering discrepancies in the conventional system of signification. It is important to recognize that he takes the existing conceptual framework as his point of departure, even when he turns its content inside out. It would be a mistake, therefore, to credit him with the discovery of the phenomenon of bipolar inversion within the jade/stone compound—for the possibility of subverting the stereotyped relations between these two objects is already suggested in the conceptual framework of Han Fei and Liu Hsieh. But while those traditional scholar-critics grumble about the unorthodox nature of such a possibility, the narrator of the *Dream* celebrates the phenomenon of inversion and considers the preservation of the prevailing order a sign of the tyranny of authority. The ceaseless shifting of the evaluative scale, which seems to Liu Hsieh an ominous sign that repudiates the value of roots and origin, appears to the nonconformist writer the only possibility for spiritual and intellectual freedom. This is a kind of freedom that always aims at transcending a completed, closed, and unified system. It consists in submitting the subject to the process of self-contradiction, rather than returning it to its root-origin.

Herein lies the supreme paradox of the *Dream of the Red Chamber*. On the one hand, our nonconformist author-narrator recognizes that any retrospective stance prompted by nostalgia for the origin signifies an obsession with fixed identity—for inasmuch as an identity is thus congealed, it remains undisturbed as a unity that may enter into conflict with others, but not with itself. Stasis is the worst malaise and the kind of danger from which the author-narrator intends to shield Pao-yü until the final climactic moments of the *Dream*—and yet those moments will deliver us nothing other than the conventional solution of identity crisis. It is at that particular juncture that we can locate the domestication of the notion of "contradictory identity." For all our narrator's earlier efforts at demystifying the concept of consistent identity, what we witness at the end is the bankruptcy of his radical vision and the resurgence of a single identity (i.e., stone) that is held to be whole and identified unambiguously as the "place of origin" (*Stone* VI: 373) for Pao-yü. For all his avowed iconoclasm, Ts'ao Hsüeh-ch'in proves as vulnerable as his fellow traveler Tung Yüeh to the Chinese return complex—a subject that will emerge again in the next chapter when we address Ts'ao Hsüeh-ch'in's conceptual revolution and its limits as revealed in the making and aborting of Pao-yü's identity quest.

Whatever our final verdict on the contradictory vision of the *Dream of the Red Chamber*, we cannot but recognize and applaud the epistemological breakthrough that the narrative fiction has achieved in delivering us, however fleetingly, an ambivalent portrait of Pao-yü. Residing in the hero is an inconsistent identity, torn not only between the essence of jade and of stone, but also between himself and his specular counterpart—Chia Pao-yü, the unreal Pao-yü. Here we are given the best footnote on the meaning of divided personality: it is a subject in process because it is a subject in crisis, and vice versa.

Chen-Chia Pao-yü 甄賈寶玉

The theme of the real (*chen*) versus the unreal (*chia*) Pao-yü forms part of Ts'ao Hsueh-ch'in's scheme of paradox aimed at laying bare and subverting our conceptual and perceptual limitations. It is a device of characterization adopted to supplement the potential dialectical relationship between bipolar pairs such as stone and jade, nature and culture, the authentic and the artificial. Like the critique of formal dichotomy, the symbolism of the double provides a subversive strategy for disclosing the problematic nature of the nuclear concepts that continue to feed the myth of bipolar classification. In our previous discussions of the paradox of *chen* and *chia*, of *yü* and *shih*, concepts such as "unity" and "identity" already loom large as integral parts of the metaphysical groundwork that presupposes a hierarchical structure within each binary opposite.

The reversibility of *chen* and *chia*, of *yü* and *shih*, challenges not only the validity of hierarchical order but also the notion of unity and identity. Each concept contains within itself a drive to contradict itself, which is a drive toward division-making. A unified entity becomes a myth, for it is forever split by a driven internal negativity that in turn triggers the identity crisis. A human subject undergoes the same permutation as the result of such psychic disorder. This process of permutation is reminiscent of the process of struggle revealed by Hegelian dialectics as essential to the concept of development. It is the "internal impulsions of development provoked by contradiction"[78] that motivate a subject's identity quest and move him or her through various stages of spiritual crisis. In the same vein, the symbolism of *Chen-Chia* Pao-yü serves as the metaphor of a divided identity that is engaged in continuous self-redefinition through self-negation.

The relativity of identity is an issue that has been explored in various discussions of the symbolic significance of Pao-yü's double identity as the Chen and the Chia Pao-yü. But it needs to be emphasized that it is not the complementary nature of doubleness, but rather the nature of internal negativity, in the hero's psychic makeup that serves to activate his spiritual quest. It is only when the double identities confront each other, and enter into an oppositional relationship that drives the one to negate the other, that the quest for identity can finally transform its momentum into action and practice. This explains the dramatic impact of the true-to-life meeting between Chen Pao-yü and Chia Pao-yü on Pao-yü's psyche. The mutual negation of the two reactivates and releases the power of internal negativity, which has always been inherent in Pao-yü, the conflicting essence torn between jade and stone. Chia Pao-yü's discovery that Chen Pao-yü is in essence the negation of himself, rather than his double, triggers the final stage of his identity crisis. Returning from his meeting with his "double," Pao-yü lapses into a spiritual limbo—"he did not speak, but smiled idiotically. . . . The next morning, he looked dull-witted as if he was sick again" (*HLM* III: 1576–77).

Wang Hsiao-lien and many other critics attribute Pao-yü's continuous spiritual transformation to the recurrent loss and recovery of his mouth-jade.[79] The hero's identity crisis is seen to be triggered by an external cause, rather than motivated by an internalized locus of change. Such a view suggests that the moment of Pao-yü's internal transformation has to coincide, and eventually to be identified, with the moment of external action that is imposed on the jade. As the external locus of change, jade is thus seen to bear the entire burden of Pao-yü's quest for identity. The concept of change revealed in this critical perspective reflects the idealist way of thinking that attributes the cause of change to a factor external to the subject itself. This external factor is often identified with a transcendental cause: jade, for example, is seen as an agent of divine machinery that operates on human reality as if it were the origin of such reality. In the light of such idealist thinking, the mysterious loss and sudden reappearance of the jade indicate a sign from

Above, which controls the system of signification by holding the ultimate authority over meaning-production and interpretation.

The *Dream*, however, is an ambitious work whose aim is to transcend the boundary of all the traditional ways of conceptualizing the nature of knowledge and the meaning of existence—and idealism is certainly among the mental handicaps to be overcome. The narrator is too mischievous a storyteller to be content with the mechanical device of using jade as the external indicator of change. To subvert the static view of change to which most of his predecessors subscribe, he attempts to depict Pao-yü's continuous psychic change through the paradox of bipolarity and the symbolism of mirror-image. By ascribing to Pao-yü a discontinuous identity made up of stone and jade at the same time, and by exploring the disunity of his identity as caught in the two Pao-yüs, the narrator introduces the dialectical process of change that the contradictory subject undergoes incessantly. By internalizing the locus of change, the narrator delivers us a subject who motivates his own transformation, thus saving him from being reduced to a mere object at the mercy of divine maneuvers.

The idea that the true hero is a subject in process is indeed a novel one in the history of traditional Chinese fiction. This attempt to continuously negate the previously established privileged point marks Ts'ao Hsüeh-ch'in's most significant contribution to the aesthetics of characterization in Chinese narrative fiction. It is probably due to his influence that there gradually developed in the late Ch'ing an aesthetics of personality appraisal that challenges the traditional dichotomy between good and evil. In his analysis of the character portrayal in the *Ju-lin Wai-shih*, an anonymous Ch'ing critic recognizes the concept of paradox as the underlying principle in the psychological makeup of individual personalities: "Chih Heng-shan's 遲衡山 pedantry and Tu Shao-ch'ing's 杜少卿 eccentricity serve as good examples that jade is not unblemished. A beautiful piece of jade is precious because it does not have a single blemish, but a piece of jade is authentic exactly because of its natural blemish."[80]

The simplistic scale of character evaluation that makes a clear-cut distinction between the perfectly good and the completely evil is in fact indebted to the Chinese historiographical tradition that serves the cause of righteous historians who turn their studios into courts of justice. In historical writings of lesser caliber, historical figures are divided into two categories—the virtuous and the vile. The purpose of history writing is to distinguish heroes from traitors by emphasizing the irreproachable conduct of the former and exposing the unredeemed debauchery of the latter. Such a historical approach to characterization has produced a symmetrical model that clearly differentiates the good from the evil, the flawless from the blemished—an aesthetic view that our anonymous Ch'ing critic clearly disputes. The paradoxical perspective he provides in evaluating the disposition of fictional characters echoes the metaphysical vision of the *Dream* that puts into question the notion of unified identity. The narrator's explicit critique of the traditional classification between the good and the evil appears as early as in chapter 2, where Chia Yü-ts'un 賈雨村 (Jia Yu-cun), serving as his mouthpiece, delivers a long-winded treatise on his own philosophy of character appraisal. In addition to the two already existing categories, a third is introduced to represent that which comes into being as the result of the clash between good and evil humors. Those who belong to this category are "incapable of becoming either greatly good or greatly bad" but are "superior to all the rest in sharpness and intelligence and inferior to all the rest in perversity, wrongheadedness, and eccentricity" (*Stone* I: 78). It is in this category that one finds the concept of paradox in whose terms the Ch'ing critic characterizes the kind of jade that is both authentic and flawed. The metaphor of the flawed jade has evolved into a new aesthetic principle that modern critics recognize as one of the most significant traits of the Chinese aesthetics of characterization.[81] It is important to note that such a metaphor makes itself intelligible through its potential capacity to reactivate the intertextual reference to the jade/stone imagery embodied in the *Dream of the Red Chamber*. The paradox of the blemished authenticity in jade has formed such an integral part of the problematics of Pao-yü's anomalous identity that it is impossible to mention the paradox without also calling into our mind the image of Pao-yü, and with it, the entire paradoxical spectrum of the *Dream*.

This brings us back to the question raised in Chapter 1 about the relations between a preexisting system of signification such as the jade lore and the jade imagery that later evolves in literature. I have posited a two-way interaction: although the jade lore serves as a structural constraint for the jade imagery, it also undergoes its own transformation by assimilating new heterogeneous phenomena that subvert its previously established totality. As the prior text-ensemble, it should by no means be identified with the ultimate text that homogenizes later texts without encountering any resistance. The interaction between metalanguage and individual speech acts is characterized by mutual accommodation, rather than by total enclosure on the one hand, and infinite dissemination on the other. When we turn to the interplay of the jade imagery in the *Dream* with the intertextual network of jade symbolism, we witness the same kind of simultaneous redistribution of meaning taking place in both textual spaces. Thus while the politico-ethical symbolism of the ritual jade releases its symbolic content of *chieh* ("purity") and, in so doing, regulates the moral vision of the *Dream*, the fiction-making of the paradox of *chen yü* ("the authentic jade") and *chia yü* ("the artificial jade") in the story has generated such a powerful momentum that it inevitably forces its way into the jade lore and readjusts its old content. Ever since the *Dream* has been accessible to the general reading public, the paradoxical nature of the literary jade imagery has transformed the formerly stable identity of the ritualistic jade into an ambiguous one. It is no longer possible to talk about jade without feeling ambivalence toward the nature of its composition, or to decide whether jade symbolizes nature or artifice and whether a flawed jade is more precious or authentic than a flawless one.

Returning to our discussion of the issue of double identity in the *Dream*, we find that the complexity of Pao-yü's psychic makeup is twofold: not only is he identical to the mouth-jade and to the Nü-kua Stone simultaneously, but, being part of jade, he is also subject to the paradox of *chen/chia* and *chieh/chuo* inherent in the jade imagery. The moral composition of such a character therefore also evolves from the principle of paradox on which is based the narrator's metaphysical vision—a vision that, by challenging the validity of any distinctive value differentiation, endorses the notion of the merging of boundaries. Herein lies the ingenious working of a writer of high literary caliber who feels compelled to articulate a moral vision that enables him to differentiate Pao-yü and Tai-yü from Pao-ch'ai and her like, yet who at the same time is capable of resolving the potential conflict between his *evaluative* moral vision and his *value-free* metaphysical vision through the symbolic characterization of double identity in Pao-yü's psyche. It is in the ambiguity of double identity that the moral vision of the *Dream* intersects the metaphysical one.

The story of the jade is indeed double-edged. It traverses the moral and metaphysical discourse of the *Dream* without shedding its original liaison with stone. The jade/stone connection in Pao-yü's psyche is as realistic and logical as it is fictional. Any other combination would have weakened the dramatic tension of Pao-yü's psychic quest and undermined the symbolism of identity crisis. Much of the fictional logic of the *Dream* rests on the simultaneously differential and analogous relationship between jade and stone. We have seen above the qualities that differentiate jade from stone as a unique mineral possessed of certain specific aesthetic content and ritualistic significance. But coming from the stone family, jade also inherits all the common properties assigned to stone: for instance, like stone, jade appears in ancient myths as the popular source of mana food, elixir, and medicine; and like stone, its sonorous quality attracts much attention. Probably the most significant point of convergence between the two consists in the potential liminal ambiguity that each is capable of generating. It is not a completely idiosyncratic idea, then, to start a story with the myth of stone and continue it with the symbolism of jade.

The jade/stone interplay brings to the fore the deep structural contradiction inherent in Pao-yü's personality. I argue that the interest of his characterization lies less in the symbolism of Chen-Chia Pao-yü, a device external to the development of his subjectivity, than in the portrayal of a subject that contains a reversible internal double—namely, jade-as-stone. Indeed, once our hero assumes the form of a handsome young man and attains the momentum of dynamic personality development that resists the instant return to his mythical origin (i.e., stone), we witness the ceaseless process of disintegration and reconstruction evoked by the tensions that the unstable stone-jade affiliation is capable of arousing. It seems difficult to define Pao-yü's subjectivity, because the subject-positions[1] of jade and stone interchange with each other unpredictably as Pao-yü exhibits or inhibits each in turn unconsciously.

At its most radical moments, the shifting structure of the interior landscape of Pao-yü's mind seems potent enough to take on a life of its own, almost capable of forgoing its ties with the original and ultimate subject-position of Pao-yü that is unambiguously spelled out by the author-narrator as that of stone. For no matter how anarchistic its vision, the *Dream of the Red Chamber* begins and ends with a transcendental metaphysics that determines that meaning is derived from the implicit assumption of a fixed origin. There is no denying that however incoherent and decentered Pao-yü's identity may appear throughout his sojourn on earth, he is always already subject-ed to the structure from which he is born. Stone as Pao-yü's pre-given identity is seen as the center that originates, organizes, and eventually constrains the endless process of structural realignment triggered by the stone-jade dialogue. Thus the *Dream* concludes with the return of jade to the foot of Greensickness Peak where its form and essence is finally restored to stone:

> An otherworldly tome recounts an otherworldly tale,
> As Man and Stone become *a single whole* once more.
> (*Stone* V: 373; italics mine)

> *Liang-fan jen tso i-fan jen* 兩番人作一番人.
> (*HLM* III: 1646)

While it may be argued that the main thrust of this couplet consists in the logic of bipolar complementarity—that is, that the real and the unreal, Stone's experience in heaven and Pao-yü's on earth, are one and the same—it is nonetheless revealing that while the narration of the *Dream* unfolds necessarily as a statement of plurality (*liang-fan*, literally "two times/lives"—i.e., the experience of Stone and the experience of Precious Jade as a man), the narrative as a final product reaffirms and retrieves the logic of unity and homogeneity (*i-fan*, here translated as "a single whole"). The *Dream of the Red Chamber* thus teaches us a paradoxical lesson that the process of unfolding is a continuous statement of difference, change, and contradiction that cannot but be closed and completed at the end.

Nowhere is this "finished" and "totalized" quality of Stone's identity more powerfully highlighted than in the soliloquy of Vanitas the Taoist, who re-encounters Stone in the last chapter:

> "When I first saw this strange tale of Brother Stone's I thought it worth publishing as a novel and copied it down for that purpose. But at that time it was unfinished; the cycle within it was incomplete. There was in the earlier version none of this material relating the Stone's *return to the source....*" (*Stone* V: 374; italics mine)

What was unfinished is now finished. Disruption is sealed up in a harmonious closure. We are informed that Stone is now "safely placed"[2] at the foot of the Peak, its life-force completely spent. In contrast to the Stone that indulges itself so energetically in earnest argument with Vanitas in chapter 1, the Stone that now greets our eyes seems divested of all its subjectivity, incapable of conversing further with Vanitas because it has already turned into a static object. Paradoxically, what becomes suppressed at the end is what the author-narrator of the *Dream* has taken such pains to emphasize earlier—namely, the notion of subjectivity, and with it, that of heterogeneity, which refutes stillness and finds the idea of (en)closure repulsive. Pao-yü's psychic journey has been propelled by qualitative breaks resulting from quantitative accumulation. But ironically, such qualitative breaks occur only to find themselves already canceled by the retrogressive motivation of the initial quality, an invariable, which mocks any possibilities of significant, deep, structural change.

Seen in this light, the *Dream* reflects two conflicting visions that fail to reconcile with each other—the structuralist, and the deconstructionist. One cannot but wonder if it is possible to answer unequivocally the questions whether Pao-yü's subjectivity is incessantly deconstructed or already pre-existent, and whether identity and structure are emphasized at the expense of process and struggle. It would be futile to seek a resolution to all the paradoxes that revolve around the issue of identity/contradiction that the *Dream* unwittingly raises. To avoid such an interpretive impasse, I would rephrase the central problematic that a critic will inevitably deal with in recognizing such an unsettled, paradoxical vision. Instead of asking the above questions, I suggest we map out the *Dream* as a narrative that can generate texts that *dramatize* its own limits. In other words, as a practice of signification, the *Dream*, however consciously it may present itself as an anomaly, is without exception built upon the limits that tradition—whether cultural, literary, or metaphysical—imposes upon itself. What distinguishes the *Dream* from other works of lesser stature is that the former defamiliarizes the elements in those traditions that subvert its radical founding presupposition, while the latter take their presence for granted as the familiar and the natural. Thus the truism of "returning to the source" takes on the guise of fictional logic in the *Dream*, demanding elucidation by those who espouse it.

It is interesting to note that the theories of identity/source, in a counter-thrust to the philosophical vision of contradiction/heterogeneity consciously spelled out by the author-narrator, are delivered by precisely those characters whose eccentric appearance and radical mentality belie the conventional wisdom they articulate at critical moments to remind us of the limits of iconoclasm. It is Vanitas who proclaims that the Stone whose identity is thus recovered "had no cause for remorse or regret" (*Stone* V: 374). It is the Buddhist monk who predicts as early as in chapter 1 of the sixteen-chapter *Chih-pen* that after Pao-yü's ordeal comes to an end, he will be "reverted to the original essence."[3] And it is with no less poignancy that Chen Shih-yin

甄士隱 (Zhen Shih-yin) concludes, not without a sense of relief, that the "substance" of Stone has "returned to the Great Unity" (*Stone* V: 371). To reinforce the truth of origin and single identity, he caps his revealing comments with the rhetorical question: "If the Fairy Flower regained its true primordial state, then surely the Magic Stone should do likewise?" (*Stone* V: 371). The nostalgia for origin, homogeneity, and totality—the cultural and religious myth rarely questioned by the Chinese, and a familiar text that needs no justification—is here turned inside out and defamiliarized into the semblance of the fictional logic of the fantastic.

When we take a close look at the symbolic stature that Vanitas, the Buddhist monk, and Chen Shih-yin embody in the *Dream*, it seems only appropriate that they should serve as ideal mouthpieces of the truth of homogeneity and the priority of origin. For as figures that transcend the temporal and spatial scheme of the human world, they themselves are homogeneous and totalized—the very "source" and terminus of being and knowledge. Each symbolizes an essence that preexists, undergoes no evolution, and requires no justification. It is no miracle that Vanitas consummates his "personality" development in the space of two couplets. His circular pilgrimage through the metaphysical categories of *se* 色 , *k'ung* 空 , and *ch'ing* 情 [4] remains an allegory meant to be grasped by a mind that does not differentiate—a mind that resolves and dissolves contradictions into a nebulous continuum, which can only be reached by a sudden hermeneutic leap that cancels the concepts of time, space, process, and struggle. Even Chen Shih-yin, who starts as a vulnerable human being, is subject to the same process of ossification. Perhaps we can assume that, given the symbolic significance of his name, Chen Shih-yin is never meant to be taken as a real character but as a mere personification of "truth concealed."

By bestowing a supernatural aura on these characters and assigning them mythological status, the *Dream* succeeds in accentuating the "dramatic" messages they deliver—words that convey nothing other than the traditional metaphysical vision of the privileged status of source and unity. In so doing, the author-narrator mystifies tradition and turns that which is originally familiar, the ideological constraints, into fiction. Herein lies the novelty and ambiguity of the *Dream*. It seems that the narrative itself is not unaware of the limits imposed by tradition and sees that the only way out of this dilemma is to turn the burden into an asset. If the tradition cannot be tamed, perhaps it can be transformed. And it is in the act of metamorphosis that the *Dream* appropriates its own limits and makes them serve its drama.

The Story of the Stone is thus a narrative capable of dramatizing its own limits at certain moments. It is certainly bound irrevocably by the constraint that turns the moment of Pao-yü's imminent emancipation into one of repression through the dramatic renewal of the metaphysics of identity. It is no small irony that the *Dream* eventually renders itself susceptible to the concepts and values from which it claims to free itself. What is no less true, however, is our irresistible fascination with the defamiliarization process that turns the problematized cultural constraint into a make-believe that can neither claim nor prove its own veracity.

In pursuing the issue of constraint, we now approach the core device of enclosure in the *Dream of the Red Chamber*. Inasmuch as the narrative fiction closes as it begins, namely, with the inaugural myth of stone, then the original and ultimate identity of Pao-yü—the essence of stone—emerges as the focal point of our discussion of the structural limits inherent in the *Dream*. And nowhere does the *Dream* hold our attention better than in its attempt to dramatize the stone imagery and bring into relief its potential for continuous evolution. In stretching stone's inherent symbolic attributes to their utmost limit, the *Dream* demonstrates, if only fleetingly, that apparant constraints can be transformed into the fictive that knows no boundary of its own laws.

San-sheng Shih 三生石 : The Stone of Rebirth

The dramatized form of stone in the *Dream* unfolds in two major metaphors: *san-sheng shih*, the "stone of rebirth" (literally, the "stone of three lifetimes"), and *t'ung-ling shih*, the "stone of divine intelligence." The first metaphor, which appears once fortuitously in chapter 1, can by no means be dismissed as unmotivated, for despite its seemingly obscure presence in the text, it nonetheless serves as the implicit context—a conceptual framework, so to speak—within which the second metaphor unfolds.

It is worth noting, moreover, that the two metaphors intersect at the axis of stone-consciousness, for both deal with the concept of the different degrees of spirituality of stone. While *t'ung-ling shih* automatically contains within itself a second metaphor—that of *wan shih* (the "unknowing stone")—the interior landscape of *san-sheng shih* encompasses three different spatial/temporal schemes—namely, this life (*chin-sheng* 今生), the previous life (*ch'ien-sheng* 前生), and the next life (*lai-sheng* 來生). In the analysis that follows, the examination of these two mataphors will bring us to a close encounter with the tension between intertextuality and dramatization, and more specifically, between the overdetermined and the contingent, and between the act of coming to terms with constraints and that of creating the illusion of fiction.

The metaphor of *san-sheng shih*, a fictionalized account of the Buddhist mythology of reincarnation, crystallizes the concept of stone-memory that seems to have grown from the primordial mythical/folkloric belief in the spiritual potency of stone. Everywhere in the ancient stone lore we find the symbolism of stone cast in the configuration of energy—from the fertility myths that celebrate its reproductive capacity to the folk legends about stone mirrors, the nodding stone, and its talking counterpart. These motifs revolve around the ancient belief that stone is the "quintessence of earth" and the "kernel of *ch'i* 氣之核,"[5] capable of engendering an intelligence grown out of highly concentrated mental/spiritual energy.

The reference to *ch'i*, "breath," and *ching* 精, a word that suggests both "spirit" and "quintessence," often conjures up an image of stone cherished and perpetuated by the elite tradition of Chinese art and literature, an image that is less associated with "energy-matter" than with the "energy-principle." There is an entire genre of rock paintings that highlights the ethereal spirit of stone with which the lone artist or writer seeks communion.[6] Cheng Pan-ch'iao 鄭板橋 had a passion for drawing deformed stones; both he and Ts'ao Hsüeh-ch'in were petrophiles who saw in grotesquely formed rocks and stones their own self-image.[7] Among the many legends celebrating rocks is a well-known anecdote about the spiritual bond between the eccentric Sung artist Mi Fu 米芾 (1051–1107) and his *shih-hsiung* 石兄, "Elder Brother Stone."[8]

The term *shih-hsiung* had probably become so popularized by Ts'ao Hsüeh-ch'in's time, among the elite circle at least, that Vanitas's greeting the Nü-kua Stone with the same appellation[9] seemed less an event than a renewal of part of the stone-cult treasured and perpetuated by Mi Fu's fellow stone-connoisseurs. Rocks that keep such spiritual communion with men of letters inevitably acquire a persona, which, combined with the long-standing folk tradition of an embryonic stone-intelligence derived from legends such as the stone mirror, the growing stone, and the talking stone, develops side by side with the highly spiritual personality of the Bodhidharma rock, the nodding stone, and other religious legends and paintings that associate the concept of enlightenment and Nirvana with stone caves and the rocky seats on which arhats and ascetics sit in meditation.[10] The literary persona of stone that slowly evolves through the centuries certainly incorporates the aesthetic, popular, and religious symbolism of its spirituality. It is not far-fetched to suggest that the Nü-kua Stone in the *Dream of the Red Chamber*, which functions as a sentient being endowed with a highly potent cognitive faculty, represents the epitome of this triplex spirituality.

It is often in light of our recognition that stone is an animate entity of consciousness that the mundane perception of unenlightened characters in the *Dream* appears ironical. Such a particularly poignant moment of irony takes place in chapter 113 when Tzu-chüan 紫鵑 (Cuckoo) undergoes an emotional reconciliation with Pao-yü through her reassessment of his true affection for Tai-yü:

> What a dreadful pity it is that our Miss Lin never had the fortune to be his bride! Such unions are clearly determined by fate. Until fate reveals itself, men continue to indulge in blind passion and fond imaginings; then, when the die is cast and the truth known, the fools may remain impervious, but the ones who care deeply, the men of true sentiment, can only weep bitterly at the futility of their romantic attachments, . . . She is dead and knows nothing; but he still lives, and there is no end to his suffering and torment. *Better by far the destiny of plant or stone, bereft of knowledge and consciousness*, but blessed at least with purity and peace of mind! (*Stone* V: 255; italics mine)

"Bereft of knowledge and consciousness" indeed! The ironic thrust of Tzu-chüan's perception does not rely solely on our recognition of the discrepancy between the mundane and the mythical understanding of the destiny of stone: on a more subtle level, it also depends upon the gap of knowledge that exists between those readers who are and those who are not informed of the intertextual reference to the mytho-folkloric stone that embodies just the opposite of what Tzu-chüan takes for granted—that is, the stone as a fully conscious entity in possession of spiritual knowledge.

Before we explore the symbolic configuration of *san-sheng shih* and *t'ung-ling shih*, in which the concept of consciousness and knowledge looms large, it may be worth taking a quick look at another revealing moment in the *Dream* that introduces a persona of stone to which Tzu-chüan is a total stranger. In chapter 18 of the seventy-eight-chapter *Chih-pen*, amidst all the din and bustle aroused by the Imperial Concubine's visit to the Garden of *Ta-kuan* 大觀園 , the Nü-kua Stone emerges all of a sudden, addressing us in a digression, and unwittingly reminds us of its role as the fictional narrator of its own story:

> At this moment I recollected the scenes that I once saw while lying underneath Greensickness Peak of the Great Fable Mountains—what a forlorn and lonely view! Were it not for the scabby monk and the crippled Taoist who brought me here to the Red Dust, how could I then witness such a magnificent spectacle![11]

Stone's soliloquy indubitably posits a central intelligence that narrates what it recollects. We are given a self-conscious stone-narrator who, because of its ability to remember, situates its subject-position consciously between the past and the present. Such a subject is narratable exactly because it has a history that keeps making sense of the present in reference to the past. In fact, Stone's autobiographical project relies on nothing other than its "historical" consciousness of its own past.

The issue of the positionality of the Nü-kua Stone, which in spatial terms can be seen as caught between stone and jade, in its *temporal* manifestation brings us to the metaphor of *san-sheng shih*—which, I argue, holds the key to our understanding of the most intriguing signifying possibilities of stone in the *Dream of the Red Chamber*. *San-sheng*, a Buddhist term based on the concept of reincarnation, prescribes a symbolic order of cyclical rebirth. The allusion of *san-sheng shih* is found in Yüan Chiao's account of the eternal friendship between Li Yüan 李源 and Yüan Kuan 圓觀 the monk.[12] According-ing to the legend, Yüan Kuan told his friend before his death that they were destined to meet again on the night of the Mid-Autumn festival twelve years later. When the prescribed time came, Li Yüan had a chance encounter with a shepherd boy who was singing a song about the mystery of karma which began with the seven-character line *san-sheng shih shang chiu ching-hun* 三生石上舊精魂 , "The old souls on the *san-sheng shih*." Coming forward to greet his friend in the spiritual persona of Yüan Kuan, the shepherd revealed his identity as none other than his old Buddhist friend reincarnated. *San-sheng shih* is thus charged with the symbolism of reincarnation, and turned into a sign that seems to imply the continuum of the old and the new, of death and life, and of the past and the present.

A close reading of the text, however, would suggest otherwise: Yüan Chiao's tale of rebirth fails to materialize the radical implications of temporality underlying the concept of *san-sheng*, inasmuch as he subjugates the instantaneous (the present) to the master plan of the past. The mapping of temporality in the tale appears to follow the principle of ceaseless transition; yet in essence, it never departs from the fixed framework of the past.

What is most interesting about this *ch'uan-ch'i* text is its simplistic interpretation—better described as a "fictional recontextualization"—of the thorny
Buddhist concept of *nien* 念 (*Smrti*, "memory").

The doctrine of rebirth, as many scholars have noted, remains controversial, for the concept of *anattā* (i.e., no permanent entity or self runs
through different lifetimes) contradicts the equally potent Buddhist belief in
"the continuity of an evolving consciousness."[13] To understand such a belief, we need to look into the theoretical implications of the concept of *nien*
and the *Alayavijnana* (the eighth consciousness, also known as the "storehouse consciousness"). Hsüan Tsang's *Ch'eng Wei-shih Lun* (*Doctrine of
Mere-Consciousness*)[14] provides the following definition of these terms:

> What is memory?
>
> It is the dharma which makes the mind remember clearly and not
> forget a thing, an event, or a situation that has been experienced. Its
> special activity consists in serving as the supporting basis for meditation
> (*samadhi*), because it incessantly recalls and retains the thing experi-
> enced in such a way that there is no failure of recollection, and thereby,
> it induces *samadhi*. There cannot be any memory of what has never been
> experienced; nor can there be any memory of the thing experienced if
> there is no clear recollection of it.[15]
>
> Considered as cause, the eighth consciousness is called *sarvabijaka* or
> the "seed consciousness," which means that it is endowed or furnished
> with all the Bijas ("seeds" or "germs"). It is capable of holding firmly
> and retaining the Bijas of all dharmas, without allowing them to be lost.
> Apart from this consciousness, no other dharma is capable of retaining
> the Bijas of all things.[16]

Underlying the above explanation is the concept of a fundamental *Alaya*
consciousness in which "memory" and the "seeds of dharma" are located—
a consciousness that evolves in a series, which, however continuous it may
appear, should by no means be envisaged as a homogeneous one.

I believe it is in the false impression of "homogeneity" evoked by Yüan
Kuan's rebirth that one can locate the traces of a fictionalized Buddhist concept of *san-sheng* in the *ch'uan-ch'i* tale. For contrary to the general Buddhist
idea of the perpetuation of character without identity of substance (as the
various incarnations of the Buddha in the *Jātaka* tales reveal), the shepherd
in Yüan Chiao's tale clearly identifies himself with his previous incarnation,

and in so doing, undermines the ambiguity that empowers the paradox of rebirth and memory. The explanatory passages in the *Ch'eng Wei-shih Lun* are occasionally very vague in exploring the strategic position of "memory" in our wakeful consciousness. The above definition of *nien* clearly suggests its intimate relationship with the practice of *samadhi* and thus promotes the belief that the recollection of one's past lives involves an arduous process of meditation, and that only the enlightened mind is capable of releasing the full power of its memory from the storehouse consciousness. Indeed, *nien*, karmic memory, should not be seen as a natural gift with which an ordinary being is endowed, but rather as the result of the spiritual cultivation of those who have gained enlightenment. As for the commoners, according to Dharmapala in the *Ch'eng Wei-shih Lun*, the first five consciousnesses "*can be* accompanied" by memory, which appears as "a *faint* recollection"; yet according to Sthirmati, the five consciousnesses are *never* accompanied by memory—"it [the memory] is lacking because they always take a new object without recollecting past objects." [17] These explications are immediately followed by the assertion in the *Wei-shih Lun* that only when one attains Buddhahood do the five consciousnesses contain and release the full potency of "memory." [18] All these illustrations serve to bear out our common understanding of "karmic memory traces," to which a layperson can be susceptible at certain illuminating but fleeting moments. They are stored in the unconscious and experienced by the unenlightened as "inexplicable, tantalizing memories, the uneasy aftermath of a dream that has been forgotten by the conscious mind but that continues to haunt the deeper mind." [19]

Seen in this light, the shepherd's effortless remembrance of the past in the T'ang tale not only falsely suggests the unlikely—that Yüan Kuan has achieved Buddhahood (a theme that the tale fails to deliver on all counts)— it also amounts to the immediate closing up of the ambivalent passage during which former consciousness is transformed into consciousness of the present existence. It is to be understood that the latter consciousness does not derive its present existence from the previous one, but from the *causes* contained in the previous existence. Thus the gatha, "Nor sameness, nor diversity / Can from that series take their rise." [20] Bearing this in mind, we would view the shepherd's unambiguous activation of his karmic memory in a problematic light: it foregrounds the identity question (i.e., the shepherd and the monk are one and *the same*), spoils the elusive imagery of the state of "continuum" of the series, and neutralizes the theoretical challenge of the Buddhist myth of the "passage" as the limbo. At the moment when the shepherd comes forward to address his old friend in the language and waking consciousness of the monk, the present is made identical to the past. The meaning of the present is to be sought in that of the past. And the progression into the future is held at bay. Yüan Chiao's citation of the term *san-sheng* thus pares down the temporal scheme of "three lifetimes" to that of two, and predates the *Dream* in its deradicalization of a concept originally meant to subvert the convention of temporality.

In chapter 1 of the *Dream*, we are informed that the aimless wandering of the Nü-kua Stone, now in the guise of the Divine Luminescent Stone-in-Waiting, brings it to the banks of the Magic River. There, we are told, "by the Rock of Rebirth [*san-sheng shih*], he found the beautiful Crimson Pearl Flower" (*Stone* I: 53). The mention of this particular rock in the *Dream* evokes rather effortlessly the intertext of Yüan Kuan's *san-sheng shih*. It is the symbolic order of reincarnation inherent in the latter that makes the citation of *san-sheng shih* immediately meaningful in the narrative fiction. We can instantly assume that this is a story about karmic ties (although to readers familiar to the Buddhist concept of "consciousness," the intertextual vision should probably involve the recognition of a more theoretical construct implicit in the *san-sheng shih*, i.e., "karmic memory") and predict, as the dying Yüan Kuan did, the reunification of the couple—in this case, the stone and the flower—in their next life. Such intertextual mechanism seems to require little explanation since the cardinal intertext not only is easily identifiable but, more importantly, appears to have undergone little content-transformation in the *Dream*.

My interest in the metaphor, however, lies elsewhere—not because the intertextuality at work above is self-evident, but on the contrary, because there seems to exist a process of intertextualization in which both versions of the *san-sheng shih* carry on a subtle dialogue with certain obscure intertexts that allow the combination of the lexeme of *shih*, "stone," and that of *san-sheng*, "three lifetimes," to hold together as a meaningful semantic unit. I am therefore less captivated by the religious symbolism that the surface-intertext of the Yüan Kuan legend triggers than by the interaction of the *san-sheng shih* with those texts in the stone lore that do not cast instantaneous imprints on the metaphor. Before we undertake the study of the intertextual permutations of the folkloric stone in the literary symbolism of *san-sheng shih*, it is important to analyze the temporal structure of such a symbolism, which, as we will see later, serves as the focal point at which the two terms, *san-sheng* and *shih*, meet to produce the metaphor of *san-sheng shih*.

The internal logic of the metaphor of the "stone of three lifetimes" posits an immense temporal and spatial content that extends the "here and now" backward and forward at the same time. It seems that the viability of the metaphor depends on the diachronic sense of progress, of the continuous evolution of one fixed moment into the next. Life is not rooted in one locale, but moves forward in a continuum. It attains a certain fluid quality that not only subverts its fixed boundary from death, but also vitiates the connotation of termination that the latter concept usually carries. In place of the one-dimensional scheme of birth and death, the "stone of three lifetimes" introduces the cycle of birth/death/rebirth. And it seems to imply that the cycle perpetuates itself. Thus, theoretically, one can assume that Yüan Kuan the monk will continuously evolve into someone else—a shepherd during this lifetime, perhaps a fisherman in the next. Transmigration is not the repetition of identity, but the transference of the karmic seeds (Bijas) that associate all three personae with each other; it guarantees that no single persona can be restored to the original because, according to the logic of *samsara*, there exist no pure originals. Yüan Kuan's tale, however, does not materialize such radical possibilities. The issue of original identity looms large instead of being overtaken, as one might expect, by the concept of the continuous evolution of a kindred carefree spirit that breaks down the fixed boundary between the identity of Yüan Kuan and that of his subsequent personae.

It is not surprising that quoting intertextually from this *ch'uan-ch'i* text, the metaphor of *san-sheng shih* in the *Dream* emerges as the same fictional construct that aborts the radical implications of the symbolism of *san-sheng*. On the one hand, it bears the vestiges of the diachronic temporal order implicit in the original Buddhist concept of *san-sheng* where, to be sure, the past leaves its indelible traces on the present, but it moves on and transforms itself not only into a different, but also into an *irreversible* form. Theoretically, Yüan Kuan should no longer be Yüan Kuan the monk. He should have evolved into a different identity—a carefree shepherd who only *unconsciously* retains the memory of his previous life and identity, as his ambiguous song seems to suggest. The past evolves into the present, and the present, into the future. Like history itself, which knows no border, the Buddhist theoretical construct of *san-sheng* suggests an endless evolution into infinity. However, the *san-sheng shih* on the banks of the Magic River introduces no such subversive perspective. Like its earlier *ch'uan-ch'i* intertext, it reveals itself as a self-bounded and self-inclusive image, paradoxically accumulating its inner immensity within its own boundary. Such a boundary is established by consecrating the past—a moment flattened out and sealed off—instead of the present, the contingent, and the experiential, as the privileged center that defines meaning. Thus while the Buddhist concept of *san-sheng* brings into relief the elusive and intangible connection that the present maintains with the past, the story that unfolds by the Rock of Rebirth sanctifies the vital claims of the past upon the present. In fact, the act of sanctification in the *Dream* goes a step further than what takes place in Yüan Kuan's story, in which the meaning of the present is repressed, but not completely subsumed in the past. It is the shepherd (i.e., the present identity), we need to recall, rather than the monk (i.e., the past identity), who is assigned a place in the chain of signification—Yüan Kuan's prediction ultimately means nothing without the reference of the shepherd's song: the meaning of the past depends as much upon the referential framework of the song sung in the present as the latter depends upon the former. In contrast, the *san-sheng shih* metaphor in the *Dream* proposes a different strategy of meaning-production. It holds under suspicion a present that does not return to the past in search for the rationale of its own existence. Thus no matter how far Pao-yü's life can evolve beyond the fixed temporal and spatial scheme, he will remain a meaningless, empty subject until the past has been not only clearly remembered and understood, but also restored in the literal sense. Pao-yü's ordeal consists in his recovery of the lost memory of his previous/past experiences—his dreamy venture into the Land of Illusions, and eventually, his loiterings by the Rock of Rebirth. Metaphorically, *The Story of the Stone* embodies the gradual process of Pao-yü's filling of an emptied vessel with the memory of a meaningful past. Deeply embedded in the metaphor of *san-sheng shih*, his personality structure and spiritual quest are not only already determined by, but also completely identified with, what has gone before—his personal past underneath Greensickness Peak.

More than any other device in the *Dream*, the "Stone of Rebirth" evokes a historical-philosophical perspective that leads the present back to the founding and inaugurating moment of being. The progressive movement promised by the metaphor is constantly arrested by a backsliding motion. A self-conscious historical formation notwithstanding, *san-sheng shih* paradoxically incapacitates its own innovative view of history—a view embedded in the religious concept of *san-sheng*—by defining and establishing history in the old triple sense of bestowing, grounding, and beginning. Within the fictional metaphor there exists a zero point, a simple beginning that contradicts the concept of history as flux—a concept that inspired the Buddhist philosophers to concoct the terminology of *san-sheng* in the first place.

As a symbolic device in the narrative fiction, *san-sheng shih* serves as a constant reminder of the importance of the previous given, and of the necessity of citing its content. The temporal and spatial scheme of the present always contains another space elsewhere. Pao-yü's life on earth is always shrouded in a cloud of disconcerting obscurity because its referents lie *elsewhere*, and they remain so as long as he fails to look elsewhere. This other locale, whether in the guise of Stone's mythical abode or of the Land of Illusions, lies beyond the conscious. Much of the dramatic interest of the *Dream* consists in the search for the other locale and, more precisely, for the entrance into the unconscious.

It is interesting to note that such entrance is almost always accompanied by a traumatic experience, often associated with the mysterious loss of Pao-yü's jade pendant, a symbol of his lucid wakeful intelligence. The disappearance of his birth-jade, however, is only an external machinery, which alone cannot conjure up the entire spectacle of the suppressed/repressed past/unconscious. It is through the voluntary act of remembering, in my opinion, that Pao-yü finally gains access to the privileged spot that connects the other locale of the past with the "here and now" and makes the latter meaningful.

Perhaps because the act of remembering has such potential to bring the narrative back to where it starts, and thus to complete the act of narration prematurely, the *Dream* does not abound in moments of remembrance until the end of the narrative. One such memorable moment, however, takes place early in the narrative to indicate that Pao-yü is endowed with the gift of retaining memories, albeit fragmentary ones, of his mythical past, even without the help of a catalyst. In chapter 3, when he first meets Tai-yü, both are haunted by the feeling of déjà-vu: Tai-yü looks at Pao-yü with astonishment because he is "so extraordinarily familiar," and Pao-yü, in turn, proclaims that "her face seems so familiar that I have the impression of meeting her again after a long separation" (*Stone* I: 101). The powerful understatement of this "strange familiarity" will emerge again toward the end of Pao-yü's spiritual journey to signal the full and unconditioned return of the past and its usurpation of the meaning of the present.

The mystery of "strange familiarity," a self-contradictory semantic construct, is finally unraveled in chapter 116 and dissolved, so to speak, when Pao-yü consciously reenters the past. For as soon as the unconscious, the

dreamy reality of the Land of Illusions, is decoded in the language and perception of the human conscious, riddles are solved, symbols exhaust their
otherworldly magic, and that which is strange in the "strangely familiar"
loses its raison d'être automatically. It seems only logical that as this chapter unfolds, Pao-yü gradually emerges from his emotional ambiguity rooted
in the sense of the ineffable, aroused by encountering persons and scenes
that he knew before but had forgotten. The process of resolving the "strange
familiar" picks up momentum, however, as he makes every conscious effort
to refamiliarize step by step what strikes him as strange. In this revisit to the
Land of Illusions, we find a self-conscious Pao-yü who now determines that
"it is time I began to learn more about the operation of fate" (*Stone* V: 285).
Each of the incidents following this decision brings him closer and closer to
the complete retrieval of a long-lost memory. At the sight of the large cup-
boards in which is deposited the "Main Register of the Twelve Beauties," he
comes to a sudden realization: "I *know* I've been somewhere like this before.
I remember it now. I was in a dream. What a blessing this is, to return to the
scene of my childhood dream!" (*Stone* V: 286). And as he holds the Register
in his hand, another remark about the urgency of remembering issues forth:
"I *do* remember seeing this . . . I think I do. . . . If only I could remember
more clearly!" (*Stone* V: 287).

From this point on, the existence of the present and the significance of this
life mean little to Pao-yü, as he concentrates his mental activity on the act
of remembering. After awakening from the dream in the Land of Illusions,
he now defines and understands the present only in terms of the past. And
he does so by abandoning himself to the act of "remembering meticulously,"
hsi-hsi-te chi-i 細細的記憶 (*HLM* III: 1588), his venture in the other world.
It is no accident that the recovery of the full potency of his memory coincides
with Pao-yü's recollection of Hsi-ch'un's would-be destiny as dictated by the
Register:

> Alas, that daughter of so great a house
> By Buddha's altar lamp should sleep alone.

> He could not refrain from uttering a few sighs. Then he remembered
> the bunch of flowers and the mat, and glanced at Aroma. Tears started
> to his eyes. When the family saw him behaving in this strange fashion,
> laughing one minute and crying the next, they could only think it a
> symptom of his old fit. None of them knew that their conversation had

sparked off a flash of illumination in Bao-yu's mind, with the result that *he could now remember word for word every poem from the registers in his dream*. (*Stone* V: 296; italics mine)

The anticipation of the future—Hsi-ch'un's conversion into a nun, and Hsi-jen's betrayal of her love for Pao-yü—can be realized only through the remembering of a past that has been suppressed. There is no authentic present, for it is already contained and appropriated into a past that is held to be the source of all that follows it. We should remind ourselves, however, of the religious significance of the full awakening of Pao-yü's recollective capacity—that is, that the complete recovery of his karmic memory coincides with the moment of enlightenment. The recontextualization in the *Dream* of the religious order implicit in *san-sheng* and *nien* nevertheless opens up other possibilities of interpretation that may contradict the original Buddhist connotations of these two concepts: to exercise one's memory is tantamount to consolidating the power of the past over the present, which no longer serves as a transition to the future, but in which times stands still. Ironically, as soon as Stone becomes conscious of its own past, the temporal evolution of *san-sheng shih* is completed. It turns back upon itself by regressing to where it was. Thus the ending of the *Dream* coincides with the triple *recovery* of Pao-yü's birth-jade, his memory, and his original identity.

The *Dream* eventually reorganizes the temporal-spatial paradigm of the religious intertext of *san-sheng*. By suppressing the progressive concept of time, it foregrounds a profoundly spatial view of existence. As the myth of *san-sheng shih* comes to a full cycle toward the end of the *Dream*, Pao-yü *sees* his own existence from the beginning: he sees his three lifetimes—the past, the present, and the future—all at once. In so doing, he transforms himself via the metaphor into an *objec*tive, a disinterested, and certainly a dehumanized spectator of the ultimately predictable vista in which temporality, with both its dangers and its possibilities, has been canceled.[21]

The metaphor of *san-sheng shih* in the *Dream* shows that the flight from time—and more specifically, from a privileged beginning, like that proposed by the author-narrator at the start of the narrative—is highly inconceivable. It is a metaphor that, by reinforcing the sense of closure and enclosure, and by privileging spatial form over temporality, delivers a tamed and popularized version of a potentially radical Buddhist cosmology.

The seemingly innocuous reference to *san-sheng shih* at the beginning of the *Dream* serves as a subtle, indeed almost imperceptible context for a narrative that spans two lifetimes, and that promises, but in the end aborts, the implicit third temporal space—namely, the future. Because most of the preceding discussion dwells on the unconsummated temporal order delivered by the concept of *san-sheng*, it remains to be seen how such a profoundly religious concept can be combined with the lexeme of stone to make sense.

As a conceptual-rhetorical apparatus, *san-sheng shih* is composed of two terms, one of which is overtly symbolic; the other, albeit content-free at first glimpse, is actually a content-repressed term. That is to say, although the second term, "stone," is as powerful and potent a signifier as the first term, its mere citation may not immediately conjure up the entire spectrum of a symbolic content that complements, if it does not exactly correspond to, the symbolic configuration of the first term. The fact that "stone" now appears as an empty vehicle carrying the weight of what *san-sheng* signifies is indeed an indication that the body of intertextual citations known as the stone lore has fallen into oblivion. However, that the semantic unit of *san-sheng shih* has been taken for granted, attracting little attention from literary critics—both traditional commentators and modern interpreters alike—gives rise to the no less significant observation that there is something immediately familiar and natural about such a combination, in contrast to which other similar combinations, such as "the wood/or metal/or jade/or pearl of three lifetimes," would appear downright absurd and completely unacceptable. Paradoxically, the lack of critical attention to the term *san-sheng shih* serves as a powerful statement that Chinese readers throughout the centuries have always unwittingly recognized and comprehended the symbolic code that stone releases in the metaphor of *san-sheng shih*.

What signifying possibilities, we may then ask, does stone find itself attached to, to make it affiliation with the religious term *san-sheng* a fictional yet an intelligent construct? Let us look at an important moment in the *Dream*, which will shed light on the nature of the particular signifying chain in the stone lore that bears on this inquiry. In chapter 98, a delirious Pao-yü comes to the realization that in a state of mental stupor he has married Pao-ch'ai instead of Tai-yü. After regaining his consciousness, he demands to be informed of Tai-yü's whereabouts. It is at this juncture that Pao-ch'ai, hoping to bring about the recovery of his sanity through shock therapy, abruptly discloses to him the news of Tai-yü's death. Unable to contain the horror and the excruciating pain this news brings, the mentally debilitated Pao-yü loses consciousness again and slips into a coma, which leads his soul to wander into the realm of the Dead in search of Tai-yü's soul. Once there, he encounters a messenger in the Netherworld who ridicules his search as a "case of futile self-delusion," for Tai-yü is no mortal being whose soul can be found in the Underworld. After advising Pao-yü to cultivate his spirit and mind so that he may one day meet Tai-yü in the celestial realm again, the messenger "took a stone from within his sleeve and threw it at Bao-yu's chest" (*Stone* IV: 373). At this instant, Pao-yü is immediately brought back and awakened to human reality.

It is intriguing that Pao-yü's transition back to the Red Dust is brought about by certain inexplicable magic of a stone. Within the grand mythical scheme of the fabulous Nü-kua Stone, this little pebble may appear no more than a contingent fictional device to bring Pao-yü from one locale to another in a quick and uninvolved manner; however, that this stone enables our hero to travel through time and space is in itself an account that cannot be attributed to the arbitrary design of the author-narrator of the *Dream*. To simply dismiss the account as such is not only to repress the chain of signification that the ritualistic-folkloric stone is capable of evoking, but to disregard the subtle affiliations that this particular account sustains with many other accounts of stone, which can only make sense insofar as they participate in a network of "reciprocal intelligibility." The context of the messenger's stone pebble in chapter 98 thus consists of other myths—that of *san-sheng shih*, as well as many other intertextual variations in stone lore.

To find the signifying links between those various intertexts is quite a task. We should perhaps satisfy ourselves with those versions that bear immediate relevance to our discussion of the *Dream of the Red Chamber*. We will start with the version of the stone in chapter 98, for this seems to consist of a single unit of meaning—namely, stone's function as a catalyst. As an agent that effects change, the stone in this incident evokes many folk legends and rituals in which it serves either as the medium for change (the symbolic beating of stones and stone bulls in rain-coercing rituals), or as the end product of such a change (T'u-shan Shih and the stone woman). Within the imagery of catalysis, stone is assigned a place between two locales and ambiguously situated at the intersection of the mutable (the rainmaking stones) and the eternal (the fossil-like stone woman). It is indeed a paradox that stone incorporates within its signifying space two opposing signs: it is an emblem of immutability (the inscribed stone tablet as well as the stone woman resists the corrosion of time and history, and guarantees the inert continuum of the verbal messages it bears), and at the same time a potential signal of transition and change. Just as the whipping of a rainmaking stone awakens its potential to activate change, so does the throwing of the stone by the underworld messenger trigger Pao-yü's entrance into another locale. It is no accident that stone chambers or stone caves serve as the favorite locale for the initiation of neophytes.[22] Both in primordial cultures and in fictional accounts, stone preserves the mythical aura of a catalyst and enacts the magic of transition.

Of course, we cannot address the concept of transition without mentioning the association of stone caves with the symbolism of the tomb. In fact, many argue that our ancestors' reverence of stones as deified objects illustrates the survival of a stone-worship that can be traced back to the Paleolithic period, when the stone cave served not only as human habitation, but also as burial ground for the deceased. The Upper Cave Man of China practiced a burial ritual that took place inside his own cave.[23] The stone cave is assigned a strange place as the point of convergence of the living and the dead. And it is in the symbolism of transition that we can find the plane of contact between *shih* 石 and *san-sheng* 三生 , the two seemingly unconnected semantic components of the "stone of three lifetimes."

The stone that sends Pao-yü back from Hell to his bedroom in chapter 98 should in this sense be taken as an intertext to the metaphor of *san-sheng shih*, for both accounts provide a fictional version of temporal relocation and reorientation, although in the case of the metaphor such relocation always signifies the return to the point of departure. In each account, the intertextual network, localized in this book as the stone lore, looms large because it has already been in place, even if we are not necessarily conscious of its particular anchored position in each given text. Such intertextual reference is useful in that it maps out semantic permutations of two different kinds. On the one hand, we can perceive the dialogue between the metaphor of *san-sheng shih* and the folkloric stone as the *sign of change*. This is not to suggest, however, that the latter's reverse image—the *immobile sign* of the inscribed stone and the petrified stone woman—does not partake of the meaning-production of the "stone of three lifetimes." It is particularly important to recognize this second kind of semantic reverberation, for it delivers the intertextuality of stone lore and a given literary text from confinement in the mechanistic model of one-dimensional correspondence.

That the conflicting symbolism of transition and immutability, embodied respectively in the rainmaking stones and the inscribed stone tablet, should simultaneously crisscross the fictional space of *san-sheng shih* serves to demonstrate that meaning is produced through the interplay between contradictory as well as homologous semantic levels. A fixed and static sign in contrast to the revolving imagery of *san-sheng shih*, the inscribed stone nonetheless reveals its intertextual connection with the "stone of three lifetimes" in that it too retains vestiges of the past. It is on the ground of the stone tablet's deeply ingrained historical obligations of remembering, and particularly of inscribing the past, that it serves as a potent sign of historical consciousness, and in this sense alone can it be seen as the mirror-image of the "stone of three lifetimes." For just as the metaphor of *san-sheng shih* perpetuates the memories of the past, so is the inscribed stone a concrete testimony to the palpable presence of the past that is already written. And yet this is not simply a past whose meaning is exhausted because it is sealed off as passé. On the contrary, it is an *enigmatized* past that demands to be deciphered and, in a paradoxical way, re-created. It is in this particular shade of meaning of the mythology of the past in *san-sheng shih* that we can perceive the subtle folkloric presence of the inscribed stone in the metaphor. To put it more specifically, it is only in light of the oracular nature of the inscribed stone that the privileging of the temporal scheme of the past in the *san-sheng shih* metaphor makes sense. For only when the past is seen as an oracular riddle does it have to be remembered, decoded, and then brought to account for the present.

At this point, we have one more variant of the stone imagery to consider in the *Dream of the Red Chamber*. This is none other than the Stone Record itself, which confronts Vanitas with its demand to be faithfully copied. Inasmuch as the Stone Record is an inscribed stone and at the same time a story about a mythical stone whose existence spans two temporal and spatial locales, we may argue that it serves as the point of contact between the inscribed folkloric stone and the metaphor of *san-sheng shih*. The fact that the story of the stone is already written as the Stone Record, forestalls the fulfillment of the temporal cycle of "three lifetimes": for the subject, Stone itself, is alrady inscribed in a frozen historical record. And precisely because the record can only be copied, not altered, it is held to be the origin of all that follows. From this perspective, the future, the third temporal space of the "stone of three lifetimes," is a return to the past, to what Stone inscribes on itself at the very beginning.

The theme of the inscribed stone is significant enough to deserve a full-length treatment. Its device as narrative closure in both the *Dream* and the *Water Margin* is a topic to which we shall return in Chapter 6. It is important at this point to bear in mind that Ts'ao Hsüeh-ch'in's Stone Record contains within itself a chain of signification that traverses the intertextual space of the "stone of three lifetimes" and that of the folkloric stone, which bears enigmatic inscriptions.

T'ung-ling Shih 通靈石 and Wan Shih 頑石 : The Stone of Divine Intelligence and the Unknowing Stone

The metaphor of *san-sheng shih* enables the *Dream* to portray Pao-yü's break with the past as a paradoxical renewal. Although the "stone of three lifetimes" eventually undermines its own logic of the temporal chain of movement, what makes such a metaphor a potent one nevertheless is both the notion of the possibility of evolution, however inadequately consummated in the *Dream*, and the re-creation of folkloric intertexts in which stone carries and contains certain forms of knowledge and consciousness. It is on such signifying ground that the metaphor of *san-sheng shih* comes to reveal itself as the absent context for the symbolism of *wan shih* and *t'ung-ling shih*—for the latter seems to enact a drama that brings into full view the silent and opaque play of the signifying possibilities inherent in *san-sheng shih*, in terms of both its evolutionary drive and its cognitive potentials.

The symbolism of *wan shih* and *t'ung-ling shih* is another metaphorical device in the *Dream* that has drawn little critical attention in the past. To the general reading public, it undoubtedly appears as the fantastic, which only makes sense if read within the fictional framework of the *Dream of the Red Chamber*. The Ch'ing commentators, however, were not unaware of the intertextual reference that the metaphor of *wan shih* makes to the popular religious legend of *tien-t'ou shih*, the "nodding stone." It is perhaps because the elite literary circle of Ts'ao Hsüeh-ch'in's time was so well informed of the stone lore that any mention of its intertextual presence in the metaphor of *wan shih* seems superfluous.

> "Pao-yü is none other than the *wan shih*, 'the unknowing stone.' The Buddhist and the Taoist made three attempts to awaken him. Surely it is not too late for [the stone] to nod its head [*tien-t'ou*]?"[24]

In this commentary on the *Dream*, Erh-chih Tao-jen unambiguously names the folkloric intertext of *tien-t'ou shih*. By associating Ts'ao Hsüeh-ch'in's account of *wan shih* with the symbolism of "head-nodding," he brings home the source-text of the "nodding stone," and along with it, the notion of the folkloric stone's potential for enlightenment. Implied in this insightful commentary is the paradoxical identification between, or more specifically the reversibility of, *wan shih* and *tien-t'ou shih*—the "unknowing" and the "enlightened" stone.

The "nodding stone" remains nevertheless an *absent* intertext in *The Story of the Stone*. Or perhaps we can argue that the metaphor of *wan shih* in the *Dream* takes on a different guise, which subsumes the earlier intertext of *tien-t'ou shih* and, more importantly, lays bare the latter's symbolic content by renaming itself *t'ung-ling*, "reaching the spirit of the Divine." The symbolic mechanism of the *wan shih/t'ung-ling shih* metaphor is of such vital importance to our understanding of the religious and metaphysical vision of the *Dream* that I will not proceed to an analysis of how such significance is made possible without first carefully examining the semantic categories of the ambiguous term *t'ung-ling*. For unless we can truly grasp the meaning of such a term, not only will we fail to appreciate the fictional logic implicit in the replacement of *tien-t'ou shih* by *t'ung-ling shih*, but the symbolic presence of the latter in the *Dream* will also make little sense.

The term *t'ung-ling* is found in the biography of Ku K'ai-chih 顧愷之, an eccentric artist-intellectual in the Chin (A.D. 165–420) court. Believing the tale of a friend who had stolen one of his paintings for a joke, K'ai-chih declared that his painted scroll was endowed with such wondrous spirituality that it was able to "reach the spirit of the divine. It thus transformed its physical substance and departed Earth" (*miao-hua t'ung-ling, pien-hua erh-ch'ü* 妙畫通靈 , 變化而去).[25] The concept of *t'ung-ling* in this text not only predicates the existence of two separate realms—the human and the divine—and the possibility of communion between the two, it also implies that such a communion can take place only through the transformation of the earthly substance of the subject in question into a celestial essence. When it is employed as a modifier qualifying another lexeme, such as stone, which already contains within itself (as our analysis of the folkloric stone has shown) the isotopy of "mediation between Heaven and Earth," the term *t'ung-ling* comes to reinforce the concept of spiritual communion. It also displaces the function of mediation onto that of transformation, and in so doing, it brings the symbolism of *t'ien-t'ou shih* into full articulation. For what makes the latter text, indeed the term *t'ien-t'ou* itself, a meaningful reference in religious and nonreligious contexts alike is the stone's signal of its own self-conscious transformation.[26]

In the context of the *Dream*, we may ask a series of questions regarding the metaphor of this transformative stone. First, from what is the *t'ung-ling* stone transformed? And how can we characterize the nature of this transformation in semantic terms? In other words, is it defined in terms of a simple semantic reversal, or in terms that eclipse any dichotomous conceptual pattern? We can perhaps go back to the intertext of the "nodding stone" in search of clues, if not answers, to these questions. The expression *wan-shih tien-t'ou*, now a familiar idiom widely used in various contexts, reveals in four characters not only stone's persona before its transformation (namely, *wan shih*), but also the fact that the relationship between this particular persona and *tien-t'ou shih* (that into which the former is being transformed) is a contradictory one—and by extension, it seems to suggest that the latter is the reversed image of the former. I would not, however, foreclose this argument, since such a hasty conclusion fails to do justice to the various signifying possibilities that the single word *wan* may suggest. The nature of the semantic transformation between *wan shih* and *t'ung-ling shih* remains an issue that cannot be fruitfully dealt with until we take a close look at the literal and symbolic meaning of these images. Having examined the semantic configuration of *t'ung-ling shih*, let us now turn to its twin imagery *wan shih*.

The allusion to *wan shih* occurs in chapter 8 in which Pao-ch'ai first examines Pao-yü's precious jade and finds its inscription a curious match to the verses on her golden locket. As she starts reading the inscriptions, the authorial voice suddenly intrudes and informs us that this precious jade is actually the "incarnation of the piece of the unknowing stone that lay underneath Greensickness Peak of the Great Fable Mountain."[27] At this juncture, a poem is cited to depict the true nature of this stone and its mythical origin. It is known to be a translucent stone, but one that, "when fate frowns, lacklustre seems" (*Stone* I: 189). The symbolism of opacity recurs in chapter 115 in the episode of Pao-yü's encounter with his double Chen Pao-yü, to whom our hero addresses himself as a piece of crude and murky stone (*HLM* III: 1573). Pao-yü's self-portrayal thus best captures one symbolic mask of *wan shih*—that its dullness, its lack of shine, connotes dull-wittedness.

A quick glimpse at the passages in the *Dream* that describe Pao-yü's temperament would seem to confirm our observation that the image of *wan shih* is not a flattering one. Indeed, Pao-yü is often associated with epithets such as "silly," "foolish," "idiotic," and "coarse," adjectives that accompany the symbol of the fool. To push the symbolism a step further, the stone in question is sometimes referred to by an even more debased epithet: *ch'un-wu* 蠢物, a "stupid thing."[28] The semantic polyvalence of the word *wan*, however, defies any attempt to pare it down to such a stable lexeme, for it also incorporates, as Lucien Miller suggests in *Masks of Fiction*, the connotation of "playfulness" (*wan* 玩).[29] By recognizing that Pao-yü's idiocy serves as the "key to his glory, as well as to his shame,"[30] and that the fool is a "symbol of imagination, intuition, and sensitivity,"[31] Miller provides us the best account of the ambiguity underlying the epithet. Thus although it is important to study the meaning of *wan* in the context of the other two recurrent words in the narrative—namely, *yü* 愚 , "foolishness," and *cho* 濁 , "opacity"—the symbolism of *wan shih* cannot be fully released until we also take into account the marginal position it occupies between "foolishness" and "intractable playfulness."

This said, we can now examine the dynamic relationship between *wan shih* and *t'ung-ling shih*. It is important, first of all, to bear in mind that the primary relationship between these two stone images is that of transformation, and that "transformation" does not necessarily signify a complete and final reversal of the prior category. The discussion above can perhaps serve to demonstrate how the semantic ambiguity of *wan shih* prevents us from predicting whether the transformation from the one to the other can indeed be complete and irreversible. It may be useful at this point to examine one more commentary, this one by Hung Ch'iu-fan, whose speculations reveal a certain subtlety that goes beyond the crude logic of *wan shih* versus *t'ung-ling shih*: "[Pao-yü was] originally a *wan shih*. After going through the process of smelting and refining, [he was] transformed into *t'ung-ling* [*shih*]; and after [another] magical metamorphosis, [he was] changed into the Divine Luminescent Stone-in-Waiting. One can thus detect that [it/he] is not senseless/ignorant."[32] The ambiguity of this commentary consists in the paradox revealed in the last sentence, which could be recuperated as *wan shih pu wan* 頑石不頑 , "the unknowing stone is not ignorant." This implies that the original category that undergoes transformation already contains within itself its mirror-image. Such a paradox immediately casts into doubt the theory of complete semantic reversal. The transformation of *wan shih*, moreover, is by no means completed with the imagery of *t'ung-ling shih*. Hung Ch'iu-fan's speculations above posit the possibility of more than one transformation of the original category—from *wan shih* into *t'ung-ling shih*, and from *t'ung-ling shih* into the Divine Luminescent Stone-in-Waiting. The symmetrical opposition between the two stone images does not hold, as a result, for the route of metamorphosis is circuitous rather than following the predictable bipolar pattern. The nature of the transformation in question thus not only transcends the dichotomous configuration that would characterize *t'ung-ling shih* as the complete reversal of *wan shih*, it also repudiates

any suggestion that the former could establish itself as the final version—
a frozen end product—which, by successfully reversing the content of the
original category, could arrest the continuous flux of transformation.

Indeed, a cruder interpretation would posit *wan shih* in direct contrast
to *t'ung-ling shih* and postulate that the former embodies what the latter is
not—that is, an entity in serious want of "knowledge" and "consciousness."
Such a scheme of bipolar opposition cannot but prove to be deceiving. We
need only recall an ambiguous comment made by the Buddhist monk during his first encounter with the Nü-kua Stone to understand the dialectical
relationship of *ling* 靈 and *ch'un* 蠢 ("stupidity"): "Your [Stone's] nature
is endowed with a certain spirituality [*ling*], yet you are so stupid [*ch'un*]
in your substance." [33] On the one hand, the peculiar "spiritual opacity" of
wan shih appears to be diametrically opposed to the "divine intelligence"
embedded in the *t'ung-ling* stone; yet, just as the fool can be seen as the
mirror-image of Pao-yü's inner self, who is caught between momentary dull-
wittedness and intuitive insight, so does *wan shih* also integrate two conflicting shades of meaning: "crude stupidity," and "mischievous playfulness."
This marginal quality of *wan*—neither here nor there—is difficult to capture
in translation. The term "unknowing stone" coined for interpretive convenience certainly falls far short of conveying the connotation of the trickster
that is built into the transformative impulse of the metaphor of *wan shih*.

When it comes to the definition of *t'ung-ling* we encounter an equally difficult situation, for the entire range of signification that these two words evoke
cannot possibly be bundled into a few words. Chou Ju-ch'ang's interpretation of the phrase *ling-hsing i-t'ung* 靈性已通 (*HLM* I: 2), for instance,
enumerates a set of four different attributes, each of which points to one
shade of meaning inherent in the lexeme *t'ung-ling*: "feelings/perceptions,"
"consciousness," "the ability to think," and "emotions." [34] The problem is
further complicated if we also want to integrate the shadow-image *wan shih*
into the lexical content of *t'ung ling*. In view of its transformative relations
with the term *wan shih*, it seems only logical that the translation of *t'ung-ling*
should incorporate connotations that would bear out these relations. The
simple term "enlightened stone" falls short of encompassing the references
of the "spiritual," the "divine," the "self-conscious," and the "transformative," all of which revolve around the fundamental concept that a seemingly
inanimate object, which bears a certain spiritual aura (Ku K'ai-chih's painting comes to mind), is now turned into a subject endowed with the power
to communicate with spirits, and in consequence, with the gift to know the

divine scheme. The "stone of divine intelligence" thus emerges as a possible translation for *t'ung-ling*.[35] Such a translation is made meaningful by the fact that it contains within itself an implicit reference to the semantic content of *wan shih*, the other metaphor it is supposed to be related to.

The reference in question here is made to the symbolism of the fool embedded in the *wan shih*, and more specifically, to the quality of "ignorance" that the latter is known to be possessed of. However, as mentioned above, we cannot separate the symbol of the fool from that of the trickster without disabling the signifying potency of the concept of *wan*. We shall now return to the semantic puzzle that *wan shih* poses and ask what it means that an entity is betwixt and between two opposing poles of signification. In a microscopic sense, I argue that the kind of semantic paradox that characterizes the signifying field of *wan shih* can be brought to bear on the transformative logic of *wan shih/t'ung-ling shih*. We now approach the heart of stone symbolism, both folkloric and fictional: the metaphor of liminality.

The Liminal Stone

Those who are familiar with the fertility cults of stone can hardly fail to perceive the shadow of the reproductive stone in the outburst of the stone egg and in the birth of the stone monkey in the *Journey to the West*. One can indeed try to map out the intertextuality of the Yü Stone, the T'u-shan Stone, and the birth-giving stones in the imagery of the stone monkey who promises endless motion and embodies the concept of change itself. Yet if Sun Wu-k'ung betrays a rather explicit folkloric identity of stone, the Nü-kua Stone under Greensickness Peak in the *Dream* seems to share few characteristics of the fertile stone. Except for the episode in the Sunset Glow Palace, the salient features of the fertile stone do not seem to have cast an indelible mark on the persona of the Stone Outcast, which, departing from the cardinal intertext of the Nü-kua myth, seems to have wandered further and further away from the heavenbound image of the fertilizing five-colored stones.

The shedding of the folkloric identity of stone in the *Dream* is an ambiguous act. On the one hand, one can argue that it never completely casts off the shadow of the primordial mythical stone: the implicit intertextuality of the life-giving stone continues to reverberate in the theme of desire that underlies the mytho-logic of the narrative, and the image of the fallen stone as the root of passion echoes the sexual understatement of Kao Mei and other ancient fertility cults of stone. On the other hand, however, the appeal of stone in the *Dream* consists less in its association with the intertextual reference to reproductive symbolism than in the transformative metaphor of *wan shih* and *t'ung-ling shih*.

The imagery of the self-conscious *t'ung-ling* stone has indeed evolved a long way from the unconscious reproductive cell. As the story of the *Dream* unfolds, we find the Nü-kua Stone transformed from the mytho-folkloric stone associated with the symbolism of healing and cosmic energy into a new fictional persona that takes upon itself two shifting, if not conflicting, guises, as the designations *wan* and *t'ung-ling* seem to indicate. The issue revolving around the stone is no longer that of its fertile potency, but rather the paradoxical nature of knowledge and the ambiguous act of knowing—paradoxical, because "ignorance" and "intelligence" emerge as two cognitive metaphors describing the transitional status that Pao-yü assumes between the moments of dull-wittedness and those of enlightenment throughout the *Dream*. To a lesser degree, Wu-k'ung's pilgrimage in the *Journey* reveals the same struggle in the matters of knowledge and enlightenment. In each case, the reproductive potency of the folkloric stone is quickly overshadowed by its intense exploration of its own cognitive potency.

The *Dream* and the *Journey* have long served as the two most celebrated showcases of a narrative mode that breaks down all the boundaries between the human and the animal, between the immortals' and monsters' domains, between mythical and mimetic discourse, and finally, between Confucianism, Buddhism, and Taoism. In addition to all these marginal modes of representation, I would include a final set of marginality—the stony mode of thinking—embodied in the ambivalent psychic makeup of Pao-yü and Wu-k'ung. Half heavenly creatures and half earthbound, half beastly or inanimate and half human, these two heroes manifest shifting phases of marginal existence. Caught in the precarious equilibrium between the conscious and the unconscious, Pao-yü and Wu-k'ung continue to talk in a double-voiced ambiguity that is built on the paradox of knowing and unknowing. Underlying the mytho-logic of the *Dream* and the *Journey* is the paradox that the most crude and ignorant is at the same time the most intelligent. As the story of Pao-yü unravels its own mystery, we come to recognize that the beginning conceals the end—the seeds of *t'ung-ling* are already contained within the crude imagery of the inept Nü-kua Stone. The inquiry into the cognitive potency of stone thus leads us to the particular mode of thinking—I would define it as the liminal mode—that the symbolism of stone is capable of evoking.

In cultural anthropology, the marginal status of neophytes is known as the "liminal phase" and is regarded as the most significant stage of rites of passage. The word *limen* is derived from the Latin; literally meaning "threshold," it marks the transitional period of the ritual subject who has just passed an earlier, fixed point in the social structure but who has not yet entered the new. Such a ritual subject resides in a symbolic ambience that surrounds both the womb and the tomb.[36] The double entendre of the liminal persona presents an ambiguity that eludes classification: "Liminal entities are neither here nor there; they are betwixt and between the positions assigned and arrayed by law, custom, convention, and ceremonial. As such, their ambiguous and indeterminate attributes are expressed by a rich variety of symbols in the many societies that ritualize social and cultural transitions. Thus, liminality is frequently likened to death, to being in the womb, to invisibility, to darkness, to bisexuality, to the wilderness, and to an eclipse of the sun or moon."[37] The attributes of liminality that characterize puberty rites and other initiation rituals seem to reinforce Lévi-Strauss's theory that the savage mind is capable of evoking mental properties (i.e., binary oppositions) that are familiar to us moderns. A study of primitive tribal ceremonies reveals that their dominant structural features can be arrayed in terms of crisscrossing dyads.[38]

The same binary composition and liminal ambivalence can be found in various ritual symbols. Both Mircea Eliade and Erich Neumann attribute the coexistence of unresolved binary opposites in archaic symbols to the manifestation of the undifferentiated unity of the primordial unconscious.[39] The snake represents both the male phallic and the female uroboric symbol; the cave is both the earth-womb and the underworld tomb; the djed pillar symbolizes not only the Great Mother but also the sun-begetting principle of Osiris.[40] The five elements and vegetation symbolism also partake of the androgynous character of primordial wholeness.

The mytho-folkloric stone is one such liminal entity that oscillates between two groups of conflicting attributes. In our discussion of the stone lore, we have noted the occasional emergence of semantic deviation that results from the coexistence of binary opposites in a given lexeme. The five-colored stone is impregnated with both solid and liquid substance; the rainmaking stones often exist in pairs, the *Yin* and *Yang* Stones, whose functions in the rain-coercing rituals are opposed to each other—the one inducing, and the other subduing, the heavenly waters; the T'u-shan Stone and the modern folk legend of the stone woman bring forth the semantic interaction between fertility and sterility; and the nodding stone assumes a liminal existence between ignorance (*wan*) and illumination (*wu* 悟), between silence and speech (nodding as a form of "body language").

Each variant of the symbolic polyvalence of the mytho-folkloric stone derives from the interaction between the static and the dynamic, and between heaven and earth. The folkloric stone thus takes on a potential liminal character and assumes a set of transitional qualities "betwixt and between" the fixed poles of meaning. The contradictory qualities of stone can be expressed in the following sets of binary discriminations:

fertility/sterility
sacredness/secularity
silence/speech
foolishness/sagacity
solidity/liquidity
stasis/dynamics
heaven/earth

Moving between the liminal status of the mytho-folkloric stone and the marginal features of Pao-yü and Wu-k'ung, we can find numerous instances of intertextuality. The various sets of opposing terms outlined above undergo subtle, and sometimes radical, transformations in the psychic composition of these two characters. The continual reversibility of *wan shih* and *t'ung-ling shih*, of the *chen/chia* Pao-yü, and of stone and jade—neither term in these pairs being ranked higher than the other—subverts, however fleetingly, the conventions of identity and unity,[41] and underlines the disseminating character of liminality that the folkloric stone is know to be possessed of.

That the folkloric stone is by itself a strong liminal entity endows the paradox of *wan-shih/t'ung-ling shih* with double poignancy. The *Dream* itself can be seen as the portrayal and celebration of the marginal as embodied in the nonconformist hero. In fact, Stone's review of its own Stone Record in chapter 1 is both a defense of a new form of fiction and, more importantly, a manifesto of the break with moral and social constraints. In terms of both its narrative logic and the new moral sensibility, the *Dream of the Red Chamber* attempts to champion the cause of the displaced and the peripheral.

At the very beginning of the *Dream*, a strong emphasis on the marginal can already be detected as the Goddess Nü-kua dismisses Stone from her service. Pattern-making produces remainders. The formation of every order engenders detritus. As the pattern of the broken firmament is restored and the cosmic order retrieved, Stone is found lying at the foot of a mountain assuming an ambiguous existence as a divine outcast, an anomaly excluded from the enclosed heaven, and a blend of lowliness and sacredness. Upon close examination, Stone's defense of its own discourse is built on a curious logic[42] that wavers between the conviction of its own worth and a rhetorical self-mockery. Placing the origin of the Stone Record in the absurd, while arguing that its editor has been engaged in the painstaking efforts of compiling the Record for ten years, the author-narrator gives us two contradictory messages and succeeds in shifting our point of view incessantly between "sense" and "nonsense" in our reading of the Record.

Victor Turner and many other structural anthropologists have studied the significance of marginal entities in the context of social mores. Based on the fundamental tenet that liminality implies that "the high could not be high unless the low exists, and he who is high must experience what it is like to be low,"[43] they expound the paradox of the powers of the weak inherent in marginal roles. By citing examples of liminal figures in folklore and literature (to name just a few: the "holy beggars," "third sons," "simpleton," the good Samaritan, and the fugitive Negro slave Jim in *Huckleberry Finn*), they observe the redeeming power of the weak strengthened by their very status of inferiority and outlawry.[44] Thus the poor and the deformed are often endowed with unusual psychic powers, spiritually elevated above their secular humility—and in structured societies, they are often those who articulate outraged morality and come to symbolize creative humanity.

This type of dialectical process that involves an alternating experience of the high and the low, the sacred and the secular, the spiritual and the earthly, comes to characterize Pao-yü's psychic journey as he travels from the lower to the higher realm of existence through the limbo of statuslessness. From the very beginning, Pao-yü's previous incarnation—the rejected Nü-kua Stone—is known to reside in a twilight zone. It is worthy enough to engage the attention of the Buddhist monk, yet not sufficiently commendable to be among the chosen few in the goddess's reconstruction of the sky. This ambivalent aura continues to surround Pao-yü as we find him embodying dull-wittedness and divine intelligence alternately throughout the entire narrative. His passage from the low to the high is a slowly progressive but continuously zigzag course between two mutually dependent personae—*wan shih* and *t'ung-ling shih*. Pao-yü's momentary transition from one persona to the other manifests the "power of the weak" and depicts the dialectical movement of liminality in motion.

One of the most transparent moments in the *Dream*, which launches and, in a sense, crystallizes the liminal metaphor of *wan shih/t'ung-ling shih*, occurs in the first chapter. Indeed, it seems that regardless of the original intention professed by an author-narrator who claims to be averse to the notion of the beginning, the "beginning" still marks the privileged locale where meaning is anchored. This is the episode in which Chen Shih-yin, upon overhearing in a trancelike delirium the conversation between the Buddhist and the Taoist monk about the "stupid thing," inquires about the object under discussion, and is shown a beautiful piece of jade upon which are engraved the four characters *t'ung-ling pao-yu*. Here we are introduced to the paradoxical identification of *wan shih* with *t'ung-ling shih*, a strange correlation that seems to contradict the oppositional relationship between these two images—an opposition based on the metaphor of darkness ("lack-lustre") and light, of spiritual dullness and numinousness.

The oppositional paradigm, however, is bound to be eclipsed by the liminal paradigm, for the former attempts in vain to summarize in a shorthand fashion a process that keeps procrastinating its consummation. The transformative passage between *wan shih* and *t'ung-ling shih* can be characterized by a variety of laborious movement rather than by a single sweeping motion of irreversible transportation. What the *Dream* enacts is exactly this lengthy and unpredictable process of vacillation between the two stone images. The enigma posed by the symbolism of *wan shih/t'ung-ling shih* can actually be recapitulated in simpler terms: what does it mean to be silly and keen in turn, or, more precisely, at one and the same time?

The interest of this question rests of course on the meaning of liminal existence, and more specifically, on how liminality, precisely because of its very slipperiness, makes the production of meaning possible. In the case of the *Dream*, and less poignantly in the *Journey to the West*, I argue that the efficacy of Pao-yü's and Wu-k'ung's spiritual quest—a privileged, if not the central, signifying locus of both narratives—rests precisely on the concept of liminality. In other words, liminality preconditions and predetermines the possibility and the nature, if not the outcome, of such quests.

In symbolic terms, it is the respective liminal attributes of *wan shih* and *t'ung-ling shih*—the ingrained playfulness-in-dullness, and the communicative potential of the secular with the divine—that make the dramatic journey of the former plausible in the first place. It is the categorical continuum of liminality and, by implication, its promise of an unbounded narrative space that can alone map out a journey that takes place in a psyche knowing no realm of its own. Only the logic of liminality can truly meet the challenge that the motif of psychic journey poses to the literary configuration of spatiality. In narrative terms, the concept of liminality makes possible the emergence and interaction of conflicting categories; and paradoxically, it also provides the local catalyst for the eventual completion of the psychic journey—that is, for the possible grand synthesis of such complementary opposites as the high and the low, the profane and the sacred, the fool and the saint, and *wan shih* and *t'ung-ling shih*.

It will be helpful, at this juncture, to take a quick look at the strategic position occupied by the concept of liminality in the fictional construct of Pao-yü's quest, and to try to understand better how the symbolic code of liminality, namely, the *wan shih/t'ung-ling shih* metaphor, can be materialized in nonsymbolic vocabulary such as "silliness" and "intelligence."

Throughout his journey on earth, Pao-yü's cognitive power reveals itself in a conflicting pattern. Before the consummation of his enlightenment ritual, he exists in the marginal passage between madness and lucidity, between humility and arrogance, and between stupidity and ingenuity. During the intervening liminal period, he passes through various ordeals of Passion. The shadows of Form (*se*) and Death have humbled him at every turn and revealed to him through his own spiritual potency, however fleetingly, the powers of the weak. The various trials he has undergone serve to awaken the dormant sacredness of the *t'ung-ling* stone, and no less significantly, to rejuvenate the elfin mental agility that, more often than not, finds itself in danger of being overtaken by its twin symbolism of the fool embedded in the metaphor of *wan shih*. Seen through the eyes of other characters in the *Dream*, Pao-yü is at once sharp and lunatic, intelligent and senseless.[45] The early chapters are indeed filled with recurrent allusions to his conflicting twin spirits—devices of characterization that serve to materialize the paradox of *wan shih* and *t'ung-ling shih*.

The overwhelmingly negative portrait of Pao-yü's recklessness and stupidity—referred to in such terms as *feng-feng sha-sha* 瘋瘋傻傻, *han-wan* 憨頑, and *ch'ih-wan* 痴頑—is, however, occasionally balanced by a different point of view, which, being introduced by Fairy Disenchantment, cannot but conjure up a stronger authority over the assessment of self-deluded mortals. Recall, for example, that Disenchantment hurriedly snaps shut the album of the Main Register for fear that she may be "in danger of becoming responsible for a leakage of celestial secrets," knowing "how intelligent and sharp witted he [Bao-yu] was" (*Stone* I: 135–36). The reversibility of bipolar terms, together with the delay of the consummation of such reversibility—captured in Disenchantment's lament, "The silly boy has not yet been illuminated!"[46]—are two important grammatical features of any liminal construction. In this respect, the *Dream of the Red Chamber*, despite its initial motivation to highlight the liminal plot of delay (e.g., Disenchantment's calculating impulse to prevent Pao-yü from perusing the Main Register), fails to bear out its radical implications by resolving and dissolving the delay impulse into the final climactic moment of Pao-yü's indubitable and irreversible evolution into the *t'ung-ling* stone. Once "perceptiveness" (re)gains the final ground, its continuous dialogue with "obtuseness" comes to be replaced by the old hierarchical relationship between the two. A "consummated" liminality, an oxymoron, forgoes the logic of process in subjugation to the movement of return. Here we arrive at the same conclusion that our previous discussions of the metaphysical vision of the *Dream* suggest—namely, it is a narrative that eventually comes to terms with that which it problematizes. The notion of the beginning and, with it, that of identity—conventions that are initially subverted—come back to haunt the new rhetoric of process and liminality. In terms of both narrative logic and the cultural unconscious, the *Dream* reveals itself as a tale about the fatal attractions of constraints and a tragedy about an aborted ideological revolution.

Although the *Dream* proper is made up of one episode after another of shifting dialogue between the signs of eccentricity and dim-wittedness, and those of penetrating shrewdness, the liminal metaphor of *wan shih/t'ung-ling shih* paradoxically brings Pao-yü's spiritual journey to a standstill. With the resolution of Pao-yü's liminal personality (stone and jade in one sense, and *wan shih* and *t'ung-ling shih* in another) into the single identity of stone and *t'ung-ling*, it is only logical that the Nü-kua Stone that greets us in the last chapter should be pared down to a mute and lifeless object, for its creative energy, known to be characteristic of any liminal entity, is now consummated, and therefore completely consumed. Seen in the context of the final resolution of the liminal paradox of *wan shih/t'ung-ling shih*, Chih-yen Chai's commentary in chapter 19 of the seventy-eight-chapter *Chih-pen* tells only the half-truth of Pao-yü's spiritual quest. Those of us who faithfully trace the liminal configuration of the *Dream* to the last page will discover that the true spirit of its negative dialectics (as Chih-yen Chai suggests in the following) is far beyond the reach of the tamed ideological vision revealed in the *Dream*:

> [Pao-yü] cannot be said to be talented, nor foolish, nor unworthy; neither good, nor bad; neither fair and frank, nor debased and despicable; neither keen and intelligent, nor vulgar and banal; neither lustful nor blinded by pure love.[47]

The metaphor of liminality, it remains to be said, is one of the most significant contributions that the *Dream* makes to Chinese narrative conventions. Given its central signifying position in the *Dream*, we should not close our discussion of the issue without mentioning in passing another intriguing metaphor—one that has less to do with stone imagery than with Pao-yü's philosophy of love. It is a metaphor characterizing the liminal nature of desire—*ch'ing pu-ch'ing* 情不情 —constructed as Ts'ao Hsüeh-ch'in's final verdict on Pao-yü's libidinal character. The metaphor appears in the now-lost Roster of Lovers in the last chapter of the original manuscript of the *Dream*.

This authorial comment, *ch'ing pu-ch'ing*, has been quoted and analyzed four times in the transcribed copies of the sixteen- and seventy-eight-chapter *Chih-pen*.[48] The commentator in the latter version seems baffled by the elusive phrase and offers no explication:

> In reading this book I only love the author's writing, really I have not been able to comment on the two characters [Pao-yü and Tai-yü]. Then later on I found that in the *Roster of Lovers* the verdict on Pao-yü is *ch'ing pu-ch'ing*, and that on Tai-yü is *ch'ing ch'ing* 情情 . These two comments are certainly better than the comment "Foolish (lover)" yet they are wholly inscrutable. Very subtle![49]

In the commentary of the sixteen-chapter *Chih-pen*, however, the quotation is given a simple definition, and Pao-yü is seen as an altruistic lover whose affection is extended to inanimate objects in the universe:

> Upon all the senseless and lifeless things in the world, he [Pao-yü] has generated a blind and silly love [*ch'ih-ch'ing* 痴情] to shower his indulgent care.[50]

It is interesting to note that a comment on Ch'ing-wen's fan-tearing episode found in chapter 31 of the seventy-eight-chapter *Chih-pen* also coincides with this interpretation:

> Tearing fans is to provide the coquettish and peevish maid a passionless object to amuse her and to induce her smile—this is the so-called

ch'ing pu-ch'ing—to move the passionless one to passion/to stir up one's passions by means of a passionless object.[51]

Finally, it is the long commentary preceding chapter 21 of the seventy-eight-chapter *Chih-pen* that offers the most profound insight into the paradoxical term:

> Boundless is the passionate love of the young lord inside the green
>   gauze window,
> Bounteous is the sorrow of the Master of the Rouge Inkslab Study
>   [Chih-yen Chai].
> Whether it be an illusion or reality [he] has in vain experienced.
> On this leisurely romantic life poems and songs have been composed
>   to no end.
> The passion-karma [*ch'ing-chi* 情機] revolves so intensely that it
>   breaks the passion sky [*ch'ing-t'ien* 情天].[52]
> Passion for love, yet no passion at all, what can you do about me?

This commentary provides a pithy footnote on the paradox of the two bipolar terms, *ch'ing* and *pu'-ch'ing*. The liminal phrase *ch'ing pu-ch'ing*, decoded above as the "passionate lover without passion"—an ambiguous appellation that participates in the overall liminal scheme of Pao-yü's attributes—translates Stone's sojourn on earth as the symbolic enactment of the *se/k'ung* ("Form/Void") paradox. The dialectics of desire contained in the libidinal metaphor recommends a different critical venture that goes beyond the scope of our present project. Suffice it to say that we find in Pao-yü a hero who wears an aura of liminality in every aspect of his existence, a hero whose ambiguous persona (stone/jade) extends to the cognitive (unknowing/intelligent) and the libidinal (*ch'ing/pu-ch'ing*).

It is worth recapitulating at this juncture that the liminal status of the Nü-kua Stone is further manifested in its physical transformation from a bare building block to a glimmering jade in the shape of a fan-pendant. Here the implications of crudeness versus refinement serve to reinforce the well-structured contrast between the "unknowing stone" and the "stone of divine intelligence." Curiously enough, Pao-yü's liminal characteristics reveal themselves not only in a shifting dialogue between *wan shih* and *t'ung-ling shih*, but also in his ambivalent physical substance as jade/stone. The two are caught in the generative imagery of birth and rebirth, dullness and translucency, and authenticity and falsehood. Our examination of the discourse of jade and stone in the previous chapter showed how each object is characterized by a problematic identity; how such double-voicedness finds its contact with their folkloric counterpart; and, most importantly, how the two discourses of jade and stone intersect each other to set loose the powerful symbolism of liminality.

The jade pendant, however, remains a surrogate spiritual guardian, a mute testimony to mystical powers. For throughout Pao-yü's pilgrimage, he never loses the memory of the stone or sheds his inane stony substance. As I argue repeatedly, however radically marginalized our hero may appear to be, the author-narrator's return complex cannot but reinforce the old conventional wisdom that conclusion not only signifies closure, it also triggers the retrogressive movement of its own enclosure by the beginning. When Pao-yü's spiritual transformation is consummated, his physical appearance is thus paradoxically reversed—or, in the metaphorical sense, made to revert—to the original substance of stone. While the symbolism of jade permeates the moral discourse of the *Dream*, it is the stone that tells the story, frames the narrative of the *Dream of the Red Chamber*, and engenders the interaction within the paradox of *wan shih/t'ung-ling shih*, and in a less telling manner, that of *se/k'ung*.

Is There a Beginning in the *Dream of the Red Chamber*?

The final reversion of the hero to his stony origin belies Ts'ao Hsüeh-ch'in's claim that he has broken away from the literary conventions (most notably, the convention of the beginning) that constrain the fictional discourse of his forebears. The priority of the discourse of stone over that of jade at the final climactic moment of the *Dream* involves more than the choice of one particular narrative strategy over the others (specifically, the option between privileging the point of origin, which dictates the return of the narrative to where it originated, and highlighting the notion of process, which interprets any form of return as structural enclosure). Ts'ao Hsüeh-ch'in's choice of a cyclical mode of narration, I would argue, articulates first and foremost the cultural myth of "returning to a stabilized and homogeneous origin," and in so doing, it reveals the constraint that the cultural unconscious exercises over his writings. The issue of the narrative beginning looms large in the ideological struggle of iconoclastic writers against tradition, be it literary or cultural. The problem of how a narrative begins and ends cannot but acquire an aura of urgency, even for those who are the least concerned about the formal structure of narrative fiction. The question "is there a beginning in the *Dream of the Red Chamber*?" is certainly value-laden and appears more implicated than ever in the issue of ideology. In what follows, I will explore how the privileged signifying position of stone enacts an ideological paradox, which the author represses, but which the narrative itself cannot help revealing.

Although we recognize that to write in general is to engage in the activity of intertextuality, the issue is particularly difficult for the Chinese poet caught in the dilemma of trying to strike original notes while being deeply immersed in an age-old poetic convention characterized by its wealth of allusions and a poetic diction made up of the citation of citations. In contrast, the situation is less treacherous for fiction-writers, for whom the burden of literary tradition—and, for that matter, that of intertextuality—seems less heavy. And indeed, Ts'ao Hsüeh-ch'in thought it possible to subvert, if not to transcend, conventional restraints. In the words of the stone, the author of the first eighty chapters of the *Dream* condemns the "stale old convention" (*Stone* I: 49) and promises to tell a story that will impart "a freshness" absent in the existing repertory of tales. Specifically under attack are the formal convention of "artificial period-setting" and the explicit socio-moral didacticism (*Stone* I: 49) of the stories of the past. Given the deeply rooted influence of historiography upon the Chinese writing tradition, we can indeed marvel at the author-narrator's radical proposal to do away with period-setting altogether. As early as in chapter 1, he has already begun to stretch the conventional concept of fictionality. To achieve this goal, the narrative voice dallies with the notion of beginning. Ts'ao Hsüeh-ch'in recognizes that embedded in the narrative convention of period-setting is not only the Chinese obsession with the notion of authenticity, but also the convention of beginning, another venerable formal constraint dictated by the historiographical tradition.

It seems that the subversion of the convention of beginning in the first chapter is successful, for Lucien Miller unveils five or six different "beginnings" of the *Dream* in his analysis.[53] The concept of a single and stable formal beginning is ridiculed and canceled. The narrator's victory over the anxiety of locating a point of origin, whether temporal or spatial, seems easily won in the prelude. The issue, however, is more complicated than it appears. Clues in the first chapter—and, in fact, throughout the remaining one hundred and some chapters—reveal the narrator's ongoing struggle to maintain his earlier claim of achieving difference. The crucial question is whether the conventional concept of beginning is subverted once and for all (or perhaps surpassed, as critics like Miller would probably argue) by means of the continuous sliding of "a beginning" in chapter 1.

Ts'ao Hsüeh-ch'in's "radical" stance and the task of subversion in question are highly ambiguous on several counts. To undertake this inquiry, we need first to examine the notion of beginning more carefully. Not only does the concept indicate a specific point in time and space, as understood by both Stone and the narrator, it also reveals a culturally endorsed vision of "origin." For the concept of "beginning" and "end" does not simply define the boundary of a text and provide a structural frame that meets the eye. It also conveys at the same time a conceptual and even an ideological framework, in that it implies the primacy and priority of such notions as "original," "transcendental," "nature," "presence," and "identity"—terms extended from the concept of beginning—over the opposite set of terms such as "derivative," "artifice," "absence," and "undecidability"—value-concepts that endanger the stability assured by the first set of terms. In other words, the beginning constitutes not only a fixed and ultimate point of reference, but also a privileged one.

A writer's decision to endorse the narrative device of beginning involves a conscious choice. One can choose to defer the beginning, or to start the story in the middle. It seems that Ts'ao Hsüeh-ch'in's narrator made the choice with little difficulty. The beginning, however, represents more than a rhetorical frame device. Transcending the concept of beginning on the stylistic level does not necessarily entail its transcendence altogether. While we may say that the narrator has made a successfully defiant gesture against the formal convention of beginning, it is a different matter when we come to assess his shedding of the ideological vision deeply embedded in the notion of beginning. The gist of the problem does not consist in whether it is possible to make the choice not to start from the conventionally expected beginning, but whether it is possible for any writer/narrator to choose to function outside the realm of the ideological or the cultural unconscious. The autonomy of the mind seems as deceptive a concept as the autonomy of the text.

One thus finds traces of the notion of "origin" here and there in the *Dream*, revealed time and again in the motivating force of its narrative structure.

Although the narrator forgoes the orthodoxy of an identifiable beginning, he never loses sight of the concept of root/origin. Throughout the narrative, he continually reminds us of the original identity/essence/nature (*pen-chih* 本質) of Chia Pao-yü. In the sixteen-chapter *Chih-pen*, the end of the story is already overdetermined both thematically and structurally as early as in chapter 1 by the Buddhist monk's revelation of a preexisting spatial and temporal point of origin. In response to Stone's eloquent plea for human reincarnation, the monk gives away the divine plan awaiting Stone: "After your [Stone's] ordeal comes to an end, you will be reverted to your original essence/nature [*Tai chüeh*-chung *chih-jih, fu*-huan *pen-chih* 待劫終之日, 復還本質]."[54] The spatial origin refers to both the physical *substance* and the physical *location* of Stone before its rebirth. A temporal reference is also set in motion by the concepts of *chung* 終 ("end") and *huan* 還 ("return"). Although the other term of each binary pair—*shih* 始 ("beginning"), as in *shih-chung* 始終 , and *yüan* 原 ("origin"), as in *huan-yüan* 還原 —is absent in the text, they nevertheless enjoy the central and privileged position in the passage, for the word *pen-chih* serves to evoke both absent terms and reinforce their paradoxical role as both the original and the final ground of Stone's existence. Thus the Buddhist monk does not simply foretell, but virtually *determines* and *dictates* the outcome of Pao-yü's journey: at his final destination he will be brought by the monk in person, just as the narrator simultaneously brings his narrative, back to the point in space and time from which both hero and narrative originated. In this enterprise of returning strategically to an origin held to be pure, intact, and forever present, we can catch a glimpse of the ideological content of that which the *Dream* represses. The narrator's efforts to vitiate the concept of beginning are successful merely at the rhetorical, and thus rather superficial, level. It appears that the Chinese literati are very often self-deluded in their attempt to escape the impalpable enclosure of the return impulse and the retrospective stance so characteristic of the Chinese writing tradition.

The search for origin, whether understood as the search for the ultimate text of the Canon or for some kind of transcendental identity that Stone exudes at the foot of Greensickness Peak, repeats the same circular movement: the return of the derivative and imitative to a preexisting pure, stable, and ideal norm. In the case of the *Dream of the Red Chamber*, the departure from such a norm is rarely appreciated as a transformation in the evolutionary sense; instead, it is considered not only a deviation from the essential but also a loss to be mourned. In chapter 8, when Pao-yü first shows Pao-ch'ai his birth-jade, the narrator emerges to give us his interpretation of its significance—or, in more accurate terms, its *lack* of significance:

> This jade is the illusory semblance [*huan-hsiang* 幻相] of that same stone block that once lay at the foot of Greensickness Peak in the Great Fable Mountains.
>
> Some jesting poet has written the following verses about it:
>
> Nü-kua stone-smelting is a story of the absurd,
> From such absurdity unravels our tale of the Great Fable Mountains.
> Losing sight of [*shih ch'ü* 失去] the pure/true realm
>   [*chen-ching-chieh* 真境界] of spirits,
> Turned into this illusory [*huan* 幻] vile bag of flesh and bone. . . .
> (*HLM* I: 123)

The earthly substance of the jade is conceived as secondary, for it is deriva-tive in nature. It assumes an illusory guise, a copy of the original heavenly stone that resides in the realm of the true and the pure. Once having left that celestial residence, the jade is believed to have lost the authentic, innocent, flawless, divine, and natural essences inherent in the stone. The implicit bi-nary opposition between stone and jade revealed in this passage rests on the correct interpretation of the two words *huan* 幻 ("the illusory") and *chen* 真 ("the real"). The recurrence of both words throughout the *Dream* points to the significant function they fulfill in its underlying conceptual framework.[55]

Although Ts'ao Hsüeh-ch'in's narrator succeeds in blurring the boundary between the true and the false in the first chapter, the diametrical relation-ship between these two terms is subtly reactivated in the above verses. Given the hidden dichotomy between *chen* and *huan*, and thus between *chen* and *chia*, the narrator's slip here leaves us little doubt as to which term is to be viewed as prior and superior to the other. Lest the argument get lost in the discussion of jade versus stone, I want to recapitulate the point of conten-tion. The issue here is not whether stone takes precedence over jade in the symbolism of authenticity versus artificiality, a thesis pursued in the previous chapter, but whether Ts'ao Hsüeh-ch'in's narrator privileges the concept of origin/beginning despite himself (i.e., "stone" as Pao-yü's true origin, and jade as an illusory image of the real stone). One should note that although the *Dream* is told without a real beginning, the narrator nonetheless ascribes primary value to Pao-yü's "original" nature (i.e., stone) and perceives the evolution of stone (i.e., Stone's reincarnation into jade and its sojourn on earth) as a departure from the authentic, to be viewed in terms of the illusory and the secondary. In such an epistemological vision the original is the eternal and the essential, and that which comes after is its surrogate, already a subordinate, both transient and accidental in nature.

In the last chapter of the narrative, we find the same conceptual framework reiterated in a conversation between Chia Yü-ts'un and Chen Shih-yin, the latter attempting to enlighten the former on the mystery of Pao-yü and Tai-yü's karma in a koan-like riddle: "If Crimson Pearl Flower has returned to the True [*chen*], how could the Magic Jade not recover [*fu-yüan* 復原]?" (*Hsien-ts'ao kuei-chen, yen-yu t'ung-ling pu fu-yüan chih li ne?* 仙草歸真 , 焉有通靈不復原之理呢?) (*HLM* III: 1645). What Chen Shih-yin says here echoes what the Buddhist monk has earlier said about the necessary "reversion" of Pao-yü. Both the monk and Chen Shih-yin bring us back to a point of view that privileges a static outside scheme, which eventually arrests the evolving inner dynamics of fictional logic. This exterior scheme is nothing other than the predictability of "recovery."

The story of the stone is thus shaped by an all-embracing mytho-logic that contradicts the spontaneous logic of fiction. The fiction motivates Pao-yü's quest in terms of self-*dis*covery and accepts the risks of rupture and discontinuity that such an unguided excursion may entail; it does not and cannot foresee the outcome of the quest, for it is a happening. The mytho-logic, on the contrary, based on terms of self-*re*covery, imposes a severe discipline on the narrative that wants to check its instantaneous momentum by thinking every turn of its thoughts from the very start. Every movement refers back to and reflects the point of origin. The narrative in progress is continuously caught in the undercurrent of regression. While the self-generating fictional logic of the *Dream*, if given free play, could lead Pao-yü to no predictable destination, the mythical scheme, being exterior to all that is changing and unreliable, cannot but curtail that movement toward dissemination by asserting its ultimate authority as an a priori fact.

To assure maximum effect, the mythical scheme has to be conveyed by the right kind of characters, and at the right moment. No one can more appropriately serve as its mouthpiece than Chen Shih-yin and the eccentric monk whose quasi-divine identity is established shortly after the narrative starts—and nowhere seems more suitable for the sanctioned scheme to be established than at the very beginning and at the very end of the narrative. Strategically, the frame-device seems the best possible solution to an author who is still helplessly caught up in the paradox of origin, essence, and beginning. Despite all the depth and ingenuity of such a complex narrative framework, he is less aware of what it will restrain than of what it can serve.

A closer look at Chen Shih-yin's rhetorical question will shed more light on our understanding of the narrator's position on the issue of beginning, and on how he limits his vision despite himself. The pun on "recovery" (*huanyüan* 還原), "return-[to]-origin," again triggers the circular and retroactive movement. Pao-yü's destiny is seen as taking place between two poles— the beginning and the end, departure and return. And it is further implied that the recovery of his true identity depends on his return to his original being, namely, stone. Not only does the point of origin assert its vantage over the ongoing process of change, but identity is also perceived as retrievable, and therefore as a seamless internalized totality that resists erosion and transformation. "Difference" as a concept is given little credit by a narrator who dwells on the authenticity of the original, who may in fact perceive that difference poses a threat to the unadulterated identity—a self-sufficient interior already completed, and therefore closed to invaders from the outside. Both Chen Shih-yin and the Buddhist monk subtly suggest that there is an end to identity crisis, that an eventual recovery holds the key to resolving the dilemma of Pao-yü's self-(r)evolution that will lead ruthlessly to the bankruptcy of the myth of a definable identity.

Every ordeal that Pao-yü goes through threatens his sense of self-integration. He is besieged by heterogeneous elements that challenge the totality of his identity. What makes our hero such an unusual character departing from previous stereotypes is exactly this intriguing process of the gradual disintegration of his stable ego-identity at each critical moment of his life. After Tai-yü's death, the core of Pao-yü's identity is prey to further destruction, and we witness his hopeless disintegration into something indefinable, purposeless, and formless. It is at this juncture, when the radicalization of Pao-yü's identity quest reaches the critical moment of genuine disorder, that the two visionaries emerge to halt the process. We cannot help speculating on the final outcome of the *Dream of the Red Chamber* if the hero were given the chance to develop within his total mental and spiritual chaos: we might be given a very different account of what true freedom means. Would it still be understood as the nihilist retreat into Buddhahood, the ascetic elimination of the self, as the narrator suggests—or could it be seen as a total indulgence in perpetual self-negation and aimlessness?

But the two prophets appear on the stage to deny any such possibility of an undecidable and unstructured outgrowth. They not only remind us of the restraining function of the narrative frame-device, but also invoke once more what the narrator has vitiated earlier, in chapter 1—namely, the traditional epistemology based on the absolute opposition between such binary terms as the true and the false, being and nonbeing, identity (similarity) and difference. That which has been opened up is closed again, and that which has fallen apart is put back in order. Heterogeneity loses its ground again as the restoration of the original essence reaffirms the priority of identity. The blurred boundary between binary opposites is once again refined.

Through the two fictional characters—the Buddhist monk and Chen Shih-yin—we have gained access to a point of view that seems to indicate the narrator's obsession with the concept of origin, and his compulsion to return. Seen in this light, what appeared an unmistakable parody of the convention of beginning in chapter 1 now strikes a note of ambivalence. Let us reconsider the opening sentence of the narrative: "What, you may ask, was the origin of this book?" (*Stone* I: 47). We have here a statement that has been taken for granted as ironic. But I argue that it carries a certain residual connotation of the narrator's well-disguised ideological orientation, whose significance can be brought to light only in retrospect. At the first glimpse, the immediate effect of the narrator's playful tone can hardly be missed. We can almost hear him saying merrily, "You expect a beginning, let me throw you one. But don't take it seriously." The distance between the two orders—the order of the original (i.e., the convention of beginning), and his point of view, which ridicules, and therefore undermines, the original—creates a sharp contrast between a literal and an alternative ironic reading. Should the reader take the narrator's opening remark seriously at this point? A definite "no" is likely to come from a first-time reader, who will be much more susceptible to an ironic reading. I suggest that a significant readjustment of this response will take place only after the reader has finished the book, for then it will be very difficult to formulate a clear "yes" or "no" answer. One might say that while it takes a sophisticated reader to delight in the irony of the sentence, it takes a real cynic to read it literally and, to use a favorite phrase of our narrator, to recover its original literal meaning, while savoring the self-defeated purpose of the narrator's original intention. In other words, the reader will have to take the narrator's opening statement much more seriously, and to meditate on, if not to revel in, the inexorable forces of self-delusion.

A retrospective reading of the convention of beginning will make more sense at this point, after our discussion of the limits confronting a writer who wages a battle against such a venerable convention. One needs to recognize in the first place that the concept of beginning will stop functioning if the beginning does not contain within itself the intention to continue and extend. The extension, however, follows a certain course, as the beginning is "the first step in the intentional production of meaning."[56]

A classic case of such a beginning intention very often gives rise to a kind of beginning that "foresees a continuity that flows from it."[57] No matter how irreverently the narrator of the *Dream* may have started his tale, and how intentionally he relegates to the winds the notion of beginning, the beginning episode of the Nü-kua myth sets up nothing less than a kind of inclusiveness within which the work develops. "Intention" is thus a tricky matter, for the intention not to begin often backfires. What is accidentally started is obliged to carry out the function of beginning once it is positionally trapped in the location designated for the beginning. To any writer who aims at subverting the convention, a beginning becomes an especial burden because of its very position of being prior to what will follow. This seems the kind of mental trap into which Ts'ao Hsüeh-ch'in's narrator falls. There is always the danger of reflecting too much upon the beginning even while relinquishing interest in the concept.

When we look at the Nü-kua episode while bearing in mind all the intricate ramifications of the paradox of beginning, we cannot help wondering whether it deserves the name of an unorthodox beginning. It is disguised in the rhetorics of the accidental, but in real "essence," it carries the same function as any other legitimate beginning that foresees and guarantees a continuity. For the myth of the Nü-kua Stone constitutes the core of the mythologic—the exterior scheme discussed earlier—that continues to guide and organize Pao-yü's psychic journey. Perhaps the narrator is fully aware of the contradiction inherent in his casual start of the beginning episode—that it is both intentional and fortuitous, a kind of mental trick that he plays on us. Perhaps he does not intend to exclude himself from his own ridicule. While laughing at all his predecessors who so deliberately began their tales in well-motivated beginnings, he intends to laugh at himself also.

Our self-conscious narrator understands the rules of the game in yet another manner. Certainly he holds no illusion that one can begin completely from nothing. He understands that even a seemingly novel start has to draw upon something old. The subsequent choice is a paradoxical one: on the one hand, the narrator undermines the convention of beginning, and with it, that of authenticity, by starting with a myth that renders the specificity of temporal and spatial reference irrelevant; on the other, this myth is not just any other myth, but one of cosmogony—"the passage from chaos to cosmos"[58]—that tells the tale of *the beginning of Creation*. The paradox seems self-explanatory: that a narrator so intent on breaking away from the conceptual enclosure of beginning would have chosen inadvertently as the starting point of his tale a myth that enacts the origin of the universe.

At a closer look, the narrator's choice of the Nü-kua episode reveals more than one instance of his attachment to convention, be it literary or cultural. One can imagine that he who is so involuntarily entrenched in the literary tradition of beginning would also find himself no less entangled in the cultural return complex, and indeed the narrator's choice of starting with the Nü-kua myth points to the manifestation of this complex in a subtle manner. For the myth enacts the symbolism of renewal and embodies one of the earliest versions of the cultural compulsion to recover. To begin with such a myth sets the tone for the act of storytelling that is to follow. It is not surprising that we will be given a tale the underlying motivation of which rests on the theme of recovery that corresponds to the mytho-logic of the Nü-kua myth. The goddess's ritualistic act of retrieving cosmic disorder is but the mythical version of our narrator's act of "recovering" the original order of the Magic Stone. What is at stake in the myth is cosmic wholeness, and in the *Dream*, individual totality. The narrator's fascination with the myth of Nü-kua thus exceeds the immediate thematic interest of the five-colored sacred stone: it serves to fulfill a deeper unconscious motivation of his storytelling.

The unconscious motivation of reversion and the problem with "origin" discussed above form a fictional version on a small scale of what we may characterize as an important problematic in the Chinese tradition of (inter)textuality: the Confucian obsession with the Canon as the ultimate text to which all later texts return in an act of conscious imitation. What Ts'ao Hsüeh-ch'in originally proposes in the *Dream* appears a viable option—the creation of an open-ended text that will depart from the familiar and the canonical. And it seems that inasmuch as our author-narrator refutes the concept of imitation and continuity in favor of change and discontinuity, such a proposal is already half fulfilled. The possibility of "open-ended textuality," however, remains a vision. For as we have already seen, the concept of origin that is ridiculed intentionally at the beginning does not lose its potency or cease to regulate the flow of the narrative. By the same token, the Nü-kua episode can by no means be seen as a radical temporal device that abolishes the concept of time, and in consequence, that of beginning and end.

What results from the confrontation between the hegemonic ultimate text and the drive for an open-ended text is rather predictable: the notion of beginning that Ts'ao Hsüeh-ch'in overcame for only a fleeting moment assumes a haunting presence in the development of the story. The aborted revolution teaches us two lessons: not only does the nonconformist writer fall short of eclipsing the convention he problematizes, he also reveals a repressed obsession with the same problematic, namely, the looking up to the point of origin as the locale to which the narrative should ultimately return. The Nü-kua myth, in a similar vein, dramatizes the act of restoration. Although mythical time exists outside the framework of a historical time scale, it validates the concept of beginning in a different manner. Just as every New Year ritual is a "resumption of time from the beginning,"[59] and a "repetition of the cosmogonic act"[60] through which concrete human time is rejuvenated and projected into mythical time, the goddess's repair of the sky acquires the significance of the ritual of regeneration. Both kinds of ritual consecrate the mythical time of the beginning—a primordial and undifferentiated state of being, pure and whole, for it is not yet divided into opposites.[61] In this sense, the Nü-kua myth repeats the mythical return to the original wholeness. Myth thus privileges the point of origin no less fervently than history. "Sacred time" may not know its end, but it reveals the same nostalgia for the beginning as its own historical time.

The narrative logic of the *Dream* is therefore a case in point of how a literary-cultural tradition is caught in the evolving contradiction of continuity and change. The binding force of the concept of origin renders creative innovation a formidable task. This is not to say that Ts'ao Hsüeh-ch'in's narrator does not succeed in transcending the limits imposed on his predecessors: he subverts the rhetorical device of the beginning, no matter how incompletely, and invites us to discover the link between originality and fiction-making. Our discussion of the concept of origin and beginning, however, reveals much of the structural and ideological constraint inherent in the *Dream*, and raises a series of questions about the function of the mythical frame-device. To cite a few: Does the myth of the Magic Stone merely restrain? Attributed as the *original* essence and *ultimate* identity of Pao-yü, is the stone in fact a static entity exterior to Pao-yü's existence? Does it serve no other function than to remind us of the hero's origin? Should we view the mythical stone as a mere supplement, a marginal and unmotivated excess, to the real existence of our hero? Eventually the above questions boil down to one: Is the myth of stone an arbitrary choice of the author to begin his tale, generating no other meaning for the story of Pao-yü than a convenient structural constraint? A great deal of our preceding discussion of the jade and stone symbolism is aimed at locating the vantage point for our speculation on these issues. Taking note of the thematic interplay between the metaphors of *san-sheng shih*, *wan shih*, and *t'ung-ling shih*, we have mapped out the central signifying position that stone occupies in the *Dream of the Red Chamber*. As the myth of Nü-kua's five-colored stone extrapolates its chain of signification into these metaphors, the frame-device appears less ungrammatical and gratuitous; it becomes part and parcel of a deeply motivated dual discourse of the fictional and the ideological.

5 THE PARADOX OF DESIRE AND EMPTINESS: THE STONE MONKEY INTERTEXTUALIZED

Like initiation ritual subjects, Wu-k'ung and Pao-yü assume a liminal existence by wandering between the mundane world and the sacred realm—the former is the prison house of *se* 色 ("Form/Passion"), and the latter, the ultimate fountainhead of all being, a paradoxical "void" (*k'ung* 空) into and out of which everything flows. Upon initial examination, the opposition of "form" and "emptiness" seems to grow out of the prototypical antagonism between fertility and sterility: "form" impregnates within itself the implications of sensual instincts and pleasures, the will to live and to procreate, while the extinction of all desires and fertilizing vitality leads to vacuity. However, unlike the other pairs in the binary series of rituals listed in the previous chapter, *se* and *k'ung* do not form two well-defined points of stasis. Each term is indeterminate. And in fact, each forms a liminal entity by itself. The two properties evolve perpetually toward infinite dissemination, according to the Taoist dialectics of "mutual arising" and the Buddhist metaphysics revealed in the Heart Sutra. Each contains within itself the seed of the other. Forever caught in the process of merging into each other, these two terms represent a continual permutation between fullness and emptiness. Herein lies the intertextual gap between the liminal paradox of *wan shih/t'ung-ling shih* and that of *se/k'ung*. The latter, precisely because of the very impossibility of finding a concrete vehicle to bear out its theoretical potentials to the full, is able to sustain perpetually the radical discourse of liminality that the former prematurely closes. While the former is recategorized and recontained within the framework of a stabilized temporal and spatial order at the end of the *Dream*, the latter disperses its content ceaselessly and commands a motion of infinite progression that subverts the bipolar concept of liminality. It is a discourse that promulgates extensively and endlessly, as follows:

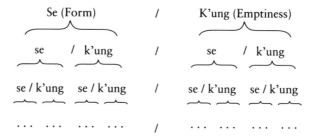

However, when such an elusive conceptual scheme is temporarily realized in a fictional character, its open-endedness suffers a predictable closure. Just as *wan shih* is bound to be enclosed by the *t'ung-ling* stone, so is Wu-k'ung, a monkey deeply enmeshed in the mind-trap of *se*—understood as both Form and Passion—overdetermined to bear witness to what his own name symbolizes: "awakened to vacuity." Once incarnated in fictional characters heavily masked in symbolism (the "Precious Jade" and "Awakened to Vacuity" serve as two prime examples), the paradoxically empty content of the *se/k'ung* metaphor becomes saturated with invariable value-terms. This very act of filling-in represents nothing other than the valorization of unstable metaphors and problematics. It is not surprising that each paradox—*se/k'ung*, and *wan shih/t'ung-ling shih*—should have undergone the same generative dilemma: instead of conjuring up an impalpable creative disorder, it transforms itself unwittingly into an omnipresent fictive constraint. In the following pages, we will trace the various citations that make the stone monkey a meaningful quest hero who, just like Pao-yü in the *Dream*, shares certain familiar features of liminality. A look at the liminal potentials inherent in the versatile stone monkey will reveal the nature of the constraint that the Form/Vacuity paradox generates despite itself.

As shown in Glen Dudbridge's analysis of the ape motif in early Chinese literature, scholars of influence-studies who have studied the *Journey* have been particularly engaged with the intertextual continuity of the fictional character of Wu-k'ung with his literary antecedents. In what way, such analyses ask, is Wu-k'ung, a demigod and a Buddhist saint, related to the legendary ape figure characterized by animal instincts and portrayed as an abductor of women and a lustful creature preoccupied with the creation of offspring?[1]

Although some scholars are inclined to accept the theory that Wu-k'ung has evolved from the folk tradition of the white ape,[2] Dudbridge refutes this hypothesis on the ground that the stone monkey bears little resemblance to the legendary white ape, whose character traits have no religious connotations.[3] He concludes: "in terms of origins and basic preoccupations the 'Tripitaka' cycle and the legend of the White Ape remain distinct. The monkey-hero in each case has its own identity—Tripitaka's disciple commits crimes which are mischievous and irreverent, but the white ape is from first to last a monstrous creature which has to be eliminated."[4] I would argue, however, in ruling out the ape solution to the folkloric origin of Wu-k'ung with a single stroke, Dudbridge has overstated his case. Driven by the zeal to search for the *complete* model, he runs the risk of dismissing significant sources in a premature fashion. In the case of the *Journey*, he should perhaps be reminded that the main difficulty in studying Wu-k'ung's origin lies in the fact that the hero is molded by no single literary influence, but by a congeries of widely disparate elements—secular as well as religious, foreign as well as indigenous—each of which leaves its imprint on the complex figure of the stone monkey-disciple. The image-making of Wu-k'ung is further complicated by an interweaving of multiple secular motifs, of which the ape legend is but *one*. It seems futile, therefore, to try to identify the ensemble imagery of Wu-k'ung—the Buddhist as well as the folk persona—with one single source.

In raising doubts about the relationship of Wu-k'ung to the white ape, Dudbridge appears to be implying that the ultimate origin of Sun Wu-k'ung can be traced only to a model that can encompass all the incongruous features in the fictional character of the monkey king; and since such a model is nowhere to be found, he finally gives up and follows other lines of inquiry.[5] I propose, on the contrary, to pursue the inquiry in a different direction by focusing on the personal traits of Wu-k'ung—namely, on the contradictory coexistence of his spiritual and animal characteristics, that is, of his religious and folkloric nature. The question should thus be reformulated—we must not ask whether a certain model can be taken as the ultimate source of the monkey king, but instead, what composite elements enter the play of signification and shape the intertextual space of Wu-k'ung's liminal personality.

The Lustful Ape: Chinese and Indian Citations

In the light of our study of intertextuality, the "superficial points of similarity"[6] between the ape-abductor and the stone monkey, however contingent they may appear, emerge as significant clues to our understanding of the problematic of liminality. We cannot ignore the implicit manifestation of the ape's carnal desire in Wu-k'ung's animal orientation. It is important, however, to recognize that the presence of other motifs in the intertextual space of the narrative (to which we will return later) serves to divert the libidinous energy of the ape into a different channel and, most significantly, introduces the other term of the liminal configuration, namely *k'ung*—the possibility of spiritual enlightenment—in a relationship of tension with its liminal opposite *se*, "desire." The discussion of such intertextual citations as the ritualistic stone and the trickster archetype will serve to illustrate how Wu-k'ung, a vainglorious stone monkey deeply enmeshed in desire, can slowly evolve into sagehood. A preliminary look at the nature of his desire—or, in symbolic terms, his obsession with Form—will curiously bring us to the other end of the liminal paradox: the Great Awakening, which is already written into the discourse of desire.

Before Wu-k'ung joins Tripitaka in the pilgrimage, he is known to be a mischievous demigod obsessed with desires of various kinds. He longs to become an immortal untouched by the iron hands of time and death. The thought of "old age and physical decay"[7] repulses him, for he desires to conquer, and not even death can stop him. Not surprisingly, after his quest for immortality is accomplished, Wu-k'ung's earlier craving is replaced by a thirst for power in the divine court. We can hardly forget those moments in the narrative when the monkey king comes alive before our very eyes, deeply entrenched in his inflated self-image and arrogant mannerisms. One of his famous outbursts occurs when he discovers that Pi-ma-wen 弼馬溫, his first office in Heaven, is nothing but an insignificant, low-ranking, horse-tending footman:

> "At the Flower-Fruit Mountain I was honored as *king* and *patriarch*. How dare they trick me into coming to look after horses for them? If horse tending is such a menial service, reserved only for the young and lowly, how did they intend to treat me? I won't do this anymore! I won't do this anymore! I'm leaving right now!" (*Journey* I: 73)

Wu-k'ung's soaring ambition for sovereignty and his egotistic self-glorification are revealed not only in his self-proclaimed title of *ch'i-t'ien ta-sheng* 齊天大聖, "Great Sage, Equal to Heaven," and in his famous battle cries at every encounter with demons as well as with the divine troops, but also in his shameless confession of his thirst for the throne of Jade Emperor, and last, but not least, in his blasphemous boasting of his own virtues. Wu-k'ung's desire for immortality and power dominates the first half of the narrative before the theme of pilgrimage is introduced. It is toned down somewhat in the latter half of the narrative, in which the persona of *hsin-yüan* 心猿, the "mind-monkey," emerges to complement that of the libidinous ape. The merging of these two personae provides the most eloquent footnote on the Buddhist metaphor that "mind" and "desire" are ultimately inseparable. Let us take a closer look at the subtle manifestations of Monkey's root of desire on two separate occasions.

The connotation of sexual desire appears in Wu-k'ung's encounter with two female demons in chapters 60 and 81. In chapter 60, Monkey's struggle with Madame Raksasi takes the curious turn of sexual adventure. In his last attempt at snatching the magic fan from Raksasi, he engages in the dangerous game of seduction and abandons himself to foreplay with her under the guise of her husband:

> After drinking a few rounds, Raksasi felt somewhat tipsy and her passion was gradually aroused. She began to move closer to the Great Sage Sun, rubbing against him and leaning on him.
>
> Holding hands with him,
> She murmured affection;
> Shoulder to shoulder,
> She whispered endearment.
>
> She took a mouthful of wine, and then he took also a mouthful of wine from the same cup. They also traded fruits with their mouths. . . .
> (*Journey* III: 163–64)

The sexual understatement in the episode seems to have caught the attention of Tung Yüeh, providing him with a starting thread in his fascinating psychological exploration of Monkey's desire in the *Hsi-yu Pu*. Tung Yüeh indeed proves himself to be ahead of his time by resorting to a train of chaotic symbols to represent "desire" in its various manifestations, among which libidinous imagery predominates: Wu-k'ung's pilgrimage is portrayed as a mind-journey through a jungle of sexual fantasies, enacting repressed desires in his unconscious.

In chapter 81 of the *Journey*, the depiction of Wu-k'ung's close encounter with carnal knowledge has lost its delicate touch of erotic romanticism as seen in the episode about Raksasi, and moved into an explicit depiction of lust:

> When the wind subsided, he [Wu-k'ung] immediately felt the fragrance of orchids and perfumes and he heard the tinkling of girdle jade. He rose slightly and raised his head to look. Ah! It was a beautiful young girl, walking straight up the hall.
>
> "Oo-li, oo-la!" chanted the Pilgrim [Wu-k'ung], pretending to recite scriptures. The girl walked up to him and hugged him, saying, "Little elder, what sort of scriptures are you chanting?"
>
> "What I vowed to chant!" replied Pilgrim. "Everyone is enjoying his sleep," said the girl. "Why are you still chanting?"
>
> "I made a vow!" replied Pilgrim. "How could I not do so?"
>
> Hugging him once more, the girl kissed him and said, "Let's go out back and play." Turning his face aside deliberately, Pilgrim said, "You are kind of dumb!"
>
> "Do you know physiognomy?" asked the girl.
>
> "A little," replied Pilgrim. "Read my face," said the girl, "and see what sort of a person I am." "I can see," said Pilgrim, "that you are somewhat of a slut or debauchee driven by your in-laws!" "You haven't seen a thing!" said the girl. "You haven't seen a thing!
>
> > I am no slut or debauchee
> > Whom my in-laws compelled to flee.
> > By my former life's poor fate
> > I was given too young a mate,
> > Who knew nothing of marriage rite
> > And drove me to leave him this night.
>
> But the stars and the moon, so luminous this evening, have created the affinity for you and me to meet. Let's go into the rear garden and make love."
>
> On hearing this, Pilgrim nodded and said to himself, "So those several stupid monks all succumbed to lust and that was how they lost their lives. Now she's trying to fool even me!" He said to her, "Lady, this priest is still very young, and he doesn't know much about lovemaking."

"Follow me," said the girl, "and I'll teach you." Pilgrim smiled and said to himself. "All right! I'll follow her and see what she wants to do with me."

They put their arms around each other's shoulders, and, hand in hand, the two of them left the hall to walk to the rear garden. Immediately tripping Pilgrim up with her leg so that he fell to the ground, the fiend began crying "Sweetheart" madly as she tried to pinch his stinky member.

"My dear child!" exclaimed Pilgrim. "You do want to devour old Monkey!" (*Journey* IV: 97–98)

What is curious about this episode is that although he has detected the fiendish nature of the beautiful girl immediately, the quick-tempered Monkey does not act according to our expectations. Instead of exposing and slaughtering her on the spot, he gives her a chance to seduce him and carries on the charade, with the "desire," as he himself proclaims, of finding out "what she wants to do with me." For several problematic moments that are riddled with libidinal understatement, Monkey's slaughtering impulse gives way to an impulse that, because of its very unfamiliarity to him, appears particularly tantalizing. The initiation into carnal knowledge begins precisely with the provocation of the novice's preliminary curiosity about what "she" wants to do with "me." The female demon thus gains the upper hand in her first encounter with Monkey by promising to "teach" what keeps his mind wandering and wondering. The sexual prelude of "hugging," "kissing," and "hand-holding," albeit seemingly innocuous, engages Monkey's mind in a manner of which he himself is not fully conscious. An ambiguous moment like this invites endless speculation but remains unaccounted for in the *Journey*. It is Tung Yüeh, the master interpreter of the unconscious, who provides us a powerful rewriting of all the passages saturated with sexual innuendo into the discourse of desire. The portrayal of Monkey's repressed sexuality in the *Tower* indeed represents the first occurrence of the psychoanalytical approach in Chinese literature.

The few references in the *Journey* to Wu-k'ung's encounter with "desire" in various guises seem to manifest the distinctive feature of the ape legend—namely, the stimulus of the libido. Wu-k'ung's (mis)adventures in the realm of *se/yü* 色欲 ("sexual desire") invariably speak of a beastly vulgarity, an inherent ape nature, which has yet to be tamed and refined by the nature of sainthood. The liminal symbolism in the very name of *wu-k'ung* 悟空,

"awareness-of-vacuity," derives its significance from the paradoxical identification of *se* and *k'ung*. It thus evokes the invisible play of *se* with all its implications of desire, both sensual and mental. The folkloric image of the lustful ape has thus participated, however subtly and fragmentarily, in the making of the symbolism of *se* that is embedded in the name of Wu-k'ung.

It is worth noting that the theoretical possibility of linking the theme of carnal desire with that of the awareness-of-emptiness had already been suggested in a Ming vernacular tale, "Ch'en Ts'ung-shan Mei-ling shih hun-chia" ("Chen Ts'ung-shan Lost His Wife on the Plum Hill"), in which Shen-yang Kung 申陽公, the ape-abductor, asks a Buddhist monk about ways of relieving his uncontrollable lust. We are informed that Shen-yang Kung often visits the temple and listens to the monks preaching sermons on the doctrines of enlightenment. One day, the ape engages in a conversation with the abbot in the following manner:

> Master Shen-yang [the white-ape spirit] said to the Buddhist Patriarch, "Your humble disciple is unable to terminate the root of love and lust. It is all because the lustful mind has confused my true nature. Who could fasten the gold bell on the tiger's neck?" The Patriarch replied, "If Your Honor wants to loosen the bell on the tiger's neck, you could solve the true nature of the lustful mind—*se* is *k'ung*, *k'ung* is *se*. If your mind is spotless, a million of the ways will appear lucid to you.[8]

By means of the paradox that "form is emptiness, and emptiness is form," the *hua-pen* tale makes the ape-abductor a potential vehicle for spiritual enlightenment. Critics have disagreed as to whether the portrayal of Wu-k'ung is modeled upon this half-human and half-beastly monster torn between lust and the yearning for enlightenment. Yet whether Shen-yang Kung proves to be Wu-k'ung's literary antecedent or his successor, the lexeme of *se*, however deeply embedded in the tradition of the ape legends, has departed from the original connotation of sexual desire and turned itself into a liminal lexeme that engages in a paradoxical dialogue with *k'ung*, thus taking upon itself various other connotations of "desire" such as the Buddhist concept of "form." Although each ape character embodies a different connotation of the concept of *se*, both Shen-yang Kung and Wu-k'ung appear as liminal entities endowed with the possibility of undergoing a semantic and eventually an ontological transformation from *se* to its bipolar opposite *k'ung*.

Critics of the *Journey* in the last few decades have consistently focused their attention on the question of Sun Wu-k'ung's genesis: is he a native product, or an imported model? Those who uphold the theory of Monkey's indigenous origin draw upon the evidence of a local monkey-cult in the Fu-chien 福建 area that is known to have existed in the late T'ang period[9] and cite the ape figure in the T'ang *ch'uan-ch'i* tale "Pu Chiang-tsung bai-yüan chuan 補江總白猿傳 as Wu-k'ung's Chinese literary antecedent. It remains difficult, however, for this school to disprove the speculations of other camps that challenge the "Chineseness" of the ape figure in the cult and in the tale literature. For those who espouse the theory of foreign influence, it is tempting to promote as the ultimate prototype for the T'ang ape figure the image of the sagacious monkey-counselor Hanuman (spelled in other versions "Hanumat") in the *Rāmāyaṇa*, who, in his many transformations in the Southeast Asian versions of the Indian epic, is "virtually always said to be a white monkey or ape" and "an abductor of wives."[10] Although the moot case of the indigenous versus the foreign model has little bearing on the present study of the intertextuality of the monkey persona, it is worth noting that the ape model for the T'ang tale can be traced as far back as the *I-lin* 易林 (Han Dynasty) and *Po-wu chih* 博物志 (Chin Dynasty).[11] These sources should serve to indicate that miscellaneous indigenous Chinese legends about lecherous ape-abductors have long existed in the mountains of Ssu-ch'uan 四川 province. If the authenticity of the Fu-chien monkey-cult is questionable, the existence of the Ssu-ch'uan apes can hardly be considered a product of Indian or Southeast Asian influence.

Although the debate over Wu-k'ung's cultural/ethnic origin has produced a wealth of source materials that have contributed considerably to the important study of premodern Chinese popular literature,[12] it often obscures significant clues that may lead us to a different mode of inquiry into the "Sun Wu-k'ung" problematic. One such clue, long buried in the dispute between the two schools of influence-study and overshadowed by some scholars' persistent emphasis on the difference in intellectual capacity between the white ape-abductor and Sun Wu-k'ung,[13] is none other than the symbolic continuum between *se*, "desire," (carnal desire, or any other form of libidinal energy), and *k'ung*, "emptiness," which points to the relationship of potential reversibility between these two personae of the ape figure—the lewd abductor of women, and the Buddhist saint.

Furthermore, it is this same symbolic valence of "desire" and its dialectic interplay with *k'ung* that sheds a different light on the intertextual relationship between Wu-k'ung and his Indian prototype(s). I need not recapitulate here all of the attributes that earn Hanuman the title of original model, according to the school of foreign influence, of the Chinese monkey-disciple. It is perhaps the self-explanatory nature of both Hanuman's role as an ideal counselor to his king and the Herculean dimension of his power [14] that renders irrefutable the hypothesis that there is a Hanuman root in the making of Sun Wu-k'ung. Based on the theory of singular identity, however, such a hypothesis precludes the discussion of other possible intertextual variants of Sun Wu-k'ung even *within* the text of the *Rāmāyaṇa* itself.

The haunting image of the lecherous white ape, I would argue, helps reformulate the terms of Wu-k'ung's identity controversy and recontextualize our reading of Vālmīki's Indian epic.[15] This is to say that when we bear in mind the "desire/emptiness" Buddhist metaphor, we are inevitably drawn to the sensuous ape-king whom Hanuman serves with such loyalty, and who reminds us both of Wu-k'ung and of the licentious Chinese ape figure. I am referring here to Sugrīva, the king of apes, who, like Hanuman, shares all the Herculean attributes of a super-monkey. Kabandha alludes to his power, which can "take any form at will,[16] and to his possession of supreme knowledge ("There is nothing whatever in any part of the world where the sun shines . . . that he does not know").[17] In this account, Sugrīva is almost indistinguishable from Hanuman in his potential display of heroism and wisdom. We may also add that Kabandha's description of the physical appearance of Sugrīva's kingdom vividly evokes the paradisal imagery of Wu-k'ung's "Water-Curtain Cave" in his primitive days.[18] There are other episodes and references in the epic—those about the animal nature of Sugrīva, and a specific reference to the perilous venture of the ape army into a mysterious stone cave [19]—that certainly bring to mind the secular image of the uncultivated Wu-k'ung and his adventure into the Water Curtain Cave in the early part of the *Journey*. The latter reference, which pertains little to our present discussion, would appeal to scholars of traditional influence-studies as an important strategic locus of the intertextuality of the Chinese and Indian texts in question. Our interest in the *Rāmāyaṇa*, however, is centered on the first set of references—namely, on the portrayal of the ethical persona of the ape, which foregrounds the same isotopy of "desire" that we have seen in the Chinese ape legends.

Sugrīva's animal nature is revealed when he abandons himself completely to the pursuit of sensual pleasures, forgetting his pledge to Rāma after the latter has helped him succeed to the throne of the kingdom of the apes. The epic provides several detailed accounts of the nature of Sugrīva's self-indulgence:

He [Sugrīva] had achieved his purpose and gained the kingdom and was wholly engrossed with women. All the desires he had harboured had been realized, and he had regained not only the wife he had longed for, but also Tārā, whom he desired. And he now gave himself up wholly to pleasure. . . . [20]

The connotation of *se* as "desire" in its crudest sense is also seen in Tārā's [21] description of Sugrīva's state of mind when she is sent by her lover to appease the anger of Rāma's messenger:

From the fact that you are in the grip of anger, it is clear that you do not know the nature of sexual passion. The man who indulges in passion does not bother about the suitability of time or place and recks little of Artha and Dharma. [22]

It seems quite clear that the ape personae in both the Chinese and Indian traditions are incarnations of sexual desire. However, while the Indian text not only overlooks the ape's spiritual acumen but also sets up the category of desire in direct opposition to that of "Artha and Dharma," the Chinese ape legends, on the contrary, have evolved into ambiguous texts such as the *hua-pen* tale, which question exactly such an oppositional relationship between *se* and *k'ung*. The Chinese challenge eventually produced the *Journey to the West*, a narrative that transforms the earlier sensual and "half-civilized [23] ape into a vehicle capable of engendering its own opposite image—the spiritual and the cultivated—while recontaining all of its original attributes of the sensual and the sexual.

I would like to point out that although the ape figure serves as a significant intertextual reference to the liminal makeup of the stone monkey, it would be reductionist thinking to assume that the mystery of Wu-k'ung's spiritual identity has been resolved. There are innumerable links in the chain that are still missing and probably will never be discovered. If the ape legends provide a clue to the folkloric connotation of *se*, what about the second term in the liminal entity—*k'ung*—the shadow-image of *se*? How do we account for the association of the stone monkey with *k'ung*? The Buddhist metaphysical framework can certainly provide a general outlook on the possibility of such an association, but it fails to answer a series of questions that seem crucial to our understanding of Wu-k'ung's ambiguous status in the *Journey*. For instance, why should a religious folk hero be an animal in origin and a comic mischief-maker by nature? And why should he be an animal of stony origin in the first place?

The Liminal Folkloric Stone

The second question brings us back to the mythical stone that harbors a latent liminal tendency. We have earlier derived a set of such liminal qualities from several highly ambiguous stone rituals. Upon close examination, the stone monkey in the *Journey* reveals certain liminal features of the ritualistic stone. The stone ovum from which Monkey is born is described as being "nourished for a long period by the seeds of Heaven and Earth, and by the essences of the sun and the moon" (*Journey* I: 67). Throughout the early chapters, we find frequent references to the divine origin of Monkey's mighty power in such terms as cosmic hierogamy—the mating between heaven and earth, and between the two heavenly bodies (*Journey* I: 82, 87, 114). As earth and moon, heaven and sun stand for the *yin* and the *yang* principle, respectively, the liminal character of the stone monkey is indubitably displayed. Since androgyny, the coalescence of *yin* and *yang*, signifies autonomy, strength, and wholeness,[24] we might say that Wu-k'ung's vitality is inherited from this undifferentiated plenitude, a neutral and creative wholeness. It seems no coincidence that the stone egg from which Wu-k'ung evolves incorporates the same liminal emphasis on the interplay between heaven and earth, and between sacredness and secularity, as the ritualistic stone. The intertextual convergences here allow us to recognize how fictionality draws its impetus from the old and the familiar, and how intertextuality works its way into the production of every text, fictional or otherwise.

In addition to the transitional attributes of heaven/earth and *yin/yang*, the stone monkey betrays yet another set of liminal characteristics of the mytho-ritualistic stone, namely, the ambiguous status of "foolishness-in-sagacity." Wu-k'ung has been portrayed on more than one occasion as the counterpart of *wan shih*, the "unknowing stone," which contains the seed of illumination but is at the same time an inert and stupid thing. This deep-seated inanity of Monkey serves as the target of ridicule in several incidents. Lady Queen Mother addresses the vanquished Wu-k'ung as *wan hou*, the "stupid monkey," after he is thrown under Five-Elements Mountain by the Almighty Buddha (*Hsi-yu Chi* 75). Throughout the pilgrimage, he often provokes Tripitaka to anger by relentlessly slaying monsters disguised in human forms. At such emotionally charged moments, Tripitaka never fails to denounce Monkey for being *hsiung-wan* 兇頑 , "violent and foolish" (*Hsi-yu Chi* 161, 221).

To understand the relevance of such an inflammatory epithet—*wan*—to the religious symbolism of the *Journey*, we must turn to the concluding authorial remarks in chapter 1:

> *Ta-p'o wan-k'ung hsü wu-k'ung* 打破頑空須悟空 . (*Hsi-yu Chi* 11)

> To break the stubborn vacuity one needs to wake to vacuity. (*Journey* I: 82)

The meaning of *wan* in this passage takes on a symbolic understatement and reveals its liminal interaction with *wu*, "illumination," in the most succinct manner. Commenting on the potential liminal symbolism embedded in Monkey's name, the narrator elicits the paradoxical correlation between *wan-k'ung* 頑空 and *wu-k'ung* 悟空 . The literal translation by Anthony Yu, however, seems aimed at deciphering the pun on the word *k'ung*, for he bypasses the second level of signification based on the binary opposition between *wan* and *wu*. The reciprocal dialectics implied in this line thus calls for a different strategy of translation—a strategy that sets *wan-k'ung* against its shadow-image *wu-k'ung* in order to release the symbolic content of each:

> To break the *wan-k'ung*, the "dull-witted" self, one needs *wu-k'ung*, the "illuminated" self.

The paradox reveals the coexistence of the conflicting twin spirits in the stone monkey. The unknowing, stubborn nature, "Wu-k'ung"'s double, awaits subjugation by the enlightened true self.

As soon as one perceives the paradox of *wan-k'ung* in Wu-k'ung's psychic makeup, the epithet *wan hou* no longer appears an unmotivated appellation but takes on a symbolic significance crucial to our appreciation of the metaphor of the "mind-monkey." The association of *wan shih* with spiritual enlightenment has come a long way since the folkloric legend of the nodding stone (*wan-shih tien-t'ou*) became widespread. Such an epithet hardly fails to evoke the folkloric texts in which the crude stones move their heads in unison in appreciation of the scriptures on the doctrine of enlightenment. The mention of the epithet *wan-shih* conjures up the missing predicate *tien-t'ou*. Wu-k'ung's seemingly innocuous epithet thus builds up our expectations of his final enlightenment, and the pilgrimage can be seen as the enactment of the process of *tien-t'ou*, of how the unknowing stone moves its head in divine empathy.

If the ritualistic/folkloric stone holds one clue to our discovery of the stony component inherent in Wu-k'ung's nature, a thorough appreciation of his equivocal sainthood cannot be gained until the key to the puzzle of his bestial/angelic liminality can be found. This brings us back to the question raised earlier, namely, how can we account for the comic and mischievous nature of this religious hero? How can we make sense out of the absurd incongruity that a saint is at the same time a beast? It is worth noting at this point that the understatement of "mischief" is already contained in the epithet *wan hou*. Anthony Yu has in fact translated the term as "mischievous Monkey" on several occasions, while ignoring its other connotation of "ineptitude." Thus *wan hou* offers us an uncomplimentary profile of Wu-k'ung: he is both ignorant and full of pranks, a stony and beastly figure— yet ironically, this same character is capable of undergoing a radical spiritual conversion.

The Trickster

In his treatise on Sun Wu-k'ung, Victor Mair makes a perceptive reformulation of the problematic of Monkey's paradoxical identity: "It might have been that there were two *related traditions* concerning the monkey figure: one which emphasizes the monkey as a demon, evil spirit . . . and one which portrays the monkey as capable of performing religious deeds.[25] Although Mair goes on to suggest that both strands derive from the "representations of Hanumat in different *Rāmāyaṇa* traditions in Central and Southeast Asia," thus reinforcing rather than challenging the theory of single identity, his speculation clearly redefines the central problematic of Monkey's character discrepancy which calls for a new interpretive strategy. In the spirit of searching for such an alternative mode of inquiry, I will suggest in the following pages that the bestial/angelic liminality grows as much out of the archetypal characteristics of the trickster as from the "two related" but vaguely conceived traditions.

The trickster is a figure of the fantastic, whose strange conversion is celebrated as much as its immeasurable energy in the folkloric literature of various cultures. It is a "mischievous supernatural figure appearing in various guises in the mythology of many primitive peoples."[26] In Chinese popular culture, the trickster is a witty figure who emerges as early as the Six Dynasties. In the *chih-kuai* tales there are numerous instances of human beings tricking ghosts; one of the most sophisticated is found in the *Lieh-i chuan* 列異傳,[27] in which a human being outwits a ghost three times and makes a big fortune by selling it as a goat.[28] A typical account of this kind in the *chih-kuai* tales makes fun of the vulnerable ghosts and highlights human wit as the most efficacious antidote for possession and for a haunted house. It is worth noting that the early Chinese trickster tale celebrates a human victory over the supernatural and reveals a merrymaking folk spirit that is oblivious to the religious symbolism derived from the possible association of the comic with the sacred. In one tale, it is the sacred tradition itself—religious Taoism, Buddhism, and Confucianism—that bears the brunt of ridicule.[29]

It is not until the blossoming of the various schools of Ch'an Buddhism in the eighth and ninth centuries that the folk element of "wit" sheds its simple pleasure-seeking principle and evolves into its religious phase. Because the concept of "wit" in the Ch'an tradition is closely intertwined with the making and unraveling of *kung-an* 公案 riddles (Zen *koans*), the Ch'an provides fertile ground for the blending of the concept of "wit" with that of "enlightenment"—the comic and the sacred. Many Ch'an masters reveal their trickster guise inadvertently. Han-shan 寒山, whom Anthony Yu cites as being of the "Zen ideal type," is remembered for the biting humor of his poetry; he always appeals to his admirers as a comic figure wrapped in the aura of the trickster.[30]

The Ch'an "definition" of *chih* 智 ("wit" or "wisdom") is a riddle by itself. In an exchange with his disciples, Master Fa Jung 法融 (593–652) of the Niu-t'ou Sect 牛頭宗 is asked "What is wit/wisdom?" He replies, "*Ching-ch'i chieh shih chih* 境起解是智 [31] ("To dissolve the arising of one's own heart and mind is *chih*"). It is said in the *Ta-ch'eng wu-sheng fang-pien men* 大乘無生方便門, "The heart/mind does not move. This is the so-called *ting* 定 ["the settled"], *chih* ["the wise"], and *li* 理 ["the principle"].[32] The simplicity of all such descriptions of "wit" leads to the most fundamental tenet of Ch'an Buddhism: *chih-fa wu-chih* 知法無知,[33] "One who knows the Dharma is unknowing." All these citations should illustrate that in the epistemological framework of the Ch'an, "wit" is seen as a paradoxical and elusive construct that reveals its efficacy only during the momentary happening of its autonomous, intuitive, and spontaneous dissolution.

The case of Sun Wu-k'ung falls somewhat short of illustrating the paramount Ch'an prototype of "wit." While the folk persona of the trickster fades gradually into the Ch'an Buddhists' persona, which is "not-knowing and knowing," both empty and saturated, perhaps at best a being "without any face to begin with" (*pen-lai wu mien-mu* 本來無面目), the process of enlightenment that Wu-k'ung undergoes in the *Journey* seems to deliver a slightly different message—"enlightenment" is not only contained in our original nature (as the Ch'an Buddhists suggest), but can even be recontained after it has been lost. It is the task of *recontainment* that Sun Wu-k'ung undertakes in the *Journey*, that distinguishes him from the eccentric real-life Ch'an masters, like Han-shan. While the latter's paradise turns out to be the *here and now* (in fact, he has never left it), it is Monkey's loss of his paradise and his initial transformation into a fraud that make the second part of his adventure meaningful—the quest for sainthood.

It is the space between "paradise lost" and "paradise regained," which Monkey has to traverse, that leads me to argue that the Ch'an model of the trickster is of secondary importance in Wu-k'ung's psychic makeup.[34] Sun Wu-k'ung remains the "trickster par excellence" precisely because his dual nature as a fraud and a savior is a novel construct in the Chinese context. The theoretical implications of such a figure in the *Journey to the West* can be best illuminated when we turn to the explanatory model of Carl Jung, who examines the trickster as an archetype that recurs in "picaresque tales, in carnivals and revels, in man's religious fears and exultations," a figure who "in his clearest manifestation" is a "faithful reflection of an absolutely undifferentiated human consciousness, corresponding to a psyche that has hardly left the animal level."[35]

In Jung's cross-cultural studies of the common denominators of human aesthetic impulses, he discovers that the motif of the trickster has recurred time and again throughout the history of literature and art. The frequency of its appearance in world literature leads him to examine the phenomenon as part of the collective psyche of humankind. Like all archetypal motifs, the continual appearance of the trickster in contemporary literature as well as in ancient mythologies provides a vital link between the predominantly conscious psyche of modern beings and the predominantly unconscious psyche of our primitive counterparts. In examining the dynamics of the trickster figure, Jung discerns a pervasive pattern that seems to govern the unfolding of the character in literary texts. He calls this pattern "the trickster cycle," the validity of which is curiously attested by the liminal character of Sun Wu-k'ung. I would suggest that the *Journey to the West* provides us the Chinese representation of the same trickster figure that prevails in myths and folk-fantasies.

Jung studies the trickster figure presented in the mythologies of the American Indians amd the Christians of the Middle Ages, and in the more modern "mythologies" found in Grimm's fairy tales. In his commentary on the subject he focuses on a fairy-tale character, the "Spirit Mercurius," to demonstrate his theory. Under his examination, Mercurius bears out the trickster motif by revealing these fundamental characteristics: he has a half-human and half-divine essence, a prankish and sometimes deviously malicious nature, an obsessive propensity for self-gratification (in other words, a psychic constitution that is predominantly unconscious and therefore subjugated to pleasure-seeking whims), and a capacity to change his physical form to accommodate his desires; yet he is a sufferer as well as an inflictor of pain, and once placed in the role of sufferer, he will find the innate capacity to transcend his own devious and self-gratifying nature by assuming the role of saint or savior—suffering for the benefit of others. The progression in the characterization of the trickster from self-fulfilling egotism to altruism marks the transformation of the primitive unconscious mind into the civilized conscious mind. Jung dwells at length on the process of humanization of the trickster from a subhuman psychological state:

> . . . the civilizing process begins within the framework of the trickster cycle itself, and this is a clear indication that the original state has been overcome. . . . the marks of deepest unconsciousness fall away from him; instead of acting in a brutal, savage, stupid, and senseless fashion, the trickster's behavior towards the end of the cycle becomes quite useful and sensible. The devaluation of his earlier unconsciousness is apparent even in the myth, and one wonders what has happened to his evil qualities. The naive reader may imagine that when the dark aspects disappear they are no longer there in reality. . . . What actually happens is that the conscious mind is then able to free itself from the fascination of evil and is no longer obliged to live it compulsively.[36]

Like Mercurius, the development of Monkey's character in the *Journey* provides an interesting footnote to Jung's theory concerning the trickster cycle. At the opening of the narrative, Monkey is magically born from a divine stone egg. He is perceived as a quasi-divine, quasi-animal creature whose birth is significant enough to catch, if only momentarily, the attention of the heavenly Jade Emperor, and yet insignificant enough that he can still commune with the unconscious animals in the forest. As his character begins to unfold, we see the extent of his unconscious orientation. In chapter 2, when he seeks out the Patriarch in order to find the secret to immortality, the Patriarch asks him, "What kind of Tao are you hoping to learn from me?" Wu-k'ung replies, ". . . Your pupil would gladly learn *whatever* smacks of

Tao." [37] It appears that any sort of wisdom is all one to Monkey, whose mind is still essentially undifferentiated in its focus. Nothing in the unconscious is clearly definable until the light of consciousness retrieves meaning from it. And Monkey's response, as insignificant as it may sound, reveals the degree to which his mind is still childishly, or primitively, unconscious. In a mildly comical fashion the Patriarch deluges Monkey with testing questions concerning his interests, and in every response Monkey obsessively clings to the single notion of attaining immortality effortlessly. He is like an insatiable child who will not be deflected from attaining what he desires. At this stage of his spiritual development, Monkey's longing for immortality has none of the garments of an intellectual pursuit; rather, it is evident that he finds life delightful and merely wishes to prolong it indefinitely. In other words, his pursuit is more of an unconscious fixation than a desire to be consciously enlightened.

After studying with the Patriarch as a disciple, Monkey acquires the skills that befit the trickster: like Mercurius he is able to transmute his physical form,[38] multiply himself, and perform a multitude of magical feats. The prankster then ascends to heaven, where his unconscious whims get him into endless mischief. The events of the Peach Banquet episode further reveal the extent to which Monkey is victimized by the whimsical indulgence of his unconscious psyche. After he overindulges himself in the elixir peaches, Monkey casts a spell of paralysis on the fairy maidens who have discovered his shameful lust for immortality. Getting away gracefully from his first scene of mischief, Monkey changes himself into a multitude of flies that land on the participants of the peach banquet rehearsal and cast the same paralysis spell on them. He then proceeds to devour the full wine jars until he is completely immersed in the mental obscurity of drunkenness. All such pranks illustrate how Monkey is completely motivated by his overwhelming need for sensual gratification—here we witness the curious merging of the lustful ape and the trickster. The pervasiveness of his antisocial behavior clearly betrays the primeval status of his psyche at this stage in the trickster cycle. While speaking of Mercurius, whose resemblance to the figure of Monkey is uncannily close, Jung writes: "On the other hand he is in many respects stupider than the animals, and gets into one ridiculous scrape after another. Although he is not really evil, he does the most atrocious things from sheer unconsciousness and unrelatedness. His imprisonment to animal unconsciousness is suggested by the episode where he gets his head caught inside the skull of an elk, and the next episode shows how he overcomes this condition by imprisoning the head of a hawk inside his own rectum."[39] After the Peach Banquet episode Monkey exerts his own brand of animal unconsciousness by pilfering Lao Tzu's 老子 elixir pills, and in doing so, he further invokes the wrath of the heavenly host against him.

When Monkey finally meets the Buddha Patriarch in battle, we see a significant progression in the trickster cycle. His confrontation with Buddha is more a battle of trickery than of brute force. And in its final outcome, we find that Monkey is victimized by his own reckless pranks. Admonishing Monkey, Buddha says:

> A fellow like you, is only a monkey who happens to become a spirit. How dare you be so presumptuous as to want to seize the honored throne of the Exalted Jade Emperor? . . . You are merely a beast who has just attained human form in this incarnation. How dare you make such a boast? Blasphemy! This is sheer blasphemy, and it will surely shorten your allotted age. Repent while there's still time and cease your idle talk! Be wary that you don't encounter such peril that you will be cut down in an instant, and all your original gifts will be wasted. (*Journey* I: 172)

This is the voice of awakened consciousness trying to check the destructive and unruly impulses of the unconscious. However, the unbridled persistence of Monkey's animal unconsciousness overrides these corrective admonitions. And in stubbornly clinging to his animal nature, he falls prey to the trap Buddha has set for him: once subdued by Buddha, he is imprisoned under the Five-Elements Mountain, where he is left to suffer for a considerable time before being rescued by Tripitaka. This episode of his defeat and subsequent confinement represents an important transition in the saga of his psychic development, for Monkey, who has previously been the inflictor of trickery, is made to be the sufferer of his own tricks. In this phase of his character development we can perceive the beginnings of his humanization, which are precursory to the culminating phase when the trickster will emerge as a saintly figure.

The episode in chapter 39 reveals Monkey's psychic transition with the greatest clarity. In this chapter Pigsy takes revenge on Wu-k'ung for a minor offense by tricking their Master into believing that Monkey has the power to resurrect the dead King of Cock-Crow. This is a particularly difficult mission, for Pigsy persuades Tripitaka not to permit Monkey to journey to the realm of Darkness where he might easily retrieve the soul from King Yama. When Monkey complains that the task is too difficult for him, Tripitaka starts chanting his disciplinarian spell, sending him into excruciating agony. In his immense suffering, Monkey submits and thinks of a plan to throw himself on the mercy of Lao Tzu who can help him with a restorative elixir. Tripitaka discontinues the spell and approves of Monkey's plans to travel to Heaven. Monkey's departing words reveal a pronounced change from the libidinous animalism that previously defined his character: in a rare moment of sincere tenderness, he asks the Master to place a mourner over the corpse and goes so far as to say that he refuses to bring the dead king back to life unless this is faithfully carried out. This shift in character from pure self-gratification to the defense of civil propriety marks Monkey's denunciation of those dark forceful impulses to which he has long been subjugated.

Without delay or deviation, Wu-k'ung then fulfills his mission of reviving the king. Although he is treated harshly by Lao Tzu, whom he has offended on a previous occasion, Monkey responds in a controlled manner, marking a further step in his humanization. And in response to the king's gratitude, instead of persisting in his old self-glorifying boasts, Monkey attributes the credit to his Master in self-deprecating modesty: "The proverb says, 'A household does not have two heads.' You [Tripitaka] should accept this bow" (*Journey* II: 218). Here we see the trickster coming around in the cycle to the locus of saint or savior figure. The emergence of Monkey's consciousness is realized in his self-control and in his ability to value and satisfy others' needs above his own.

In contemplating the elements of the trickster in the figures of the shaman and the medicine-man, Jung provides the following analysis that bears relevance to our discussion of Monkey: "At all events the 'making of medicine-man' involves, in many parts of the world, so much agony of body and soul that permanent psychic injuries may result. His 'approximation to the savior' is an obvious consequence of this, in confirmation of the mythological truth that the wounded is the agent of healing, and that the sufferer takes away suffering." [40]

With the emergence of the metaphor of the mind-monkey, [41] and its gradual culmination in the final enlightenment of Wu-k'ung at the end of the *Journey*, we see the trickster cycle fulfilled. In light of this discussion, Monkey's elevated title of *tou-chan-sheng-fo* 鬥戰勝佛, "Buddha Victorious in Strife," is particularly meaningful for it speaks to the developmental process of Monkey's psyche. In essence, his conscious mind finally emerges victorious over the mischievous instincts of the unconscious. As the pilgrims draw closer and closer to their journey's end, Monkey's transformation grows more and more transparent:

> By then, Pa-chieh [Pigsy] was clamoring not at all for food or tea, nor
> did he indulge in any mischief. Both Pilgrim [Monkey] and Sha Monk
> behaved most properly, for they had become naturally quiet and re-
> served since the Tao in them had come to fruition. They rested that
> night. (*Journey* IV: 419)

In this description, the insatiable needs that previously dominated Monkey's character have been pacified by the enlightened mind. He has freed
himself from sensual attachments and achieved a state of wholeness and
spiritual clarity. His thoughts are concentrated and controlled, rather than
impulsively fragmented. Perhaps the best indication of Monkey's liberation
from the usurping tendencies of the unconscious is found in the symbolic
implications of the removal of the golden fillet from his head.

As one may recall, Monkey's curiosity and covetousness for the golden fillet caused his enslavement to it: his own desires and animalistic attachments
bestowed upon it its punitive power over him. Its removal at the end of the
pilgrimage shows that the rectification of Monkey's mind is what ultimately
liberates him from imprisonment. Thus in response to Monkey's request to
remove his fillet, Tripitaka says:

> "Because you were difficult to control previously," . . . "this method had
> to be used to keep you in hand. Now that you have become a Buddha,
> naturally it will be gone. How could it be still on your head? Try touch-
> ing your head and see." Pilgrim raised his hand and felt along his head,
> and indeed the fillet had vanished. (*Journey* IV: 426)

The disappearance of the fillet signifies the complete integration of the super-
ego into the psychic constitution of Monkey. Previously the fillet has served
as an external master over his unruly impetuosity, but with Monkey's illumination, its controlling function has been internalized—hence, its disappearance as an exterior ruling force. By the end of the narrative, with Monkey's
initiation into Buddhahood, we witness the completion of his psychic development, which began with the unconscious and ends in deified consciousness.

It is part of the Jungian hypothesis that the progressional development of
the trickster cycle correlates directly with the evolution of the human psyche from its primitive origins to a highly developed status. Seen in this light,
each stage of Monkey's mythological journey may serve as an elaborate allegory for the evolution of the human mind. And his quest is indeed that of
the mind. The trickster cycle thus provides the missing links in our investigation of the significance of Monkey's psychic liminality. Interwoven into

other intertextual references, such as the legendary ape figure and the liminal folkloric stone, the trickster archetype introduces a different stratum of signification into the image-making of the stone monkey. It is worth reiterating at this point that textuality is intertextual by nature, and that intertextuality sets before us an untamable series, a motley of homogeneous and disparate prior-texts, lost origins as well as endless horizons. Any single text, or even a cluster of homogeneous texts, is therefore inadequate to bear out complex imagery. For that matter, neither the folkloric stone by itself, nor the text of the ape and the trickster alone, suffices to answer all the mysteries that encircle the character of the stone monkey. One might argue that each of the three intertextual references sheds light on certain facets of Monkey's threshold personality. But no ultimate source can be sought in any direction without undermining the anonymous nature of intertextuality.

The discussion of the three intertextual references serves to remind us of the complex mechanism of textual production and of the multiple threads of intertextuality that are woven into an image as seemingly simplistic as that of the stone monkey. Such a critical exercise also demonstrates that it is the ceaseless dialogue between heterogeneous intertextuality rather than a single unified intertext that makes the stone monkey signify as it does. The subtle intertextual dialogue between the ape, the folkloric stone, and the trickster, in their production of Monkey's liminal characteristics, can be mapped out as follows:

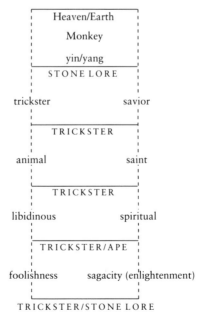

The occasional overlapping of the above liminal sets illustrates the law of mutual dependency characteristic of intertextuality. And the absence of a complete three-way convergence in any liminal series casts doubts upon the argument that an ultimate prototype of Wu-k'ung's psychic composition can be sought in any single source. Moreover, in view of the frequent interplay between the trickster and the folkloric text in producing Wu-k'ung's liminal personality, we may suggest that their predominant intertextual presence in the *Journey* may have accounted for the weakening of the third intertext—the lustful ape figure—and as a result, for the neutralization of the theme of carnal desire in Wu-k'ung's characterization.

The Knowing Stone

While examining the crucial role played by the animated stones in generating the spiritual awakening of Wu-k'ung and Pao-yü, I discussed the intertextual reference of the sacred ritualistic stone whose dynamic and fertilizing capability culminates in the spiritual potency of the nodding stone (*tien-t'ou shih*). In the literary texts, the accretion of the folkloric "enlightened" stone is manifested in the vivacious image of the "knowing" stone. Betraying the unmistakable imprint of the folkloric stone at intervals, the enlightened stone monkey and the mythical *t'ung-ling* stone come to embody a logical culmination of the primitive stone-cult. From the primordial stone of five colors, an inanimate object, to the sonorous stone chime, a sound-making instrument, and finally to the talking and nodding stone—the animate subject of divine intelligence—we can fully recognize the discursive and spiritual developmental potentials of stone. We can also anticipate that the verbal expressions of the folkloric stone, as found in the inscribed stone tablet and in the legend of the talking stone, will eventually evolve into a higher level of cognitive activity that gives birth to two prototypes of the "intelligent" stone—one motivated by an external human force (the nodding stone), the other informed, it appears, by its own acumen (the knowing stone).

The theme of the knowing stone occupies a central position in the symbolism of quest underlying the *Dream* and the *Journey*. As incarnate stones, both Wu-k'ung and Pao-yü have undergone the earthly form of existence and come to an awakening. In each case, the knowing stone symbolizes the potentiality for enlightenment. The fact that Monkey is born from a divine stone ovum already foretells his later illumination; and by the same token, the hermeneutic code implied in the title of the Stone Record signifies to the perceptive reader as early as in chapter 1 that this is a story of enlightenment, namely, of the "nodding" of a block of unknowing stone. The recognition that the intertwining relationship between the knowing stone and the theme of illumination serves as an important structuring force guides us through our reading and helps us identify and classify relevant thematic sequences.

In discussing the liminal implications of the *se/k'ung* paradox, I have shown how the Buddhist metaphysical framework motivates the theoretically perpetual dissemination of these two binary terms. I would propose that it is this Buddhist paradox of Form/Vacuity that interacts with the folk imagination and adds a radical dimension to the already existing liminal scheme of the nodding stone. The mutual reinforcement of the imagery of the illuminated *tien-t'ou shih* and the Buddhist paradox gives birth to the imagery of the knowing stone ensemble.

This intertwining of the *tien-t'ou* stone with the Buddhist allegory is demonstrated in the choice of locus for the process of enlightenment in the *Journey to the West*: for instead of Tripitaka, the legendary saint, it is the *stone* monkey who propagates the paradox of the Heart Sutra and thus serves as the very locus where the spiritual eye of the pilgrimage is located. In my earlier interpretation of Wu-k'ung's liminal status, I showed how the seeds of illumination are already implied in the metaphor of his Buddhist name *wu-k'ung* and symbolically impregnated within the stone ovum. This deeply ingrained divine root—the marriage of sun and moon, of heaven and earth— seems to account for Monkey's instinctual and precocious understanding of the sutra. And throughout the journey, we find him engaged in a continual explication of the *se/k'ung* paradox to his master, hoping the latter will open his eyes to the illusory nature of all the calamities they have encountered on the road. In chapter 24, Monkey evokes the metaphor of the "Spirit Mountain" which does not exist in an earthly form but stands in the inner recess of one's mind—the very source of the Void (*Hsi-yu Chi* 266). The discussion of the paradox continues during intervals between their adventures, sometimes in the form of elaborate philosophical treatises, and at other times in improvised aphorisms. On one occasion, Monkey roars with laughter, saying:

> "When you [Tripitaka] achieve your merit, then all the nidanas will cease and all forms will be but emptiness. . . ." (*Journey* II: 99)

In the following chapters we find Monkey at one time indulging in a lengthy explication of the changing phases of the moon as a symbol for the process of mind-cultivation (*Hsi-yu Chi* 411), and on another occasion making a repeated attempt to warn Tripitaka of the illusory nature of the six senses (*Hsi-yu Chi* 485). In chapter 85 he recapitulates the metaphor of the Spirit Mountain, pinpointing its intimate relationship with the quest of the mind (*Hsi-yu Chi* 959).

Monkey's spiritual rebirth is therefore partially fulfilled all along the pilgrimage. And he has died two spiritual deaths: one takes place at the Five-Element Mountain underneath which he loses his libidinous self, another at the divine Ling-yün Ferry 凌雲渡, where all four pilgrims witness the miraculous extinction of their earthly forms with a mixed feeling of fear and wonder. Seen in the light of the metaphor of "passage," death and rebirth merge into each other at a single moment in a scene of poignant simplicity:

> Immediately the boatman punted it up to the shore. "Ahoy! Ahoy!" he cried. Terrified by what he saw, Tripitaka said, "How could this bottomless boat of yours carry anybody?" The Buddhist Patriarch said, "This boat of mine
>
> > Since creation's dawn has achieved great fame;
> > Punted by me, it has e'er been the same.
> > Upon the wind and wave it's still secure;
> > With no end or beginning it's still secure;
> > With no end or beginning its joy is sure.
> > It can return to One, completely clean,
> > Through ten thousand kalpas a sail serene.
> > Though bottomless boats may ne'er cross the sea,
> > This ferries all souls through eternity."
>
> Pressing his palms together to thank him, the Great Sage Sun said, "I thank you for your great kindness in coming to receive and lead my master. Master, get on the boat. Though it is bottomless, it is safe. Even if there are wind and waves, it will not capsize."
>
> The elder still hesitated, but Pilgrim took him by the shoulder and gave him a shove. With nothing to stand on, that master tumbled straight into the water, but the boatman swiftly pulled him out. As he stood on the side of the boat, the master kept shaking out his clothes and stamping his feet as he grumbled at Pilgrim. Pilgrim, however, helped Sha Monk and Pa-chieh [two other disciples] to lead the horse and tote the luggage into the boat. As they all stood on the gunwale, the Buddhist

Patriarch gently punted the vessel away from shore. All at once they saw a corpse floating down the upstream, the sight of which filled the elder with terror.

"Don't be afraid, Master," said Pilgrim, laughing. "It's actually you!"

"It's you! It's you!" said Pa-chieh also.

Clapping his hands, Sha Monk also said, "It's you! It's you!"

Adding his voice to the chorus, the boatman also said, "That's you! Congratulations! Congratulations!" Then the three disciples repeated this chanting in unison as the boat was punted across the water. (*Journey* IV: 383–84)

With this concluding passage that arrests the ceaseless evolution of Form and Emptiness, the mirage of the liminal stone monkey is materialized in a frozen image where the *se/k'ung* paradox resolves itself by coinciding with the folkloric *tien-t'ou shih* in the single orbit of the knowing stone.

It is interesting to note that, like the *Dream of the Red Chamber*, such a resolution reveals a spatial concept of existence—a concept that is subject either to a vicious circularity by recovering the logocentric origin of the subject in crisis, as in the case of the *Dream*, or to a single climactic identification of the ultimate, as in the *Journey*. Both strategies close off the phenomenological understanding of the temporal mode of existence. As Pao-yü is returned to a static point of origin—a senseless block of stone—the pilgrims, in an even more dramatic manner, denounce not only their temporal being, but also their existence as single individual entities. What they leave behind after reaching the "other shore" is not only their previous sensual being, but that which differentiates them from each other. The symbolic death they die is therefore more than the death of ignorance. The chanting in unison and the identification of the corpse as the undifferentiated incarnation of all four of them cannot but reiterate the tyranny of homogeneity, since difference and plurality are now reduced to a single identity. The comic exclamations made by Monkey, Pa-chieh, and Sha Monk deliver a message that is not so congratulatory after all—the extinction of the boundaries between the self and the other, and the renewed consecration of collective, albeit spiritually potent, identity.

Thus however radical it may first appear, the infinitely extending liminal passage in the *Dream*—and, to a lesser degree, in the *Journey*—cannot, and does not, perpetuate its course within the narrative framework. In the case of the *Journey*, the *se/k'ung* paradox is settled at the moment when Form yields to Emptiness at the Ling-yün Ferry. And as I have argued in previous chapters, the possibility of the radical dissemination of Pao-yü's character is also brought within the confines of a writing tradition deeply immersed in the retroactive complex. Thus the narrative logic of "return" characterizes and predetermines the Nü-kua Stone's final destination, and in a less dramatic manner, it also foretells how and where Wu-k'ung's journey will come to an end. In each case, we witness the disseminating impulse held in check and eventually tamed by the nostalgic urge to retrieve and regress. The progressive narrative movement comes full cycle, and the indefinitely dispersed liminality is transformed into a *cyclical* liminality at the last moment.

Thus Monkey is seen as a divine stone egg that undergoes successive transfigurations—first into an animal endowed with human consciousness, then into a quasi-divine creature, and finally, back to its original stature of innocence, now in the guise of a Buddhist saint. Pao-yü emerges as a heaven-born stone incarnate that moves through different stages of psychic death and evolution until he reverses back to the earliest incarnation. In each case, the stone incarnate travels back to its original point of departure and enacts the metaphor of spiritual *rebirth*.

The circuitous tour of the novice may seem less distinctly manifested in the *Journey*, since Monkey's illumination appears to have taken place long before his journey is consummated and the passage at the Ferry simply adds a formal finishing touch to a fait accompli. However, this is hardly the case with the *Dream of the Red Chamber*. The cyclical nature of Pao-yü's quest underlies both the thematic and structural framework of the narrative in a much more involved and sophisticated manner. In the composite makeup of the Nü-kua Stone, we witness the equally intimate interaction of the liminal stone with the Buddhist *se/k'ung* allegory. The process of Vanitas's mock enlightenment through the maze of "desire" (*se*) and "emptiness" (*k'ung*) in chapter 1 already specifies the roundabout path upon which our hero will travel later. In the text of the *Dream*, the stone plays an even more crucial role in the cycle of spiritual growth—Pao-yü is born with a piece of jade that signifies the possibility of his eventual enlightenment; losing it results in the fading of his consciousness, and finding it again engenders a psychic rejuvenescence. While the choice is left open for the author-narrator to decide whether the retrieval of the lost jade will lead to a psychic saga that bears no memory of the Nü-kua Stone, the *Dream* fails the expectation of the radical reader by treading a path that eventually leads us back to where it starts. Thus each recovery of Pao-yü's jade leads him a step closer to where he originates—that is, to a gradual recovery of his lost divine wisdom. Throughout the narrative, we witness the potential dispersal of Pao-yü's liminal persona accompanied by, and finally enclosed within, the shadows of a circular motion.[42] It should perhaps be mentioned in passing that the continuous re-emergence of the varius incarnations of Buddha in the Indian *Jātaka* tales parallels the continuum of the life-cycles of the Christian God and the Greek vegetation deity.[43] In Chinese as well as in Western literature, the cyclical symbolism is religious in origin, stemming either from the popular Buddhist doctrine of reincarnation (as distinct from the Zen Buddhist doctrine of the *se/k'ung* paradox), or from the Christian myth of rebirth and the Greek Cult of the Year-Daimon.

Seen in this light, the cyclical resolution of Pao-yü's spiritual crises should be considered the natural realization of a predetermined mytho-logic, rather than a case of moral redemption, as Yü P'ing-po argues. Based on the deeply ingrained anti-Confucian mentality reflected in Pao-yü's early apathy to fame-seeking and serious learning, Yü accuses Kao O, the reputed author of the last forty chapters, of deviating from the original authorial plan by arbitrarily changing the rebellious hero into a self-rectified pedantic whose pursuit of the Confucian ideal culminates in his successful performance in the civil service examination on the eve of his spiritual enlightenment. Repulsed by the "didactic spirit" implied in the hero's later conversion to conformist ideals, Yü P'ing-po proclaims that the dramatic reversal of Pao-yü's temperament appears most unconvincing, and that it only reveals Kao O's own ideological commitment to Confucianism.[44] Pursuing the same argument, he interprets Pao-yü's spiritual transformation in terms of a reductionist moral scheme, thus completely depriving it of its underlying mythological implications.[45] The negative undertone revealed in Yü P'ing-po's critique of Pao-yü's "rectifying process" further extends itself to the critic's evaluation of the plot development in the last thirty chapters of the *Dream*. In the latter discussion, he questions the relevance of the loss and retrieval of Pao-yü's jade pendant to the narrative in general, thus dismissing once more the important issue of the cyclical mytho-logic: "The most peculiar passage in the last forty-chapter sequel is the episode of Pao-yü's loss of his magic jade and the monk's returning of the jade (i.e., chapters 90 and 116). Since the author arranged the episode of the loss of the jade, why did he make Pao-yü retrieve it later? Moreover, the coming and going of the jade was without a single trace;

it is indeed very strange. To put it in compromising terms, it is very mysterious; to put it in relentless terms of criticism, it is simply unreasonable and
ridiculous.[46] Here Yü P'ing-po is obviously baffled by the plot of "cyclical
return," not recognizing it as a phenomenon that is neither "mysterious" nor
"unreasonable," but one that can be reformulated in the spirit of the above
quotation: to put it in compromising terms, it follows the archetypal pattern
of the myth of the eternal return; to put it in relentless terms of criticism, it is
simply a reflection of the retrospective narrative tradition that always looks
back in nostalgia, and that yields to the yearning for retrieval and privileges
the original point of departure.

Chen Shih-yin's concluding remark in the last chapter thus hits home the
fictional logic of the *Dream*. It answers Yü P'ing-po's complaints with a rhetorical question that serves as the simple reminder of an urge that is as old as
the history of humankind itself:

> The celestial plant returned to where she came from, how could the
> *t'ung-ling* stone not retrieve its original form? (*HLM* III: 1645)

To recapitulate our previous discussion, the symbolism of the knowing
stone that underlies Pao-yü and Wu-k'ung's psychic makeup serves to demonstrate the sometimes subtle, and sometimes predictable interplay between
the folkloric text of the *tien-t'ou* stone and the Zen Buddhist paradox of
Form/Vacuity. As the potential reincarnation of the *tien-t'ou* stone, the
knowing stone reenacts the latter's liminal principle, while undergoing the
process of domesticating the radical implications of the *se/k'ung* paradox.
Thus while the fictional logic of the knowing stone makes possible the full
display of the infinitely regenerated discursive energies, it is also capable
of subjugating them by reactivating the all-powerful return impulse. That
which is progressing is often brought to a standstill—or rather, back to
where it starts. Instead of releasing the energy, the point now is to "restore
the energy." This is particularly true in the case of the *Dream*, where the
reversion in question appears all the more disconcerting since the author-
narrator has promised, and indeed delivered, such a merry spectacle of radical possibilities, before the nostalgia for the beginning sets in and encloses
what has been set loose.

By now the haunting resemblance between the two divine stone incarnates
in the *Dream* and the *Journey* seems to need no further justification. We
have seen how each is characterized by a dynamic capacity that gives impetus to the transformative energy of Monkey and the fertilizing power of

250 The Story of Stone

the Nü-kua Stone. The biological manifestation of this inexhaustible thrust of vigor is at the same time extended to the psychic field from which the stone monkey derives his yearning for power, immortality, and enlightenment, and the Nü-kua Stone, its will to live an earthly life in all its glamor and intensity. The story of their stony origin continues as each stone incarnate evolves into the image of the knowing stone that provides the pivotal structural framework for the quest of the mind.

It is important to recognize that while the *Journey to the West* serves to illustrate the intertextual constraints that the folkloric texts impose upon the "stony" persona of Monkey, the making of the literary stone symbolism therein has undergone a rather complex process which cannot be understood simply in terms of the generative grammar of the stone lore. A close examination of the paradox of the knowing stone in both the *Dream* and the *Journey* demonstrates that its complete intertextual convergence into the folk legend of the nodding stone has never been fulfilled. What comes to characterize the uniqueness of the Nü-kua Stone and the stone monkey is not only the simple revelation of their liminal passage, but also their *theoretical* potential of undergoing a dissemination that transcends the folk-formula of binary opposition in its barest and crudest terms. Any study of intertextuality is bound to account for two contradictory mechanisms at work in textual production—in other words, how intertextual citations manifest themselves in the dual but simultaneous operation of reiteration and transformation. In the case of the motif of the knowing stone, it is important for us to acknowledge that at its roots lies the haunting presence, sometimes reactivated and sometimes radically transformed in its encounter with other intertexts, of an ancient stone lore, whose devious excursions into and out of the cultural unconscious can be detected in creative ventures that traverse different epochs and different generations.

6 THE INSCRIBED STONE TABLET

In the previous chapters I have discussed the significance of jade symbolism in the *Dream of the Red Chamber*, and the folkloric character of "stone-intelligence" that serves as a point of contact between the Nü-kua Stone and the stone monkey in the *Journey*. We now turn to the other dominant stone imagery, namely, the inscribed stone, to study its generative power in motivating the cyclical narrative structure of the *Water Margin* and the *Dream*.

Both works illustrate a completed mythological cycle in bringing the denouement of the narrative to its original point of departure—the myth of the inscribed stone. The *Dream* in one of its many beginnings unfolds with the discovery of an engraved stone block by a Taoist monk, Vanitas, and ends with his reencountering the same shiny but now illuminated stone; the dramatic action in the *Water Margin* originates in Commander Hung's 洪太尉 excavation of an underground inscribed stone tablet and concludes with the descent of another such tablet from Heaven. The fictional logic of the *Dream* rests on the reenactment of the record engraved on the Nü-kua Stone, and that of the *Water Margin*, on the unraveling of riddles found on the underground stone tablet and the execution of the dictates of Heaven inscribed on the celestial tablet. The enigma-ridden stone tablet that precipitates the drama of the Liang-shan rebels also appears in the *Dream*, where it assumes a minor, but nonetheless significant, role. It emerges in chapter 5 when Pao-yü enters the Realm of Illusions and undergoes the initiation ritual at the hands of Fairy Disenchantment. There the hero's failure to decipher the riddles on the stone tablet serves as a prelude to his subsequent abortive attempt to come to grips with the meaning of the Twelve Register Books.

In both narratives, the solution of the mystery results, on the one hand, in the disclosure of the karmic operation, and thus, of the will of Heaven; and on the other hand, in the revelation (i.e., the 108 heroes of Liang-shan) and reactivation (i.e., Chia Pao-yü, the "unreal" precious jade) of the hero's/ heroes' true identity—whether that be meteoroids, or a piece of "authentic" precious jade.

The stone tablet buried in the "Subdued Fiends Hall" and the stele erected in the Land of Illusions are emblems of divine instruments that serve to mediate between heaven and earth. The riddles inscribed on each tablet are presented to human beings as divine oracles, the prophetic nature of which clearly demands interpretation and dictates devoted human observation. In the demythologized world, the Mandate of Heaven can only reveal itself to humans in paradoxes, the successful resolution of which may result in the reunion of the human and the divine intelligence. The mysterious stone tablet therefore serves as a challenge to limited human wisdom. In the fated encounter with the mute message-bearer, the human hero often responds inadequately or consciously bypasses it. Thus both Commander Hung and Pao-yü fail the divine revelation, as one (mis)interprets, and the other ignores, the ironic truth inscribed on the oracular stone tablet.

At the entrance to the dream territory, Pao-yü beholds a stone archway on which are written four large characters—"The Land of Illusions"—whose significance is explicated in a couplet of small characters inscribed on either side of the vault: "Truth becomes fiction when the fiction's true; Real becomes not-real when the unreal's real" (*Stone* I: 130). In light of the fictional logic of the *Dream*, the truth/fiction paradox, which is built into the name of Chia Pao-yü and points to the illusory nature of reality, proves to be an esoteric divine message that is beyond the comprehension of our hero. In the *Water Margin*, the failure to respond to the divine point of view takes an ironic twist. For while Pao-yü never reacts to the riddles, Commander Hung deciphers them in all earnest—but in his fit of human self-righteousness he fails to perceive the paradox that in meeting the challenge of interpretation, he will fall out of divine favor and become the arch-culprit for releasing the demon spirits sealed underneath the stone slab. What is revealed in this episode is a curious human dilemma: the Mandate of Heaven demands human interpretation and execution, yet at the same time it ridicules and defies mortal intelligence. Commander Hung is depicted as the victim of this paradox. Falling into a trap too ingeniously arranged to be avoided by any vainglorious mortal, he violates a divine taboo by faithfully implementing the heavenly decree. Thus, having fulfilled the imperial mission of searching for the Taoist Master to relieve the nationwide plague, the Commander plunges himself unconsciously under the wheel of divine machinery. Embarking upon a sight-seeing trip during his stay at the Taoist monastery, he comes to a sinister-looking hall and feels attracted by its mysterious aura:

> It was surrounded by a red mud wall; the entrance had a large red door with two leaves which were fastened by a very big lock. There were about ten strips of paper sealing the door, and these were all stamped with red seals; above the door was a board with four gilt characters, "The Subdued Fiends Hall." The envoy asked what the Hall was used for, and was informed that a previous Head Taoist had subdued many fiends, and imprisoned them there.
>
> "But why are there so many seals on the door?"
>
> "During the T'ang dynasty the Head Taoist Tung Hsuan subdued the king of the devils, and locked him up inside this Hall. The succeeding generations have each added another seal so that it may never be opened. If those devils ever got out there would be a great calamity. . . .
>
> Hung felt very curious at this, and had a desire to investigate so he said to the superintendent, "Please open the door, and I will see what this king of the devils is like." . . .
>
> The priests were all afraid of his great influence, and therefore they summoned servants to tear off the seals and break the big lock. This was done, and when the door was opened they all went inside, but could not see anything because it was pitch dark there. So Hung ordered the servants to light about ten torches, and with these he made a close examination. There was not a single thing except a stone tablet in the center of the hall. It was about six feet in height, and was resting on a stone tortoise which was almost half in the soil. On the tablet were characters of the very ancient style, and they could not make out any of them. But upon examining the other side of the tablet they found four characters which read, "Open when Hung comes." The Imperial Envoy Hung was much pleased at this, and turning to the taoists said, "You tried to obstruct me, but many hundred years ago they wrote my name here, and predicted that I would come here, and open the door. The fiends, I see, are imprisoned under this tortoise. Dig out the stone tortoise for me!" (*Water Margin* vii–viii)

So they remove the tortoise and unearth another square slab of stone, under which have been confined for generations the evil spirits of antiquity. Despite the warnings and protests of the god-fearing Taoists, Hung has it lifted up, thus releasing the 108 stars that become reincarnated as the legendary Liang-shan bandits.

In examining this episode, we are struck by the recurrence of the stone motif in the guise of the inscribed tablet and the apotropaic slab. Here we encounter the transformation of a folkloric image into a literary theme. That the stone slab is invested with the magic formula for holding malign spirits at bay unmistakably reveals the traces of the T'ai-shan Stone in folk legends. Placed at sites that are exposed to harmful spirits, the T'ai-shan Stone stands for the guardian spirit endowed with a mystic power to avert malevolent influences. Before the fatal excavation, the slab in the *Water Margin* has wrought the same spell on the evil spirits and bound them in eternal imprisonment. At this moment we may also recall yet another embodiment of such evil-warding stones in the *Dream of the Red Chamber*—namely, the precious jade pendant born with Pao-yü that carries the inscription "Dispel the harms of witchcraft" (*HLM* I: 124). Following this line of argument, Pao-yü's loss of consciousness can be seen as a sign of his affliction by evil spirits, for the loss of his jade amulet vitiates the charm of protection and exposes him to pernicious phantoms of all sorts.

It is ironic, I noted earlier, that the Imperial Envoy Hung cancels the charm of the apotropaic slab by following the exact dictates written on the stone tablet erected at the center of the "Subdued Fiends Hall." It is a familiar folk motif, however, that stone serves as the mouthpiece of Heaven. Innumerable instances of the inscribed stone can be found in the stone lore, bearing the same enigmatic verbal messages that evade human intelligence. In my discussion of the engraved stones in Chapter 2, I bore witness to the intimate relationship between the riddle-like messages and the irrevocable Mandate of Heaven. It suffices to say that the representation of stone as an instrument of cosmic design seems a remnant of the ancient belief that stone is a substitute for divinity. As the sanctity of stone gradually wears away, its affiliation with Heaven remains intact in the inscriptions, which emit an aura of spurious sacredness. The enigma—and sometimes, the nonsensical paradox—carved on the stone is therefore regarded by god-fearing people as the revelation of the will of Heaven.

The essentially folkloric character of the inscribed stone may have appeared self-explanatory in the *Water Margin*, but it has undergone a certain transformation in the *Dream*. We encounter in the latter not only two such stones, each exhibiting a different mediating function, but also the convergence of oral and written discourse embodied in the *talking inscribed stone*.

The magic jade pendant serves as a mediator between Heaven and Earth not only in the sense that its prophetic inscriptions represent divine communications with humans, but also in that it is literally a secular representation of the sacred Nü-kua Stone. Transformed by the Buddhist monk, the jade serves as the only link between the mythical and the mundane world. By fulfilling the mediating function between the human and the supernatural, the engraved magic jade betrays its folk origin. As we turn to the other inscribed stone, the Stone Record itself, which greets our eyes in the very beginning and at the very end of the *Dream*, we find that the folkloric imagery no longer dominates but often yields to the law of fiction-making. The Stone Record is, after all, as the narrator jestingly says, "a fictional account and an inept legend." [1] That the entire narrative of the *Dream* is derived from an inscribed stone record strikes us as not only unfamiliar, but also an improbable narrative device. For the eighteenth-century reader, who is best represented in the fictional character of Vanitas, fiction must subjugate itself to the supremacy of truth. Evolved from the historiographical tradition, the generic convention of narrative fiction up until Ts'ao Hsüeh-ch'in's time is still made up of various make-believe devices. Among these, the most familiar is the use of external narrators as eye-witnesses who truthfully record and transmit their stories, which are usually framed within a "discoverable dynastic period" to further reinforce their veracity. Like eighteenth-century English realism, which introduces such devices as diaries and letters, the Chinese narrator, in order to vouch for the truth of his fiction, is preoccupied with the task of explaining how a manuscript or a story has come into his possession. All such conventions are aimed at convincing the reader of the probability of the source from which a tale or a novel is born. Naturally, when the fictional inscriber belongs to an absurdly nonhuman category—namely, mineral— whose existence cannot be traced to any dynastic period, the narrative enters the realm of pure fiction, which breaks down all the literary conventions of the past and asserts its own "poetic truth" in the very name of improbability. Yet in doing away with the old literary norms, the author does not exempt himself from the challenge of justifying his claims to a different order of truth. The beginning chapter of the *Dream* therefore dramatizes this process of naturalizing the fictitious, which involves a critique of the previous generic convention and a defense of the authority of fiction in its own right—a procedure clearly laid bare in the debate between Stone and his first reader, Vanitas.

In responding to Vanitas's stereotypical accusations of the invalidity of the Stone Record, the Nü-kua Stone not only "cites" the stale old narrative conventions but also "exposes" them to a relentless critique. Taking stock of the vice of each popular narrative genre, Stone dismisses historical romance, erotic novels, and boudoir romances as trivial clichés, which the fresh note of its own story will revitalize. In the ensuing recommendations of its own fiction-making, we find the nonhuman narrator eager to assure the reader of the reliability of its story:

> Surely my "number of females," whom I spent a lifetime studying with *my own eyes and ears,* are preferable to this kind of stuff? . . .

> All that my story narrates, the meetings and partings, the joys and sorrows, the ups and downs of fortune, are *recorded exactly as they happened.* I have not dared to add the tiniest bit of touching-up, for fear of losing the *true picture.* . . . (*Stone* I: 50; italics mine)

This concern with making clear the origin of the story involves the process of naturalizing what seems strange at first sight. By appealing to our common notions of "true picture," Stone makes sure that the conventional reader will voluntarily suspend disbelief, come to appreciate the narrator's frankness, and be convinced of the truth of the sad confessions.

In arguing with Vanitas—the immediate reader of the memorable Record of Love—the stone is actually addressing the invisible general public, in the hope that a different orientation of their reading will facilitate their appreciation of this new mode of fiction. Here we witness another form of deviation of the inscribed stone from its folkloric counterpart, not in the sense of its narrative mode, but in the very content of its inscription. In other words, the fictional stone departs from its folkloric antecedent by assuming a mediating function that goes beyond that between Heaven and human beings: it is first and foremost a stone that bears human-made—or, one might say, stone-made—*fiction,* serving as the mouthpiece of a central intelligence that is no longer identified with the invisible Heaven itself. The potency of such an inscribed stone resides within the framework of a verbal transmission that mediates between the reader and the fiction-maker. The divine logic of the Mandate of Heaven gives way to the code of reader reception. The inscribed stone thus moves from the confined order of folk culture into a free and imaginative order of fiction.

These illustrations of the two inscribed stones in the *Dream* should serve to demonstrate that while the jade pendant reveals its affiliation with the folkloric stone by serving as the mouthpiece of the willful Heaven, the Nü-kua Stone, on the contrary, enacts the radical point of view of a self-reflexive inscriber and follows the self-regulating law of literature. One stone mediates between heaven and earth in the form of impersonal oracle; the other, between the reader and the writer in the mode of autobiography.

The subtle interaction of the folkloric conventions with literary imagery is indeed one of the many virtues of the *Dream*. It is a truly ingenious device that the inscribed Nü-kua Stone should serve as a means of exploring the possibility of self-conscious metafiction that exposes its own artificiality by laying bare the very process of fiction-making. Ts'ao Hsüeh-ch'in's experiment with the narrative point of view cannot be fully appreciated, however, until we bring to light another narrative strategy closely related to that of the inscribed stone.

In discussing the value of its own inscriptions, the Nü-kua Stone comes to life as an eloquent preacher who talks Vanitas into accepting the *Story of the Stone* as a "true record of real events" (*Stone* I: 51)—a paradoxical designation whose irony lies in the interplay between the "true" and the "false." In this dispute we encounter the double of the stone-inscriber, namely, the stone-narrator, who constantly intersects the written record of his own inscription. At those moments when the stone breaks its silence, a curious interaction takes place between the talking stone and the inscribed stone. The language-making capacity of the stone reaches its culmination as the role of the story-*teller* merges into that of the story-*inscriber*. And this combination of the oral and written discourse constitutes the narrative ensemble of the *Dream of the Red Chamber*.

The persona of the stone-narrator emerges unexpectedly in several chapters and interrupts the flow of the transcribed third-person inscription with critical comments of all kinds. The digression of Stone often releases the reader temporarily from the intensity of the human drama and reminds us of its authorial omniscience in the first-person voice. In chapter 6 of the sixteen-chapter *Chih-pen*, the entrance of Liu Lao-lao 劉姥姥 (Grannie Liu) into the Garden is preceded by the teasing remark of Stone:

> If you think that this work is petty and despicable, then put it aside right
> away, and look for a good one to attract your attention.[2]

While the purpose of starting a new narrative thread seems to underlie the insertion of this rejoinder, in chapter 18 of the seventy-eight-chapter *Chih-pen* the description of the flowery scenery of the Garden is suddenly interrupted, with no real justification, by Stone's recollection of its previous existence, a retroactive stance released in an outburst of sentimental soliloquy:

> At this moment I recollected the scenes that I once saw, lying underneath Greensickness Peak of the Great Fable Mountains—what a forlorn and lonely view! Were it not for the scabby monk and the crippled Taoist who brought me here to the Red Dust, how could I then witness such a magnificent spectacle! I thought of composing a *fu* 賦 of "Lanterns in the Moonlight" and a panegyric of her [Yüan-ch'un] Homecoming to celebrate today's occasion, but I was afraid that they would fall into the clichés of other banal works. Moreover, even if I were inspired by the spectacle greeting my eyes now, how could I grasp the ineffable essence of this splendid scene were I to sing a *fu* or a panegyric! And yet on the other hand, even if I did not compose anything, my dear readers would surely still be able to envision its grandeur and luxury. Therefore I now save my energy. Well, let us now quit this digression and go back to our main topic. . . .[3]

In chapter 78 the playful undertone of the stone recurs as Pao-yü recites the essay lamenting the death of his favorite maid Ch'ing-wen:

> When you gentlemen come to this passage, just take it as a joke, and it will keep you from getting drowsy.[4]

The sporadic comic relief provided by the stone-narrator is not always well motivated. As the continuity of the inscribed record is arbitrarily broken to accommodate the whimsical monologue of its "author," a discrepancy between the oral and written discourse sometimes takes place, and the dialogue of the stone often appears nonsensical and superfluous—as shown in the above quotations.

The most significant and justifiable "authorial" comment made by Stone is found in chapter 15 in which Hsi-feng 熙鳳 (Phoenix) keeps Pao-yü's jade beside her pillow for fear that it might get lost during the night. As a result, the central intelligence of the jade loses the opportunity to witness the mysterious rendezvous between Pao-yü and his male confidant Ch'in Chung 秦鐘 (Qin Zhong); and in faithfully observing the generic convention that governs the narrative point of view, Stone cannot but honestly confess that it is totally ignorant of the whole dramatic episode, thus leaving the relationship between the two adolescent boys purposefully ambiguous:

> As for the "settling of accounts" that Bao-yu had proposed to Qin Zhong, we have been unable to ascertain exactly what form this took; and as we would not for the world be guilty of a fabrication, we must allow the matter to remain a mystery. (*Stone* I: 300)

Chao Kang and Ch'en Chung-i recommend this particular authorial intrusion and regard it as an ingenious suspense-building device.[5] For the bypassing of the crucial information in this account not only creates the innuendo of a homosexual relationship between the two men (which, if explicitly brought to light, would certainly result in a breach of the code of decorum), it also obeys a fundamental narrative convention that dictates authorial silence in the absence of the first-person eyewitness. Although Stone's authorial comment rarely appears in such a meaningful light, the *Dream* presents a unique case of the ingenious transformation of two manifestations of folkloric stone imagery—the talking and the inscribed stone—into the single persona of the Nü-kua Stone.

The talking stone of the *Dream* deviates from its folkloric antecedent in two respects: it verbalizes its *own* speech rather than delivering a message from Heaven; and the miraculous aura surrounding the talking folkloric stone is now naturalized within the framework of fictional logic. The initial question addressed to the legend of the talking stone in the *Tso Chuan*—"Why does the stone talk?"—loses the edge of its irony, for the mode of intelligibility in the *Dream* is clearly that of the fantastic.[6] The talking literary stone is self-explanatory. Its verbal message is too articulate to require human justification. Why does the stone talk?—it thinks, therefore it talks.

In the first chapter of the *Dream*, we can thus find several layers of signification that reverberate within the semantic field of a single character—the Nü-kua Stone. It understands the meaning of its own story and demands that it be made known. Stone amuses us by talking sense and nonsense at the same time. It is above all the actor and inscriber of its own story. These complementary sets of talking and knowing, of knowing and being known, of story-making and story-telling, of making sense and nonsense, are all curiously intermingled in the complex ensemble of the magic *t'ung-ling* stone in the *Dream of the Red Chamber*.

The stone tablet in the *Water Margin*, which also serves as a curtain-raiser and, moreover, an enclosing narrative device, establishes with Heaven a bond of a different order. Critics often disagree as to whether the Liang-shan heroes are just bloodthirsty followers of gang morality or faithful instruments of the heroic code prescribed by Heaven. Modern readers often feel repulsed by the ritualistic vengeance carried out by the bandits. The heroes' intense hatred of adulterous women is especially hard to stomach because the sin of sexual indulgence invariably entails reprisals of the most sadistic kind. C. T. Hsia's comment on this aspect of the Liang-shan heroism serves to articulate the repulsion felt by many critics and readers toward the self-righteous "merry men" of the Liang-shan-po: "When such episodes were first told in the market place, they were meant to be entertainment and the storytellers probably could see little difference between deeds of individual heroism and collective acts of sadistic punishment. The continued popularity of such stories to the present day, however, does speak for a peculiar insensibility to pain and cruelty on the part of the Chinese people in general.[7] In the same vein of compassion, Hsia finds it hard to admire Li K'uei's 李逵 "calculated cannibalism" as well as Wu Sung's 武松 "impetuous massacre."[8] Yet however unreasonable the demonic fury of the heroes may appear to the sensitive readers of today, there is little doubt that within the framework of the fictional logic of the *Water Margin*, this particular code of heroism is endorsed by Heaven.

In chapter 47 of the seventy-chapter edition by Chin Sheng-t'an 金聖嘆 (ca. 1610–1661), the bandit chieftain Sung Chiang 宋江 encounters the mystical Goddess of Paradise 九天玄女 in a dream and is given three divine volumes as a token of divine patronage. Upon bestowing the divine gift on the hero, the goddess delivers the following dictate:

> ". . . in future you [Sung Chiang] can act as the agent of Heaven. In all affairs be honest and upright. In official affairs support the emperor and tranquilize the people. When affairs are wrong rectify them. . . ." (*Water Margin* 589)

This episode serves as a prelude to the miraculous descent of the stone tablet from heaven in chapter 70, which brings the novel back to its mythological point of departure and reveals the heroes' identities as none other than the evil stars released by Commander Hung from underneath the apotropaic stone tablet. The completion of the narrative in the same image of the inscribed stone thus ends a mythological cycle and creates a kind of textual symmetry that the 120-chapter edition of the *Water Margin* fails to achieve. Let us temporarily bypass the question of narrative cycle and the virtues of the truncated 70-chapter version edited by Chin Sheng-t'an and turn our attention instead to the tablet that falls from the sky as the 108 heroes are assembled at Liang-shan-po to conduct a grand memorial service for the dead.

The dramatic function of this heavenly stone tablet cannot be brought to light until we have laid bare the real significance of the sacrificial memorial. Sung Chiang himself clearly indicates that it is being held in order to appease the souls of innocent victims, on the one hand, and to thank Heaven for protecting their welfare and blessing their military feats, on the other. However, his reasons for undertaking the religious service go beyond these allegedly altruistic motives. The real purpose will not be revealed until the ceremony draws to an end. On the last day of the ritual, Sung Chiang and his subjects are seen united in a single-minded effort to pray for the divine revelation of Heaven: "All the men prayed to Heaven in earnest for a divine manifestation." [9] Their prayer, as well as the particular manner of the bandits' communion with Providence, betrays a pattern reminiscent of the ancient *feng-shan* ritual performed by emperors at the beginning of their reigns to consolidate their bond with the male sovereignty of Heaven.

As discussed above in Chapter 2, the royal cult often takes place right after the king has completed his exploits: he rules his kingdom fresh from his military victories. The ritual therefore stands for the ceremony of inauguration in which the emperor announces his success to Heaven and at the same time seeks divine sanction of his kingship in a symbolic communion with the gods. Sung Chiang's proposal to hold a sacrifice can therefore be interpreted as a self-serving act, indicating the same desire of a mortal chieftain to evoke the Mandate of Heaven to consecrate his throne. He is more concerned with ensuring the legitimacy and the future prosperity of his reign than with making offerings to the dead and being absolved by Heaven of the sins he and his brothers have committed in battles.

The *feng-shan* rite consists of the imperial prayer and the inscribing as well as the erecting of a stone tablet, and sometimes it also involves the sealing of jade plates that record the emperor's devout supplication to the divine sovereignty. The literary version of the *feng-shan* ritual in the *Water Margin* reveals its folkloric affiliation by placing a significant weight on the theme of the inscribed stone—which, however, culminates in a radical transformation of the original folk motif.

In the historical ritual, the petition of the emperor remains a one-way communication. Although aimed at soliciting the Mandate of Heaven, the verbal message sent by the emperor is destined to evaporate in a monologue. Heaven on His part always remains inscrutably silent. The fulfillment of the reciprocal speech act can only be envisioned by the pious petitioner in a private imaginary world. As we turn to fiction, however, the channel of communication is opened, and we come to witness a literal response of Heaven to the human prayer. The episode of divine disclosure in the *Water Margin* is imparted with such dramatic force that it is equaled only by the biblical episode of the descent of Moses' stone tablet bearing the Ten Commandments:

> About one o'clock a sharp noise was heard in the sky as though a huge piece of silk was being torn apart. Gazing upward the assembled mass saw in the sky a golden tray with two sides elongated. This was known as "Heaven's Gates Opened," or "Heaven's Eye Opened." In the bright gap there shone a dazzling blaze of light. Circling around it were clouds of variegated colors. From the middle of the lights came a ball of fire which descended on the first floor of the terrace. It circled round the other two floors and then went to the south side where it disappeared. The Heaven's Gates were now closed. The priests and leaders descended from the terrace. Sung Chiang called for shovels and spades to dig the ground where the fire had disappeared. They had dug down only about three feet when they found a stone tablet on which characters were engraved. Orders were given for incense and paper to be offered to Heaven for this gift. (*Water Margin* 915)

On the stone tablet are found not only the names of the 108 heroes of Liang-shan-po, but also the Mandate of Heaven written in a four-character couplet—"Carrying out Heaven's Wish / Loyalty and Justice Achieved" (替天行道 , 忠義雙全)—a sacred instruction that coincides with the dictates Sung Chiang has received earlier from the Goddess of Paradise. From now on we shall find that the heroes hold "loyalty" to be a no less important cause than "justice." Sung Chiang's secret wish for imperial amnesty has thus acquired a "theoretical" basis through the divine revelation. The fall of the stone tablet serves to reinforce and accelerate the rebels' voluntary conversion into loyal subjects of the imperial court. On the one hand, the tablet reveals the mechanism of cosmic design, for the identity of each hero is spelled out in none other than the meteoric appellation assigned to each of the 108 "evil stars"; on the other hand, the tablet is also seen as the emblem of a covenant made between these heroes and the Supreme Heaven. From now on the sanctified rebels will carry out the divine cause and execute justice on behalf of heavenly as well as human sovereignty.

By entering into a secret pledge with Heaven through the *feng-shan* ritual, Sung Chiang finally casts off the evil aura surrounding the meteorite-born. The successful performance of the rite, completed by the answer from Heaven, appears as a fictional device aimed at resolving the paradox that reincarnated evil spirits can project themselves into the virtuous images of high-minded heroes. By dramatically transforming the malignant meteor-oids of the prologue into the honorable recipients of divine favor in the epilogue, the author-narrator attempts to abolish the ambiguity inherent in the moral code of the *Water Margin*. One wonders if the author-narrator has determined whether the gang of Liang-shan-po should be regarded as violent bandits or valiant heroes. If they are to be perceived as invincible folk heroes, as portrayed in the *Water Margin*, the question then remains as to how best to account for their evil origin and for the narrator's earlier prediction that these released "demons" will bring calamity to the human world.

The only possible solution to this contradiction seems to lie in a genuine conversion of the Liang-shan heroes—but this entails the problem of how to convince the reader of the plausibility of a change of gang morality to the code of imperial service. If we recall how fiercely the gang have resisted the corrupt local officials and the evil prime minister throughout the narra-tive, it seems rather odd that a sudden change of circumstances would bring them to accept the decree of a previously discredited sovereignty. Perhaps such a conversion can only be economically and convincingly achieved in a highly symbolic manner. And the epilogue of the seventy-chapter edition of the *Water Margin* offers just such a solution—a clean-cut supernatural solution that dismantles in the most effective way the ambiguity surrounding the heroes' moral character. The symbolism of the *feng-shan* ritual is thus introduced. And the fall of the stone tablet serves as a powerful device for reinforcing the rationale of conversion. The deus ex machina manifests the Mandate of Heaven, to which all human beings, whether good or evil, sur-render in docile obedience. Seen in this light, the divine scheme counteracts the whimsical and contingent nature of the gang's nascent pledge of loyalty to the emperor. It revokes in an arbitrary, albeit self-justifying, manner the deeply ingrained evil spell inflicted earlier upon the heroes. Such is the fictional logic that underlies the work: only Heaven can retrieve the iniquity that has been sown by no other force than Heaven itself.

In the drama of the transformation of the Liang-shan heroes' spiritual and political orientation, the inscribed stone plays a crucial role that has drawn little attention from the critics of the *Water Margin*. In addition to its mediating function, the tablet dispels the evil persona of the heroes by imposing upon them an aura of sacredness. And apart from serving as an ideological instrument, the tablet performs yet another function that can be particularly held to account for Chin Sheng-t'an's controversial emendation of the 120-chapter text of the *Water Margin*.

Chin Sheng-t'an affiliation with the *Water Margin* is manifested not only in his prolific commentaries on the work but also in his revolutionary truncation of the original text to seventy chapters, combining the original prologue and chapter 1 into a single episode in the name of *hsieh-tzu* 楔子, "preamble." To conclude the narrative, he improvises an episode of Lu Chün-i's 盧俊義 dream vision, which enacts the execution of all the Liang-shan heroes by the imperial court. An extensive corpus of criticism has been devoted to debating the merits of Chin Sheng-t'an's monumental editing effort. While most scholars agree that the editor in question should undoubtedly be credited with the deletion of many superfluous and incoherent passages in the original text,[10] and that an apparent deterioration of the author's skill beyond chapter 70 has severely impaired the overall artistic appeal and the achievement of the first part of the work,[11] nevertheless, when it comes to the ideological underpinning of Chin's truncation, the critical response is in the main negative. There is general agreement that by casting aside the theme of the rebels' pacification, which dominates the dramatic action in the last fifty chapters, Chin Sheng-t'an revealed his own loyalist ideology and feudalistic moral sensibility.

In order to better understand the nature of this charge, we have to examine why Chin Sheng-t'an's deletion of the second half of the original text is seen as a highly complex ideological choice rather than a simple aesthetic one. Like all traditional men of letters in China, Chin was closely affiliated with the court and its Confucian orthodoxy. As a rule, his duty as a loyal official overshadowed his other professional commitments, among which the pursuit of a literary career was probably no more autonomous than the official one. Under the control of Confucian moral didacticism, literature never gained autonomy from its age-old cohabitation with politics. Even the best literary sensibility could not evade the haunting influence of the historio-graphical tradition. Chin Sheng-t'an was certainly not alone in experiencing the internal conflict of his literary commitment with the political one.

Going through his *Shui-hu* commentary, one is often struck by his conflicting moods that vacillate between sympathy with the individual bandit-heroes, and a resolute condemnation of their collective outlawry. His ambivalent attitude toward the Liang-shan heroes is best illustrated in the following commentary: "*Shui-hu* condemned only Sung Chiang—this is meant to punish and annihilate the ringleader. The rest of the gang was there-fore pardoned." [12] We can recognize in Chin Sheng-t'an a confusion of the role of literary critic with that of Confucian historian—for while he readily endorses the vivid portrayal of banditry by assigning to the work the honor-ary title of the "Fifth Book of Genius 第五才子書," he finds the idea of im-perial amnesty intolerable and blasphemous.[13] Living in a turbulent era when China was being torn apart by the rebellious forces led by two formidable outlaws, Chang Hsien-chung 張獻忠 (1605–47) and Li Tzu-ch'eng 李自成 (1605–45), Chin firmly believed that even a fictional treatment of rebels in a favorable light could further encourage the spread of gang morality, and that the imperial pardon of evil brigands was definitely a compromise that would only foster the growth of corrupt moral influence on the common folk.

Appalled by the description in the *Water Margin* of the royal peace treaty sealed between the emperor and the Liang-shan rebels, Chin Sheng-t'an de-cided to truncate the remaining fifty chapters to salvage the moral integrity of the work. His relentless condemnation of the bandits as a group is further revealed in the editorial insertion of the short dream episode that foretells the tragic outcome—a well-deserved one, from Sheng-t'an's viewpoint—of the rebels in the form of allegory. By pronouncing the death sentence on the 108 heroes in Lu Chün-i's dream, Chin Sheng-t'an has taken poetic justice into his own hands, and as a result, he has seriously compromised his integ-rity as a literary critic. Chin's ideological tampering with the original text is regarded as the most unredeeming quality of the 70-chapter edition. Hu shih's critique of Chin Sheng-t'an represents perhaps the most insightful evaluation of this kind of political enthusiasm led astray: "Sheng-t'an was an extremely sharp person, therefore he could appreciate *Shui-hu*. However, the literary critic Chin Sheng-t'an was unavoidably misled by Chin Sheng-t'an the historian who followed the tradition of the 'Spring and Autumn Analects.' He could appreciate the literary merits of *Shui-hu*, but he misunderstood the moral message of the work. Little did he realize that the truncation of the entire plot of amnesty in the 70-chapter edition is on the contrary more anti-authoritarian in nature.[14]

While political ideology stood in the way of Chin Sheng-t'an's appreciation of the 120-chapter edition, we may ask if his bold revision illustrates any noticeable aesthetic merits. Most critics agree that although the anticlimactic last fifty chapters certainly fail to "attain the artistic level of the early episodes,"[15] their relentless truncation is nonetheless hardly justifiable on the grounds of redeeming the overall artistic design of the work.[16] In view of the difficulty of defining such terms as "aesthetic quality" and "artistic design," I would evade this loaded critical idiom and suggest a different evaluative strategy: it is possible to reformulate the central issue that underlies Chin Sheng-t'an's editing as the choice of a cyclical narrative plot-structure over a linear one.

That Chin Sheng-t'an was preoccupied with the technical devices of the *Water Margin* is revealed in his discussions of the fifteen contrivances used by Shih Nai-an 施耐庵 in plot development and characterization.[17] For such a critic who deplored the general reader's ignorance of the art of narrative and propagated the subtlety of story-telling techniques, the structural framework of the *Water Margin* must have seemed a crucial component of artifice and have gripped his critical attention with the same intensity as the moral discourse underlying the *Water Margin*. It is most likely that Chin regarded his revision as a worthy cause in terms not only of moral rectification, but also of aesthetic merit. In his commentary on the last chapter of the *Water Margin*, the overriding concern with structural unity obviously emerges as a powerful rationale for the editing project:

> Some may want to raise questions about the divine message on the in-scribed stone as to whether it is true or fabricated by Sung Chiang. This kind of inquiry is in my opinion nonsensical and dull-witted. The author simply aimed at closing the narrative by rearranging and listing one by one the names of the one hundred and eight heroes—literally, "adding eyeballs to the unfinished picture of the dragon and covering up the pit." For to start and end with the stone tablet is the [completion of] the so-called big cycle [*ta-k'ai-ho* 大開闔 , "grand opening-closing"].[18]

As manifested in this passage, Chin Sheng-t'an is not concerned with whether the fall of the heavenly tablet is true or false, but rather with the fictional machinery of literature that accords structural unity a paramount place. The enclosure of the seventy-chapter edition within the mythological framework of the inscribed stone tablet serves to fulfill the self-generated drive of the mytho-logic of "return."[19] At this juncture, we should recall that both the Nü-kua Stone and the monkey-disciple enact the drama of birth-death-rebirth and bear out such a mytho-logic. In the *Water Margin*, we witness a weaker thematic manifestation of the cyclical grammar, since the earthly adventures of the 108 evil spirits culminate, in one edition, in unredeemed tragic deaths, and in another, in an ideological conversion that only ambiguously suggests the mythical "ascent to the new ideal state."[20] What Chin Sheng-t'an chooses to accomplish, then, is to restore the mytho-logic to the narrative. By ending the legend of the outlaws in the twice-recurring myth of the stone tablet, he succeeds in turning our attention from the unfulfilled thematic cycle of the narrative to a structural symmetry that bespeaks no less vigorously the developmental logic of mythical narrative.

Aesthetically speaking, Chin Sheng-t'an's decision to discard the gradual evolution of the Liang-shan heroes' tragic course can be seen as an unconscious choice to recontain the narrative fiction into myth. What he may not have realized is that by making such a choice, he privileged the mythic mode over the literary exigencies of realism and tragedy. We can claim that his editing of the *Water Margin* reveals not only his personal literary taste and political ideology, but also his choice for a particular narrative genre. The project as a whole should therefore not be lightly dismissed as whimsical, nor should its underlying artistic motivation be underestimated. I argue that it is precisely on that ground that Chin Sheng-t'an's literary sensibility and critical acumen can best be assessed and justified.

In the preceding discussion, I have shown how the motif of the inscribed stone tablet generates both the thematic and the structural coherence of the *Water Margin*. Such a tablet reiterates the seme of "riddle," "oracle," "mediation between heaven and earth"—all the dominant semantic properties of its folkloric counterpart. The double function of the stone—mediating, and message-bearing—is crucial to the evolution of the plot of the *Dream* and the *Water Margin*. There is little doubt that the myth of the stone tablet is not merely a gratuitous and "ungrammatical" occurrence: in its playful dialogue with the stone lore, it represents a rejuvenated literary treatment of a popular folk motif. It is thus not too far-fetched to conclude that the significance of the stone imagery in the three narratives cannot be adequately understood without examining them in the light of intertextuality.

The intertext of the stone lore reveals time and again the dynamic process of the transformation, accretion, and refinement of folk prototypes into literary themes. Our inquiry into the stone lore not only sheds light on the signifying possibilities of the sacred stone of liminal persona and the oracular stone tablet, it also exposes us to the moral and ideological discourse and the circular labyrinth of the narrative structure that underlies the three literary works under discussion. By studying these three texts as an ensemble, we encounter the recurrence of the stone motif in different guises. In the *Dream of the Red Chamber*, the stone discarded by Goddess Nü-kua acquires Nirvana and resumes its stony existence to tell its own story of disillusionment and enlightenment; in the *Water Margin*, the formidable-looking stone tablet that seals up the 108 evil spirits descends again from heaven to reaffirm the cause of heroism; in the *Journey to the West*, the sacred stony essence that Monkey possesses at the very beginning of the narrative foreshadows his later spiritual attainment. In each literary transformation, stone plays a significant role in generating the thematic and structural circularity of the narrative. The denouement of each narrative not only corresponds to, but also inverts, in a paradoxical manner, the initial state of affairs. Both the enlightenment of Monkey and Pao-yü and the revelation of the Liang-shan heroes' karmic origin have, on the one hand, nullified their ignorant state of mind as embodied in the initial situation; and on the other hand, they have also resulted in a return to an "organized" innocence, a mirror-like image of their original form of existence.

Given the semantic ambiguity of stone as an entity of both fertile and sterile, both divine and secular, substance, it is perhaps futile to conclude a discourse that perpetuates itself in liminal progression. Should we then emulate Lévi-Strauss's rhetoric by saying that stone can be viewed as a liminally structured property that mediates between life and death—an insoluble opposition with which the human mind is eternally obsessed, which it is impelled to resolve? Does stone then represent another "point of repose or equilibrium" at which human beings become more aware of the fix they are in and come to grips with the crucial components of all the intriguing dilemmas?

John B. Vickery, in his study of the literary impact of *The Golden Bough*, contemplates the issue of the haunting presence of the past and comes to an insight reminiscent of Lévi-Strauss's theory of mediation.[1] According to Vickery, the continual emergence of the mythoi in literary creations that focus on ancient myths/rituals is intended to achieve an existential as well as a cultural instrospection, and to not only realize the role of the literary works "in the ordinary, daily existence of their time," but also "to relate them to an even more remote and primitive past; or to find in them metaphors whose continuation into the present illumine its central dilemma."[2] The mythopoeic imagination reflected in the contemporary literary works inspired by *The Golden Bough* crystallizes in various guises the enduring dilemma of the cultural present that bears out the "anthropological vision of the primitive past."[3]

The issue of the claims of the remote and archaic cultural past on a culturally different present certainly poses an urgent question to anthropologists, mythologists, folklorists, and those in classical studies. We may ask, with regard to the particular critical practice in which this present book is engaged, whether the metaphor of the sacred stone that perpetuates its fertilizing efficacy sheds the same illumination on the philosophical quest for the significance of human existence. Or, to put it more specifically, whether the liminal ambiguity of the ritualistic stone that is both static and dynamic, unknowing and intelligent, earth-destined and heavenbound, serves as a metaphor for the insoluble dilemma of human beings whose soaring spirits aspire to tear themselves from the confinement of their fragile and mortal flesh in an everlasting struggle. And, most important, whether the fictional resolution of the ultimate triumph of the stone—i.e., the final enclosure of the *Dream* and the *Water Margin* by the discourse of stone—serves to remind those who dare to envision a future free of constraints of the weight of the haunting past.

This is the set of inquiries we can ultimately derive from the study of the intertextuality of mythology and literature. Raising these questions should not only help us understand the open-ended nature of interpretation—we can extrapolate an endless series of such speculations, the nature of which can shift from the purely linguistic to the allegorical, philosophical, metaphysical, and political—but should also reveal that any interpretive methods, be they *explication de texte*, semiotic, (post)structuralist, or mythological, will eventually bring us back to the ideological implications of the text under examination. The last question posed above thus emerges as the most fascinating and the most urgent, because the issue it discloses—namely, that of ideological enclosure—which has tamed the best talents of China's classical period, Ts'ao Hsüeh-ch'in and Chin Sheng-t'an included, continues to characterize the dilemma in which modern and contemporary Chinese elite intellectuals have found themselves. And most significantly, it is precisely at this last question that the two distinctly different critical paradigms— one established by traditional scholars of *HLM* studies,[4] and the other still under construction by text-oriented Chinese and Western literary critics of the younger generation—will eventually converge.

Nothing concerns traditional scholars of *HLM* studies more than the issue of authorship. Because Ts'ao Hsüeh-ch'in is generally acknowledged as the author of the first eighty chapters, and Kao O as the author of the remaining forty chapters, much scholarly work in the past has been concentrated on the study of textual discrepancies between the two parts and on the retrieval of Ts'ao Hsüeh-ch'in's "original authorial intention." Deeply entrenched in the perspective and methodology of traditional historiography, most traditional *HLM* scholars carry the heavy ideological baggage that subjugates the worth of a sequel (*hsü-shu* 續書) to the original parent narrative because the sequel is seen as epistemologically inferior to begin with. What is worth noting is the equally popular tendency among these scholars to condemn Kao O on the grounds of his political ideology. Wu Shih-ch'ang complains that Kao O turns Pao-yü into a Confucianist by forcing him to take the civil-service examination.[5] Yü Ying-shih, who is more concerned with setting up a new critical paradigm that would shift from an author-oriented perspective to a text-oriented one, nevertheless concurs with the general opinion that the "total meaning" of the first eighty chapters suffers "distortion" in Kao O's hands.[6] It is Chou Ju-ch'ang who stands out as the most vehement critic of Kao O, attributing the making of the sequel to a political conspiracy. He attacks Kao not simply for his betrayal of Ts'ao's original design for Pao-yü's final destiny, but more importantly, for his hidden "political agenda" for editing and completing the unfinished manuscript.[7] Quoting from Kao's preface to Ch'eng Wei-yüan's printed edition, Chou Ju-ch'ang claims that such an agenda can ony be defined in terms of ideological censorship, set up by the defenders of feudal ideology with the aim of "not compromising Confucianism."[8] He then speculates that Kao O was most likely commissioned by the power elite of the imperial court to undertake such a task.[9] Regardless of their differing degrees of rhetorical offensiveness, underlying all these critiques of the ill-fated sequel is the fundamental assumption that there exists a huge ideological gap between Ts'ao Hsüeh-ch'in the iconoclast and Kao O the conformist, and that the central locus of such an ideological difference resides in each author's professed ideological affiliation with or deviation from certain Confucian values.

The point of contention could then be summarized as follows: On ideological grounds, does Kao O's sequel deviate drastically from what Ts'ao Hsüeh-ch'in laid out in the first eighty chapters? To examine this question, I suggest first of all that we carefully distinguish minor textual discrepancies from the ideological ones,[10] since the former pertain to the issues of linguistic expertise and artistic vision and, although they should by no means be dismissed as innocuous, they appear nevertheless as a lesser evil than "ideological expurgation." Leaving the aesthetic issues aside, we can now focus on the central problematic posed by traditional *HLM* scholars. At first glance, it seems a convincing argument that Ts'ao Hsüeh-ch'in, who dwelled so painstakingly on the nonconformist mentality of both the Nü-kua Stone and Chia Pao-yü, would be much repulsed by Kao O's notion of sending his hero to the civil-service examination and making him pass with an unexpectedly high ranking. I would argue, however, that even the issue of the civil-service examination falls far short of defining the ideological center of the *Dream*. Just as "the subjective intention of an author may or may not be compatible with the objective realization of the meaning of his/her work,"[11] the notion of a single, self-contained "authorial intention" can no longer hold its ground. Perhaps the best political reading of the illusory nature of "authorial intention" can be found in Lu Hsün's interpretation of the *Dream*. On the ideological struggle of premodern writers with China's feudal past,

he offers few complimentary remarks. Well aware that even the most enlightened could not be exempted from the socio-cultural constraints of imperial
China, Lu Hsün draws our attention to the ideological paradox that is well
hidden in the self-styled and self-conscious iconoclasts. In the case of Ts'ao
Hsüeh-ch'in, he points out that such an ideological contradiction resides in
the author's deep-seated fatalism as revealed in the prescribed content of the
Main Register of Fairy Disenchantment: "the final destiny [of those maid-
ens] embodies nothing but a return/closure: it signifies the conclusion of
problems, not the beginning of problems." [12]

Lu Hsün's comment on Ts'ao Hsüeh-ch'in's ideological ambiguity coincides in spirit with what I have observed about the repressed ideological
centers in the *Dream*. A great deal of our earlier discussion of the jade
and stone symbolism reveals just that—the deep structure of the ideological
unconscious that the text itself represses, and reveals, at times. One such
repressed "center" that keeps reemerging during the course of our critical
venture is the return complex that celebrates the origin, defining it as the
pure, the authentic, the homogeneous, and, in short, as a singular recuperable identity. Instead of showing us the story of a stone that is caught in the
unforeseeable outcome of its adventures on earth, what the *Dream* enacts
is the recovery of the logocentric origin—the safe and predictable reversion
of the jade/stone double identity to a singular and lifeless block of stone.
What the Nü-kua Stone and Pao-yü himself come to embody is none other
than the idealistic mind-set that enables human beings to look over the whole
of life and to grasp its totalized order, to make sense of its origin and end,
to assume a stance of disinterest—in other words, to subscribe to the spatial
view of existence. This cannot simply be relegated to the global artistic vision
that the author conjures up in the creative process of writing fiction. Just
as the making of the fictitious is inseparable from our perception of where
reality begins and ends, so is the aesthetic deeply implicated in the ideological. In this regard, the deconstructionist notion of a free play of discourses
seems out of the question. What this book argues is that inasmuch as an
author is subjugated to certain forms of ideological constraint, only a limited range of signifying practices will ultimately make itself available. This
implies that Ts'ao Hsüeh-ch'in's Confucianist heritage and his Taoist and
Buddhist spiritual orientation eventually narrow down his choice of narrative strategy to one particular formula—namely, that of *fan-pen kuei-chen*
返本歸真 , "returning to the source and to the authentic."

I will not reiterate my earlier discussion of the Confucian obsession with the concept of origin and the privileged position occupied by the return complex in its overall ideological framework. What remains to be examined is the meaning of *pen* 本 and *chen* in the Buddhist cosmology; the Taoist concept of *huan-yüan* 還原 ; and the significance of the ideological correspondence between the Confucian, Ch'an Buddhist, and Taoist views in regard to our interpretation of Ts'ao Hsüeh-ch'in's narrative logic.

To examine the Taoist fascination with the notion of *kuei-ken* 歸根 ("returning to the roots") and *kuei-p'u* 歸樸 ("returning to the unpolished") there can be no better place to start than the *Tao-te Ching*, which provided inspiration for later Taoist alchemists who, according to Joseph Needham, envisaged a "thought-system" that advocates "a frank reversal of the standard relationships of the five elements" in such a way that "the normal course of events could be arrested and set moving backwards."[13] The embryonic theoretical underpinning for such an alchemical practice can in fact be found in the Taoist Canon:

> A myriad creatures grow and rise together,
> I observe their return.
> The growing and flourishing creatures,
> Each returns to its separate roots [*fu-kuei ch'i-ken* 復歸其根].
> Returning to its roots is called "stillness,"
> This is what one means by "returning to the essence of one's life.[14]
>
> Not departing from the Constant,
> Returning to the state of the infant [*fu-kuei yü ying-erh*
>   復歸於嬰兒].[15]

These quotations reveal that the privileged stage of one's life in the Taoist conceptual scheme is infancy, which exuberates a physical and mental euphoria that corresponds to the metaphor of the new(ly)-born, the pure, the spontaneous, the authentic, the uncarved—in short, the metaphor of the natural and the inexhaustible.

If the symbolism of the infant serves as a concrete manifestation of the Taoist fascination with the concept of "origin" and "roots," then the Buddhist metaphor of similar concepts is cast in much more abstract terms. Fundamental to Ch'an Buddhism is the doctrine of *pen-hsing*, "the original nature." Whether it is designated *pen-hsin* 本心 , *pan-jo* 般若 , *tzu-hsing* 自性 ,[16] *pen-hsing* 本性 ,[17] *chen-k'ung* 真空 ,[18] or *pen-lai mien-mu* 本來面目 ,[19] such a nature is seen as the pure and the empty. It is spontaneous and self-sufficient because it always and already contains the wisdom of *pan-jo* effortlessly.[20] Thus, "as soon as one recognizes and comprehends one's self-nature, one arrives at the Land of Buddha instantly";[21] and "if one knows one's original mind, one frees oneself instantaneously."[22] All these elucidations point to the single truth that the "original nature" is the same as the Buddha nature, which "neither grows nor dies away" (*pu-sheng pu-mieh* 不生不減).[23] Perhaps the best metaphor for such a state of nonbeing can be found in the last couplet of Hui-neng's 惠能 famous gatha: "it originally contains no substance / how can there emerge any dust?" (*pen-lai wu i-wu / ho-ch'u je ch'en-ai* 本來無一物 ，何處惹塵埃).[24] The metaphors of "cleanliness" and "emptiness" thus combine to characterize the essence of purity that the original nature is known to possess. In its underlying epistemology, Buddhism privileges the concept of the original and assigns its symbolic content as *chen* ("the authentic"), *ching* 靜 ("the nonactive"), *hsü* 虛 ("the empty"), and *wu* 無 ("nothingness").

All these illustrations should make it clear that Buddhism bears a certain correspondence to Confucianism and Taoism in its making of an epistemological vision that privileges the origin as the authentic and, most significantly, dictates the necessary return to the original point of departure. It is always the elucidation of the original nature rather than the process of enlightenment that forms the focal point in Buddhist scriptures. For the Confucianist and the Buddhist, and to a lesser extent for the Taoist as well,[25] the notion of "deviation" from the source suggests not only the inevitable fall into impurity, but also the dissolution of a totalized and homogenized being epitomized in the Confucian tradition as *tao-t'ung* 道統 , in the Buddhist as *pen-hsin/hsing* 本心/性 , and in the Taoist as *yüan* 元 , "the profound."[26] The issue of deviation is thus a spiritual dilemma for the Buddhist and the Taoist, and a social problem that carries far-reaching political implications for the Confucianist. What deviates must be brought back. In this sense, the popular idiomatic expression *mi-t'u chih-fan* 迷途知返 , "those who went astray [will] return," is imbued with strong Confucian and Buddhist connotations.

Returning to our discussion of the *Dream of the Red Chamber*, the fictional logic of *fan-pen kuei-chen* delivered through the mouthpiece of the Buddhist monk reveals Ts'ao Hsüeh-ch'in's triple ideological affiliation with the Confucian return complex, the Taoist yearning for the "zero degree," and in particular, the Buddhist obsession with the "original nature." The rationale that underlies such a logic is the impulse of rectification, whether it be ethical, spiritual, or religious. The fact that the major spokesmen for such a logic are those from the Land of Buddha (Chen Shih-yin and Miao-yü included) may lead us to take its formulaic content at face value (i.e., treating it as a self-justifiable religious truism) and may divert our attention from its deeply embedded secondary ideological implications. But it is this second level of signification that allows us to undertake an ideological reading of a fictional logic that, I argue, holds an important key to our examination of the Ts'ao Hsüeh-ch'in-versus-Kao O controversy.

If we characterize the fictional logic in question as the thematic, structural, and ideological center of the *Dream* all at once, it follows that Kao O has faithfully executed the original "authorial intention." We should note that such a logic is enacted as early as in chapter 1 in the Ch'eng edition, and it is clearly emphasized by the Buddhist monk in the sixteen-chapter *Chih-pen*. In the last chapter, when Chen Shih-yin informs Chia Yü-ts'un of the logic of *hsien-ts'ao kuei-chen / 't'ung-ling' fu-yüan* 仙草歸真 / 通靈復原 (*HLM* III: 1645), he is merely reiterating what the Buddhist monk prescribed earlier in chapter 1. This indicates that it is Ts'ao Hsüeh-ch'in, not the author of the sequel, who frames the entire narrative in an ideological framework that can by no means justify its total departure from the Confucian vision. The issue of the ideological discrepancies between these two authors should therefore be contemplated in a different light from that suggested by traditional *HLM* scholars: instead of condemning either author, or even both, as "Confucianist," we should recognize that as a socio-political being, no writer is immune to cultural and ideological constraints, and that interpretation always presupposes the working of ideological repression. For that matter, the ideological difference between Ts'ao Hsüeh-ch'in and Kao O resides less in their professed attitude toward civil-service examination than in the ideological unconscious that each reveals in his own writing.

This discussion of the ideological horizon of a literary work should serve to indicate that the study of intertextuality always extends its critical practice into the broader domain of politics, history, and ideology with which traditional critics in particular feel most concerned. In a much narrower sense, on the other hand, the study of the intertextuality of the stone lore and the literary stone/jade symbolism also illustrates the interplay between the deeply ingrained mythological consciousness and the artistic vision of the author-narrators of the three narratives.

The study of the intertextual relations between the mythic/folkloric stone and its literary counterpart demonstrates various literary manifestations of mythopoeic imagination. The meaning of the past in the present is an intriguing question that continuously engages the attention of the intellectual community of various disciplines. An investigation of the interlocking of the anthropological vision with the literary one must also incorporate the joint efforts of cultural anthropologists and intellectual historians. It is a domain that the present study cannot reach. Suffice it to say that what has been mapped out in this book elucidates only one aspect of the significance of the meaning of the past in the present. By bringing to light how the vast intertextual space of the three narratives is traversed by a corpus of identifiable myths and rituals, I have illustrated how the present is made intelligible in the reverberation of the collective (un)conscious. The vivid images of the Nü-kua Stone, the mischievous Monkey, and the enigmatic tablet of the Liang-shan heroes evoke the haunting vignette of the folkloric stone that is both preserved and gradually eroded in the process of its continuous citation in various genres of writings.

The infiltration of the ritualistic stone into the complex fictional discourse of the literary stone reveals how the mechanism of intertextuality continues and subverts the past simultaneously. Because no writer can avoid finding his or her identity in the ancients' while differing from them at the same time,[27] the traversal of conflicting as well as compatible intertextual homologues in the immediate space of a literary work creates signs of disparity as well as points of connection. In my analysis, the latent intimations of the link of the literary stone with its folkloric antecedent are often supplemented, and even overridden, by intertextual permutations of other kinds. The Buddhist allegory of Form/Vacuity and the archetype of the trickster represent two of the most intriguing intertextual models that undertake a shifting dialogue with the stone lore in generating the liminal complexity of the Nü-kua Stone and the stone monkey.

Through the close examination of the composite stone symbolism in the three narratives, I have shown that the stone lore is not merely a stable remnant of a bygone monument, it is also a shifting intermixture that renews its vitality through the continuous assimilation of other pertinent materials. It is a process of self-renewal by means of transformation and multiplication—a process that every viable symbol and text undergoes in order to resist total immersion in the powerful matrix of a metalanguage that divests creativity of its uniqueness and homogenizes irregularities in the name of convention.

This continuous struggle against enclosure finds its most poignant illustration in the contradictions that the stone myth evokes in the *Dream of the Red*

Chamber. As a frame-device, the myth of the Nü-kua Stone regulates the narrative movement and predicts Pao-yü's return to its point of origin. Any frame-device in fact guarantees the circularity of narration. But the *Dream* is not concerned merely with the myth of a rock, but also with the rise and fall of a "precious jade." It is the integration of the jade motif that situates the narrative in a double bind: is Pao-yü a free subject under his own influence, or an agent manipulated by the divine scheme?

The tragic dimension of the *Dream* achieves its depth and magnitude because of the structural tension that exists between stone and jade, between the divine and the secular, between the myth of stone and the drama of an individual. Pao-yü's tragedy consists not only in the perpetual struggle of a heterogeneous entity (elements of stone intermingled with those of jade) in search of an elusive totality, but also in his doomed struggle against the enclosure of a fictional device that continually defeats the autonomous evolution of the hero as a *self*-contradictory human subject. By starting the *Dream* with the myth of stone, the narrator triggers the process of paradox: in portraying Pao-yü, should he stress process rather than identity, his ongoing struggle rather than a recuperable structure? Is it possible to allow Pao-yü to evolve his own identity out of the unpredictable dialogue between jade and stone? Or should Pao-yü be subordinated to the structural limitations imposed by the stone framer that waits to cancel his split subjectivity by returning it to a single static identity—namely, a piece of stone lying immobile and resigned at some mythic locale?

The structural tension between the divine myth and the human drama gives rise to a discrepancy in the narrative that often raises doubts about the effectiveness of the mythical framework in question. But it is precisely this tension of the incompatible scale of things that creates the depth and complexity that characterize monumental works such as the *Dream of the Red Chamber*. By the same token, it is the absence of such a contradictory vision that transforms a potentially viable beginning in the *Journey* into a fortuitous and less-motivated frame-device. Wu K'ung's divine stone ovum reminds us of the homogeneous identity of the primordial stone of fertility. It remains such—the verbatim citation of an image that has turned static because of its imagistic purity. The comparison between these two mythical frameworks suggests that the more heterogeneous and contradictory elements a discourse appropriates, the more multiplied its signifying practices, and the more enduring its appeal.

The nature of this appropriation that takes place in every discourse reiterates the underlying principle of the trigram: "Phenomena are entangled with one another [*wu hsiang-tsa*], this is called '*wen*' (pattern/text)."[28] Whether cast in the Chinese metaphor of *tsa* 雜 ("mixture/entanglement"), or in Wittgenstein's metaphor of the thread, the concept of textuality tells the same story: it is a heterogeneous assemblage—it is intertextual. Just as the strength of the thread "does not reside in the fact that some one fibre runs through its whole length, but in the overlapping of many fibres,"[29] so should our attempt at highlighting the semantic play of the stone lore in the three narratives not be taken as a claim to the uniformity of signification. The encounter between a preexisting network of meaning and an idiosyncratic creative genius does not end in the absolute domination of one over the other. It embodies the subtle interplay, in Gérard Genette's terms, between the "infinite shock" that an individual talent provokes and the fulfilled expectations that convention perpetuates.[30] In this study of the topos of stone, intertextuality does not merely serve to provide a contextual framework of meaning that penetrates the density of a text in order to reach "what remains silently anterior to it"[31]—most important of all, it also makes the text "emerge in its own complexity" and tell its own story of how meaning is shifted and differentiated in its flight toward playfulness.

Abbreviations

Chih-yen Chai	Yü P'ing-po, *Chih-yen Chai "Hung-lou Meng" chi-p'ing*
CKKTSH	Yüan K'o, *Chung-kuo ku-tai shen-hua*
HLM	Ts'ao and Kao, *Hung-lou Meng*
HLMC	I Su, *"Hung-lou Meng" chüan*
HLM hsin-pien	Chao and Ch'en, *"Hung-lou Meng" yen-chiu hsin-pien*
HNT	Liu An, *Huai-nan-tzu*
Hsi-yu Chi	Wu Ch'eng-en, *Hsi-yu Chi*
HWHHLC	*Hai-wai hung-hsüeh lun-chi*
Journey	Wu Ch'eng-en, *Journey to the West*
KSH	Yüan K'o, *Ku shen-hua hsüan-shih*
Rāmāyaṇa	Vālmīki, *Srimad Vālmīki Rāmāyaṇa*
SCHCKC	Takigawa, *"Shih Chi" hui-chu k'ao-ch'eng*
SHC	*Shan-hai-ching*
SHCCC	Hung Pei-chiang, *"Shan-hai-ching" chiao-chu*
SHTLHP	*"Shui-hu" tzu-liao hui-pien*
Shuo-wen	Hsü Shen, *Shuo-wen chieh-tzu*
SPLC	*"Shih Pen" liang-chung*
SSCCS	*Shih-san-ching chu-shu*
Stone	Cao and Gao, *Story of the Stone*
TCC	Ch'en Yao-wen, *T'ien-chung chi*
TCSSCCW	*Tuan-chu "Shih-san Ching" ching-wen*
TPKC	*T'ai-p'ing kuang-chi*
TPYL	*T'ai-p'ing yü-lan*
Water Margin	Shih Nai-an, *Water Margin*

1 Intertextuality and Interpretation

1 Shih Nai-an, *Water Margin* (hereafter *Water Margin*), trans. J. H. Jackson, prologue (n. pag.).
2 Wu Ch'eng-en, *Journey to the West* (hereafter *Journey*), trans. Anthony C. Yu, I: 67.
3 Cao Xueqin and Gao E, *The Story of the Stone* (hereafter *Stone*), trans. David Hawkes (I–III) and John Minford (IV–V), I: 47. While relying on the translations by Jackson, Yu, Hawkes, and Minford, I have also rendered my own translation whenever a different interpretation of the original text appears preferable.
4 Kristeva, *Semeiotiké*, 146; according to Kristeva, "tout texte se construit comme mosaïque de citations, tout texte est absorption et transformation d'un autre texte."
5 This is hardly the place to deliver a full-length treatise on the modern understanding of a "text." However, for those traditionalists to whom a text means something identical to a "work" bound between two covers (and hence the conception of "intertextuality" means nothing more than the study of the relationship between two specific written samples), a more elaborate discussion of the issue is in order. First of all, it is crucial to differentiate the traditional concept of "text" from the one to which I subscribe in this book. The traditional concept of a text as a self-contained entity with a beginning and an end, self-evident between covers, and distinguishable by a title, has long been questioned by post-structuralists. Jacques Derrida and Roland Barthes provide the best footnotes on the evolution of the concept of "text" from a self-sufficient and finite product to an open-ended field of signifying process. The following quotations should provide some clues to the new understanding of a text: (1) ". . . a 'text' is no longer a finished corpus of writing . . . but a differential network, a fabric of traces referring endlessly to something other than itself, to other differential traces" (Derrida, "Living On/Border Lines" 84). (2) Barthes's classic definition of "work" versus "text" is worth quoting at some length because of its significance to contemporary theories: "One must take particular care not to say that works are classical while texts are avant-garde. Distinguishing them is not a matter of establishing a crude list in the name of modernity. . . . A very ancient work can contain 'some text,' while many products of contemporary literature are not texts at all. The difference is as follows: the work is concrete, occupying a portion of book-space (in a library, for example); the Text, on the other hand, is a methodological field. . . . While the work is held in the hand, the Text is held in language. . . . It follows that the Text cannot stop, at the end of a library shelf, for example; the constitutive movement of the Text is a *traversal* [traversée]: it can cut across a work, several works" (Barthes, "From Work to Text" 74–75). These illustrations should make it clear that a text is situated in an endless chain of semiosis. In other words, it contains different signifying structures that open it up constantly to an "outside" that is "never properly external to it" (John Frow, "Intertextuality and Ontology," in Worton and Still 48–49).

If some complain that this new concept of "text" is an imported critical category alien to the Chinese writing convention, I would argue that the earliest appearance of the notion of *wen* 文 (*wen* contains the earliest concept of the Chinese script and signifies a wide spectrum of meanings: script / sign / pattern / configuration / text / textuality / literature / culture) in the "Hsi-tz'u" Commentaries 繫辭 (the most authoritative among the ten

Confucian Commentaries on the *I Ching*) by no means suggests that the Chinese concept of "script/text" is from the very beginning enclosed within the boundary of the monologic written space. The origin of *wen* is found in a myth recorded in the "Hsi-tz'u": "When in early antiquity Pao Hsi Shih 包犧氏 ruled the world, he looked upward and contemplated the images in the heavens; he looked downward and contemplated the patterns on earth. He contemplated the markings of birds and beasts and the adaptations to the regions. He proceeded directly from himself and indirectly from objects. Thus he invented the eight trigrams in order to enter into a connection with the virtues of the light of the gods and to regulate the conditons of all beings" ("Hsi-tz'u" II: 8/3b).

This frequently cited passage seems to support the widely held view that the birth of script is generated by the analogical mode of thinking. It is indeed this fateful Confucian analogy between *t'ien-wen* 天文 ("the signs of heaven [earth and nature]") and *jen-wen* 人文 ("the configurations of human beings") that reduces Pao Hsi's original vision of an infinitude of semiotic happenings in nature—mysterious "markings of birds and beasts," and the kaleidoscopic vista of the "images" of sun and moon—to something equivalent to a closed "outside," a superstructure that is not only capable of determining the human base structure, but is also self-determined as a finished product. But *t'ien-wen* contains within itself both the real and the symbolic, the base and the superstructure, and only when it is brought to serve as the model for *jen-wen* does it begin its descending journey from the open space of plurality to that of *wen-te* 文德, *wen-t'i* 文體, and *wen-chang* 文章 —concepts that cancel out the ambiguity and fluidity of the innate (a)moral and spatial vision of *t'ien-wen*. This discussion does not bring us to the conclusion that the Chinese concept of *wen* and the post-structuralist term "text" can be considered and evaluated in equal terms. It only serves to illustrate that while Pao Hsi's unconstrained vision of *t'ien-wen* can be seen as a prototype for *jen-wen*, it at the same time problematizes the very logic of the self-containedness of the latter. The working of the analogical metaphor should suggest something other than what the Confucian commentaries imply. It suggests the opening up of the conceptual category of the twin image of *t'ien-wen—jen-wen*—"the written configurations of human beings."

6 "Kuei-mei 歸妹," *Chou-i cheng-i* 5/19a. This quotation is taken from the Confucian commentary "T'uan Chuan" 彖傳 ("Commentary on the Decision") on Hexagram "Kuei Mei" in the *I Ching*. The metaphor of marriage and sexuality seems self-explanatory here. Richard Wilhelm's annotation on this particular entry of the "T'uan Chuan" Commentary provides further insight into the significant connection between human and cosmic sexuality underlying the hexagram: "Heaven, *Ch'ien* 乾, has withdrawn to the northwest, and the eldest son, *Chen* 震, in the east, is the originator of life. The earth, *K'un* 坤, has withdrawn to the southwest, and the youngest daughter, *Tui* 兌, in the west, presides over harvest and birth. Thus the present hexagram indicates the cosmic order of the relations of the sexes and the cycle of life" (R. Wilhelm 665).

The same concept of the relationship between pattern-making and sexuality is indicated in the "T'uan Chuan" Commentary on Hexagram "Kou" 姤 (the character *kou* certainly carries the connotations of sexual encounter, if not the consummation of marriage): "When heaven encounters earth, all things are settled into distinct patterns" (*Chou-i cheng-i* 5/3a.) The commentaries quoted here on both hexagrams carry the notion of *wen* beyond its mental configuration into that of a sensual body. Whether *wen* is seen as cosmic order or pattern of things—imperceivable and intangible—we should nevertheless be reminded that such abstraction is sometimes cast in the concrete imagery of "marriage," and naturally, in that of sexuality of the body.

It is worth mentioning that in the Western tradition "intertextuality" as a poststructuralist idiom also contains the connotations of "intersexuality." Roland Barthes is the most notable theorist elucidating the intertwining of these two concepts. His attempt at eroticizing "intertextuality" is seen in his theory of the reversible figure of body-as-text/ text-as-body, in his earlier image for the writer as a prostitute at the crossroads of discourse, and in his idea of conducting a series of "promiscuous" relationships with the discourses of his day. See Barthes, *Roland Barthes*, and *Pleasure of the Text*. Also see Diana Knight, "Roland Barthes: An Intertextual Figure," in Worton and Still 92–107. In the *I Ching*, there are other passages that emphasize the interchange between cosmic and human pattern in metaphors of sensuality and sexuality. Controversial as it may sound to many, it is a phenomenon worthy of our attention and exploration.

7   Chiang Shu-yung 113 (quoting Chu Hsi).

8   "Hsi-tz'u" II: 8/13b.

9   Tso-ch'iu Ming, *Kuo Yü* II: 16/516.

10   Wu Chün 2/7a.

11   It is worth noting that the vague Chinese notion of intertextuality has undergone its gradual evolution simultaneously with that of textuality. Both were born from the embryonic notion of *wen* ("pattern") and *hsiang* 象 ("the image") as conceived in the trigram and the hexagram. In the history of Chinese culture, the development of the tradition of *wen* has not always followed the well-regulated course channeled by the orthodox Confucian heritage. Although Confucianism is certainly a recurrent theme in the evolution of the concept of (inter)textuality, it has nevertheless encountered many countercurrents throughout the dynastic history, particularly at those moments when socio-political instability coincided with the heavy influence of foreign cultures to challenge the ideological hegemony of Confucianism and give birth to alternative modes of thinking such as Taoism and Ch'an Buddhism. The Eastern Han (25–220) and Wei-Chin (220–420) periods mark one such decentered moment of Chinese literary history: although this was by no means the earliest era in China to witness the blossoming of various schools of thought, the late Han and Wei-Chin literati and philosophers represent the first generation of scholars who sowed the seeds of diverse theories of (inter)textuality and paved the way for the continuous emergence of contradictory elements in Chinese writing conventions. Regardless of the peripheral or mainstream position each of the literary figures occupied during that period, and regardless of how orthodox some of their views may appear at first glance, Wang Ch'ung, Wang Pi, Li Chih, Liu Hsieh, Chung Hung, and Ko Hung have all generated the burgeoning of ideas counter to the Confucian literary tradition. Each has contributed to the emergence of a cluster of ideas that not only contradicts the well-established convention of root-searching and continuity, but also disrupts the Confucianist efforts at homogenizing and domesticating the notion of (inter)textuality. The seeds of the prominent ideas of *i* 異 ("difference") and *pien* 變 ("transformation") form the nuclei of an intertextual mechanism that is transformative rather than confluent.

12   When we contemplate the sacred aura surrounding the Confucian Classics, we can hardly fail to recognize the significant role that the concept of "personal context" has played in the process of canonization. We should note that it is not the aesthetic evaluation of a text alone, but the appraisal of the personality of its writer that comes to play a significant role in the canonization of the writings of sage-kings. The notion of "personal context" exerts an undeniable influence upon the text and eclipses the concept of textual autonomy. Personal integrity, *jen-ko* 人格 , is perceived as a prerequisite for textual integrity, *wen-ko* 文格 . Mou Tsung-san divides the Chinese tradition of personality appraisal into two schools—one evolving from Confucian ethics, the other from the aesthetic appreciation of a writer's *ts'ai-hsing* 才性 , "artistic and spiritual temperament" (Mou 46), a trend deeply rooted in the *hsüan-hsüeh* 玄學 tradition of the Wei-Chin period. However, it is also worth noting that the Confucian endorsement of the priority of a writer's moral personality over the aesthetic one was firmly established before the Wei-Chin, and that it continued to assert its influence upon the mainstream personality appraisers, and in particular, upon the folk tradition throughout the later ages. The Wei-Chin school of personality appraisal gained its popularity primarily among elite intellectual circles. Its influence upon the popular literary tradition was limited. Underlying the myth of *jen-ko* is the notion that the strength of a writer's moral caliber—namely, his fruitful practice of asceticism and temperance—can lend an aura to his writing, thus heightening and defining its aesthetic appeal. The literary paradigm of the Confucian Classics comes into being as the personal/ethical merges into the textual/aesthetic. The domesticated is virtuous and the virtuous is artistically exquisite. This is an example of how personal context eclipses textual autonomy.

13   The Five Classics are the *I Ching*, *Shih Ching*, *Li Chi*, *Ch'un-ch'iu*, and *Shang Shu*.

14   I would like to acknowledge Joseph Allen as the coiner of this term in his discussion of "intratextuality" in *In the Voice of Others: Chinese Music Bureau Poetry* to be published by the Michigan Papers in Chinese Studies of the University of Michigan.

15   Chiang K'uei 63. This is my own translation.

16   Alter 115.

17   Ts'ao Hsüeh-ch'in's life span remains controversial to this day. There are two sets of dates: 1724–64, argued by Chou Ju-ch'ang, and 1715–63, advocated by Yü P'ing-po. See Chou Ju-ch'ang, "*Hung-lou Meng*" *hsin-cheng* I: 173–82; Yü Ying-shih, " 'Mao-chai shih-kao' " 245–58; Chao Kang and Ch'en Chung-i I: 27–29.

18   See "*Tien-t'ou Wan-shih* 點頭碩石 " in Chap. 2 for the description and analysis of this legend.

19   It is worth noting that this kind of interpretive self-indulgence was by no means unfamiliar to traditional Chinese commentators of narrative fiction—especially to those who attempted a close reading of the *Dream of the Red Chamber*. While modern critics often disparage the impressionistic critical discourse produced by premodern scholar-commentators, one can hardly fail to reexperience the pure delight of the latter in free-floating from one literary association to another—particularly at those fruitful but rare moments when the issue of "authorial intention" was inadvertently put aside. The infinite multiplicity of intertextual references in many such *HLM* commentaries serves to illustrate that the fundamental notion of intertextual reading—that the "appearance of a word

reactivates a history"—was not only well understood but also earnestly practiced by some well-known *HLM* commentators. The fluidity of their critical discourses is often suggested by their titles: "Yüeh *HLM* sui-pi 閱紅樓夢隨筆 " ("Random Notes on *HLM*"); "Ch'ih-jen shuo-meng 癡人說夢 " ("Notes on 'Dream' by a Daydreamer"); "Tu *HLM* tsa-chi 讀紅樓夢雜記 " ("Miscellaneous Notes on *HLM*"); and "*HLM* tsa-yung 紅樓夢雜詠 " ("Assorted Notes on *HLM*"), to name just a few.

20   The concept of intertextuality, which emerged in the 1970s, has been widely discussed throughout the 1980s. It is premature to conclude that the concept has become a passing vogue, even if the term itself has gradually faded into the general critical vocabulary of literary studies in the academy. The growing anonymity of the term, however, demonstrates that it has already been assimilated into the critical canon. The concept for which it stands—the reader/text-oriented critical perspective—continues to dominate the field of literary criticism to this day. It represents the root concept on which many theories of post-structuralism and postmodernism are based. The familiarity of the concept itself speaks of its acceptance by the generation of critics and readers who have been exposed to the theoretical assumptions of the post-structuralist age. It is therefore not surprising that books discussing and utilizing the concept of intertextuality for the reinterpretation of traditional and modern classics continue to appear in the market. To cite a few titles: O'Donnell and Davis, *Intertextuality and Contemporary American Fiction* (1989); Worton and Still, *Intertextuality: Theories and Practices* (1990); Gelley, *Narrative Crossings* (1987); Caws, *Textual Analysis: Some Readers Reading* (1986); and Hutcheon, "Literary Borrowing . . . and Stealing: Plagiarism, Sources, Influences, and Intertexts" (1986).

21   For the convenience of the reader, the citation of the names of the major characters in the *Dream of the Red Chamber* in this book is accompanied by the *pin-yin* romanization used by David Hawkes and John Minford in their translation published by Penguin.

22   For my discussion of the recontextualization of *san-sheng* in Ts'ao Hsüeh-ch'in's metaphor of *san-sheng shih*, see Chap. 5.

23   One of the few illuminating moments of such a double bind reveals itself in Huang T'ing-chien's 黃庭堅 (1045–1105) poetic theory. Fundamentally a Confucian classicist, Huang uses the Ch'an approach to rejuvenate the old concept of imitation. He redefines the literary exercise as a form of spiritual exercise. His solution to the dilemma of inanimate imitation—and for that matter, that of citing allusions—is to introduce a mode of communion whose momentum originates from the spiritual rather than the formal identity between the old poet and the new. His subtle denial of the notion of originality is paradoxically mixed with his search for "creativity" in terms of alchemical and magical transformation. In the following passage, one can perceive the dilemma of a Confucian literary man who is intensely aware of the conflict between this impossible yearning for originality and the necessity to come to terms with the recognition that writing is essentially an act of copying: "To create one's own diction is the most difficult task. In Tu Fu's 杜甫 poetry and Han Yü's 韓愈 essays, there is not a single word that does not have a source. However, as those of later generations are not well read, they think Tu and Han are original. The literary masters in olden times knew how to mold and smelt a myriad of matters. Although they borrowed hackneyed expressions from the ancients and put them

into their own writings, what was picked was like an elixir with a mere touch, iron was turned into gold" (Huang T'ing-chien 316).

Some of the later critics see nothing but a more refined poetics of imitation behind Huang's metaphors of transformation. I would point out, however, that his ideas suggest an innovative view of poetic intertextuality. Writing is perceived as the activation of a complex historical archive that imposes ultimate limitation upon the flight of new diction. The activities of molding, smelting, casting, and transforming thus all serve as metaphors for the verbal permutation and redistribution that characterize the inner dynamics of intertextuality. In Huang's poetics, the making of poetry is no longer conceived as a momentary and unconscious outburst of divine inspiration, nor as a heroic gesture of capturing the inexhaustible; at best, it is seen as a painstaking effort to appropriate prior verbal codes and come to terms with intertextual constraints.

24 These two sentences—*tzu-ch'ü tzu-lai* 自去自來 and *k'o-ta k'o-hsiao* 可大可小 —were added by Kao O 高鶚 to the original *Chih-pen* 脂本 text. Chou Ju-ch'ang cites this addition to illustrate how the Ch'eng-Kao edition is inferior to the *Chih-pen* text. Chou argues that Kao O made a poor editorial decision to bestow such transformative attributes upon the Nü-kua Stone. He insists that the stone is incapable of "moving" and "transforming" itself according to the "original intention" of the author. By adding these eight characters, Chou argues, Kao O "almost turned the Nü-kua Stone into the stone monkey in the *Journey*." This last comment is particularly illuminating in that it shows Chou Ju-ch'ang's lack of awareness of the mechanism of intertextuality. The activity of both writing and reading is unavoidably intertextual. That the stone monkey may serve as the blueprint for the Nü-kua Stone is hardly as sinful as Chou suggests: it only serves to demonstrate the natural process of writing. I find it ironic that while Chou argues for the autonomy of Ts'ao Hsüeh-ch'in's Nü-kua Stone, he himself practices the intertextual reading that makes it possible for him to take note of the intertextual relationship of the two stones in the *Dream* and *Journey* in the first place. See Chou Ju-ch'ang, *"Hung-lou Meng" hsin-cheng* I: 14–15.

25 Foucault, *Archaeology of Knowledge* 130–31, 206–7. Foucault's archive is defined as "the general system of the formation and transformation of statements" (130), a system too vast and fragmentary to be recuperable, for it cannot be described in its totality. This definition, however, often meets Foucault's other contradictory statements about the concept of historical context. Foucault works within the framework of a determinable historical text, yet he is highly conscious of its differentiation and discontinuities. On the one hand, his notion of context is a "definable systematically abridged paradigm—a set of prescribed epistemic structures" (Leitch 150)—in other words, an all-embracing transcendental structuralist network that assures that textuality functions within the cultural and historical archive; on the other hand, he proclaims that the horizon and context of every text cannot be conceived as a comprehensive and continual whole (Foucault, "Nietzsche, Genealogy, History"). Foucault's definition of the archive embodies a conceptual vacillation that should perhaps be taken as the self-critical awareness of structuralist thought at its best.

26 See Barthes, *S/Z*: this term embodies the sum total of the fragments of "something that has already been read, seen, done, experienced" (20). The body of the *déjà lu* consists

of five major categories: the hermeneutic, semic, symbolic, proairetic, and cultural. Each code itself is a mirage of quotations. Barthes's aim is to produce the orchestration of these various codes—in other words, the disintegration of the text in slow motion (12).

27   Riffaterre, "Textuality" 2.

28   Riffaterre, *Semiotics of Poetry* 23. "Hypogram" is defined as a preexistent word group. It is the product of "past semiotic and literary practice" (83).

29   Culler, *Structuralist Poetics* 138–60. Literally, "vraisemblance" means "true semblance, what tradition makes suitable or expected in a particular genre" (139). "Vraisemblance" is the sum total of knowledge that appears natural because it is cultural—a "general and diffuse text which might be called 'public opinion' " (139). In reading a text, we tend to recuperate and naturalize, whether consciously or not, the strange, the unfamiliar, and the fictional. In other words, the unfamiliar elements in a text are brought into contact with "vraisemblance," that with which we are already familiar.

30   Liu Hsieh 6/519.

31   "Hsiang Kung erh-shih-pa nien," Wang Po-hsiang 464. The concept of context perceived here is curtailed and merely confined to the intratextual space of the *shang-hsia wen* 上下文 —the written or spoken statements that precede or follow a specific word or passage within the text.

32   Liu Hsieh proposes the concept of *t'ung pien* 通變 in *Wen-hsin tiao-lung*, which deals with the issue of generic change and continuity (i.e., the question of the relationship of a text to its literary conventions). The conceptual framework of Liu's *t'ung-pien* chapter is derived from the "Hsi-tz'u":

> Thereupon closing/enclosing the gate is called *k'un* 坤, "the Receptive"; opening the gate is called *ch'ien* 乾, "the Creative." The alternation of opening and (en)closing is called *pien* 變, "change"; the continuous coming forward and going backward is called *t'ung* 通, "channeling." ("Hsi-tz'u" I: 7/17a)

The alternation of *t'ung* and *pien* is perceived as a movement between two different kinds of movement. One is illustrated by a temporal metaphor of continuous traffic (*wang-lai* 往來, "forward and backward"), and the other, by a spatial metaphor of transformative relocation (*ho-p'i* 闔闢, "the [en]closing and opening"). The motion of change thus perceived is never unidirectional. The concept of *t'ung*, in particular, emphasizes the simultaneous motion of progression and regression. The traffic between the past and the future needs to be incessantly channeled to ensure continuity.

The concept itself appears to be a paradox for it contains two conflicting notions: *pien* ("change") and *t'ung* ("continuity"). On the one hand, Liu Hsieh maintains that the renewal of literary expression depends upon the writer's flexibility in adapting to changing literary trends; on the other, we can also perceive in his discussion the heavy influence of Confucian formalism that stresses the drive to emulate and preserve rather than the incentive of bringing about difference. His classicist spirit often stands in his way and prevents him from appreciating the new, even though the historical necessity of stylistic changes is well recognized. He complains that "a rivalry in producing something new, to the neglect of ancient values, has lulled the wind and sapped vitality" ("T'ung-pien" ["Flexible Adaptability to Varying Situations"], in Liu Hsieh, *Literary Mind* 321). He eventually propagates the merits of preservation, emphasizing the importance of "striking a middle road" and of the acquisition of a "synthetic outlook." In his definition of *t'ung pien*, he clearly modifies and qualifies the concept of change to suit the eclectic view of literature characteristic of the Confucian tradition. "Flexible adaptability" is therefore formulated as the ability of a writer to "know which elements to preserve and which to change" (323).

33 Leitch 124.

34 Heath 74.

35 Traditional studies of *Hung-lou Meng* (*hung-hsüeh* 紅學, hereafter *HLM* studies) utilize the methodology of historiography in setting up their theoretical paradigm. Two major schools dominated the field in the early twentieth century: the school headed by Ts'ai Yüan-p'ei 蔡元培 (Ts'ai's *"Shih-t'ou Chi" so-yin* 石頭記索隱 [1915] established itself as the canon for the school) focused on the author's political motivation by interpreting the *Dream* as a political novel aimed at propagating Han nationalism against the rule of the Manchu; the other school, headed by Hu Shih and Yü P'ing-po (Hu's *"Hung-lou Meng" k'ao-cheng* 紅樓夢考証 [1921] served as the model for his followers), advocated the paradigm of autobiography in interpreting the *Dream*. Seen in the light of the latter school, Chia Pao-yü is none other than the author Ts'ao Hsüeh-ch'in himself. Both schools overlap the real with the symbolic, the historical with the contemporary. Extrapolating from these two competing historiographical paradigms, scholar-critics are most concerned with issues such as the identity of Ts'ao Hsüeh-ch'in, Chih-yen Chai 脂硯齋, and Chia Yüan-ch'un 賈元春 (Jia Yüan-chun); the physical location of Ta-kuan yüan 大觀園; and the dating and comparison of various *Chih-pen* texts, etc. For a more detailed discussion of the various theoretical paradigms of *HLM* studies, see Yü Ying-shih, "Chin-tai hung-hsüeh."

36 In addition to the two paradigms discussed in n. 35 above, there emerged in Mao's China during the 1950s another paradigm derived from the political ideology of Marxism. The leading spokesman of the new school is Li Hsi-fan, who published *Ts'ao Hsüeh-ch'in ho t'a-te "Hung-lou Meng"* in 1973, sharply criticizing the autobiographical paradigm advocated by Hu Shih and Yü P'ing-po. Li Hsi-fan subscribes to the Marxist concept of class struggle and argues that Ts'ao Hsüeh-ch'in wrote the *Dream* with the purpose of exposing the social injustice and the ruthlessness of class struggle in eighteenth-century China. Seen in this light, Ts'ao emerges as a great "antifeudal" and revolutionary writer. For a summary of Li's perspective, see Li Hsi-fan and Lan Ling I: 1–17.

37 Although the device of stone-as-narrator is by no means consistent throughout the *Dream*, the persona of the stone-narrator does not simply disappear after its lengthy argument with Vanitas in chapter 1: it reemerges unexpectedly on several occasions to interrupt the flow of the third-person narration. See Chap. 6, "The Inscribed Stone Tablet," for a discussion of the narrative function or dysfunction of the "talking stone."

38 Derrida, *Speech and Phenomenon* 141. Also see Derrida, "Différance" 396–420.

39 Anthony Yu, "Introduction" 58. Also see Yu, "Religion and Literature in China" 130 ff. Yu points out that Tripitaka's quest for the scripture is a symbolic journey of his return to the land of purity where he resided in his previous incarnation as the second disciple of Buddha, Gold Cicada. He also observes (in a later communication with the author) that

"the pilgrims' apotheosis should be seen as a reversion to the original exaltation in both Buddhist and Taoist terms." Also see "The Knowing Stone" in Chap. 5 for my discussion of the ideological implications of the pilgrims' dramatized apotheosis at the end of their journey in terms of the narrative logic of "return."

40   Yu, "Religion and Literature in China" 130–33.

41   See n. 9, above.

42   Culler, *Pursuit of Signs* 110.

43   Chou Ch'un 77.

44   Quoted in Jameson, *Prison-House of Language* 6.

45   In a slightly different manner, Lévi-Strauss offers a subtler apology and more modest claim for the work he did on South American mythology—a posture that approaches mine in coming to terms with the interpretive dilemma posed by the evolving contradiction of the open/enclosed duality of intertextuality. According to him, "If critics reproach me with not having carried out an exhaustive inventory of South American myths before analyzing them, they are making a grave mistake about the nature and function of these documents. The total body of myth belonging to a given community is comparable to its speech. Unless the population dies out physically or morally, this totality is never complete. . . . Experience proves that a linguist can work out the grammar of a given language from a remarkably small number of sentences, compared to all those he might in theory have collected, . . . in no instance would I feel constrained to accept the arbitrary demand for a total mythological pattern, since such requirement has no meaning" (*The Raw and the Cooked* 7).

46   The controversial nature of metalanguage has invited much speculation in the West over the last few decades. Roland Barthes's insight conciliates more than resolves the incompatible views surrounding the issue: "We are beginning to glimpse (through other sciences) the fact that research must little by little get used to the conjunction of two ideas which for a long time were thought incompatible: the idea of structure and the idea of combinational infinity" ("Textual Analysis" 137).

47   To cite a pair of examples: When Kongas and Pierre Maranda take Lévi-Strauss's formula as the absolute structural model for all folkloric items, they have gone to an extreme by enthroning the concept of "system"; for a detailed description of their interpretive procedures, see *Structural Models in Folklore and Transformational Essays*. With a similar structuralist formula, William Hendricks pares the text of "A Rose for Emily" down to a bare skeleton of several syntactic chains; see his "Methodology of Narrative Structural Analysis," *Essays* 175 ff.

48   Jameson, "Foreword," xv.

49   This observation leads us to yet another inherent problematic of interpretation: just how scientific can an interpretive system be, and how far can it replace intuition and intelligence? Barthes asks in *Critique et vérité* how one can "discover structure without the help of a methodological model" (19). This blind faith in the omnipotent function of systematically derived models appears to be a malaise prevalent in the age of structuralism. But is interpretation impossible without maps, squares, or formulas? It is Heidegger, perhaps, who drives the issue home by bringing forward the prestructured nature of understanding: "All prepredicative simple seeing of the invisible world of the ready-to-hand is in itself

already an 'understanding-interpreting' seeing" (Heidegger, *Sein und Zeit* 149; trans. in
R. Palmer 135). As a result, he plainly concludes that "interpretation is never a presuppo-
sitionless grasping of something given in advance" (Heidegger 150; see Palmer 136). The
problem of most criticism results from the abuse of this presupposition rather than from
its presence.

50 Lévi-Strauss, *From Honey to Ashes* 356. Lévi-Strauss explained the multidimensional
nature of the mythical field in which a single myth is related to a group of myths of which
it is a transformation. The structural approach to such a myth involves the study of its
cross-connections to the other paradigmatic sets.

51 In Lévi-Strauss's terms, "If one aspect of a particular myth seems unintelligible, it can
be legitimately dealt with, in the preliminary stage and on the hypothetical level, as a
transformation of the homologous aspect of another myth" (*The Raw and the Cooked* 13).

52 Consider, for instance, the lexeme "bark." It is composed of the semic core of "a sharp
vocal noise" and supplemented by such contextual semes as "human" and "animal." The
correct reading of "bark" in a given context depends upon the combination of the relevant
contextual seme with the invariant semic core. Consider the following sentence: The man
barked at his wife. The proper reading of "bark" in this context calls for the selection of
"human" rather than "animal" as the contextual variant to be combined with the semic
core of "a sharp vocal noise." Thus Greimas suggests that a series of alternative contextual
semes can account for the variations in meaning.

53 Greimas, *Structural Semantics* 46ff.

54 Maurice Merleau-Ponty, *Le visible et l'invisible* (Paris: Gallimard, 1964) 243; trans. in
Merleau-Ponty, *The Visible and the Invisible* 189.

55 Culler, *Structuralist Poetics* 87.

56 Greimas, *Structural Semantics* 102. "Cultural grid" is the cultural *vraisemblance* that a
reader possesses. The existence of such prescribed knowledge seems to put into question
the possibility of objective semantic analysis. Greimas offers no quick solution to this
paradox. Following the line of Culler's argument, one might say that the operation of a
cultural grid does not necessarily cancel the validity of an objective semantic analysis. On
the other hand, the most refined sensibility and cultural memories interact with, and often
coincide with, the theories of semantics in interpretive procedures.

57 Greimas, *Structural Semantics* 59. Greimas holds that the concept of classemes, characterized by their iterativity, provides a clearer explanation for the vague concept of "the
meaningful whole," which was defined as a prerequisite in Hjelmslev's theory. "The meaningful whole" of a given text is the "global signified of a signifying ensemble" manifested
by a homogeneous semantic coherence, rather than a preexistent undifferentiated entity.
Furthermore, in recognizing the illusions of objective reading, he says: "For the fact that
such a grid is, in the present state of our knowledge, difficult to imagine for the purposes
of mechanical analysis signifies that the description itself still depends, in large part, on
the analyst's subjective appreciation" (102).

58 Riffaterre, "Textuality" 2.

59 While the school of imitative poetics dominated the literary field of traditional China, it
has also served as a stimulus for the periodic emergence of a cluster of ideas evolved from
the notion of *pien*, "change." Throughout the history of premodern literature, one can find

many literati fascinated with the concept of *pien*, the origin of which can be traced back to the great Chinese sourcebook of knowledge, the *I Ching*. As early as the Han Dynasty, Wang Ch'ung was betraying an awareness of historical relativism. According to him, the writings of the Classics are no better than, but simply different from, modern texts. His perception of "change" is primarily based on an evolutionary theory of language. Literary history is understood in concrete terms of the succession of one literary idiom by another. The implications of Wang Ch'ung's aesthetic relativism remained unremarked until the Ming Dynasty (1368–1644), when literary eccentrics such as Li Chih and Yüan Hung-tao raised their voices against the old agenda of both moral and literary conformity. Yüan's contribution to the poetics of *pien*, though fragmentary, nonetheless poses a serious challenge to the poetics of imitation. Yüan Hung-tao is certainly not a pioneer in advocating the concept of *pien*; his relentless attack on the movement of archaism and on the practice of imitative poetics propagated by the "Former and Later Seven Masters" was preceded by other notable examples in earlier literary history. But he is the first to capture the notion of change in terms of the concept of *shih* 史, "historical period." He attributes the permutation of aesthetic values to the changing course of history. According to him, the contact with history does not necessarily entail an obsessive return. It involves the active cultivaton of a kind of historical consciousness that recognizes in history the promise of change as well as the drive toward continuity. I should point out, however, that neither Yüan Hung-tao nor his brother Tsung-tao 袁宗道 is an uncompromising critic of old paradigms; both consider the writings by the ancients to be supreme embodiments of the ideal text. For the analysis of the two Yüans' literary theories, see Chou Chih-p'ing 1–20, esp. 10–11.

60 The concept of change contained in the *I Ching* accommodates two primary semes that appear to be at odds with each other—*pien-i* 變易 ("change") and *pu-i* 不易 ("the unchangeable"). The unchangeable refers to the positions of heaven and earth, and the hierarchy of human relationships (preface, *Chou-i Cheng-i* 3a). It suffices to note that the concept of *t'ung* 通, which the *I Ching* elucidates, introduces the notion of a ceaseless, but ordered, textual trafficking that takes place in a self-conscious intertextual space. The radical possibility that intertextual permutation follows no predictable laws is alien to the *I Ching* tradition. In the "Hsi-tz'u," one finds that the principle of *t'ung-pien* is assigned a boundary: "The operation of *pien* and *t'ung* cannot find a better illustration than in that of the four seasons" [*pien-t'ung mo ta hu ssu-shih* 變通莫大乎四時]" ("Hsi-tz'u" I: 7/17b). In other words, the case of *t'ung-pien* is to be found in the predictable and self-contained alternation of four seasons. The notion of self-containment introduces a mode of (inter)textuality that is controllable and ultimately traceable. Thus the concept of change in the *I Ching* constantly meets the challenge of its opposite drive to stabilize.

61 See, for example, H. Wilhelm 20.

62 Yang Hsiung 179.

63 Tu Wei-ming, "Profound Learning" 12.

64 In his commentary on the *I Ching*, Wang Pi succeeds in transplanting the paradox of language suggested by Chuang Tzu into the explication of the loaded concept of the *hsiang*. Whether or not Wang Pi is essentially a Taoist under the Confucian cloak or a Confucianist in Taoist disguise is an issue that needs to be explored elsewhere. Ch'ien Mu argues

that although commonly acknowledged as the pioneers of the *hsüan-hsüeh* tradition, both Wang Pi and Ho Yen 何晏 should be regarded more as Confucianists than Taoists. Ch'ien, however, offers little explanation as to why both men interpret the Confucian Classics from the Taoist perspective. See Ch'ien Mu 68–73.

65 Wang Pi 609.

2   The Mythological Dictionary of Stone

1 *Tung-fang kuo-yü tz'u-tien* 680.

2 Shimmura Izuru 106.

3 *Random House College Dictionary* 1294.

4 Greimas, *On Meaning* 3–4.

5 Perron xxv.

6 F. R. Palmer 30. In Palmer's words, "sense deals with semantic structure, and reference deals with meaning in terms of our experience outside language" (31)—that is to say, one refers to intralinguistic relationship, the other to the function of language on the experiential level.

7 Even though Palmer indicates that only when the scope of semantic theory encompasses the study of the "referential" aspect of language can it be considered a comprehensive theory, he nevertheless devotes only one chapter in his book to the investigation of the referential content of language. See "The Non-linguistic Context," in *Semantics* 43–58.

8 See F. R. Palmer 93: "By syntagmatic is meant the relation that a linguistic element has with other elements in the stretch of language in which it occurs, while by paradigmatic is meant the relationship it has with elements with which it may be replaced or substituted."

9 Palmer 94–96, citing Firth, *Papers in Linguistics.*

10 Lévi-Strauss, *From Honey to Ashes* 356.

11 Greimas is not unaware of the insufficiencies of Lévi-Strauss's paradigmatic approach to discourse analysis. In "The Interaction of Semiotic Constraints" and "Elements of a Narrative Grammar," Greimas acknowledges his debt to both Vladimir Propp and Lévi-Strauss for the shaping of his own methodological perspective, which links the study of syntax with that of semantics and projects the paradigmatic axis onto the syntagmatic axis (*On Meaning* 48–83). For the theoretical model of such a synthetic approach, see his "Toward a Semiotics of the Natural World," which, according to Perron, presents a "syntactic and semantic (actantial) theory of discourse" (*On Meaning* xxvi).

12 Greimas, *On Meaning* 4.

13 Ibid.

14 Katz 33.

15 Katz 33–34.

16 The identification of semes, "minimal semantic units," is based on the working of binary oppositions. Thus we are able to derive the seme of "hardness" from a lexical item because of our recognition of its potential binary relationship with the seme of "softness." Other semic groups include "human/animal," "earth/heaven," "male/female," and "birth/death."

17 Katz 37.

18 Saussure 122ff.

19   Lehrer 71–72.

20   Karlgren took issue with Granet because the latter had selected his source materials without discretion to reconstruct the social and religious history of ancient China. See Karlgren 346–49. ,

21   Chü Yüan (340–278 B.C.) 3/16b. Also see Yüan K'o, *Ku shen-hua hsüan-shih* (hereafter *KSH*) 16.

22   Karlgren 229.

23   Yüan K'o, *KSH* 16; Plaks, *Archetype and Allegory* 30.

24   Chü Yüan 3/16b.

25   Liu An (d. 122 B.C.), *Huai-nan-tzu* (hereafter *HNT*) 17/4b.

26   Hsu Shen (A.D. 55–149) is the compiler of *Shuo-wen chieh-tzu* (hereafter *Shuo-wen*), the earliest Chinese etymological dictionary, which consists of thirty volumes.

27   Yüan K'o, *KSH* 19.

28   *Shuo-wen* 12b/4b.

29   "Ta-huang hsi-ching," *Shan-hai-ching* (hereafter *SHC*), in Hung Pei-chiang, *Shan-hai-ching chiao-chu* (hereafter *SHCCC*) 16/839. Also see Yüan K'o, *KSH* 39.

30   Neumann, *Great Mother* 29.

31   Yüan K'o, *KSH* 20, quoting from *Feng-su t'ung*, comp. Ying Shao (fl. A.D. 189–194); the extant text is quoted in the *T'ai-p'ing yü-lan* (hereafter *TPYL*), comp. Li Fang (A.D. 925–996) et al., I: 76/5a.

32   It is also interesting to note that this myth presents an explanation for the phenomenon of social inequity. Nü-kua's playful experimentation with clay involves the operative motions of "patting" and "dragging through/shaking off" the yellow earth: the former movement produces images of beings of the upper class; the latter, those of the lower class. While the motion of "patting" imparts a conscious design to a piece of matter, the "dragging through and shaking off" of the mud suggests just the opposite; in the given context, it conjures up the image of a lackadaisical craftworker who allows the matter to scatter and form its own shape without any preconceived blueprint in mind. Clearly the quality control of such mass production is more difficult to maintain than that of the highly concentrated individual effort that the action of "patting" seems to suggest. Thus in the mythic origin of humankind, the seeds of inequity have already been sown. In a seemingly innocuous manner, then, the mytho-logic underlying the creation myth serves to justify the existence of social inequity.

33   Hsu Shen in the *Shuo-wen* defined Nü-kua as "an ancient divine woman" (12b/4b).

34   Karlgren 229.

35   "Lan Ming," *HNT* 6/7b; also see Yüan K'o, *KSH* 23 (trans. in Bodde 386–87).

36   Yüan K'o, *Chung-kuo ku-tai shen-hua* (hereafter *CKKTSH*) 46 nn.9, 10, 11.

37   Kung Kung was portrayed in several texts as an ugly creature, half-human and half-beast. Kuo P'u's 郭璞 annotation on "Ta-huang hsi-ching" in the *SHC* quotes from *Kuei Tsang* 歸藏: "Kung Kung had a human face, snake body, and red hair" (*SHCCC* 16/388). In "Hsi-pei-huang ching," it says that "there was a human trace in the wasteland of the Northwest—dull and unruly as an animal, his name was Kung Kung" (Yüan K'o, *CKKTSH* 60 n.16).

38   Yüan K'o, *KSH* 32–33. Yüan K'o interpreted Kung Kung's battle with Chuan Hsü as a

revolt against the old rotten political order and as a challenge against the old monarchy established by Chuan Hsü. Kung Kung was therefore hailed as the champion of the oppressed.

39 Yüan K'o, *KSH* 29, quoting from "T'an-t'ien" of *Lun Heng*, comp. Wang Ch'ung (A.D. 27–97).

40 Lieh Yü-k'ou (4th cent. B.C.), *Lieh Tzu* 5/60.

41 Ssu-ma Chen, "San-huang pen-chi," in *"Shih Chi" hui-chu k'ao-cheng* (hereafter *SCHCKC*) 11c.

42 Yüan K'o, *KSH* 39, quoting from the *Shih Pen* (*"Shih Pen" liang-chung* [hereafter *SPLC*] 1).

43 Plaks, *Archetype and Allegory* 28.

44 Yüan K'o, *KSH* 21 n.6.

45 "Mei Shih," *Chou Li* in *Shih-san-ching chu-shu* (hereafter *SSCCS*) 14/15a–16b; trans. in Plaks, *Archetype and Allegory* 31.

46 "Sheng Min," "Ta Ya," in *Shih Ching* 17a/1b; trans. in Waley 5.

47 The interpretations of the *Shih Ching* were made by four different schools: Ch'i, Lu, Han, and Mao. With the loss of the texts of the first three schools, the extant annotations and interpretations of Mao Kung became the orthodox text.

48 *Shih Ching* 17A/1b.

49 *TPYL* III: 529/4a.

50 See "Li-i chih 2," in *Sui Shu* I: 7/146.

51 Wen I-to 110 n.30. Also see Yüan K'o, *CKKTSH* 56.

52 Wen I-to 97–99. In his article Wen I-to traces the gradual convergence of the three terms— "Kao T'ang," "Kao Mi," and "Kao Mei."

53 See annotations on "Hsia pen-chi," in *Shih Chi*, *SCHCKC* 41c. According to the source, both Yü and his kingdom are identified as "Kao Mi." Also see Wen I-to 99.

54 "Wu-hou tai-fu p'u," in *SPLC* 20. Also see "Ti Hsi," *SPLC* 3, 4, 8.

55 *Ch'ing-hua tsa-chih* 19 (1935): 827–65, quoting "Yüeh-wang wu-yü wai-chuan," in Chao Yeh (fl. A.D. 40–80), *Wu-yüeh ch'un-ch'iu* 4/124. Also see Wen I-to 99.

56 Sung Yü 19/393–97.

57 Wen I-to 99. According to Wen, *kao* is the variation of *chiao*. And the character *t'ang* 唐 corresponds to *tu* 杜, which shares the same phonetic root with *she* 社; hence *t'ang* also corresponds to *she*.

58 "Hou-chi 2," in Lo Pi 2/11a, quoting *Feng-su t'ung*; also see Yüan K'o, *KSH* 20.

59 Lo Pi 2/12b.

60 Cheng Hsüan (A.D. 127–200), *Cheng Chih* c/31.

61 Wen I-to 100–102.

62 Wen I-to 98.

63 Neumann, *Great Mother* 260.

64 Annotations on "Hsia pen-chi" (*So-yin*) in *SCHCKC* 38c.

65 "Ti Hsi," *SPLC* 8. Also see Wang Hsiao-lien 66. Wang Hsiao-lien's quotation from the *Shih Pen* is different from the original text: "T'u-shan Shih was designated as Nü-kua."

66 Yüan K'o, *KSH* 309–30, quoting from "Yüeh-wang" (Chao Yeh 4/129).

67 *Nü-chiao* is seen in "Ti Hsi" of the *Ta-tai-li*, quoted in an annotation on "T'u-shan Shih"

in "Ti Hsi" of the *Shih Pen* (see *SPLC* 8); *Nü-ch'iao* is seen in "Ku-chin jen-piao," *Han Shu* II: 20/880; *Yu-chiao Shih* is seen in "Chin-yü 4," Tso-Ch'iu Ming II: 35b; *Yu-kua Shih* is seen in "San-huang pen-chi," *Shih Chi, SCHCKC* 11d.

68   Wang Hsiao-lien 66. Wang identifies Nü-chiao and Nü-ch'iao with Nü-kua.

69   Wen I-to 116.

70   Yen Shih-ku's annotations on "Wu-ti chi," *Han Shu* I: 6/190.

71   Wen I-to 116.

72   Neumann, *Origins* 102ff.

73   Ssu-ma Chen, *SCHCKC* 11c.

74   Karlgren 303.

75   Neumann, *Origins* 131.

76   Neumann, *Origins* 133.

77   "Hai-nei-ching" of *SHC*, quoting from *K'ai Shih* 開筮, *SHCCC* 18/473.

78   *Ch'u-hsüeh-chi*, comp. Hsü Chien (A.D. 659–729) et al., 22, quoting from *Kuei Tsang*.

79   Chü Yüan, "Tien Wen," 3/5b.

80   "Hsiu-wu," *HNT* 19/7b.

81   Karlgren 309.

82   Wang Ch'ung, "Ch'i-kuai-p'ien," *Lun Heng* pt. 1, 3/19b.

83   Wang Fu, "Chiao-chi" ("P'ien" 30), *Ch'ien-fu lun* 8/30a.

84   Annotations on "Hsia-pen-chi" in Chang Shou-chieh, *"Shih Chi" cheng-i*, quoting from "Ti-wang chi," see *SCHCKC* 41c.

85   Hao I-hsing's annotations on "Hsi-shan-ching" of *SHC* in *SHCCC* 50.

86   "Hsia pen-chi," *SCHCKC* 49b.

87   Yüan K'o, *CKKTSH* 230 n.2, quoting from Lin Ch'un-p'u 1/9.

88   Wang Chia (d. 2 B.C.), *Shih-i chi* 38.

89   "Pen ching," *HNT* 8/6b–7a. According to this source, "At the time of Shun, Kung Kung tossed and stirred up the flood, and it reached K'ung-sang."

90   In Hsün K'uang's "Ch'eng-hsiang," *Hsün Tzu* 18/4a, it says: "Yü has achieved great exploits. He checked the flood on earth, extinguished the enemy of the people, and expelled Kung Kung."

91   "Li T'ang," in *T'ai-p'ing kuang-chi* (hereafter *TPKC*), ed. Li Fang (925–96), et al., 467/2b; also see Yüan K'o, *KSH* 305–6. Both sources give a detailed account of how Yü subdued the water god Wu-chih-ch'i.

92   "Hai-wai pei-ching," *SHCCC* 8/233; trans. in Karlgren 309.

93   "Fan-lun hsün," *HNT* 13/22b.

94   "Pa I," *Lun Yü* in *Ssu-shu chi-chu*, annot. Chu Hsi (1130–1200), 17–18.

95   *TPYL* III: 532/3a, based on a quotation from "Wai-chuan" of *Li Chi; TPYL* 532/5b mentions "the Stone host-god of the Imperial She temple."

96   "Ch'i-su hsün," *HNT* 11/8a.

97   "Li Chih" (*Chih* 55), *Sung Shih* IV: 102/2484.

98   Karlgren 308.

99   "Mei Shih," *Chou Li* (*SSCCS* III) 14/17a.

100 Wang Hsiao-lien 48.

101 See Po Chü-i (A.D. 772–846), *Pai-k'ung liu-t'ieh* 2/7b for dragon images, and 82/5b for

both clay dragons and painted images; also see Eberhard 462. For detailed discussion on the subject, see Cohen 246 n.6.

102 Wang Ch'ung, "Shun ku," *Lun Heng* pt. 2, 15/14b.

103 Wang Hsiao-lien 51.

104 Sheng Hung-chih (fl. Liu Sung Dynasty, 420–79), *Ching-chou chi* 2/10b. This lost work is partially reconstructed in the *Lu-shan ching-she ts'ung-shu*, comp. Chen Yün-jung, based on the quotations in the *Pei-t'ang shu-ch'ao*, comp. Yü Shih-nan (558–638), II: 158/12b–13a. For information about the source and the translation of the above passage, see Cohen 250 n.20.

105 Cohen 250.

106 *TPYL* I: 52/2b; also see Ch'en Yao-wen, *T'ien-chung chi* (hereafter *TCC*) 3/31b, based on a quotation in the *Ching-chou chi* 2/10b.

107 *TCC* 3/31b, based on a quotation from the *Kuang-chou chi*, comp. Ku Wei of Chin Dynasty (A.D. 265–420).

108 James George Frazer argues in his study of magic and primitive religions that the sacrifices of the high priests and tribal kings in primitive societies reveal the existence of a prevailing institution of fertility rituals. Such an institution requires the periodic execution of a community scapegoat or representative in order to reassure the renewal of the life-force. See *Golden Bough* 308–668.

109 Annotations on "Feng-shan shu" in Chang Shou-chieh, *SCHCKC* 496b.

110 Annotations on "Feng-shan shu," *SCHCKC* 496c, based on a quotation from the *Wu-ching t'ung-i*.

111 Li Tu 14–15. The Chou rulers used the doctrine of the Mandate of Heaven to consecrate their victory over Shang Dynasty and thus perpetuated the myth that the monarch ruled by the decree of Heaven. The religious doctrine served the political interest of the human sovereign, as well as serving as the moral law of cause and effect.

112 "Wen Wang," *Ta-ya* in *Shih Ching* (*SSCCS* II) 16.1/10a–11a.

113 "Hao-t'ien yü ch'eng-ming," in the "Ch'ing-miao" chapter of *Chou Sung, Shih Ching* 19.2/1b.

114 "K'ang Kao," *Shu Ching* 97.

115 "Yün Han" in the "Tang" chapter, *Ta-ya* in *Shih Ching* (*SSCCS* II) 18.2/17a.

116 "Chao Kao," *Shu Ching* 117.

117 Annotations by Takigawa on "Feng-shan shu" in *SCHCKC* 496c. According to the annotator, the *feng-shan* ritual started in Ch'in Dynasty and reached its popularity during the time of Emperor Wu of Han. Marcel Granet seems inaccurate in suggesting that "The first of the *feng-shan* ceremonies was carried out by the Emperor Wu of Han in 110 B.C." (113).

118 "Ch'in Shih-huang pen-chi," *SCHCKC* 119a–b.

119 "Wu-ti chi," *Han Shu* I: 6/191.

120 *Ch'u-hsüeh chi* II: 13/26b, based on quotations from Ying Shao, *Han-kuan-i* B/42.

121 *Shuo-wen* 1.1/7a.

122 *Li Chi* (*SSCCS* V) 30/12b.

123 *Li Chi* 30/13b.

124 "Ch'un-kuan ta-tsung-po," *Chou Li* (*SSCCS* III) 18/24a–b.

125 Williams 235.

126 Feng Yen (of T'ang Dynasty) 4/22b.

127 Shih Yu (fl. 48–33 B.C.) 1/24b.

128 Wang Hsiang-chih II: 135/8a.

129 *Fan-ku ts'ung-pien* 36/14a.

130 Wang Hsiao-lien 71.

131 *TCC* 8/34d, quoting from the *Ching-chou chi*; *TCC* 8/37b, quoting from the *Ch'ia-wen chi*, comp. Cheng Ch'ang (of T'ang Dynasty).

132 *Chiu T'ang-shu* IV: 37 (*Chih* 17)/1350; also see *TCC* 8/39b–40a.

133 *TCC* 8/31b–32a.

134 *TCC* 8/39b.

135 *TCC* 8/34b.

136 "*Lieh-chuan* 119," *Chiu "T'ang-shu"* XIII: 169/4407; also see *TCC* 8/43a–b. The quotation from the *TCC* differs from the original text in two details: the name of Wang Fan's son Hsia-hsiu (退休) was changed into Hsia-hsiu (瑕休), and the conclusion of the old man—"This is by no means a good omen"—was replaced by "How can it be taken as a good omen?"

137 *TCC* 8/32a, quoting from *Tung-ming chi*, comp. Kuo Hsien (of Han Dynasty).

138 Li Shih-chen (of Ming Dynasty) VIII: 84–133 (K'un-yü tien, 9/43a–13/10b).

139 "Chung-shan ching," *SHCCC* 5/141.

140 *TCC* 8/52b, quoting from the *T'ai-p'ing huan-yü chi*, comp. Yüeh Shih (930–1007).

141 Wang P'u (922–82), I: 28/534.

142 Tuan Ch'eng-shih (d. 863), 2/182.

143 *TCC* 8/47b, quoting from *Chi-ku lu*, comp. Ou-yang Hsiu (1007–72).

144 Tuan Ch'eng-shih 10/80.

145 "*Lieh-chuan* 54," *Pei Shih* VIII: 66/2322.

146 *TPYL* I: 52/4a, quoting from the *Chün-kuo chih*, comp. Yüan Shan-sung (of Chin Dynasty).

147 *TCC* 8/50b, quoting from the *Huan-yü chi*.

148 "Chung-shan ching," *SHCCC* 5/138.

149 Ibid. Kuo P'u's source was derived from "Wu-hsing chih," *Chin Shu* II: 28 (*Chih* 18)/854.

150 *TCC* 8/36a, quoting the *I-yüan*, comp. Liu Ching-shu (of Liu-Sung Dynasty).

151 *TCC* 8/40a, quoting the *Yü-chang chi*, comp. Lei Tz'u-tsung of Liu-Sung Dynasty.

152 *TPKC* 231/1b–2a, quoting from the *Chao-yeh ch'ien-tsai*, comp. Chang Cho (660–732), 3/36.

153 "Yü Kung," *Shang Shu* (*SSCCS* I) 6/11a.

154 *TCC* 8/46a, quoting from the *Chia-shih t'an-lu*, comp. Chang Chi (of Sung Dynasty).

155 *TCC* 8/51a, quoting the *Ch'ia-wen chi*.

156 Todorov 25–26. Todorov quotes the Russian mystic Vladimir Solovyov: "In the genuine fantastic, there is always the external and formal possibility of a simple explanation of phenomena, but at the same time this explanation is completely stripped of internal probability" (25–26). Once we choose one realm over the other, we leave the fantastic for "a neighboring genre"—either the natural, or the marvelous. Therefore the genre of the fantastic rests on the indeterminacy of one's reading experience.

157 *Tso Chuan* (*SSCCS* VI) 44/21b–22a.

158   Wang Chia 5/116.

159   *TCC* 8/33a, quoting from the *Hsi-ching tsa-chi*, comp. Liu Hsin (45 B.C. to A.D. 23), 1/3b.

160   *TCC* 8/54a, quoting from the *Hsün-yang chi*, comp. Chang Seng-chien (of Chin Dynasty).

161   *TCC* 8/54a, quoting the *Yu-ming lu*, comp. Liu I-ch'ing (403–44), 241–42.

162   Miao T'ien-hua 839, quoting "Ti-li" in the *T'ung-su pien*, comp. Chiao Hao (of Ch'ing Dynasty).

163   Hay 64.

164   *Tz'u Hai* 2066.

165   Eliade, *Myths, Dreams* 174.

166   According to Neumann, "It is an essential feature of the primordial archetype that it combines positive and negative attributes and groups of attributes. This union of opposites in the primordial archetype, its ambivalence, is characteristic of the original situation of the unconscious, which consciousness has not yet dissected into its antitheses. Early men experienced this paradoxical simultaneity of good and evil, friendly and terrible, in the godhead as a unity" (*Great Mother* 12).

167   Wang Hsiang-chih 81/5a; *TCC* 8/53a, quoting from the *Shih-shuo*.

168   *TCC* 8/49b, quoting from the *Huan-yü chi*.

169   *Tung-fang kuo-yü tz'u-tien* 680.

170   Hay 18.

171   Plaks, *Archetype and Allegory* 170.

172   Plaks argues that the Chinese garden evokes a vision of cosmic completeness that is projected by the compositional symmetry of the garden landscape, achieved through the interplay of bipolar concepts such as hardness and softness, light and shadow, high and low, nearness and distance, panoramic and close-up views, inside view and outside view, etc. See "The Chinese Literary Garden," *Archetype and Allegory* 146–77.

173   Hay 86.

174   Hay 84.

175   Hay 100.

176   Tu Wan 72 (K'un-yü tien I, t'se 51, 8/37b).

3   Stone and Jade

1   Chang Hsin-chih, "*Hung-lou Meng* tu-fa," in I Su, "*Hung-lou Meng*" *chüan* (hereafter *HLMC*) I: 154. Chang Hsin-chih was one of the traditional commentators who interpreted the *Dream* from the moralist point of view and wrote his commentaries for didactic purposes. In "Miao-fu Hsüan *Shih-t'ou Chi* tzu-chi," he claimed that his mission as a commentator was to "remedy the harms that this book did [to the readers], and to rectify the "human heart and the way of the world" (34). For a more detailed discussion of Chang's interpretive stance, see Han Chin-lien 125–33. Also see Chou Ju-ch'ang, "*Hung-lou Meng*" *hsin-cheng* II: 1139. The entry on the intertextual relationship of the *Dream* with the other three narratives cited above represents one of the small handful of observations made by Chang Hsin-chih on the literariness and structure of classical narrative fiction.

2   Chao Kang and Ch'en Chung-i, "*Hung-lou Meng*" *yen-chiu hsin-pien* (hereafter *HLM hsin-pien*) 177.

3   In chapters 23 and 26, Pao-yü and Tai-yü cite verses from *The Romance of the Western Chamber* to tease each other; in chapter 49, Tai-yü and Pao-ch'ai discuss passages from the drama. In addition to the direct quotations, there are innumerable references in the narrative that allude to the drama in question. See note 5 below.

4   The Chih-yen Chai commentaries on the *Dream of the Red Chamber* were originally written in red ink, hence the self-designation of "the Red-ink Studio." The original manuscript of the *Dream*, with its commentaries, was transcribed into different copies later. And the Chih-yen commentaries were copied down in two colors—red and black. The commentaries consist of a variety of styles: (1) specific comments on individual passages or phrases, in double columns of small characters (in black ink); (2) general comments that occur in eighteen chapters, written on separate pages placed before each chapter (in black ink); (3) additional remarks at the end of each chapter (in black ink); (4) upper marginal comments (in red ink); (5) comments in between the columns of the text (in red ink); (6) general remarks at the end of the text of each chapter, which occur in six chapters (in red ink).

The identity of Chih-yen Chai has been a controversial issue. There are two main hypotheses: both Chou Ju-ch'ang and Wu Shih-ch'ang postulated that Chih-yen and Ch'i-hu 畸笏 (the other major commentator of the original manuscript) should be taken as one single individual who used two different designations, while Yü P'ing-po and Chao Kang/Ch'en Chung-i argued that Chih-yen should by no means be confused with Ch'i-hu. Within the theory of "single identity," however, Chou identified Chih-yen with Shih Hsiang-yün 史湘雲 (Shi Xiang-yun) (see Chou Ju-ch'ang, *HLM hsin-cheng* I: 833–940), while Wu repudiated such a conclusion and insisted that Chih-yen was actually Ts'ao Hsüeh-ch'in's paternal uncle Ts'ao Shih 曹頎 (see Wu Shih-ch'ang, "*Hung-lou Meng*" *t'an-yüan wai-pien* [hereafter *HLM t'an-yüan wai-pien*] 1–18). Within the theory of "two identities," Yü P'ing-po was not sure about Chih-yen's real identity (see Yü, *Chih-yen Chai "Hung-lou Meng" chi-p'ing* [hereafter *Chih-yen Chai*] 6–9), while Chao and Ch'en argued that Chih-yen was Ts'ao Hsüeh-ch'in's cousin Ts'ao T'ien-yu 曹天佑 (see *HLM hsin-pien* 73–138). Although it is difficult to tell which hypothesis is correct, we can nevertheless conclude that Hu Shih's speculation (that Chih-yen was Ts'ao Hsüeh-ch'in) is quite far-fetched. Chou Ju-ch'ang's speculations also sound less convincing than Wu Shih-ch'ang's.

5   Chih-yen Chai pointed out in his commentaries several passages in the *Dream* that showed Ts'ao Hsüeh-ch'in's conscious imitation of the *Western Chamber* and *The Golden Lotus* in creating the characterization and the tone of the major characters' discourse in the *Dream*. For instance, Chih-yen's commentary on chapter 25: "The fantastic passages from the work [*Dream*] quoted from [earlier] poems and the *t'zu* songs are all passages of the finest caliber like this one. May I ask you readers, isn't this [passage] an allusion to *ko-hua jen yüan t'ien-yai chin* 隔花人遠天涯近 " (*Chih-yen Chai* 344) (here the allusion is to the episode of "*Ssu Jing* 寺警 " in the *Western Chamber*). For further discussion of the influence of *The Golden Lotus* and the *Western Chamber* on the *Dream*, see *HLM hsien-pien* 177–78.

6   See *HLM hsin-pien* 177; Yü P'ing-po, "*Hung-lou Meng*" *yen-chiu* 226. Also see Hu Shih 405, in which he points out that the Roster of Lovers resembles the "stone tablet" in the

Water Margin and the "posthumous Honors List" in the *Ju-lin wai-shih* (*The Scholars*). It is worth noting that the most interesting treatise on the origin of the "Roster of Lovers" was contributed by Chou Ju-ch'ang: in "*Hung-lou Meng* 'ch'ing-pang' yüan-yüan lun" Chou suggests that Ts'ao Hsüeh-ch'in's idea of the Roster came from Feng Meng-lung's 馮夢龍 (1574–1646) *Ch'ing-shih* 情史, an anthology of love stories collected and compiled in the early seventeenth century. The anthology consists of twenty-four chapters, each of which is organized around a particular category of *ch'ing* 情. To name just a few: *ch'ing-yüan* 情緣 ("conjugal destiny and affinity"), *ch'ing-ai* 情愛 ("passion"), *ch'ing-ch'ih* 情癡 ("infatuation"), *ch'ing-han* 情憾 ("pathos"), *ch'ing-huan* 情幻 ("illusion"), and *ch'ing-ling* 情靈 ("efficacy"). Very few materials are available for us to reconstruct Ts'ao Hsüeh-ch'in's criteria for the composition of his "Roster of Lovers." Yü Ying-shih, quoting a commentary ("The case of passion/desire in the entire narrative has to be viewed according to the manner in which each maiden is enrolled in Pao-yü's heart" [*Chih-yen Chai* 449]) transcribed in the seventy-eight-chapter *Chih-pen* (*Chia-hsü-pen* 甲戌本 in Hu Shih's terms, and *Chih-ching-pen* 脂京本 in Wu Shih-ch'ang's terms), came up with a very convincing argument that the ranking of each maiden was decided according to her relationship with Pao-yü in matters of the heart (Yü Ying-shih, "*Hung-lou Meng* te liang-ko shih-chieh" 40–42; also see Yü, "Yen-ch'ien wu-lu hsiang hui-t'ou" 91–113). Although the origin of the actual ranking still remains controversial, one can nonetheless argue that Ts'ao Hsüeh-ch'in was heavily influenced by Feng Meng-lung's system of classification in the *Ch'ing-shih*. Ts'ao's categories of *ch'ing-ch'ing* 情情 and *ch'ing-lieh* 情烈 clearly echo Feng's combinatorial logic. The hypothesis of influence is further strengthened by the correspondence between the alternate titles of the *Ch'ing-shih* and the *Dream*: the former is also known as *Ch'ing-t'ien pao-chien* 情天寶鑑 ("A Mirror for the Passion Sky"), and the latter as *Feng-yüeh pao-chien* 風月寶鑑 ("A Mirror for the Romantic"). For the introduction to the *Ch'ing-shih* and the translation of excerpts from the anthology, see Mowry, *Chinese Love Stories*.

7   *Chih-yen Chai* 228, 256.

8   See Wu Shih-ch'ang, *Red Chamber Dream* 157–58.

9   Wu Shih-ch'ang, *Red Chamber Dream* 266. See Hu Shih's comment on the structural device of the Roster of Lovers as narrative enclosure in note 6 above.

10 Wu Shih-ch'ang argues that the Roster of Lovers brings the narrative back to the "mythological, preincarnation story in the Introduction of the book," and that the grand cycle of the "Other-World—This World—the Other-World" is thus completed (*Red Chamber Dream* 160).

11 The scholars of *HLM* studies who belong to the school of the "autobiographical approach" provide a different interpretation of the Nü-kua Stone's complaint about the goddess's neglect of its merits. From this perspective, the phrase *wu-ts'ai pu-t'ien* 無材補天, "unfit to repair the azure sky" (*Stone* I: 49), can be seen as Ts'ao Hsüeh-ch'in's self-portrayal as an outcast in a society from which he was alienated. Stone's indulgence in self-pity thus appears in a different light: it is the author's complaint about such an ostracism in mythological terms. See Chou Ju-ch'ang, "*Hung-lou Meng*" *hsin-cheng* I: 15. I should also mention a poem whose authorship, a subject of controversy among *HLM* scholars, may be attributable to Ts'ao Hsüeh-ch'in. In this five-character poem, we find two cou-

plets that seem to bear out the hypothesis of the autobiographical school, if the poem was indeed written by Hsüeh-ch'in: *yu-chih kuei wan-p'u, wu-ts'ai ch'ü pu-t'ien / pu-ch'iu yao chung-shang, hsiao-sa tso wan-hsien* 有志歸完璞，無才去補天；不求遠衆賞，瀟灑做頑仙 ("Intent on returning thither as a polished jade, unfit to repair the azure sky / Seeking no mundane appreciation, without restraint roaming like a playful fairy"). See Yü Ying-shih, "Chin-tai hung-hsüeh" 28.

12 The various copies of the *Dream of the Red Chamber* now exist in two major systems—the transcribed copies (usually designated as the *Chih-pen*), and the printed editions. The transcribed copies exist in eight different versions, each of which contains Ts'ao Hsüeh-ch'in's original manuscript together with the commentators' texts written by Chih-yen Chai, Ch'i-hu, and the other commentators of Ts'ao Hsüeh-ch'in's contemporaries. Among those eight transcribed copies, the sixteen-chapter copy, the seventy-eight-chapter copy, "Chi-mo 己卯" (1759), and the Ch'i Liao-sheng 戚寥生 (1732–92) copy (*Yu-cheng-pen* 有正本) were most frequently cited and discussed. The dating of the first two copies caused many controversies among scholars of *HLM* studies. Hu Shih first assigned the two dates *Chia-hsü* (1754) and *Keng-ch'en* 庚辰 (1760) to the sixteen-chapter copy and the seventy-eight-chapter copy respectively. The designations gained such popularity that even after Wu Shih-ch'ang made a convincing critique of Hu Shih's dating method, scholars continued to use Hu's naming system for these two transcribed copies. To rectify Hu's mistakes, Wu coined two different names to replace Hu's designations—*Chih-ts'an-pen* 脂殘本 for the sixteen-chapter copy, and *Chih-ching-pen* for the seventy-eight-chapter copy—and suggested two different dates. According to Wu, the *Chih-ching-pen* was copied after 1767, and the *Chih-ts'an-pen* after 1774 (141). For a detailed discussion of Wu's argument and his critique of Hu Shih's views, see Wu Shih-ch'ang, *HLM t'an-yüan wai-pien* 96–200. The printed editions were edited by Kao O and Ch'eng Wei-yüan. They consist of two main versions: *Ch'eng-chia-pen* 程甲本 (1791), and *Ch'eng-i-pen* 程乙本 (1792). For detailed discussion of the virtues and vices of each version, see *HLM hsin-pien* 73–111, 245–58. Also see Wu Shih-ch'ang, *Red Chamber Dream* 1–11, 267–77.

13 *Ch'ien-lung chia-hsü Chih-yen Chai ch'ung-p'ing "Shih-t'ou Chi"* (hereafter *Ch'ien-lung chia-hsü*) 6. The translation was quoted from Miller 37–39.

14 This translation of mine is more literal than Miller's. It brings into focus the Taoist concept of "mutual arising."

15 Yeh Chia-ying discredits Wang Kuo-wei's intent of associating "jade" with "desire," and proclaims that the critic misinterpreted the philosophy that underlies the *Dream*. She argues that the symbolism of "precious jade" is not to be understood within the framework of Schopenhauer's philosophy of desire and free will, but is built on the Buddhist metaphysics that emphasizes the potential of the original nature (*pen-hsing* 本性) for enlightenment. Yeh seems unwilling to acknowledge the dialectical nature of Buddhist metaphysics, which is concerned with the nature of desire as much as with the means of our liberation from it. One might say that the Chinese fascination with the *Dream of the Red Chamber* has more to do with Ts'ao Hsüeh-ch'in's depiction of the process of the hero's passion (*ch'ing/yü* 情/欲) journey than with the underlying religious "truth" about the "original purity of the human mind." The *Dream* would certainly appear less novel if the emphasis of the narrative is placed on the familiar theme of Buddhist enlightenment.

While numerous Buddhist treatises dwell on the topic of "original nature," what makes the *Dream* a narrative fiction to be distinguished from such treatises is the fact that it deals with the "fallen nature" of desire rather than reiterating a religious truism that has been echoed for thousands of years by priests, Ch'an poets, philosophers, and fiction writers such as Wu Ch'eng-en. See Yeh Chia-ying 141–44.

16   Wang Kuo-wei 11.

17   *Chih-yen Chai* 3.

18   Wang Kuo-wei 12.

19   *Limen* is a Latin word which literally means "threshold." In cultural anthropology, it refers to the transitional period during which the ritual subject is situated between the old social structure and the new into which he or she is being initiated. For a detailed discussion of the concept, see "The Liminal Stone" in Chap. 4, below.

20   Na Chih-liang, "Ku-tai te tsang-yü" 332.

21   Goette 35.

22   Laufer 103.

23   "Ch'un-kuan tsung-po," *Chou Li*, in *Tuan-chu "Shih-san Ching" ching-wen* (hereafter *TCSSCCW*) 30.

24   Hansford 86.

25   The third role assigned to jade in this particular text relates to divination, which seems to have originated from one of the important roles that the ritual jade played in the imperial cosmic rituals mentioned above. The six jade vessels in question—especially the *pi*, a perforated disk—were used to invoke the help of spirits to relieve natural disasters. See Rawson 29.

26   Laufer 299. It was believed that by closing up all apertures of the body with jade, the essence of the *yang* would triumph over the destructive underworld *yin* elements. This practice betrays the heavy influence of religious Taoism during the Han Dynasty.

27   Ts'ao Hsüeh-ch'in and Kao O, *Hung-lou Meng* (hereafter *HLM*) I: 28.

28   *Ch'ien-lung chia-hsü* 6b–7a.

29   Na Chih-liang, "Ku-tai tsang-yü" 103–4.

30   The association of *han-ch'an* 含蝉 , the mouth-pupa, with the concept of resurrection has been discussed in various treatises on jade. See Laufer 299–301.

31   Lyons 4.

32   Rawson 64.

33   T'ung Chung-t'ai 8.

34   Laufer 325.

35   Na Chih-liang, "Chi-ssu t'ien-ti ssu-fang te liu-ch'i" 8.

36   *Chou Li* (*TCSSCCW*) 30.

37   Hansford 59–60.

38   "P'ing-i," *Li Chi*, *TCSSCCW* 133.

39   *Shuo-wen* I: 1/7a.

40   Lo Man-li 29.

41   Coward and Ellis 78.

42   It is worth noting that the association of the names of Tai-yü and Pao-ch'ai with the Taoist theory of five elements has been elaborated in critical treatises written by both traditional

Chinese commentators and contemporary American scholars. See Plaks, "Allegory" 195–96; also see Plaks, *Archetype and Allegory* 54–83. It is possible that Plaks was inspired by the traditional commentator Chang Hsin-chih's analysis of Tai-yü's and Pao-ch'ai's last names in the context of the theory of five elements; see Chang Hsin-chih, "*Hung-lou Meng* tu-fa" 156. According to those critics, the interaction among five elements, which takes the dominant pattern of complementary bipolarity and multiple periodicity, can best account for the ill-fated love between Pao-yü and Tai-yü. For a detailed analysis of such critical perspective, see Jing Wang, "Poetics of Chinese Narrative."

43   The majority of traditional commentators condemned Pao-ch'ai for her devious-mindedness. Chih-yen Chai's commentaries seem to represent the orthodox view. Both the sixteen-chapter and the seventy-eight-chapter transcribed copies contain Chih-yen's remarks on the episode of Hsiao-hung ·小·紅 (Crimson) (chapter 27) and his criticism of Pao-ch'ai's calculating mind—"Could we interpret her action as coming from someone who is a learned and judicious female Confucianist? The way the author portrays her is indeed very appropriate" (*Chih-yen Chai* 377). Now to cite a few examples of similar assessment of Pao-ch'ai, made by other commentators collected in the "*Hung-lou Meng*" *Chüan*: Hsü Ying, "*Hung-lou Meng* lun-tsan," HLMC I: 127; Hua-shih Chu-jen, "*Hung-lou Meng* pen-i yüeh-pien," I: 181; Hsieh-an Chü-shih, "Shih-t'ou i-shuo," I: 191–92, 195; Hsi-yüan Chu-jen provides a detailed analysis of Pao-ch'ai's scheming nature and her stupidity in "*Hung-lou Meng* lun-pien," I: 201–2; Hsü Yeh-fen, "*Hung-lou Meng* pien," I: 229. Pao-ch'ai had fewer defenders. One of them, Wang Hsi-lien, complains about Tai-yü's narrow-mindedness in favor of the "virtuous and talented" Pao-ch'ai ("*Hung-lou Meng* tsung-p'ing," I: 150). Another commentator, Chang Hsin-chih, denounces both maidens and concludes that "Neither serves as a desirable model [for maidenhood]" ("*Hung-lou Meng* tu-fa," I: 155–56). An impartial account of the virtues and vices of both maidens is offered by Chu Tso-lin, "*Hung-lou Meng* wen-k'u," I: 160–61. Yeh Ho differs from all the other commentators by suggesting that we should not assess Pao-ch'ai and Tai-yü against each other ("Tu *Hung-lou* cha-chi," I: 286).

Modern commentators are equally divided in their evaluation of these two maidens. T'ai Yü (Wang K'un-lun) designates Pao-ch'ai as "an orthodox utilitarian" and Tai-yü as "an unorthodox emotionalist" (see T'ai Yü, "Hua Hsi-jen lun," "*Hung-lou Meng*" *jen-wu lun*). Yü P'ing-po argues that Ts'ao Hsüeh-ch'in did not intend to rank one maiden above the other, for "the book always places Pao-ch'ai and Tai-yü on equal footing, describing them as two peaks facing each other and as two streams channeled in two different water-courses—each works wonders in its own way. We cannot compare the one with the other" (Yü, "*Hung-lou Meng*" *yen-chiu* 112). Han Chin-lien characterized Pao-ch'ai as a feudal conformist, and Tai-yü as an antifeudal rebel (241).

Some critics still subscribe to the theory of the double, *chien-mei* 兼美, by taking Pao-ch'ai and Tai-yü as two complementary faces of a single ideal beauty. This idea was suggested in one of the original prefaces written by Ts'ao Hsüeh-ch'in's brother T'ang-ts'un for the older manuscript of the *Dream*: "Although *ch'ai* 釵 and *yü* 玉 appear as two different names, they actually make up one single individual. This is an 'illusory touch'" (*Chih-yen Chai* 434). Wu Shih-ch'ang provides a convincing argument against the rationale underlying this particular entry of T'ang-ts'un's commentaries. According to Wu, T'ang-ts'un's remark, like some of his other prefaces, pertains only to the original design in Hsüeh-ch'in's older manuscript. Since T'ang-ts'un died young he did not have the opportunity of reading the revised manuscript, in which the characterization of Pao-ch'ai and Tai-yü differs significantly from what Hsüeh-ch'in first envisioned. See Wu Shih-ch'ang, *HLM t'an-yüan wai-pien* 182–97.

44   Those who are well aware of the relations of sexual politics to the historical construction of such an aesthetic bias may feel free to readjust their personal preferences for our two heroines. This is a topic that goes beyond the scope of my present project, but I would like to mention in passing several intriguing issues that the perspective of gender studies inevitably elicits. The politics of the body not only poses a set of behavioral standards for the female gender in particular, it also conditions and thus manipulates the ruling of poetic justice and public opinion. In light of this perspective, the nature of the competition in which Tai-yü and Pao-ch'ai are involved appears even more complicated than what is already implied. It is not just a competition in love, but one in public appeal. Throughout the ages, Tai-yü has emerged as the real victor in the poll of public opinion, thanks to the Chinese sexual politics that prescribes, as far as the female gender is concerned, that the small and the weak is beautiful, and that the victimized gains in a paradoxical way. But our awareness that sexual politics manipulates public appeal cannot but raise the question whether Tai-yü is as much a victor as such politics recommends. I would suggest that perhaps Tai-yü is as great a loser as Pao-ch'ai, not simply because she loses Pao-yü, but because she is trapped in a cultural aestheticism that endorses the sexual politics that recompenses, by means of an illusory poetic justice, the physically weak female for her loss in real-life battles. As if by placing her upon the pedestal of the ideal feminine, poetic justice succeeds in elevating her status from that of loser to that of victor.

The cult of Lin Tai-yü serves as an excellent example of the compensatory psychology in question. This is the woman who has been celebrated as the most attractive female literary personality in traditional Chinese literature. This is the ideal model for elite womanhood. The morality play enacted in the *Dream* thus reads as follows: It matters little if Tai-yü lost Pao-yü in real life to her rival, for it was she, rather than Pao-ch'ai, who had possessed his heart and achieved a spiritual union with him. Therefore, although abused and victimized, she emerges as the ultimate *heroine* in the *Dream of the Red Chamber*. This is the dominant interpretation accepted by the general reading public since the eighteenth century. The legitimacy of Tai-yü's cult symbolism remains intact as long as one evades the issues raised by gender politics. Such issues indeed proliferate rapidly when we launch into a mode of thinking that emphasizes the politics of critical methodology. We need to look into, for instance, the political implications of idealizing a beauty that is frail and defenseless, and of constructing her rival in a physique that is her opposite. The inquiry will eventually lead us to challenge the problematic perception: the victim is our ideal hero(ine). How is any aesthetic or moral evaluation possible when such criteria are infiltrated by the political unconscious? This new conceptual framework may give rise to interpretations that will lead us in a different direction. The role of victim assumed by Tai-yü may invoke sympathies of a different nature, while the condemnation of Pao-ch'ai's manipulative nature may also lose some of its edge.

45   Kang Lai-hsin 60.

46   See "Is There a Beginning in the *Dream of the Red Chamber*?" in Chap. 4, below.

47   See T'ang Ch'ang-ju 298–310.

48   For the definition of the four virtues *jen, i, chih,* and *yung,* see "The *Feng-shan* Ritual" in Chap. 2, above.

49   See "Story of Jade" 904.

50   Hsü Shou-chi IV: 28.

51   Hay 122.

52   As mentioned earlier, the intellectual trend against the ideological domination of Confucianism emerged in the late Ming with the development of Wang Yang-ming's (1472–1506) School of the Mind known as the *hsin-hsüeh* 心學 . This school, which evolved from the idealist view of the Sung philosopher Lu Chiu-yüan 陸九淵 (1139–93), placed the emphasis on the a priori nature of subjectivity over objectivity. Starting from the premise that the locus of subjectivity is to be found in the mind, one can define the physical nature of external matters only through the perception of the mind. In Wang Yang-ming's epistemological framework, the mind is seen as a self-defined and self-sufficient totality that "knows about itself naturally," *liang-chih tzu chih chih* 良知自知之 (Wang Yang-ming II: 211). The rectification of the mind in Wang Yang-ming's tradition means simply getting back in touch with the mind in its original and undifferentiated state. This emphasis on the intuitive knowledge of the mind about its own nature marks the deviation of the Wang-Lu School from the orthodox Ch'eng-Chu 程朱 School of Principle (*li-hsüeh* 理學), known for its rationalist approach to the Confucian tradition of self-cultivation.

53   De Bary II: 196.

54   For a discussion of the lack of significance of childhood in Confucian ideology, see Jing Wang, "Rise of Children's Poetry" 57.

55   Li Chih, "T'ung-hsin shuo" 368.

56   Li Chih 370.

57   Ts'ao Hsüeh-ch'in's intellectual affiliation with Li Chih may go deeper than has been recognized. Lin Tai-yü's famous elegy to the fallen flowers contains allusions to the two lines Li Chih wrote in lamenting the inconstancy of human life: *k'an-hua pu shih chung-hua jen* 看花不是種花人 ("Those who look at the flowers now are not those who planted them"), and *hua k'ai hua hsieh tsung pu chih* 花開花謝總不知 ("Nobody knows when the flowers bloom and fade"); see Li Chih, "Ch'i-yen ssu-chü" and "Mu-tan shih," 6/243.

58   References to *sha* and *feng* and *tai* can be found in the *Dream* abundantly, especially in the first eighty chapters. The simultaneous reference to all three epithets appears in chapter 71, HLM II: 1014.

59   Sun T'ung-sheng, quoting Chang Hsin-chih (self-designated as T'ai-p'ing Hsien-jen), I: 40.

60   In Ch'eng Wei-yüan's printed edition, the phrase is slightly different: *chuang-yü* ("pretending to be inane"). While *ts'ang-yü* depicts Pao-ch'ai as falling short of being a genuine soul, *chuang-yü* is an even less complimentary description. See Ch'eng Wei-yüan 65.

61   "P'ing-i," *Li Chi, TCSSCCW* 133.

62   "Chün-tzu," "*Hsün Tzu*" hsin-chu 408.

63   Hsün Tzu defined *chieh* in "Chün-tzu" as the attribute "of living and dying for the sake of

defending it [the ruling principles of ancient sage-kings]" (*"Hsün Tzu" hsin-chu* 408). In another chapter, he made a similar statement: ". . . thereby none of the Confucian scholars would fail to value the code of honor and to die in its defense" ("Wang-ba," *"Hsün Tzu" hsin-chu* 187).

64   Kan Pao 11/137.

65   Liu Hsieh, "Tsung-shu," *Literary Mind* 447.

66   See Han Fei 4/13 (I: 238). According to the legend, Ho Shih found an unpolished jade disc which he offered as a tribute to the court. The imperial jade-craftsman failed to identify the value of the disc and insisted that what Ho Shih had brought was simply a piece of stone. After suffering the punishment of amputation twice, Ho Shih eventually proved that his disc was truly made of jade.

67   Ko Hung 194 (3/18a).

68   For a more detailed analysis of the interpretive framework of Western scholars of *HLM* studies, see Jing Wang, "Poetics of Chinese Narrative" 255–68.

69   See Wong Kam-ming, "Narrative Art of *Red Chamber Dream*" and "Point of View."

70   See Plaks, *Allegory and Archetype*.

71   See Miller, *Masks of Fiction*.

72   "Yen Yüan," *Lun Yü* 77.

73   Ryan 10.

74   According to Kang, "seen from the point of view of his affiliation with the inane stone, Pao-yü appears as none other than a pure simplicity, a primordial origin" (Kang Lai-hsin 234).

75   K'ang Lai-hsin 231.

76   *I-wen lei-chü* II: 83/142b.

77   For a detailed discussion and definition of *t'ung-ling shih*, see "*T'ung-ling Shih* and *Wan Shih*: The Stone of Divine Intelligence and the Unknowing Stone," in Chap. 4 below.

78   Lenin 196.

79   See, for example, Wang Hsiao-lien 88–91.

80   "Wo-hsien ts'ao-t'ang," Li Han-ch'iu 118.

81   See Wu Kung-cheng 596.

4   The Story of Stone

1   "Subject-position" is a term used by Paul Smith in his discussion of the concept of "subject" in *Discerning the Subject*. He argues against the totality of subjectivity, since the subject is always subjected to more than one constraining social formation and to political discourses that are changing at the same time. Each such formation and discourse can be mapped out as a subject-position that competes with others to subjugate the individual. These various subject-positions never cohere to constitute a single, uncontradictory individual. (See Smith's "Note on Terminology," xxxiii–xxxv.) It is worth mentioning that contemporary Chinese theorists have also made some significant contributions to the discussion of "subjectivity" (*chu-t'i* 主體). The "human subject" became the catch-phrase of the 1980s as China underwent economic and cultural modernization following the collapse of the ultra-leftists' monopoly on power. The controversy over Chinese modernity revolves around the discovery of a creative—and, arguably, an autonomous—subjectivity

in post-Mao literature. The topic of the meaning of socialist humanism has been widely addressed by Marxist theorists, dogmatic and unorthodox ones alike, and also by creative writers. By far the most significant theorist is Liu Tsai-fu, whose writings on this subject heralded a period of prolific discussions of the aesthetic, ontological, and political implications of "subjectivity." Liu's *Hsing-ko tzu-ho lun* is a substantial work on the bipolar structure of personality. His conceptual framework, which represents a momentous breakthrough in the Chinese aesthetics of one-dimensional characterization, is based on the underlying assumption and affirmation of a coherent subjectivity that is "made up of" (*tzu-ho* 組合), as the title of his book suggests, rather than infinitely divided or disseminated into, various sets of opposites, such as the "hidden" and the "apparent," the "contingent" and the "determined," the "sublime" and the "absurd," the "good" and the "evil." His emphasis on the mechanism of bipolar composition reflects a philosophical vision that is based on the dichotomous perception of being and knowledge, and confined within a highly consistent paradigm of predictable totality.

2 John Minford rendered the two words *an-fang* 安放 into "lying still." (*Stone* V: 374). My translation comes closer to the original. While "lying still" retains the sense of stone as a subject, albeit a lifeless one, *an-fang* certainly turns Stone into an object syntactically. The syntax of objectification implicit in "safely placed" is significant in that Stone is ontologically no longer a subject, but an object not responsible for its own activity, not even for that of "lying still" at the foot of Greensickness Peak.

3 *Ch'ien-lung Chia-hsü* 6.

4 After discussing the value of the Stone Record with Stone, Vanitas attains a sudden illumination. The "process" is described as follows: Starting off "in the Void (*k'ung*) [he] came to the contemplation of Form (*se*); and from Form engendered Passion (*ch'ing*); and by communicating Passion, entered again into Form; and from Form awoke to the Void" (*Stone* I: 51).

5 *Ch'u-hsüeh chi* 24a, quoting *Wu-li lun* 物理論 by Yang Ch'üan 楊泉 of Chin Dynasty.

6 Painters of the Ming and Ch'ing dynasties seem to be concerned more with the interior landscape of the natural objects they portray than with what meets the eye. John Hay argues that the Ch'ing painters are particularly drawn to the foraminal structure of rocks (Hay 118–19). They appear interested in capturing the internal empty space rather than the solid texture of the rock.

7 In one of the inscriptions on his paintings of rocks, Cheng Pan-ch'iao wrote: "This stone of Pan-ch'iao, a grotesque stone. Grotesque, therefore heroic; grotesque, therefore delicate" (see Chang Wei-yüan, "Wen jen yü ch'ou shih"). Ts'ao Hsüeh-ch'in's Manchu friend, Tun Min 敦敏 (1729–1786?) described one of Ts'ao's paintings of stone as a symbolic statement of the iconoclastic artist himself: "Such proud bones like you are rare, disjointed and rugged [like the stone]" (Tun Min, "T'i Ch'in P'u hua-shih").

8 See Mi Fu's biography in the *Sung shih*, ed. T'o-t'o et al., 1st ed., 496 vols. (Peking: Chung-hua shu-chü, 1977), 444: 5620; Yeh Meng-te (1077–1148), X: 155.

9 In his debate with Stone on the value of the Stone Record, Vanitas addresses the latter as "Elder Brother Stone" (*HLM* I: 4).

10 John Hay describes paintings in which eccentric arhats are portrayed as "bizarre forma-

tions of trees and rocks" (Hay 63). Among such paintings are *The Sixteen Arhats*, dated 1591, exhibited in the Metropolitan Museum; *The Five Hundred Arhats* handscroll in the Nelson-Atkins Museum; and an anonymous seventeenth-century *Shakyamuni under the Bodhi Tree*.

11 *Chih-yen Chai* 132; also see *HLM* I: 245.

12 See *Yüan Chiao* 258–59.

13 Jayatilleke 82, 128ff, 152ff.

14 *Ch'eng Wei-shih Lun*, a doctrinal Canon of the Wei-shih (Yogacara) School, is a complete Chinese version of the *Trimsika*. Hsüan Tsang also incorporates the explanations of ten Indian commentaries into this canonical work.

15 Hsüan Tsang 377.

16 Hsüan Tsang 107.

17 Hsüan Tsang 385.

18 Hsüan Tsang 385–87.

19 O'Flaherty 220.

20 Translated in *Visuddhi-Magga* 239.

21 The Buddhist interpretation of such a vision is contained in the concept of *ta tz'u-pei* 大慈悲 (*mahakaruna*, "grand compassion"). And according to Professor Roger Corless of the Department of Religion at Duke University, the equivalent Taoist explication of this vision is framed in the negative concept of "crystallization," a term for the kind of existence that is eternally immobile, such as the stone. Corless credits this notion of "crystallization" to Edward Schafer.

22 In "Tu Tzu-ch'un," a T'ang *ch'uan-ch'i* tale, the hero undergoes his initiation ritual in an enclosed stone chamber; see Li Ching 230–33. *Ming-pao Chi* provides an account of a Buddhist monk who copies scriptures in a stone chamber; see Tang Lin (fl. ca. 660), 51: 789. In Central Australia during the Pleistocene epoch, an old religious ceremony still survived, in the course of which a tribal procession was formed to fetch sacred objects from stone caves that were regarded as holy sanctuaries (see Levy 36). The Australian medicine-men of the Ice Age were also known to retire to a cave for their ritual death-slumber and subsequent rebirth (see Spencer 480–84). G. R. Levy pointed out that "later civilized races also performed such ceremonies in caves or crypts and considered the cave as the mother from whom they are born again" (Levy 53). In discussing the association of the stone cave with the symbolism of womb/tomb, William Irwin Thompson cites the archaeological evidence of the megalithic stone temples on Malta, the architectural plan of which betrays an "outline of the old Paleolithic obese Great Goddess" (Thompson 264n). The Maltese temples and other such ancient temples on Skara Brae, in Wales, and in Egypt reiterate the same formula that the tomb is the womb, the paradox of which is manifested in the dual character of the Great Mother.

The association of stone caverns with holiness in both the Chinese and the Australian case seems to indicate that such symbol-making evolved from the earlier prototype of the cave as both the hearth and the sanctuary in the Stone Age. I should point out, however, that while the Chinese shared the Western fascination with the stone cave as the locale for initiation and religious activities, the Chinese attachment to the womb symbolism inherent in the image of the cave was not nearly as strong as the Westerners'. It is possible that the symbolism of the cave as Mother is a phenomenon unique to Western civilization. This is not to negate the divine potency of the few Chinese Mother Goddesses such as Nü-kua, Hsi-wang-mu 西王母 , and the Goddess of Kuan-yin 觀音 —but each of these mother figures seems to reign autonomously, and is very rarely conceptualized in the single body of the Great Mother. The cult of the Great Goddess as a universal religion that survived in Indo-Europe is not found in China. It suffices to say that although the Chinese cave wo/men must have worshipped, with an intensity equal to that of their Western counterparts, the caves in which they found shelter and buried the dead, the Western Chalcolithic pre-occupation with the cave-womb symbolism has no obvious contemporaneous counterpart in China. It seems that the obsession with the cave-form as womb, and consequently as the body of the Mother, is not so much a universal phenomenon as reminiscent of Western Neolithic-Chalcolithic mentality.

23   Cheng Te-k'un, *Prehistoric China* 35.

24   Erh-chih Tao-jen 102.

25   "Lieh chuan 62," *Chin Shu* 2405.

26   In the present-day context, the expression *wan-shih tien-t'ou* "the crude/unknowing stone nodded its head" often refers to self-rectification and to the genuine conversion of an individual who has gone astray.

27   This is my own translation. Hawkes fails to bring out the symbolic meaning of the term *wan shih*; his translation reads: ". . . this jade was a transformation of that same stone block which once lay. . ." (*Stone* I: 189).

28   The term "ch'un-wu" is translated by David Hawkes as "absurd creature" (*Stone* I: 54), thus losing the connotation of foolishness. In general, Hawkes fails to evoke the symbol-ism of dullness and opacity implied in the epithet *wan shih* by rendering it simply into a "lifeless stone block." The same blunder occurs when he deals with the term *t'ung-ling*. By translating the term as "Magic Stone," he aborts the subtle interplay between *ch'un*, *wan*, and *t'ung-ling*. His translation of *t'ung-ling* also revokes the intertextual reference of the folk legend of the nodding stone, and in so doing, cancels the possibility of dramatic transformation originally implied in the juxtaposition of the two conflicting epithets, *wan* and *t'ung-ling*. Inasmuch as the paradoxical identification between these two stones con-stitutes the epistemological as well as the symbolic framework of the *Dream*, Hawkes's misinterpretation of the epithets not only weakens the force of the allegory underlying the *t'ung-ling* stone, it also annuls the liminal characteristics of Pao-yü's psychic makeup.

29   Miller 36 37 n.76.

30   Miller 82.

31   Miller 179.

32   Hung Ch'iu-fan 238.

33   This comment appears in chapter 1 of the sixteen-chapter transcribed copy; see *Ch'ien-lung Chia-hsü* 6b.

34   Chou Ju-ch'ang, *"Hung-lou Meng" hsin-cheng* I: 14.

35   Anthony Yu suggests that the term is associated with the "sense of numinous intelligence," but his emphasis is more on the trancelike process of how such an intelligence, when

granted to a fictive subject, can be arrived at. I would suggest that this "illusory" and "dreamlike process" that leads the subject into communion with the divine can be characterized in terms of liminality—a concept I will deal with in the next section. See Yu, "History" 17.

36   According to Victor Turner, "During the intervening 'liminal' period, the characteristics of the ritual subject ('the passenger') are ambiguous; he passes through a cultural realm that has a few or none of the attributes of the past or coming state" (94).

37   Turner 95.

38   Turner 38.

39   See "*Shih-nü*: Stone Woman" in Chap. 2, above.

40   Neumann, *Great Mother* 242. The ancient Egyptian myth of Osiris is closely related to the fertility ritual. In the myth, Isis, Nephthys, Set, and Osiris were two brothers and two sisters. Isis married Osiris. Osiris was killed twice by his hostile brother Set—the first time, he was drowned in the Nile or imprisoned within a cedar chest that corresponded to the symbolic djed pillar; the second time, he was dismembered. Isis found the coffin and brought Osiris back to life again. To ancient Egyptians, wood symbolized organic living duration. By ascending from the wood coffin, a mixed imagery of life and earth, Osiris became the emblem of transformation and rebirth. The djed pillar therefore became the symbol of the Egyptian God Osiris, identified with the male phallic symbol. The wood pillar is, however, also identified with the Great Tree Goddess. Thus Neumann concludes in *The Great Mother* that "in the symbolic equations of a Feminine that nourishes, generates, and transforms, tree, djed pillar, . . . belong together" (243).

41   Also see "Between Stone and Jade" in Chap. 3, above.

42   Lucien Miller gives us a detailed analysis of this "curious logic." He interprets the narrator's tendency to debunk himself as a mask-device through which the author-narrator presents his own revolutionary concept of fiction. See Miller 206, 221–22.

43   Turner 97.

44   "All these mystic types are structurally inferior or 'marginal,' yet represent what Henri Bergson would have called 'open' as against 'closed morality,' the latter being essentially the normative system of bounded, structured, particularistic groups" (Turner 110).

45   Hawkes's lack of awareness of the semantic tension between *wan* and *t'ung-ling* results in his occasional misinterpretation of the significant phrases that portray Pao-yü's character. For instance, *han-wan*, "silly mischievous," is rendered as "wilful" (*Stone* I: 98). *Ch'ih-wan*, "silly and dull-witted," is translated as "silliness" (*Stone* I: 137). The same term *ch'ih-wan* is translated by Lucien Miller as "silly dullness," which comes closer to the original; see Miller 94.

46   This is my own translation. Hawkes fails to grasp the deep meaning of *wu*, "illuminated." His translation reads: "Silly boy! You still don't understand, do you?" (*Stone* I: 145).

47   *Chih-yen Chai* 256.

48   The Chih-yen Chai commentaries on this phrase occur in chapter 8 of the sixteen-chapter *Chih-pen*, and in chapters 19, 21, and 31 of the seventy-eight-chapter *Chih-pen*.

49   *Chih-yen Chai* 256. This translation was rendered by Wu shih-ch'ang, *Red Chamber Dream* 155. I have purposefully omitted his translation of the two terms *ch'ing pu-ch'ing*

and *ch'ing ch'ing*, since their meanings incorporate multiple references. The former was translated by Wu as "Lover with Pure Love," and the latter as "Passionate Lover yet without Passion At All."

50 *Chih-yen Chai* 135. According to Wu Shih-ch'ang, this summary commentary placed at the beginning of chapter 31 was not written by Chih-yen, but by Hsüeh-ch'in's brother T'ang-ts'un 棠村 , who wrote a handful of prefaces summarizing his readings of each chapter and copied them into the old manuscript of the *Dream*. Wu argues that it is for sentimental reasons that Chih-yen kept all T'ang-ts'un's earlier prefaces. For his argument, see *HLM t'an-yüan wai-pien* 11.

51 *Chih-yen Chai* 405.

52 *Chih-yen Chai* 287. This verse was translated by me. For the most part I used Wu Shih-ch'ang's translation (*Red Chamber Dream* 93), polishing it here and there; however, he left the penultimate line untranslated.

53 Miller 35–36.

54 *Ch'ien-lung Chia-hsü* 6.

55 The word *huan* is pinpointed as a specific reminder of the "main theme" of the *Dream* in the seventy-eight-chapter *Chih-pen*. The passage in question sounds like an unpolished authorial intrusion: "Words such as *meng* 夢 ('dream') and *huan* ('illusion') in this chapter serve as reminders for the reader. They also point out the main theme of this book" (*HLM* I: 1). Wu Shih-ch'ang argues that the commentary is actually one of the early prefaces that T'ang-ts'un wrote for the old manuscript of the *Dream* (Wu, *HLM t'an-yüan wai-pien* 184). Given the importance of the word *huan* to the understanding of the authorial intention, David Hawkes's translation seems highly questionable: he renders it as "transformation" in lieu of "illusion." This slip of the hand seems a problematic one, because such a translation bypasses the hidden dichotomous relationship between *chen* and *huan*, and thus between *chen* and *chia*.

56 Said 5.

57 Said 76.

58 Eliade, *The Myth of the Eternal Return* 56.

59 Eliade, *The Myth* 54.

60 Eliade, *The Myth* 20.

61 See Neumann, "The Creation Myth: the Uroboros," *Origins* 5–38. According to Neumann, the evolution of consciousness begins with the submersion of the ego in the unconscious, the mythical symbol of which is the circle. He named it the Uroboros, which represents all the aspects of the Self-contained—the perfect state in which duality has not yet been born from the original undifferentiated unity. It is only when humankind discovers its ego consciousness that the wholeness of the mythical unconscious is sundered into opposites.

5 The Paradox of Desire and Emptiness

1 Dudbridge 116.

2 Dudbridge 126–27. According to Dudbridge, Ōta Tatsuo claims that there is an intimate

relationship between the legendary white ape and the fictional character of Sun Wu-k'ung. Ōta argues that the connotation of the name "Wu-k'ung" derives from this particular context of the sexual overtones of the white ape woman-abductor (Ōta 11).

3   Dudbridge 126–27.

4   Dudbridge 128.

5   Dudbridge 166. Dudbridge raises other questions, such as why the religious folk-hero Tripitaka should be accompanied by animal-attendants, and why Monkey plays the most important role among them.

6   Dudbridge 128.

7   Wu Ch'eng-en, *Hsi-yu Chi* (hereafter *Hsi-yu Chi*) 5.

8   "Chen Ts'ung-shan Mei-ling shih hun-chia" 11.

9   Mair 694, citing K'ung Ling-ching 孔另境 and Akira Isobe's 磯部彰 studies.

10 Mair 670–71. One of Mair's central arguments is that the making and accretion of Wu-k'ung in the *Journey* "occurred centuries before his [Wu Ch'eng-en's] time" and that it took place during the process of the oral transmission of Hanuman's legends from Southeast Asian countries to China. He also cites Liu Ts'un-yan's statement that the T'ang tale provides the evidence that "Hanumat cloaked in a Chinese robe does exist in our tales" (712).

11 See annotations on "Pu Chiang-tsung bai-yüan chuan" 18. Chiao yen-shou in the *I-lin* records the following: "There were big apes in the southern Mountains who abducted [our] beautiful wives." Chang Hua in *Po-wu chih* provides the following account: "On the high mountains south of the Ssu-ch'uan mountain range, there were animals which looked like apes, seven feet tall, which could walk fast like humans. . . . Beautiful women who traveled the same path were often abducted by them. And nobody would know their whereabouts."

12 The questions that arise from influence-studies of this nature—how and when a monkey assumes a key role in the *Journey to the West*, and different versions of the *Rāmāyaṇa* in Chinese Buddhist texts and in Southeast Asian oral literature and performing arts—are extremely important. They not only provide a potent point of departure for comparative studies of Chinese, Indian, and Southeast Asian popular literature, they also contribute to a more thorough understanding of the *Journey*. For the most comprehensive study of Sun Wu-k'ung's problematic origin, see Mair 659–752.

13 See Mair 718, quoting Huang Meng-wen 黃孟文 , who states that "In every way, he [the lecherous demon] is truly unlike the 'white-robed scholar' [Wu-k'ung]." Mair also quotes Dudbridge on this matter: "the essential role of the white ape . . . is one of the abductor and seducer of women, a characteristic *foreign* to the Monkey of the JW" (Mair 719–20).

14 For a detailed description of the full gamut of Hanuman's magic power—his power of leaping, velocity, and transformation—see Jambavna's portrayal of Hanuman in Canto LXVI, "Jambavna Persuades Hanuman," of Vālmīki, *Srimad Vālmīki Rāmāyaṇa*, trans. N. Raghunathan (hereafter *Rāmāyaṇa*) II: 320–22.

15 It goes beyond the scope of this book to study the other versions, both written and oral, of the *Rāmāyaṇa* in India, Southeast Asia, and China, to see whether Sugrīva always bears the same guise as in Vālmīki's account.

16   Canto LXXII, "Kabandha Asks Rāma to Make Friends with Sugrīva," *Rāmāyaṇa* II: 154. Also in Canto V, "Rāma and Sugrīva Form a Compact," it is said that "the great ape, Sugrīva, took the guise of a man of attractive appearance" to address Rāma (II: 178).

17   *Rāmāyaṇa* II: 155.

18   "In that mountain . . . there is a great cave, which is closed by a rock and difficult to enter. At its eastern entrance there is a big pool of cool water. The place abounds in fruits and roots and is delightful, and many kinds of beasts are to be found there" (*Rāmāyaṇa* II: 157).

19   This episode took place in Canto L, "The Rkshabila," *Rāmāyaṇa* II: 294–96.

20   *Rāmāyaṇa* II: 241.

21   It is worth noting here that Tārā, Vāli's devoted wife, now becomes Sugrīva's mistress. Neither the author-narrator nor the characters in the epic make any remarks about Sugrīva's "abduction" of Tārā after his brother's demise. I would suggest that Sugrīva's possession of her can be seen as a subtle variation of the ape-abductor theme.

22   *Rāmāyaṇa* II: 259.

23   Vālmīki described Sugrīva's ape-clan as "half-civilized." See Sarma, *Ethico-Literary Values* 201.

24   Eliade, *Myths, Dreams* 175. Eliade cites examples of various mythological figures, such as Attis, Adonis, Dionysus, and Cybele, who show traces of androgyny. For Eliade, androgyny symbolizes the perfection of a primitive nondifferentiated status. This is why our mythical ancestors, as well as the Supreme Being, were androgynous.

25   Mair 720.

26   *Random House College Dictionary* 1403.

27   The compiling of the *Lieh-i chuan* was attributed to Emperor Wen of Wei (186–226) or Chang Hua (232–300).

28   "The Man Who Sold a Ghost," in *The Man Who Sold a Ghost* 1–2.

29   "The New Ghost," *Yu-ming lu* in *The Man Who Sold a Ghost* 105–6.

30   Yu, "Religion and Literature" 137.

31   Yin Shun 116, quoting Yen Shou 延壽 *Tsung-ching lu* 宗鏡錄, vol. 97.

32   Yin Shun 145.

33   Yin Shun 126, quoting Fa Jung's *Hsin-ming* 心銘.

34   For a detailed discussion of the association of the Ch'an Buddhist practice and Monkey's riddle-solving activities—the enigmatic dialogue and witty repartee between Monkey and his first teacher, his intuitive understanding of the religious significance of the slaying of the Six Robbers, etc.—see Yu, "Religion and Literature" 136–38.

35   Jung 260/465.

36   Jung 266/477.

37   *Journey* I: 84. This is my own translation. Anthony Yu renders it as ". . . Your pupil would gladly learn whatever has a smidgen of Taoist flavor."

38   I should also mention that Wu-k'ung's "seventy-two transformations" are seen by many scholars as growing out of the *Jātaka* tradition and other Indian fables and miracle tales (see Mair 716). These foreign motifs, whose oral transmission into popular Chinese literature took place during the T'ang, serve to complement our discussion of the trickster archetype.

39   Jung 264/473.

40   Jung 253/455.

41   I should point out that the term "*hsin-yüan*" contains within it not only Buddhist connotations of the "restless mind," but also the common folk understanding of the "flighty
disposition" of the monkey. In the *Rāmāyaṇa*, for instance, Hanuman exposes Sugrīva's
instability of mind as something typical of his monkey nature (Canto II, "Sugrīva Sends
Hanuman to Meet Rāma," II: 172).

42   A few comments need to be made at this point about Wang Hsiao-lien's analysis of the
cyclical mytho-logic underlying the *Dream*. He divides the narrative structure into three
parts—origin, ordeal, and return (Wang Hsiao-lien 91). Each stage generates a plot cen-
tering on the variation of stone symbolism—the birth of jade (*han-yü* 含玉), the loss of
jade (*shih-yü* 失玉), and the return of jade (*huan-yü* 還玉). Wang's discussion seems to
overemphasize the role of stone as a structuring component of the *Dream*. And his exploration of the folkloric origin of the cyclical pattern in question also betrays a reductionist
mode of thinking:

> The Chinese myths and legends of love are usually embodied in invariable formulas.
> The formulaic composition is often presented as follows:
>   mythic origin—ordeal—the eternal return
> Many legends tell the stories of the primitive origins of legendary figures, for instance,
> the fairies in Heaven or meteorite-borns, or the stone at the foot of Greensickness
> Peak; and then of the ordeals of love—the process of a kind of tragic love; and lastly,
> of the ultimate return—the fairy who has descended from Heaven returns there,
> the dragon princess who came from the sea returns to the dragon palace, or [the
> stone woman] assumes a fossil-like existence that transcends time and space through
> physical transformation. (Wang 75–76)

The critic's argument seems stretched as he turns to the legend of the stone woman to
account for the narrative cycle of birth and rebirth manifested in the *Dream*. For the folklore about the stone of the chaste woman hardly contains the theme of "mythic return," for
Wang implies. The tranformation of the woman standing in wait for her absent husband/
lover can hardly be interpreted in cyclical terms. Her rocky existence signifies much less a
return to earth than a silent token of her aborted fertility as well as a testimony to an everlasting spiritual bond with the absent beloved. The marble-like immobility reiterates the
same liminal logic engraved on Keats's Grecian urn, where human yearnings are set loose
in a moment of intensity but frozen in eternal stasis. In a similar manner, the folk legend of
the "female fossil" serves as an eloquent expression of desire and sterility simultaneously.
Failing to recognize that such liminal characteristics underlie the pathos of the chastity
stone, Wang Hsiao-lien overstretches the folkloric text to justify the so-called invariable
formulaic expression for all Chinese legends of tragic love.

43   See Northrop Frye's theory of mythos, *Anatomy of Criticism* 158–59. He offers the interpretation of the mythic model of trinity as follows: "In the divine world the central
process or movement is that of the death and rebirth, or the disappearance and return,
or the incarnation and withdrawal, of a god. This divine activity is usually identified or
associated with one or more of the cyclical processes of nature. The god may be a sun-god,
dying at night and reborn at dawn, or else with an annual rebirth at the winter solstice; or

he may be a god of vegetation, dying in autumn and reviving in spring or (as in the birth stories of the Buddha) he may be an incarnate god going through a series of human or animal life-cycles."

44 Yü P'ing-po, *"Hung-lou Meng" yen-chiu* 51, 68.

45 According to Yü, Kao O "was also poisoned by the cliché of 'moral rectification' in popular novels, and felt impelled to transform Pao-yü into a different person" (Yü P'ing-po 68).

46 Yü P'ing-po 40.

6 The Inscribed Stone Tablet

1 Miller renders the phrase *chia-yü ts'un-yen* 假語村言 as "fictive language and vulgar words" (see Miller 112).

2 *Chih-yen Chai* 132.

3 *Chih-yen Chai* 281–82.

4 *Chih-yen Chai ch'ung-p'ing "Shih-t'ou Chi"* 1925; trans. in Wu Shih-ch'ang 204.

5 *HLM hsien-pien* 193.

6 It is worth noting that several scholars of the *HLM* studies interpret the device of the "talking stone" as allegorical. Wu Shih-ch'ang points out that the allusion of the "talking stone" appeared in many early Ch'ing poems; he quotes one of Ming I's 明義 commentary poems on the *Dream of the Red Chamber* and draws our attention to the particular couplet: "The stone lost its numinous energy after returning to the foot of the mountain / In vain it assumed the name of the 'talking stone'" (*Lu-yen so-ch'uang chi* 綠煙瑣窗集). Based on this couplet and several other allusions to the talking stone in T'ang poetry, Wu argues that the talking stone in the *Dream* performs the same function as its original counterpart in the *Tso Chuan*: it serves as the mouthpiece of social critics. Seen in this light, the story that the stone tells is not its own story (i.e., Ts'ao Hsüeh-ch'in's own life story), nor even a fictional one, but a social critique that carries far-reaching political implications. See Wu Shih-ch'ang, *HLM t'an-yüan wai-pien* 77–78.

7 Hsia 96.

8 Hsia 96.

9 Chin Sheng-t'an, *Shui-hu chuan* II: 785.

10 Lu Hsün, *Chung-kuo hsiao-shuo shih-lüeh* 154.

11 Wang Ching-yu, *Chin Sheng-t'an* 59. Also see Irwin 91.

12 Chin Sheng-t'an, "Tu ti-wu-ts'ai-tzu-shu fa," *Shui-hu tzu-liao hui-pien* (hereafter *SHTLHP*), 32.

13 See Chin Sheng-t'an, "Ti-wu-ts'ai-tzu-shu Shih Nai-an *Shui-hu Chuan* hsü-erh," "hsü-san," "Sung-shih-kang p'i-yü," "Sung-shih-mu p'i-yü," "Tu ti-wu-ts'ai-tzu-shu fa," *SHTLHP* 24–38.

14 Hu Shih 52.

15 Irwin 91.

16 For instance, both Richard Irwin and John Wang problematize the aesthetic effect of Chin's "righteous" editing of the 120-chapter version. Irwin accuses Chin Sheng-t'an of ruining the effect of unity underlying the narrative fiction: ". . . did he [Chin Sheng-t'an] not realize that the underlying unity of the story was as truly a feature of its greatness

as the details of presentation? For the sake of preserving that unity he might have been content to leave the text unchanged, since his own talents were clearly not sufficient to improve upon it" (Irwin 91).

Upon close examination, Irwin is rather vague as to what the real nature of this so-called "underlying unity" is—is it a thematic or a structural unity? The same ambivalent negative response is echoed in John Wang's appraisal of Chin Sheng-t'an, in which the critic reiterates his concern with the unity of the work in impressionistic terms: "Apart from the elementary consideration that we as readers of an exciting story would naturally wonder what happens once the 108 heroes gather in Liang-shan-po, Ch'in's truncation has destroyed the basic design of the novel as a whole. Although episodic in structure, the novel is yet informed by 'a magnificent literary conception' as Shih Nai-an builds 'his materials up into a great mass tragedy. The rebels are successful so long as they do not make peace with the court and are not pardoned; then they die off one by one'" (Wang Ching-yu, *Chin Sheng-t'an* 59; Wang is citing Jaroslav Prusek, "Boccaccio and His Chinese Contemporaries," *New Orient* 7/3 [June 1968]: 68).

Although John Wang attempts to focus more clearly on the nature of the "underlying unity" of the *Water Margin*, he appears uncertain as to whether it should be seen in a structural or a thematic light. The ambivalence of Wang's critical perspective is reflected in his equation of the "basic design" to the "literary conception" of the narrative—critical terms too vaguely defined to be of any significant explanatory value. At first Wang seems to aim at distinguishing a common reader's desire to know what happens next— a plot-centered concern—from the critic's interest in an artistic unity explained in terms of the "basic design" and the "literary conception" of the author. He blunders at the next moment by linking the concept of "episodic structure" with the thematic components of "tragedy," thus equating "basic design," "narrative structure," "literary conception," and the generic concept of "tragedy" in an undifferentiated conceptual mass. The lack of focus of Wang's critical perspective greatly impairs the validity of his evaluation of the aesthetic merits of Chin Sheng-t'an's 70-chapter edition.

17   Chin Sheng-t'an, "Tu ti-wu-ts'ai-tzu-shu fa" 36–38.

18   Chin Sheng-t'an, "Kuan-hua-t'ang k'o ti-wu-ts'ai-tzu-shu *Shui-hu* ch'i-shih-hui tsung-p'ing" 224.

19   Both Northrop Frye and Robert Scholes in their studies of the theory of mythos claim that "cyclical movement" (Frye 158; Scholes and Kellogg 220) and "symmetrical cosmology" (Frye 161) characterize the basic structural principles of myth. According to Scholes and Kellogg, the sacred myth—the most ancient form of narrative—is a "gloss" on rituals that are closely related to the primitive human worship of Nature. Of those rituals which enact the cyclical processes of Nature, the most important type celebrates the cyclical movement of vegetation. Frye studies the movement of the narrative from one form to another and comes to the conclusion that the fundamental form of such narrative movement is cyclical—i.e., the alternation of success and decline, effort and repose, and life and death.

Following this line of argument, the three critics proclaim that the plot elements in mythical narrative unfailingly involve a circular journey in terms of both theme and plot structure. Scholes ascribes this recurring ritualistic pattern to the human celebration of the annual cycle of seasons and vegetative life (Scholes and Kellogg 220). Frye traces the rotary movement of mythos in four major categories of cyclical symbols (Frye 160; the four categories are the four seasons of the year, the four periods of the day, four aspects of the water cycle, and the four periods of life).

20   Scholes and Kellogg 224. According to the two critics, the narrative pattern of sacred myth is symmetrical: it involves the rotary movement of descent from celestial perfection and ascent to the new ideal stage.

Conclusion

1   Lévi-Strauss believes that myth provides a logical model, "an intermediary entity," capable of overcoming contradictions in social reality through the mechanism of paradoxes and reversals; see "Structural Study of Myth" 229–30. Also see Douglas 52–56. According to Douglas, Lévi-Strauss's concept of the mediating function of myth reveals his debt to the dialectical method of Hegelian philosophy. She recapitulates his thoughts as follows: ". . . the structure of myth is a dialectic structure in which opposed logical positions are stated, the oppositions mediated by a restatement, which again, when its internal structure becomes clear, gives rise to another kind of opposition, which in its turn is mediated or resolved, and so on" (52).

2   Vickery 143.

3   Vickery 149.

4   "Traditional scholars of *HLM* studies" refers specifically to the autobiographical school headed by Hu Shih and Yü P'ing-po, and to those modern and contemporary Chinese scholar-critics who are engaged in "textual research" (*k'ao-chü hsüeh* 考據學)—among whom are Chou Ju-ch'ang, Wu Shih-ch'ang, Chao Kang/Ch'en Chung-i, and to a lesser degree, Yü Ying-shih.

5   Wu Shih-ch'ang, *HLM t'an-yüan wai-pien* 272.

6   Yü Ying-shih, "Chin-tai hung-hsüeh" 27.

7   Chou Ju-ch'ang, *"Hung-lou Meng" hsin-cheng* II: 875–927, 1153–67.

8   Kao O, *"Hung-lou Meng hsü"* 18.

9   Chou Ju-ch'ang II: 1161–62.

10   Chou Ju-ch'ang enumerates the discrepancies, both textual and ideological, in Kao O's later text; they range from minor changes, additions, or deletions of certain words and phrases to the major editing of passages that are considered "ideologically problematic." For specific examples of those discrepancies, see Chou, *HLM hsin-cheng* I: 15–27.

11   Ch'eng Pu-K'uei 119, quoting from Chang Pi-lai 94.

12   Lu Hsün, "Lun cheng-le-yen k'an" 220.

13   Needham VI/5: 25.

14   Lao Tzu 9.

15   Lao Tzu 16.

16   All three terms are quoted from "Hsing-yu p'ing I," *"Liu Tzu t'an-ching" chien-chu* 7a.

17   "Hsing-yu p'ing I" 23b.

18   "Pan-jo p'ing II," *"Liu Tzu t'an-ching" chien-chu* 27a.

19   "Hsing-yu p'ing I" 17b.

20   "Pan-jo p'ing II" 30a.

21 "Pan-jo p'ing II" 33a.

22 "Pan-jo p'ing II" 33b.

23 "Hsing-yu p'ing I" 11a.

24 "Hsing-yu p'ing I" 13a. The story about Hui-neng succeeding his master Hung-jen as the Sixth Patriarch of the Ch'an school is a widely circulated Buddhist legend. Hui-neng won his master's recognition by composing a gatha that parodied one written by a fellow-disciple, Shen-hsiu. Hui-neng's gatha reads as follows: "The tree of Perfect Wisdom is originally no tree. Nor has the bright mirror any frame. Buddha-nature is forever clear and pure. Where is there any dust?" (trans. quoted from De Bary I: 351).

25 Although the manifestation of Taoist metaphysics in the *Dream* seems overshadowed by the Buddhist metaphor of *wan shih tien-t'ou*, I should point out that Pao-yü is a fervent admirer of *Chuang Tzu* and other Taoist treatises. It is especially interesting to note that toward the end of his earthly sojourn, we are told that Pao-yü's favorite leisure readings consist of nothing other than books on religious Taoism. To better prepare himself for the impending civil-service examination, he removes "his copy of *Zhuang-zi* from the table, collecting up at the same time some of his other favourite esoteric [*author's note*: the word "esoteric" is absent in the original; the translator has taken the liberty of inserting the word as a footnote on Pao-yü's penchant for the writings on secret religious practices] books (a collection that included *The Hermetic Clavicule* [*Ts'an-t'ung-ch'i* 參同契], *The Secret of the Primordial Flower* [*Yüan-ming pao* 元命苞], and *The Compendium of the Five Lamps* [*Wu-teng hui-yüan* 五燈會元]). He gave instructions to Musk, Ripple 秋紋 (Ch'iu-wen), and Oriole 鶯兒 (Ying-erh) to store all of these away" (Minford, *Stone* V: 332). With the exception of the last title, Pao-yü's favorite collection consists of writings on alchemy and Taoist secret talismans. See *HLM* III: 1615 n.1 for the details on the Taoist nature of *Ts'an-t'ung-ch'i* and *Yüan-ming pao*.

26 Lao Tzu 1. *Yüan* is identical to the concept of *hsüan* 玄, "the mysterious," "the profound," "the dark," and "the zero degree which is both the beginning and the end at the same time."

27 Chiang K'uei 1175: 63.

28 "Hsi-tz'u" II: 8/13b.

29 Wittgenstein 32.

30 Gérard 16–17.

31 Foucault, *Archaeology of Knowledge* 47.

Chinese and Japanese Sources

Chang Cho, comp. *Chao-yeh ch'ien-tsai*. In *Ts'ung-shu chi-ch'eng chien-pien*. Ed. Want Yün-wu. 860 vols. Taipei: Shang-wu yin-shu kuan, 1965–66. Vol. 723.
　　張　鷟．朝野僉載．叢書集成簡編．王雲五編．

Chang Hsin-chih. "*Hung-lou Meng* tu-fa." *HLMC* I: 153–59.
　　張新之．紅樓夢讀法．紅樓夢卷．

———. "Miao-fu Hsüan p'ing *Shih-t'ou Chi* tzu-chi." *HLMC* I: 34–35.
　　張新之．妙復軒評石頭記自記．紅樓夢卷．

Chang Pi-lai. *Man-shuo "Hung-lou"*. Peking: Jen-min wen-hsüeh ch'u-pan she, n.d.
　　張畢來．漫說紅樓．

Chang Shou-chieh. "*Shih Chi* cheng-i. SCHCKC.
　　張守節．史記正義．史記會注考證．

Chang Wei-yüan. "Wen-jen yü ch'ou-shih." *Ch'ien-chiang wan-pao* 23 September 1990.
　　張維元．文人與醜石．錢江晚報．

Chao Kang and Ch'en Chung-i. "*Hung-lou Meng*" hsin-t'an. 2 vols. Hong Kong: Wen-i shu-wu, 1970.
　　趙岡．陳鐘毅．紅樓夢新探．

———. "*Hung-lou Meng*" yen-chiu hsin-pien. Taipei: Lien-ching ch'u-pan she, 1975.
　　趙岡．陳鐘毅．紅樓夢研究新編．

Chao Yeh, ed. *Wu-yüeh ch'un-ch'iu*. In *Kuo-hsüeh chi-pen ts'ung-shu*. Ed. Wang Yün-wu. Taipei: Shang-wu yin-shu kuan, 1968. Vol. 395.
　　趙曄．吳越春秋．國學基本叢書．王雲五編．

"Ch'en Ts'ung-shan Mei'ling shih hun-chia." *Ku-chin hsiao-shuo*. Ed. Feng Meng-lung. Photo reprint of the T'ien-hsü Chai inscribed copy of Ming Dynasty. 2 vols. Taipei: Shih-chieh shu-chü, 1958. I: 20/1b–15b.
　　陳從善梅嶺失渾家．古今小說．馮夢龍編．

Ch'en Yao-wen, ed. *T'ien-chung chi*. Taipei: Wen-hai ch'u-pan she, 1964.
　陳耀文．天中記。

Cheng Hsüan, ed. *Cheng Chih*. In *Ts'ung-shu chi-ch'eng chien-pien*. Vol. 100.
　鄭玄．鄭志．叢書集成簡編．

Ch'eng Pu-k'uei. "*Hung-lou Meng* yü she-hui shih." *HWHHLC* 117–26.
　程步奎．紅樓夢與社會史．海外紅學論集．

Chiang K'uei. Preface. *Pai-shih Tao-jen shih-chi t'i-yao*. In *Ching-yin Wen-yüan Ko "Ssu-k'u ch'üan-shu"*. Comp. Chi Yün et al. 1st ed. 1500 vols. Taipei: Shang-wu yin-shu kuan, 1983. 1175:63.
　姜夔．白石道人詩集提要．景印文淵閣四庫全書．紀昀等編．

Chiang Shu-yung. "Chung-kuo ku-tai i-shu pien-cheng ssu-hsiang te che-hsüeh ch'uan-t'ung." *Ku-tai wen-hsüeh li-lun yen-chiu*. Shanghai: Shanghai ku-chi ch'u-pan she, 1986. XI: 111–24.
　蔣樹勇．中國古代藝術辯證思想的哲學傳統．古代文學理論研究．

Ch'ien-lung chia-hsü Chih-yen Chai ch'ung-p'ing "Shih-t'ou Chi". 3rd ed. Taipei: Hu Shih Memorial Society, 1975.
　乾隆甲戌脂硯齋重評石頭記．

Ch'ien Mu. "Wei-Chin hsüan-hsüeh yü nan-tu ch'ing-t'an." *Chung-kuo hsüeh-shu ssu-hsiang shih lun-ts'ung*. 7 vols. Taipei: Tung-ta shu-chü, 1977. III: 68–76.
　錢穆．魏晉玄學與南渡清談．中國學術思想史論叢．

Chih-yen Chai ch'ung-p'ing "Shih-t'ou Chi". Peking: Ku-tien wen-hsüeh ch'u-pan she, 1955.
　脂硯齋重評石頭記．

Chin Sheng-t'an. "Kuan-hua-t'ang k'o ti-wu-ts'ai-tzu-shu *Shui-hu* ch'i-shih-hui tsung-p'ing." *SHTLHP* 128–225.
　金聖嘆．貫華堂刻〈第五才子書〉水滸七十回總評．水滸資料彙編．

——— . "Sung-shih-kang p'i-yü." *SHTLHP* 29–30.
　金聖嘆．宋史綱批語．水滸資料彙編．

——— . "Sung-shih-mu p'i-yü." *SHTLHP* 30–32.
　金聖嘆．宋史目批語．水滸資料彙編．

——— . "Ti-wu-ts'ai-tzu-shu Shih Nai-an *Shui-hu Chuan* hsü-erh." *SHTLHP* 24–25.
　金聖嘆．〈第五才子書〉施耐庵水滸傳序二．水滸資料彙編．

——— . "Ti-wu-ts'ai-tzu-shu Shih Nai-an *Shui-hu Chuan* hsü-san." *SHTLHP* 25–29.
　金聖嘆．〈第五才子書〉施耐庵水滸傳序三．水滸資料彙編．

——— . "Tu ti-wu-ts'ai-tzu-shu fa." *SHTLHP* 32–38.
　金聖嘆．讀〈第五才子書〉法．水滸資料彙編．

——— , ed. *Shui-hu chuan*. 2 vols. Kowloon: Yu-lien ch'u-pan she, 1967.
　金聖嘆．水滸傳．

Chin Shu. Comp. Fang Hsüan-ling (of T'ang Dyansty) et al. 5 vols. Peking: Chung-hua shu-chü, 1974.
　晉書．房玄齡等撰．

Chiu T'ang-shu. Comp. Liu Hsü (of Chin Dynasty) et al. 16 vols. Peking: Chung-hua shu-chü, 1975.
　舊唐書．劉昫等撰．

Chou Chih-p'ing. "*Kung-an p'ai" te wen-hsüeh p'i-p'ing chi ch'i fa-chan*. Taipei: Shang-wu yin-shu kuan, 1986.

周質平．公安派的文學批評及其發展．

Chou Ch'un. "Yüeh *Hung-lou Meng* sui-pi." *HLMC* I: 66–77.

周春．閱紅樓夢隨筆．紅樓夢卷．

Chou-i cheng-i. Annot. Wang Pi and Han K'ang-po. 3rd ed. Taipei: Chung-hua shu-chü, 1977.

周易正義．王弼．韓康伯注。

Chou Ju-ch'ang. "*Hung-lou Meng* 'ch'ing-pang' yüan-yüan lun." *Chin wan-pao* 8 October 1987.

周汝昌．紅樓夢情榜淵源論．今晚報．

———. "*Hung-lou Meng" hsin-cheng*. 2 vols. Peking: Jen-min ch'u-pan she, 1976.

周汝昌．紅樓夢新證．

Chou-li. *SSCCS*. Vol. III.

周禮．十三經注疏．

Ch'u-hsüeh chi. Comp. Hsü Chien et al. Photo reprint of the 1531 inscribed ed. Taipei: Hsin-hsing shu-chü, 1966.

初學記．徐堅等撰．

Chu Tso-lin. "*Hung-lou Meng* wen-k'u." *HLMC* I: 159–63.

朱作霖．紅樓夢文庫．紅樓夢卷．

Chu Yüan. *Ch'u Tz'u*. In "*Ch'u Tz'u*" *pu-chu*. Ed. Hung Hsing-tsu. 3rd ed. Taipei: I-wen ch'u-pan she, 1968.

屈原．楚辭．楚辭補註．洪興祖撰．

Erh-chih Tao-jen. "*Hung-lou Meng* shuo-meng." *HLMC* I: 83–103.

二知道人．紅樓夢說夢．紅樓夢卷．

Fan-ku ts'ung-pien. In *Shuo Fu*. Ed. T'ao Tsung-i. Photo reprint of the Han-fen-lou ed. 8 vols. Taipei: Shang-wu yin-shu kuan, 1972. Vol. IV.

繙古叢編．說郛．陶宗義撰．

Feng Yen. *Feng-shih wen-chien chi*. In *Shuo Fu*. Vol. I.

封演．封氏聞見記．說郛．

Hai-wai Hung-hsüeh lun-chi. Ed. Hu Wen-pin and Chou Lei. Shanghai: Shanghai ku-chi ch'u-pan she, 1982.

海外紅學論集．胡文彬．周雷編．

Han Chin-lien. *Hung-hsüeh shih-kao*. Shih-chia-chuang: Hopei jen-min ch'u-pan she, 1982.

韓進廉．紅學史稿．

Han Fei. "Ho-shih p'ien." "*Han-fei tzu*" *chi-shih*. Annot. Ch'en Ch'i-yu. 2 vols. Shanghai: Jen-min ch'u-pan she, 1974. I: 238–39.

韓非．和氏篇．韓非子集釋．陳奇猷校注．

"Hsi-tz'u I & II." *Chou-i cheng-i* 7 / 1b–8 / 15a.

繫辭．周易正義．

Hsi-yüan Chu-jen. "*Hung-lou Meng* lun-pien." *HLMC* I: 198–205.

西園主人．紅樓夢論辨．紅樓夢卷．

Hsieh-an Chü-shih. "*Shih-t'ou i-shuo*." *HLMC* I: 184–97.

解盦居士．石頭臆說．紅樓夢卷．

Hsü Shen. *Shuo-wen chieh-tzu*. Peking: Chung-hua shu-chü, 1963.

　　許慎．說文解字．

Hsü Shou-chi, ed. *Yü p'u lei-pien*. 4 vols. N.p., 1889.

　　徐守基．玉譜類編．

Hsü Yeh-fen. "*Hung-lou Meng* pien." *HLMC* I: 227–32.

　　許葉芬．紅樓夢辨．紅樓夢卷．

Hsü Ying. "*Hung-lou Meng* lun-tsan." *HLMC* I: 125–46.

　　徐瀛．紅樓夢論贊．紅樓夢卷．

Hsüan Tsang. *Ch'eng Wei-shih Lun*. Trans. Wei Tat (Hong Kong: The Ch'eng Wei-shih lun Publication Committee, 1973).

　　玄奘．成唯識論．

Hsün K'uang. *Hsün Tzu*. 3rd ed. Taipei: Chung-hua shu-chü, 1970.

　　荀況．荀子．

"*Hsün Tzu*" *hsin-chu*. Ed. "Hsün Tzu" Annotation Committee at Peking U. Peking: Chung-hua shu-chü, 1979.

　　荀子新注．北京大學荀子注釋組．

Hu Shih. "Pa Ch'ien-lung Keng-ch'en-pen Chih-yen Chai ch'ung-p'ing *Shih-t'ou Chi* ch'ao-pen." In *Hu Shih wen-ts'un*. 4 vols. Taipei: Yüan-tung t'u-shu kung-ssu, 1961. Vol. IV, pt. 2: 396–407.

　　胡適．跋乾隆庚辰本脂硯齋重評石頭記抄本．胡適文存．

Hua-shih Chu-jen. "*Hung-lou Meng* pen-i yüeh-pien." *HLMC* I: 179–83.

　　話石主人．紅樓夢本義約編．紅樓夢卷．

Huang T'ing-chien. "Ta Hung Chu-fu shu." *Chung-kuo li-tai wen-lun hsüan*. 4 vols. Shanghai: Ku-chi ch'u-pan she, 1979. II: 316–17.

　　黃庭堅．答洪駒父書．中國歷代文論選．

Hung Ch'iu-fan. "*Hung-lou Meng* chüeh-yin." *HLMC* I: 235–42.

　　洪秋蕃．紅樓夢抉隱．紅樓夢卷．

Hung Pei-chiang, ed. "*Shan-hai-ching*" *chiao-chu*. 2nd ed. Taipei: Le-t'ien shu-chü, 1981.

　　洪北江．山海經校注．

I Su, ed. "*Hung-lou Meng*" *chüan*. 2 vols. Peking: Chung-hua shu-chü, 1963.

　　一粟．紅樓夢卷．

I-wen lei-chü. Comp. Ou-yang Hsün (557–641) et al. 2 vols. Shanghai: ku-chi ch'u-pan she, 1965.

　　藝文類聚．歐陽詢等撰．

Kan Pao. *Sou-shen Chi*. Annot. Wang Shao-ying. Peking: Chung-hua shu-chü, 1979.

　　干寶．搜神記．汪紹楹校注．

Kang Lai-hsin. *Shih-t'ou tu-hai*: "*Hung-lou Meng*" *san-lun*. Taipei and New York: Han-kuang ch'u-pan she and Highlight International, 1985.

　　康來新．石頭渡海：紅樓夢散論．

Kao, O. "*Hung-lou Meng* hsü." In Ch'eng Wei-yüan ed. Ts'ao Hsüeh-ch'in's *Hung-lou Meng*. Taipei: Wen-hua t'u-shu kung-ssu, 1980. 18.

　　高鶚．紅樓夢序．程偉元印．紅樓夢．

Ko Hung. "Shang-po p'ien." *"Pao-p'u-tzu" wai-p'ien*. In *Ching-yin Wen-yüan Ko "Ssu-k'u ch'üan-shu"*. Ed. Chi Yün et al. 1st ed. 1500 vols. Taipei: Shang-wu yin-shu kuan, 1983. 1059: 193–95.

　　葛洪．尚博篇．抱朴子外篇．景印文淵閣四庫全書．

Lao Tzu. *Tao-te Ching*. 3rd ed. Taipei: Shih-chieh shu-chü, 1969.

　　老子．道德經．

Li Chi. SSCCS. Vol. V.

　　禮記．十三經注疏．

Li Chih. "Ch'i-yen ssu-chü." "Mu-tan shih." *Fen Shu hsü "Fen Shu"*. Taipei: Chung-hua shu-chü, 1975. 6/243.

　　李贄．七言四句．牡丹詩．焚書．續焚書．

———. "T'ung-hsin shuo." *Ku-tai wen-lun ming-p'ien hsiang-chu*. Ed. Huo Sung-lin. Shanghai: Shanghai ku-chi ch'u-pan she, 1986. 368–72.

　　李贄．童心說．古代文論名篇詳註．霍松林編．

Li Ching. "Tu Tzu-ch'un." *T'ang-jen ch'uan-ch'i hsiao-shuo*. Tainan: P'ing-p'ing ch'u-pan she, 1975. 230–33.

　　李靖．杜子春．唐人傳奇小說．

Li Han-ch'iu, ed. *"Ju-lin wai-shih" yen-chiu tzu-liao*. Shanghai: Shanghai ku-chi ch'u-pan she, 1984.

　　李漢秋．儒林外史研究資料．

Li Hsi-fan and Lan Ling. "P'ing *"Hung-lou Meng" hsin-cheng*." *"Hung-lou Meng" hsin-cheng*. 2 vols. N.p.: n.p., n.d. I: 1–17.

　　李希凡．藍翎．評紅樓夢新證．紅樓夢新證．

Li Shih-chen. *Pen-ts'ao kang-mu*. In *Ku-chin t'u-shu chi-ch'eng*. Comp. Ch'en Meng-lei et al. 100 vols. Taipei: Wen-hsing shu-tien, 1964. VIII: 84–133.

　　李時珍．本草綱目．古今圖書集成．陳夢雷等編纂．

Li Tu. *Chung-hsi che-hsüeh ssu-hsiang-chung te t'ien-tao yü shang-ti*. Taipei: Lien-ching ch'u-pan she, 1978.

　　李杜．中西哲學思想中的天道與上帝．

Lieh Yü-k'ou. *Lieh Tzu*. In *Kuo-hsüeh chi-pen ts'ung-shu*. Ed. Wang Yün-wu. 2371 vols. Taipei: Shang-wu yin-shu-kuan, 1968. Vol. LV.

　　列禦寇．列子．國學基本叢書．

Lin Ch'un-p'u, ed. *"Chu-shu chi-nien" pu-cheng. 'Chu-shu chi-nien' pa-chung*. 2nd ed. Taipei: Shih-chieh shu-chü, 1967.

　　林春溥．竹書紀年補證．竹書紀年八種．

Liu An. *Huai-nan-tzu*. 2nd ed. Taipei: Chung-hua shu-chü, 1971.

　　劉安．淮南子．

Liu Hsieh. *Wen-hsin tiao-lung*. 1st ed. Taipei: Ming-lun ch'u-pan she, 1974.

　　劉勰．文心雕龍．

Liu Hsin. *Hsi-ching tsa-chi. Ssu-pu ts'ung-k'an ch'u-pien*. Taipei: Shang-wu yin-shu kuan, 1965. Vol. XXVII.

　　劉歆．西京雜記．四部叢刊初編．

Liu I-ch'ing, ed. *Yu-ming lu*. In *Ku-hsiao-shuo kou-ch'en*. Ed. Lu Hsün. 2 vols. Hong Kong: Hsin-i ch'u-pan she, 1976. Vol. I.

劉義慶．幽明錄．古小說鈎沉．魯迅編．

Liu Tsai-fu. *Hsing-ko tzu-ho lun*. Shanghai: Shanghai wen-i ch'u-pan she, 1985.

劉再復．性格組合論．

"*Liu Tzu t'an-ching*" *chien-chu*. Annot. Ting Fu-pao. Taipei: T'ien-hua ch'u-pan shih-yeh yu-hsien kung-ssu, 1979.

六祖壇經箋註．丁福保箋註．

Lo Man-li. "Yü-ch'i te ch'i-yüan ho fa-chan." *I-shu chia* 30 (1977): 26–31.

羅曼莉．玉器的起源與發展．藝術家．

Lo Pi. *Lu Shih*. *Ssu-pu pei-yao*. 611 vols. Taipei: Chung-hua shu-chu, 1965. Vol. 88.

羅泌．路史．四部備要．

Lu Hsün. *Chung-kuo hsiao-shuo shih-lüeh*. Peking: Pei-hsin shu-chü, 1923–24.

魯迅．中國小說史略．

———. "Lun cheng-le-yen k'an." *Fen*. In *Lu Hsün ch'üan-chi*. Ed. Lu Hsün chi-nien wei-yüan-hui. 20 vols. Peking: Jen-min wen-hsüeh ch'u-pan she, 1973. I: 217–22.

魯迅．論睜了眼看．墳．魯迅全集．

Lun Yü. *Ssu-shu chi-chu*. Annot. Chu Hsi. Taipei: Shih-chieh shu-chü, 1974.

論語．四書集注．朱熹注．

Miao T'ien-hua, ed. *Ch'eng-yü tien*. 5th ed. Taipei: Fu-hsing shu-chü, 1980.

繆天華．成語典．

Mou Tsung-san. *Ts'ai-hsing yü hsüan-li*. Taipei: Hsüeh-sheng shu-chü, 1980.

牟宗三．才性與玄理．

Na Chih-liang. "Chi-ssu t'ien-ti ssu-fang te liu-ch'i." *Hua-hsia Weekly* No. 105. *Chung-yang jih-pao* 5 June 1988: 8.

那志良．祭祀天地四方的六器．華夏週刊．中央日報．

———. "Ku-tai te tsang-yü." *Ta-lu tsa-chih*. 5.10 (1952): 330–35.

那志良．古代的葬玉．大陸雜誌．

———. "Ku-tai tsang-yü." *Ku-yü lun-wen chi*. Taipei: National Palace Museum, 1983. 101–9.

那志良．古代葬玉．古玉論文集．

Ota Tatsuo. "Boku tsūji genkai shoin Saiyūki Kō," *Kōbe gaidai ronso* 10.2 (1959): 1–22.

太田辰夫．朴通事諺解所引西遊記考．神戸外大論叢．

Pan Ku, ed. *Han Shu*. 8 vols. Peking: Chung-hua shu-chü, 1975.

班固．漢書．

Pei Shih. Li Yen-shou (of T'ang Dynasty) ed. 10 vols. Peking: Chung-hua shu-chü, 1974.

北史．李延壽撰．

Po Chü-i. *Pai-k'ung liu t'ieh*. Taipei: Hsin-hsing shu-chü, 1969.

白居易．白孔六帖．

"Pu Chiang-tsung bai-yüan chuan." *T'ang-jen ch'uan-ch'i hsiao-shuo*. Ed. Ts'ui-wen-t'ang. Tainan: P'ing-p'ing ch'u-pan she, 1975. 15–18.

補江總白猿傳．唐人傳奇小說．

Sheng Hung-chih. *Ching-chou chi*. In *Pei-t'ang shu-ch'ao*. Ed. Yü Shih-nan. 2 vols. Taipei: Wen-hai shu-chü, 1962. II: 158/12a–13b.

盛弘元．荆州記．北堂書鈔．虞世南撰．

Shih Ching. SSCCS. Vol. II.

詩經．十三經注疏．

"Shih Pen" liang-chung. Annot. Sung Chung. Ch'ang-sha: Shang-wu yin-shu kuan, 1937.

世本兩種．宋衷注．

Shih-san-ching chu-shu. 3 ed. Taipei: I-wen ch'u-pan she, 1965.

十三經注疏．

Shih Yu. *Chi-chiu p'ien.* In *Yü Hai.* Comp. Wang Ying-lin. 8 vols. Facsimile of a 1337 ed. Taipei: Hua-wen shu-chü, 1964. Vol. VIII.

史游．急就篇．玉海．王應麟撰．

Shimmura Izuru, ed. *Kojien.* Tokyo: Iwanami Books Co., 1976.

新村出．広辞苑．

Shu Ching. In *'Shang Shu' chin-chu chin-shih.* Ed. and annot. Ch'ü Wan-li. 2nd ed. Taipei: Shang-wu yin-shu kuan, 1970.

書經．尚書今註今釋．屈萬里編註．

"Shui-hu" tzu-liao hui-pien. Ed. Ku-tien wen-hsüeh yen-chiu tzu-liao. Taipei: Li-jen shu-chü, 1981.

水滸資料彙編．古典文學研究資料彙編．

Ssu-ma Ch'en. "San-huang pen-chi." *SCHCKC* 11–12.

司馬貞．三皇本紀．史記會注考證．

Ssu-ma Ch'ien. *Shih Chi. SCHCKC.*

司馬遷．史記．史記會注考證．

Sui Shu. Comp. Wei Cheng (of T'ang Dynasty) et al. 3 vols. Peking: Chung-hua shu-chü, 1973.

隋書．魏徵等撰．

Sun T'ung-sheng. "Miao-fu Hsüan p'ing *Shih-t'ou Chi* hsü." *HLMC* I: 39–41.

孫桐生．妙復軒評石頭記敘．紅樓夢卷．

Sung Shih. Comp. T'o T'o (of Yüan Dynasty) et al. 20 vols. Peking: Chung-hua shu-chü, 1977.

宋史．脫脫等撰．

Sung Yü. "Kao T'ang fu." *Wen Hsüan.* Ed. Hsiao T'ung. 2nd ed. 2 vols. Hong Kong: Shang-wu yin-shu kuan, 1960. I: 19/393–97.

宋玉．高唐賦．文選．蕭統撰．

T'ai-p'ing kuang-chi. Comp. Li Fang et al. Taipei: Hsin-hsing shu-chü, 1973.

太平廣記．李昉等撰．

T'ai-p'ing yü-lan. Comp. Li Fang et al. 4 vols. Peking: Chung-hua shu-chü, 1960.

太平御覽．李昉等撰．

T'ai Yü. *Hung-lou Meng jen-wu lun.* Shanghai: Kuo-chi wen-hua fu-wu she, 1948.

太愚．紅樓夢人物論．

Takigawa Kametaro, ed. *"Shih Chi" hui-chu k'ao-cheng.* Taipei: Hung-shih ch'u-pan she, 1981.

瀧川龜太郎．史記會注考證．

Tang Ch'ang-ju. "Wei-Chin ts'ai-hsing lun te cheng-chih i-i." *Wei-Chin Nan-Pei-Ch'ao shih lun-ts'ung.* Peking: San-lien shu-tien, 1955. 298–310.

唐長儒．魏晉才性論的政治意義．魏晉南北朝史論叢．

Tang Lin. *Ming-pao chi.* In *Ta-cheng hsin-hsiu "Ta-tsang Ching".* Reprint of 1928 ed. 85 vols. Tokyo: Ta-cheng hsin-hsiu "Ta-tsang Ching" k'an-hsing-hui, 1973. 51: 787–802.

唐臨．冥報記．大正新脩大藏經．

Ts'ao Hsüeh-ch'in and Kao O. *Hung-lou Meng*. 3 vols. Peking: Jen-min wen-hsüeh ch'u-pan she, 1982.

曹雪芹．高鶚．紅樓夢．

Ts'o-ch'iu Ming. *Kuo Yü*. 2 vols. 3rd ed. Shanghai: ku-chi ch'u-pan she, 1978.

左丘明．國語．

———. *Tso Chuan*. SSCCS vol. VI.

左丘明．左傳．十三經注疏．

Tu Wan. Preface. *Yün-lin shih-p'u*. In *Ku-chin t'u-shu chi-ch'eng*. VIII: 72.

杜綰．雲林石譜．古今圖書集成．

Tuan Ch'eng-shih, ed. *Yu-yang tsa-tsu*. In *Ts'ung-shu chi-ch'eng chien-pien*. Vols. 116–17.

段成式．酉陽雜俎．叢書集成簡編．

Tuan-chu "shih-san Ching" ching-wen. Annot. Tuan Yü-ts'ai. 3rd. Taipei: K'ai-ming shu-tien, 1968.

段注十三經經文．段玉裁．

Tun Min. "T'i Ch'in P'u hua-shih." *HLMC* I: 6.

敦敏．題芹圃畫石．紅樓夢卷．

T'ung Chung-t'ai. "Kang-jou hsiang-chi te ai-yü hsin-li." *Chung-yang jih-pao* 15 March 1987: 8.

童中台．剛柔相濟的愛玉心理．中央日報．

Tung-fang kuo-yü tz'u-tien. Taipei: Tung-fang ch'u-pan she, 1976.

東方國語辭典．

Tz'u Hai. 3rd ed. Taipei: Chung-hua shu-chü, 1969.

辭海．

Wang Chia. *Shih-i chi*. Taipei: Mu-t'o ch'u-pan she, 1982.

王嘉．拾遺記．

Wang Ch'ung. *Lun Heng*. *Ssu-pu pei-yao* vol. 125.

王充．論衡．四部備要．

Wang Fu. *Ch'ien-fu lun*. *Ssu-pu pei-yao* vol. 123.

王符．潛夫論．四部備要．

Wang Hsi-lien. "*Hung-lou Meng* tsung-p'ing." *HLMC* 146–53.

王希廉．紅樓夢總評．紅樓夢卷．

Wang Hsiang-chih, ed. *Yü-ti chi-sheng*. Taipei: Wen-hai ch'u-pan she, 1962.

王象之．輿地紀勝．

Wang Hsiao-lien. "Shih-t'ou te ku-tai hsin-yang yü shen-hua ch'uan-shuo." *Chung-kuo te shen-hua yü ch'uan-shuo*. Taipei: Lien-ching ch'u-pan she, 1977.

王孝廉．石頭的古代信仰與神話傳說．中國的神話與傳說．

Wang Kuo-wei. "*Hung-lou Meng*" *p'ing-lun*. Taipei: T'ien-hua ch'u-pan she, 1979.

王國維．紅樓夢評論．

Wang Pi. "Ming *Hsiang*." "*Chou-i* lüeh-lieh." In *Wang Pi chi chiao-shih*. Ed. Lou Yü-lieh. 2 vols. Peking: Hsin-hua shu-chü, 1980. II: 609.

王弼．明象．周易略例．王弼集校釋．樓宇烈校釋．

Wang Po-hsiang, ed. "*Ch'un-ch'iu Tso Chuan*" *tu-pen*. Hong Kong: Chung-hua shu-chü, 1959.

王伯祥選注．春秋左傳讀本．

Wang P'u, ed. *T'ang hui-yao*. Taipei: Shih-chieh shu-chü, 1968.

王溥．唐會要．

Wang Yang-ming (Shou-jen). "Ta-hsüeh-wen." *Chung-kuo che-hsüeh shih chiao-hsüeh tzu-liao hsüan-chi*. 2 vols. Peking: Chung-hua shu-chü, 1982. II: 207–12.

王陽明．大學問．中國哲學史教學資料選輯．

Wen I-to. "Kao T'ang shen-nü ch'uan-shuo fen-hsi." *Wen I-to ch'üan-chi*. 4 vols. Shanghai: K'ai-ming shu-chü, n.d. Photo-offset. Hong Kong: 1972. 1: 81–113.

聞一多．高唐神女傳說分析．聞一多全集．

Wu Ch'eng-en. *Hsi-yu Chi*. Taipei: Wen-yüan shu-chü, 1975.

吳承恩．西遊記．

Wu Chün. *Hsi-ching tsa-chi*. In *Ssu-pu ts'ung-k'an*. 2100 vols. Comp. and reproduced in a photolithographic ed. Shanghai: Shang-wu yin-shu kuan, 1920–22. Vol. 27.

吳均．西京雜記．四部叢刊．

Wu Kung-cheng. *Hsiao-shuo mei-hsüeh*. 2nd ed. Nanking: Chiang-su wen-i ch'u-pan she, 1987.

吳功正．小說美學．

Wu Shih-ch'ang. "*Hung-lou Meng*" *t'an-yüan wai-pien*. Shanghai: Shanghai ku-chi ch'u-pan she, 1980.

吳世昌．紅樓夢探源外編．

Yang Hsiung. "Hsüan li." *T'ai Hsüan*. In *Chung-kuo hsüeh-shu ming-chu chin-shih yü-i*. 6 vols. Ed. Editorial board of Hsi-nan shu-chü. Taipei: Hsi-nan shu-chü, 1972. III: 179–81.

楊雄．玄理．太玄．中國學術名著今釋語譯．

Yeh Chia-ying. "Ts'ung Wang Kuo-wei '*Hung-lou Meng*' p'ing-lun chih te-shih t'an-tao *Hung-lou Meng* chih wen-hsüeh ch'eng-chiu chi Chia Pao-yü chih ch'ing-kan hsin-t'ai." *HWHHLC* 141–44.

葉嘉瑩．從王國維〈紅樓夢評論〉之得失談到紅樓夢之文學成就及賈寶玉之情感心態．海外紅學論集．

Yeh Ho. "Tu *Hung-lou* cha-chi." *HLMC* I: 285–92.

野鶴．讀紅樓箚記．紅樓夢卷．

Yeh Meng-te. *Shih-lin Yen-yü*. Peking: Chung-hua shu-chü, 1984.

葉夢得．石林燕語．

Yin Shun. *Chung-kuo ch'an-tsung shih*. 3rd ed. Taipei: Cheng-wen ch'u-pan she, 1983.

印順．中國禪宗史．

Ying Shao. *Feng-su t'ung*. *TPYL* vol. I.

應劭．風俗通．太平御覽．

———. *Han-kuan-i*. In *Ts'ung-shu chi-ch'eng chien-pien*. Vol. 279.

應劭．漢官儀．叢書集成簡編．

Yü P'ing-po, ed. *Chih-yen Chai "Hung-lou Meng" chi-p'ing*. Hong Kong: T'ai-p'ing shu-chü, 1975.

俞平伯．脂硯齋紅樓夢輯評．

———. "*Hung-lou Meng*" *yen-chiu*. Peking: T'ang-ti ch'u-pan she, n.d.

俞平伯．紅樓夢研究．

Yü Ying-shih. "Chin-tai hung-hsüeh te fa-chan yü hung-hsüeh ko-ming." *HWHHLC* 10–30.

余英時．近代紅學的發展與紅學革命．海外紅學論集．

———. "*Hung-lou Meng* te liang-ko shih-chieh." *HWHHLC* 40–42.

余英時. 紅樓夢的兩個世界. 海外紅學論集.

———. " 'Mao-chai shih-ch'ao' chung yu-kuan Ts'ao Hsüeh-ch'in sheng-p'ing te liang-shou shih k'ao-shih." *HWHHLC* 245–58.

余英時〈懋齋詩鈔〉中有關曹雪芹生平的兩首詩考釋. 海外紅學論集.

———. "Yen-ch'ien wu-lu hsiang hui-t'ou." *HWHHLC* 91–113.

余英時. 眼前無路想回頭. 海外紅學論集.

Yüan Chiao. "Yüan Kuan." *Kan-tse yao. T'ang-jen ch'uan-ch'i hsiao-shuo chi.* Taipei: Shih-chieh shu-chü, 1962. 258–59.

袁郊. 圓觀. 干澤謠. 唐人傳奇小說集.

Yüan K'o. *Chung-kuo ku-tai shen-hua.* Shanghai: Shang-wu yin-shu kuan, 1951.

袁珂. 中國古代神話.

———. *Ku shen-hua hsüan-shih.* Peking: Jen-min wen-hsüeh ch'u-pan she, 1979.

袁珂. 古神話選釋.

Western Language Sources

Alter, Robert. *The Pleasure of Reading: In An Ideological Age.* New York: Simon & Schuster, 1989.

Barthes, Roland. *Critique et vérité.* Paris: Seuil, 1966.

———. "From Work to Text." In *Textual Strategies: Perspectives in Post-Structuralist Criticism.* Ed. Josue V. Harari. Ithaca, N.Y.: Cornell UP, 1979.

———. *The Pleaure of the Text.* Trans. Richard Miller. New York: Hill and Wang, 1975.

———. *Roland Barthes by Roland Barthes.* Trans. Richard Howard. New York: Hill and Wang, 1977.

———. *S/Z.* Trans. Richard Miller. New York: Hill and Wang, 1974.

———. "Textual Analysis of Poe's 'Valdemar.' " In *Untying the Text: A Post-Structuralist Reader.* Ed. Robert Young. Boston: Routledge & Kegan Paul, 1981, 133–61.

Bodde, Derk. "Myths of Ancient China." In *Mythologies of the Ancient World.* Ed. S. N. Kramer. New York: Doubleday, 1961, 369–405.

Cao Xueqin and Gao E. *The Story of the Stone.* Trans. David Hawkes (I–III) and John Minford (IV–V). 5 vols. 6th ed. New York: Penguin Books, 1973–86.

Caws, Mary Ann, ed. *Textual Analysis: Some Readers Reading.* New York: Modern Language Association of America, 1986.

Cheng Te-k'un. *Prehistoric China.* In *Archaeology in China.* Cambridge: U of Toronto P, 1959. Vol. I.

Cohen, Alvin P. "Coercing the Rain Deities in Ancient China." *History of Religions* 17.3–4 (1978): 245–65.

Coward, Rosalind, and John Ellis. *Language and Materialism: Developments in Semiology and the Theory of the Subject.* London: Henley, and Boston: Routledge & Kegan Paul, 1977.

Culler, Jonathan. *The Pursuit of Signs: Semiotics, Literature, Deconstruction.* Ithaca: Cornell UP, 1981.

———. *Structuralist Poetics: Structuralism, Linguistics, and the Study of Literature.* Ithaca: Cornell UP, 1975.

De Bary, Wm. Theodore, et al., eds. *Sources of Chinese Tradition.* 2 vols. New York and London: Columbia UP, 1964.

Derrida, Jacques. "Différance." In *Deconstruction in Context: Literature and Philosophy.* Ed. Mark C. Taylor. Chicago: The U of Chicago P, 1986, 396–420.

———. "Living On/Border Lines." Trans. James Hulbert. In *Deconstruction and Criticism.* Ed. Harold Bloom et al. New York: Continuum, 1979, 75–176.

———. *Speech and Phenomenon: And Other Essays on Husserl's Theory of Signs.* Trans. David B. Allison. Evanston: Northwestern UP, 1973.

Douglas, Mary. "The Meaning of Myth, with Special Reference to 'La Geste d'Asdiwal.'" In *The Structural Study of Myth and Totemism.* Ed. Edmund Leach. London: Tavistock Publications, 1967, 49–69.

Dudbridge, Glen. *The "Hsi-yu Chi": A Study of the Antecedents to the 16th Century Chinese Novel.* London: Cambridge UP, 1970.

Eberhard, Wolfram. *The Local Cultures of South and East China.* Leiden: E. J. Brill, 1968.

Eliade, Mircea. *The Myth of the Eternal Return.* 2nd ed. Trans. Willard R. Trask. Princeton: Princeton UP, 1974.

———. *Myths, Dreams, and Mysteries.* Trans. Philip Mairet. New York: Harper & Row, 1960.

Firth, J. R. *Papers in Linguistics: 1934–1951.* London: Oxford UP, 1957.

Foucault, Michel. *The Archaeology of Knowledge and the Discourse of Language.* Trans. A. M. Sheridan Smith. New York: Pantheon Books, 1972.

———. "Nietzsche, Genealogy, History." In *Language, Counter-Memory, Practice: Selected Essays and Interviews.* Ed. and trans. Donald F. Bouchard. Ithaca: Cornell UP, 1977, 139–64.

Frazer, Sir James George. *The Golden Bough.* Abridged ed. New York: MacMillan Publishing, 1922.

Frow, John. "Intertextuality and Ontology." In Worton and Still, *Intertextuality: Theories and Practices,* 45–55.

Frye, Northrop. *Anatomy of Criticism.* Princeton: Princeton UP, 1957.

Gelley, Alexander. *Narrative Crossings.* Baltimore: Johns Hopkins UP, 1987.

Genette, Gérard. *Figures of Literary Discourse.* New York: Columbia UP, 1982.

Goette, J. "Jade and Man in Life and Death." *T'ien Hsia Monthly* 3 (1936): 34–44.

Granet, Marcel. *The Religion of the Chinese People.* Ed. and trans. Maurice Freedman. Oxford: Blackwell, 1975.

Greimas, Algirdas Julien. *On Meaning: Selected Writings in Semiotic Theory.* Trans. Paul J. Perron and Frank H. Collins. Minneapolis: U of Minnesota P, 1987.

———. *Structural Semantics.* Trans. Daniele McDowell et al. Lincoln and London: U of Nebraska Press, 1983.

Hansford, S. Howard. *Chinese Carved Jades.* Greenwich, Conn.: New York Graphic Society, 1968.

Hay, John. *Kernels of Energy, Bones of Earth: The Rock in Chinese Art.* New York: China House Gallery, China Institute in America, 1985.

Heath, Stephen. "Structuration of the Novel-Text." *Signs of the Times.* Ed. Stephen Heath et al. Cambridge: Granta, 1971.

Heidegger, Martin. *Sein und Zeit.* Tubingen: Niemeyer, 1963.

Hendricks, William O. *Essays on Semiolinguistics and Verbal Art*. Paris: Mouton, 1973.

Hsia, C. T. *The Classic Chinese Novel*. New York and London: Columbia UP, 1968.

Hsüan, Tsang. *Ch'eng Wei-shih Lun*. Trans. Wei Tat. Hong Kong: The Ch'eng Wei-shih Lun Publication Committee, 1973.

Hutcheon, Linda. "Literary Borrowing . . . and Stealing: Plagiarism, Sources, Influences, and Intertexts." *English Studies in Canada* 12.2 (1986): 229–39.

Irwin, Richard. *The Evolution of a Chinese Novel: "Shui-hu Chuan"*. Cambridge, Mass.: Harvard UP, 1953.

Jameson, Fredric. Foreword. Greimas, *On Meaning* vi–xxii.

———. *The Prison-House of Language: A Critical Account of Structuralism and Russian Formalism*. Princeton: Princeton UP, 1972.

Jayatilleke, K. N. *The Message of the Buddha*. London: Allen & Unwin, 1975.

Jung, Carl. "On the Psychology of the Trickster Figure." Trans. R. F. C. Hull. *The Archetypes and the Collective Unconscious. Collected Works of C. G. Jung*. Bollingen Series XX. 2nd ed. New York: Pantheon Books, 1968. Vol. IX, pt. 1, 255–70.

Karlgren, Bernhard. *Legends and Cults in Ancient China. Bulletin of the Museum of Far Eastern Antiquities* XVIII (1946): 199–356.

Katz, J. J. *Semantic Theory*. New York: Harper & Row, 1972.

Kristeva, Julia. *Semiotiké: Recherches pour une sémanalyse*. Paris: Seuil, 1969.

Laufer, Berthold. *Jade: A Study in Chinese Archaeology and Religion*. Anthropological Series Vol. X. Chicago: Field Museum of Natural History, 1912.

Lehrer, Adrienne. *Semantic Fields and Lexical Structure*. Amsterdam and London: North-Holland Publishing Co., 1974.

Leitch, Vincent B. *Deconstructive Criticism: An Advanced Introduction*. New York: Columbia UP, 1983.

Lenin, Vladimir. "Philosophical Notebooks." *Collected Works*. London: Lawrence & Wishart, 1972. Vol. 38.

Lévi-Strauss, Claude. *From Honey to Ashes*. Trans. John and Doreen Weightman. London: Jonathan Cape, 1973.

———. *The Raw and the Cooked*. Trans. John and Doreen Weightman. New York: Harper Colophon Books, 1975.

———. "The Structural Study of Myth." *Structural Anthropology*. Trans. Claire Jacobson and Brooke Grundfest Schoepf. New York: Basic Books, 1963.

Levy, G. R. *The Gate of Horn: A Study of the Religious Conceptions of the Stone Age and Their Influence upon European Thought*. London: Faber and Faber, 1948.

Liu Hsieh. *The Literary Mind and the Carving of Dragons*. Trans. Vincent Yu-chung Shih. Hong Kong: Chinese UP, 1983.

Lyons, Elizabeth. "Chinese Jades: The Role of Jade in Ancient China." *Expedition* 20.3 (Spring 1978): 4–20.

Mair, Victor H. "Suen Wu-k'ung = Hanumat? The Progress of a Scholarly Debate." Reprinted from Proceedings of the 2nd International Conference on Sinology, Academia Sinica. Taipei, 1989. 659–752.

The Man Who Sold a Ghost: Chinese Tales of the 3rd–6th Centuries. Ed. and trans. Yang Hsien-yi and Gladys Yang. Hong Kong: Commercial Press, 1958.

Maranda, Pierre and Kongas. *Structural Models in Folklore and Transformational Essays*. Paris: Mouton, 1971.

Merleau-Ponty, Maurice. *The Visible and the Invisible*. Trans. Alphonso Lingis. Ed. Claude Lefort. Evanston: Northwestern UP, 1968.

Miller, Lucien. *Masks of Fiction in the "Dream of the Red Chamber"*. Arizona: U of Arizona P, 1975.

Mowry, Hua-yüan Li. *Chinese Love Stories from "Ch'ing-shih."* Hamden, Conn.: Archon Books, 1983.

Needham, Joseph. *Science and Civilisation in China*. 6 vols. Cambridge: Cambridge UP, 1954–83. Vol. V.

Neumann, Erich. *The Great Mother: An Analysis of the Archetype*. Trans. Ralph Manheim. Princeton: Princeton UP, 1972.

———. *The Origins and History of Consciousness*. Trans. R. F. C. Hull. Princeton: Princeton UP, 1970.

O'Donnell, Patrick, and Robert Con Davis, eds. *Intertextuality and Contemporary American Fiction*. Baltimore and London: Johns Hopkins UP, 1989.

O'Flaherty, Wendy Doniger. *Dreams, Illusion, and Other Realities*. Chicago and London: U of Chicago P, 1984.

Palmer, F. R. *Semantics: A New Outline*. Cambridge: Cambridge UP, 1976.

Palmer, Richard. *Hermeneutics*. Evanston: Northwestern UP, 1969.

Perron, Paul J. Introduction. Greimas, *On Meaning* xxiv–xlv.

Plaks, Andrew H. "Allegory in *Hsi-yu Chi* and *Hung-lou Meng*." *Chinese Narrative*. Ed. Andrew Plaks. Princeton: Princeton UP, 1977, 163–202.

———. *Archetype and Allegory in the "Dream of the Red Chamber"*. Princeton: Princeton UP, 1976.

The Random House College Dictionary. Ed. Jess Stein. Revised ed. New York: Random House Inc., 1975.

Rawson, Jessica. *Chinese Jade: Throughout the Ages*. London: Drydens Printers, 1975.

Riffaterre, Michel. *Semiotics of Poetry*. Bloomington: Indiana UP, 1984.

———. "Textuality: W. H. Auden's 'Musée des Beaux Arts.'" In Caws, *Textual Analysis*, 1–13.

Ryan, Michael. *Marxism and Deconstruction: A Critical Articulation*. Baltimore and London: Johns Hopkins UP, 1982.

Said, Edward W. *Beginnings: Intention and Method*. 2nd ed. New York: Columbia UP, 1985.

Sarma, Binod. *Ethico-Literary Values of the Two Great Epics of India: An Ethical Evaluation of the Two Great Epics of India: An Ethical Evaluation of the "Mahabharata" and the "Rāmāyaṇa"*. New Delhi: Oriental Publishers & Distributors, 1978.

Saussure, Ferdinand de. *Course in General Literature*. Trans. Wade Baskin. New York: McGraw-Hill, 1966.

Scholes, Robert, and Robert Kellogg. *The Nature of Narrative*. New York: Oxford UP, 1971.

Shih Nai-an. *Water Margin*. Trans. J. H. Jackson. Shanghai: Commercial Press, 1937. Facsimile reprint, Cambridge, Mass.: C. & T. Co., 1976.

Smith, Paul. *Discerning the Subject*. Minneapolis: U of Minnesota P, 1988.

Spencer, Baldwin. *Native Tribes of the Northern Territory of Australia*. Oosterhout: Anthropological Publications, 1966.

"The Story of Jade: A Chinese Tradition and a Modern Vogue." *Living Age* 332 (May 15, 1927): 903–8.

Thompson, W. I. *The Time Falling Bodies Take to Light: Mythology, Sexuality, and the Origins of Culture.* New York: St. Martin's Press, 1981.

Todorov, Tzvetan. *The Fantastic: A Structural Approach to a Literary Genre.* Trans. Richard Howard. London: P of Case Western Reserve U, 1973.

Tu Wei-ming. "Profound Learning, Personal Knowledge, and Poetic Vision." In *The Vitality of the Lyric Voice.* Ed. Shuen-fu Lin and Stephen Owen. Princeton: Princeton UP, 1986, 3–31.

Turner, Victor. *The Ritual Process: Structure and Anti-Structure.* Ithaca: Cornell UP, 1969.

Vālmīki. *Srimad Vālmīki Rāmāyana.* Trans. N. Raghunathan. 3 vols. Madras and Bangalore: Vighneswara Publishing House, 1981.

Vickery, John B. *The Literary Impact of "The Golden Bough".* Princeton: Princeton UP, 1973.

Visuddhi-Magga. Chapter xvii, "Buddhism." Ed. and trans. Henry Clarke Warren. New York: Atheneum, 1977. 238–41.

Waley, Arthur. Translation of excerpts from *Shih Ching.* In *Anthology of Chinese Literature.* Ed. Cyril Birch. 2 vols. New York: Grove Press, 1965–72, I: 5–29.

Wang Ching-yu. *Chin Sheng-t'an.* New York: Twayne Publishers, 1972.

Wang Jing. "The Poetics of Chinese Narrative: An Analysis of Andrew Plaks' *Archetype and Allegory in the 'Dream of the Red Chamber.'*" *Comparative Literature Studies* 26.3 (1989): 252–70.

———. "The Rise of Children's Poetry in Contemporary Taiwan." *Modern Chinese Literature* 3.1–2 (1987): 57–70.

Wilhelm, Hellmut. "The Concept of Change." *Change: Eight Lectures on the "I Ching".* Trans. Cary F. Baynes. New York: Harper Torch Books, 1960.

Wilhelm, Richard. *The I Ching.* Trans. Cary F. Baynes. 3rd ed. Princeton: Princeton UP, 1967.

Williams, C. A. *Outlines of Chinese Symbolism and Art Motives.* New York: Dover, 1976.

Wittgenstein, Ludwig. *Philosophical Investigations.* Trans. G. E. M. Anscombe. 3rd ed. New York: Macmillan, 1968.

Wong Kam-ming. "The Narrative Art of *Red Chamber Dream*." Diss. Cornell U, 1974.

———. "Point of View, Norms, and Structure: *Hung-lou Meng* and Lyrical Fiction." In Plaks, *Chinese Narrative* 203–26.

Worton, Michael, and Judith Still, eds. *Intertextuality: Theories and Practices.* Manchester and New York: Manchester UP, 1990.

Wu Ch'eng-en. *The Journey to the West.* Ed. & trans. Anthony C. Yu. 4 vols. Chicago: U of Chicago P, 1977–83.

Wu Shih-ch'ang. *On the "Red Chamber Dream": A Critical Study of Two Annotated Manuscripts of the Eighteenth Century.* Oxford: Clarendon Press, 1961.

Yu, Anthony C. "History, Fiction and the Reading of Chinese Narrative." *Chinese Literature: Essays, Articles, Reviews* 10.1–2 (1988): 1–19.

———. Introduction. Wu Ch'eng-en, *Journey to the West,* I: 1–62.

———. "Religion and Literature in China: The 'Obscure Way' of *The Journey to the West*." In *Tradition and Creativity: Essays on East Asian Civilization.* Ed. Ching-I Tu. New Brunswick and Oxford: Transaction Books, 1987. 109–54.

Note: English alphabetization is letter-by-letter. Endnotes are signified by "n." following page references. Chinese entries follow Chinese alphabetization.

Jing Wang is Assistant Professor of Chinese Language and
Literature at Duke University.

Library of Congress Cataloging-in-Publication Data
Wang, Jing, 1950–
The story of stone : intertextuality, ancient Chinese stone
lore, and the stone symbolism : in Dream of the red
chamber, Water margin, and The journey to the west /
Jing Wang.
— (Post-contemporary interventions)
Includes bibliographical references and index.
ISBN 0-8223-1178-X (cloth). — ISBN 0-8223-1195-X (paper)
1. Chinese literature—History and criticism. 2. Stone in
literature. 3. Stone—Folklore. 4. Ts'ao, Hsüeh-ch'in,
ca. 1717–1763. Hung lou meng. 5. Chin, Sheng-t'an, ca.
1610–1661, ed. The water margin. 6. Wu, Ch'eng-en,
ca. 1500–ca. 1582. Hsi yu chi. I. Title.
II. Series.
PL2265.W28   1992
895.1'09—dc20   91-12211 CIP